MUSLIMS AND
IN NORTH AMERICA:
PROBLEMS AND PROSPECTS

EDITED BY
AMBER HAQUE

Published by
amana publications
and
A.S. NOORDEEN

© 1420 A.H. / 1999 A.C. by
amana publications
10710 Tucker Street
Beltsville, Maryland 20705-2223 USA
Tel: (301) 595-5777 Fax: (301) 595-5888
E-mail: igamana@erols.com
Website: www.amana-publications.com

Library of Congress Cataloging-in-Publication Data

Muslims & Islamization in North America : problems and prospects /
edited by Amber Haque
p. cm.

Includes bibliographical references

ISBN 0-91-595791-4

1. Islam - North America. 2. Muslims - North America I. Haque,
Amber. II. Title: Muslims and Islamization in North America

BP67.A1 M86 1999   99-30397
297.2'7'0973 - dc21   CIP

CONTENTS

List of Contributors   vi

1. Introduction...1
   Amber Haque

I. Islamization of Knowledge in North America

2. History of Islamization of Knowledge and Contributions
   of the International Institute of Islamic Thought....................13
   Jamal Barzinji
3. The Transforming Experience of American Muslims: Islamic
   Education and Political Maturation....................................33
   Louay M. Safi
4. A Critical Review of Islamization of Knowledge in the
   American Perspective...49
   Shujaat A. Khan

II. Economic Contributions

5. Perspective in Islamization of the Labour Market:
   The Occupational Composition of Canadian Muslims..........69
   Masudul Alam Choudhry
6. Three Billion Dollar U.S. 'Halal' Food Market....................95
   Mohammad Arif Zakaullah
7. Islamic Banking in North America :
   Growth and Obstacles...101
   Abdulkader Thomas
8. Islamic Home Financing in North America........................117
   Syed E. Hasan

III. Political Awareness

9. Awareness and Consciousness of Muslims in Canada...........131
   Syed Serajul Islam

10. Collective Identity and Collective Action:
    The Case of Muslim Politics in America............................ 147
    M.A.Muqtedar Khan
11. Islamic Activism: Organizing Lobbying Efforts for Muslim
    Influence in America... 161
    Ejaz Akram

IV. Mass Media

12. Hollywood's Reel Arabs and Muslims.................................179
    Jack Shaheen
13. Islam, Muslims, and the American Media............................203
    Ahmadullah Siddiqi
14. Media Relations Tips for Muslim Activists..........................231
    Ibrahim Hooper

V. Educational Concerns

15. Islamic Studies in America..257
    Seyyed Hossein Nasr
16. The Curriculum Challenge for Islamic Schools in
    America..273
    Freda Shamma
17. Toward an Integrated Program of Islamic Studies:
    A Systematic Approach..297
    Abidullah Ghazi

VI. Social Issues and Concerns

18. Islamic Fundamentalism 311
    Ahmad H. Sakr
19. Muslim Youth of North America: Issues and Concerns..........323
    Riyad Shamma
20. Islamic Estate Planning: Using Wills and Living Trusts..........331
    Kareem Irfan and Nasrul Huq
21. Muslim Women in Dialogue : Breaking Walls,
    Building Bridges...337
    Ghazala Munir
22. The Lawful and the Prohibited: Our Need, Our Obsession.....343
    Shahid Athar

VII.   Works of Da'wah

23. Islamic Movement in America - Why?............... 355
    Shamim A. Siddiqi
24. Marketing Islam in the United States: A Strategy
    for Dignity, Harmony, and Prosperity.............................363
    Aqueel Ansari
25. The Future of *Da'wah* in North America..........................383
    Larry Poston

VIII.   American Muslims at the Millennium and Beyond

26. *Saiyad Fareed Ahmad* and *Saiyad Nizamuddin Ahmad*....... 399

APPENDIX I Islamic Center Directory, United States.................. 427
APPENDIX 2 Islamic Center Directory, Canada...........................474
APPENDIX 3 Islamic School Addresses in North America..........479
APPENDIX 4 Media Directory..490
APPENDIX 5 Muslim Financial Institutions.................................491

List of Contributors*

Jamal Barzinji, Ph.D., Former Dean of the Faculty of Islamic Revealed Knowledge and Human Sciences, International Islamic University, Malaysia, and Director of the International Institute of Islamic Thought (IIIT), Malaysia.

Louay M. Safi, Ph.D. Associate Professor, Department of Political Science, and Dean of the Research Center. International Islamic University, Malaysia.

Shujaat A. Khan, Ph.D., Professor of Economics, St. John's University, New York, and Editor of the quarterly newsletter, ILM, published by the Islamic Research Foundation, based in Louisville KY, USA.

Masudul Alam Choudhry, Ph.D., Professor of Economics at the University College of Cape Breton, Nova Scotia, Canada.

Abdulkader Thomas, General Manager of the United Bank of Kuwait, – New York Branch and Chairman of the Editorial Board, *The American Journal of Islamic Finance.*

Muhammad Arif Zakaulla, Ph.D., Associate Professor, Department of Economics and Management Sciences, International Islamic University Malaysia. He also served as a former Director of Public Relations & Interfaith Affairs, Islamic Society of Greater Worcester, Worcester, MA USA.

Syed E. Hasan, Ph.D., Associate Professor, Geo-Sciences Department and Director of the Environmental Sciences Project. University of Missouri, MO USA.

Seyyed Hossein Nasr, Ph.D., University Professor of Islamic Studies at George Washington University, Washington D.C. He is author of many books on Islam and on philosophy of science.

---

* Name listing is based on order of chapter presentation in the book.

Freda Shamma, Ph.D., Curriculum Coordinator, Islamic School Project, International Islamic University, Malaysia. She has many years of experience in the area of curriculum development for part time and full time Islamic schools in North America.

Abidullah Ghazi, Ph.D., Executive Director of the Iqra' International Educational Foundation, Chicago, USA.

Syed Serajul Islam, Ph.D., Professor of Political Science, formerly Associate Professor, McGill University, now working at the International Islamic University, Malaysia.

M. A. Muqtedar Khan, Editor of the *American Muslim Quarterly,* Editorial Assistant *American Journal of Islamic Social Sciences* and also a doctoral candidate in international relations at Georgetown University, USA.

Ejaz Akram, doctoral candidate in world politics at Catholic University and also serves as Assistant Editor of the *American Muslim Quarterly*.

Jack Shaheen, Ph.D., Professor Emeritus in the Midwest and a well-known writer on Arabs and Muslims of North America.

Ahmadullah Siddiqi, Ph.D., Associate Professor of Journalism and Public Relations at Western Illinois University and Secretary General of the North American Association of Muslim Professionals and Scholars, Chicago, USA.

Ibrahim Hooper, National Communications Director for the Council on American Islamic Relations (CAIR).

Ahmad H. Sakr, Ph.D., President of the Foundation for Islamic Knowledge based in Chicago. Dr. Sakr is also a Muslim activist and has been involved in many *Dawah* related TV and radio programs over the years.

Riyad Shamma, Editor, *Musings*, a youth magazine published from Cincinnati, OH. He is also the founder and director of *Muslim Writers Guild*, and the national adviser for MYNA (Muslim Youth of North America).

Shahid Athar, M.D., Physician and a Muslim activist from Indiana. He has written several books on Muslims and Islam and has also served as the Director of Interfaith Program, Indianapolis, IN USA.

Kareem Irfan, J.D., Senior Intellectual Property Attorney in Chicago and M. Nasrul Huq, M.D., eye surgeon, also the Chairman of the Living Trust and Estate Planning Committee of the North American Islamic Trust, Indianapolis, IN.

Ghazala Munir, Founding member of the Interfaith Dialogue Association in Grand Rapids, MI, and a Muslim activist who was awarded a fellowship at Yale University in 1996.

Aqeel Ansari, M.A., Economist, specializing in investment banking, environmental and land-use planning. He has been writing and publishing on Islamic issues, since 1990.

Larry Poston, Ph.D., Writer and Associate Professor at Nyack College, New York, USA.

Shamim A. Siddiqi, President, Forum for Islam Work. He is a Muslim activist in the New York area. He has written several books on Islamic propagation in the West, especially the United States.

Saiyad Fareed Ahmad, Ph.D., Associate Professor of Sociology, International Islamic University, Malaysia. He taught in India, USA, and Saudi Arabia. He has been associated with the Islamic movements of North America since 1966.

Saiyad Nizamuddin Ahmad, Doctoral candidate in Islamic Philosophy at Princeton University. He was awarded CASA Fellowship in 1995 – 96 and he also taught at the University of Texas at Austin, in 1998.

INTRODUCTION

Amber Haque

The present volume, **Muslims and Islamization in North America: Problems and Prospects,** is solely devoted to studies of Muslim profiles and problems. It is a record of the struggle of "Islamization," a chronicle of its ups and downs, its achievements and challenges; in a way, it is a sort of stock-taking of how American Muslims have fared thus far and what the future holds for them.

The central unifying theme that ties every article of this volume into a unified whole is the process of Islamization—a term, which is more, misunderstood than understood in the present American context. The reasons for choosing Islamization as our main focus are many. The Muslims of North America represent an active, vibrant, growing and expanding segment of the American society. Some of the questions that loomed large in the Muslim consciousness in the 1950's and 60's, like whether Islam will survive in America or whether recent migrants will be absorbed like the earlier slave immigrant groups are not accorded as much interest now and have only academic value. Islam has not only arrived in America and the West, but it is growing and beginning to make its presence felt. On the verge of the millennium, it is not only poised to strike deeper roots, but has become the second largest religious minority group in North America.

Despite prejudice, discrimination, conflict and hatred, the Islamic community is on the move. The American Muslim community is making significant contributions in the areas of economics, politics, and education. This opportunity has also brought frustration and challenges to the fore: the pains and frustrations of acceptance by the larger local community, issues of identity, community building, institutionalization, setting up of schools, human rights and political representation, mass media and its attitudes towards Muslims, and many other social issues. All these issues have been covered to give our readers a chance to understand the broad-spectrum situation of Muslims in America.

1

The present work however, goes beyond the layman's approach and understanding of the picture of Muslims and Islamization. Essays presented in this volume not only record an insider's account, but are scholarly attempts to move away from the subjective to the objective, the critical, and the analytical. In brief, for the first time, this volume brings original information about the Muslims of America, which is unavailable from other sources. It also covers some fresh ground in some fresh ways.

The book was initially conceptualized in early 1997. A chapterization scheme was developed and changes and revisions of the list of chapters were made a few times to make it as representative of the situation of American Muslims as possible. Titles and topics were plugged in later to give it as broad and comprehensive a scope as was practical. The authors for the articles included were apprised of the plan of the book and they knew what they were expected to write. They were given complete freedom and autonomy to write what they wanted to say. Authors' analyses of various issues will hopefully be taken as positive feedback, rather than criticisms of a particular Muslim group or organization.

The selection of the authors to match the topic was attempted on the basis of the expertise and experience they had in their area and of course, their willingness to write a fresh chapter. Except for a couple, all papers compiled here are original and, unpublished writings. Nearly all the authors, are currently domiciled in North America.

Chapter I begins by introducing "Islamization of Knowledge," a concept alien to many Americans but one that has challenged Western philosophy and theories from many angles. In his essay, Jamal Barzinji presents the chronological events shaping the movement of "Islamization of Knowledge." He points out that, after many years of work in this area, the conclusion drawn was that the *Ummah* is facing a "crisis of thought." The International Institute of Islamic Thought (IIIT) was thus formed in 1981 in the U.S. to combat this crisis through various means. In this chapter, the author discusses the role of IIIT in the Islamization process and also describes how IIIT has been involved in an in-depth analysis of the *Ummah's* crisis of thought, through conducting ongoing worldwide research and coming up with ways to solve problems in continuous interaction with Muslim communities around the world. Special emphasis is given on developing a comprehensive Islamic approach in the various human sciences and publishing textbooks and other

2

literature from an Islamic perspective. Some of the more specific achievements of the IIIT have also been highlighted.

Louay Safi points out that not only the growth of Muslim community in America has been significant in the last 3 decades; America has actually transformed the Muslims in numerous ways, and in turn, it stands ready to be profoundly influenced by the Muslim presence in America. He hails the autonomy, equality, and freedom, exercised in America and how Muslims have learned to assert their rights in protecting their interests. He is optimistic about the Muslim immigrants, their personal and collective achievements, and their efforts toward Islamic cause. He also highlights the importance of "Integration of Knowledge" and why Muslims need to be organized and make more concerted efforts toward their involvement in the American political process. Dr. Safi places special emphasis on "spiritual and technical" strengths, rather than simply numbers of Muslims and reiterates the value of unity and cooperation in enchancing the Muslim voice in America.

Shujaat A. Khan discusses the decline of Islamic Civilization in the past 500 years followed by a political stagnation and how the materialistic outlook of the West has influenced Muslim thought and practice. He reiterates the beliefs of Muslim scholars, reformists and activists by pointing out that without the transformation of the existing political and economic structures in accordance with the *Shariah*, the *Ummah* cannot make real progress in today's world and cannot spread the essence of Islam to others effectively. His paper critically examines the process of Islamization of knowledge in general as well as in the North American perspective, focusing on its purpose, potential, and prospects.

Chapter II is devoted to the economic contributions and concerns for the Muslims of North America. Masudul Alam Choudhry examines two perspectives on Islamization of knowledge and their implications on the organization of the occupational composition of the Muslim labor force in Canada. This attempt is made at conceptual as well as an empirical level. He critically evaluates the experience of approaches to Islamization in North America and draws inferences at the global level. The author proposes the epistemological approach to Islamization.

Muhammad Arif Zakaullah discusses the large potential for the *halal* food market for the Muslim business community in the U.S. and suggests ways to improve the *halal* food distribution network. He also presents a brief result of his economic survey, which he conducted in the New England area in 1987.

Abdulkader Thomas analyzes the Muslim economic surveys done in 1992 by the *American Journal of Islamic Finance* and, in early 1997, by the United Bank of Kuwait, (New York Branch) to understand the financial capacity, sophistication, and needs of Muslims in North America. He also briefs us on two newer surveys on the economic demographics of Muslims conducted by the Arab American Anti-Discrimination Committee and the Dallah Albaraka Corporation, in collaboration with the AT&T. His stance is cautionary but optimistic in regards to the economic and political maturity of the Muslims as increasing growth of Muslims in North America is drawing the attention of banks, businesses, and governments.

Syed E. Hasan summarizes the main features of all Islamic Housing projects in North America, from their origination—the works of Dr. Jamal Badawi in Halifax, Canada—to present day organizations; their membership requirements, number of houses bought and current financial strength. Based on his interviews with project directors, he gives recommendations on how to choose and invest in the available Islamic financing institutions.

Chapter III is concerned with the political maturity and involvement of the Muslims in the political process. In his paper, Syed Serajul Islam, raises some basic questions regarding Canadian Muslims. Who are these Muslims? Are they conscious of their Islamic heritage? What factors are responsible for their consciousness and in what areas are they more conscious? What is the future of Canadian Muslims? The author discusses issues of identity crisis, conflict between the old and new generations, and discrimination and racism. He also deals with Muslim obligations of prayers and *Ramadhan*, marriage related practices, food and drinks, burial, and education. He sheds some light on the institutional mechanisms for preserving consciousness, for example, the role of mosques, Islamic Centers and the Islamic Associations. He concludes that the future of Muslims depends on their ability to keep Islamic consciousness throughout generations. This can only be accomplished by developing institutions for Muslims that are adaptable and suitable to the North American environment.

Mohammed A. Muqtedar Khan writes on the issue of collective identity of Muslims in North America. He criticizes the Muslims heavily for their lack of participation in the American political process because of their inability to organize themselves, even at the community level. He believes in the collective action of Muslims and says that it is definitely there as seen in the Muslim's rituals and religious activities. However,

4

Muslims are seriously divided on ethnic and nationalistic grounds. He blames the Muslims for importing traditional *Ulema* and criticizes Muslims' conscious attempts to resist assimilation into American culture or system, especially from groups like *Tablighi Jamaat*. He offers a plan for American Muslims to view themselves as America's Muslims with unique needs and a common identity and exploit the opportunities to create a microcosm of a global *Ummah* in America.

In his chapter, Ejaz Akram claims that present American Muslims have a defeatist attitude and poor understanding of Islam, as Islam requires participation in the immediate surroundings to make them conducive for the Muslims, yet Muslims are rarely involved in the American political process. He suggests the use of pedagogical means to improve Muslim involvement in the politics of America. He emphasizes the need for organization and chalks out the strategic direction Muslims should take. The author also describes the lobbying tactics relevant for Muslim participation in American politics.

Chapter IV addresses the issues in mass media and information technology as they relate to the Muslims of North America. Jack Shaheen enumerates contributions of Muslims to the American society and laments the lack of recognition given to the Muslims by the American people, especially from the media. The writer cites over a hundred TV programs in what he calls, "Hollywood Reels," educating the reader on stereotypes and biases presented against Muslims, everyday. He is severely critical of the media authorities who create biases and anti-Muslim sentiments among the public. He contends that, in order to promote the interest of collective America, prejudices must be removed. He further says that, "nothing percolates unless you apply heat," indicating that the media itself, for instance, "the Disney Studios, should take the lead in debunking the harmful myths."

Ahmadullah Siddiqi presents a rather pessimistic, but perhaps, a real picture of Islam, Muslims, and the American Media in the North American context. He raises many practical questions related to the topic and gives a historical view of media bashing of various ethnic groups in the American context. He also gives quotes from books defaming Muslims, as well as, information that is prejudiced and inaccurate, that has resulted in crimes against Muslims. Towards the end of his paper, the author highlights what the various Muslim organizations are now doing to prevent the situation.

Ibrahim Hooper, emphasizing the importance of the Muslim image and the role of media, explains what media relations is, who are the media "gatekeepers," and how his organization carries out its mission. From starting a media watch committee to an action alert network and organizing a phone tree, the author walks us through many practical tips and guidelines on dealing with the media. His emphasis is working with media at the local level and he also explains how journalists really work, from creating news until its publication or broadcast. Some more tips are given on what to say or not say in a phone conversation or media interview, and how to deal with the tough questions.

Chapter V deals with educational achievements and future plans. In his paper on Islamic Studies in North America, Seyyed Hossein Nasr, points out that the issue of Islamic Studies is not only a matter of theoretical or academic concern, but the future of the Islamic world and North America depends upon that knowlegde. The world of Islam is too large and the force of Islam too strong to be rejected by America. He reminds us that the contributions of Muslim scientists and philosophers, words of Arabic and Persian origin, and the influence of Islamic architecture are in one way or the other, embedded in the Western world. Yet, the situation of Islamic studies as a discipline and an entity is far from satisfactory. He describes causes for this deficiency, from historic to modern times and offers suggestions for inclusion of Islamic sciences, philosophy and arts, not only as a separate entity but also as a part of general education and liberal arts program at the university level. He places special emphasis on the fact that Islam should be studied more as a religion, rather than a field or discipline.

Freda Shamma gives a brief history of the arrival of Muslim in America and then introduces the rise of Islamic schools in North America. She makes a distinction between the indigenous and immigrant Muslim's perspective, pointing out that Sister Clara Muhammad Schools were developed with concern of providing children a physically and morally safe environment and also with the concern of teaching the existing Western curricula. Immigrant Muslims, on the other hand, generally fail to see any relationship between a secular curriculum and the commitment of their children as Muslims and, consequently, rely only on home and/ or weekend Islamic instruction. She addresses the advantages of the secular curriculum but, at the same time, also raises serious concerns about itsappropriateness for Muslim children. After highlighting the needs for Islamic curriculum, she presents detailed instruction methods for the arts and sciences, based on the *Tawhidic* paradigm. She calls the work a challenge and invites Muslims to reach beyond their personal needs to join hands in designing and developing a curriculum that will truly meet the needs of the larger *Ummah* in a primarily non-Muslim society.

Abidullah Ghazi gives some background on the curriculum of schools in the West and claims that children there are more enthused about school than in places where the curriculum is not based on well-researched and integrated programs. The author describes the goals of education in Western countries, where it is conceived around some philosophy in order to develop particular kind of citizens. He says that Muslims must also work together in developing not only Islamic literature for children but an Islamic system of education, with the goals of developing Islamic personalities. He presents the perspective of Islamic education with brief statements of need. He is especially concerned about the Muslims living as tiny minorities in the West and describes the role which Iqra' Educational Foundation plays in assessing and fulfilling the changing needs of Islamic education worldwide.

Chapter VI covers social issues important to Muslims. This chapter begins with the issues and concerns Muslims have regarding the image of Islam in North America. Ahmad H. Sakr explains how Islam is a total way of life, rather than a religion. He addresses many different terms used in relation to Islam that connote negative image of Muslims and Islam. He gives "internal" and "external" reasons for the fear of Islam, which the West has often portrayed incorrectly. The author tries to remove misconceptions about Islam and stresses the positive relationship and commonalties between Muslims and Christians and suggests ways to improve the situation.

Riyad Shamma talks very frankly about the way Muslim youth are discussed in regional conventions, Islamic Center dinners, and *Khutbas*. He takes the readers' attention toward the Muslim youth; who these youth really are, and exactly what is being done for or by them that addresses the future, which is in their hands. He discusses the "threats," which youth get from their parents and the society at large, and contends that it is this threat which causes a majority of the problems among the youth. He offers suggestions on what Muslim youth really need today in America and educates readers on what things are being done today by various youth groups, Muslim organizations, and Islamic schools. He also discusses the future plans, support needed, and what every Muslim can do to help.

The next major issue, which every Muslim American is facing, is that of *halal and haram*, written by Shahid Athar. The author starts his essay by making a remark that, what makes Muslim-living difficult in a non-Muslim country, is enjoying the "permissible" and avoiding the "forbidden." He says that it is sometimes hard to make the distinction between the two. He addresses issues that Muslims are facing, starting from diet and social mixing, to the dress code for both, men and women. He also talks about interaction issues with non-Muslims. He deals with many personal experiences, which he has faced over the last 25 years living in North America, and calls them "Horror Stories." An interesting aspect of his writing is the result of a survey, which he had sent to 20 "prominent" Muslims of U.S., to "assess their opinion of the lawful and the prohibited." After giving the expert opinions, he discusses the issues from his own perspective.

Kareem Irfan and M. Nasrul Huq describe "Islamic Estate Planning Using Wills and Trusts." Intricate details of the inheritance laws from an Islamic perspective and laws of the land are dealt with, in brief, and simple to understand language. The pros of having a Living Trust and an Islamic Will are emphasized.

Ghazala Munir begins by highlighting the role of women in building families, communities and societies, and what Muslim women of America are doing in terms of *da'wah* efforts. The author says that, in order to have dialogue with peoples of other religions, it is important for Muslims to understand other faiths. A true dialogue can take place on the basis of mutual respect and trust; nevertheless, we have to be well grounded in our own ideology so that we don't see others as threat to our belief system. She names women of modern day America and on the international scene, who are extending the message of Islam in various spheres of life. She also discusses the aims and methods in interfaith dialogues gaining popularity and controversy on the American soil.

Chapter VII deals with the Works of *da'wah*. Aqeel Ansari, while acknowledging the influence of the West (and especially of the U.S.) over today's man, writes that, the seller who can market his product effectively in the U.S. opens up tremendous opportunities worldwide. In his philosophical essay, he deals with the topic of *da'wah* from a marketing angle, contending that Muslims need to understand the nature of their product, they need to identify direction of their efforts, and they also need to develop strategies consistent with those directions. He describes the lifestyle of submission and offers a "marketing strategy" based on revealed knowledge. He indicates that the buyer who has the freedom of choice for our product, should be made aware of the accountability for the choices he makes. The author also offers an approach different than slogan and speeches; harmony and prosperity. He considers "one buyer at a time" as the best approach of extending *da'wah*.

Larry Poston begins by asking whether Muslim *Da'is* will become successful in their missionary work and strengthen Islam or will the growth of Islam be only temporary. He distinguishes between two general philosophies of *da'wah*, the "defensive-pacifist" approach and the "offensive-activist" approach. He says that Muslim organizations are increasing, but for the most part they are still small, unorganized, poorly staffed and poorly funded. He criticizes the Muslims who refuse to adapt any Qur'anic precept to Western ways, requiring instead the non-Muslim society be transformed to accommodate to Muslim law. He notes that although some important windows for conversion of non-Muslims have closed, there are still some ways of improving the situation. One major way is for the Muslims of North America to develop and follow an indigenous American leadership. Other ways are influencing the media, avoiding direct attacks upon Christian teachings, improving *da'wah* at the local level, rather than national level, and adoption of the missiological approach. It is educational to read his report, based on research, on why non-Muslims convert to Islam.

Shamim A. Siddiqui starts by saying that after the collapse of Soviet Union, the U.S. is championing the cause of freedom, free market, democracy, and human rights in the world, amidst their philosophy of liberalism. This, the author believes, is a double standard, as can be seen through numerous examples around the world. He also criticizes the Muslim countries for their inability to produce a practical model of Islam and its teachings. He considers North America as an ideal place for implementation of the American as well as the Islamic ideologies that could benefit the peoples of the world.

In the last chapter, Saiyad Fareed Ahmad and Saiyad Nizamddin Ahmad offer an analysis of the problems and prospects for North American Muslims at the millennium and beyond. They explain the term "millennium" from Islamic perspective and acknowledge that accurately predicting the future is nothing but a hazardous venture. On the future of Islamic religiosity, the authors write that Islam will not only survive but flourish given certain conditions, which the present day American Muslims must meet - a critical one of which is raising Muslim children

"Islamically." Especially interesting is the authors' contention that despite the religious freedom guaranteed in the American constitution, there remains a tendency in the American social institutions undermining all religions, in general. The authors address the issue of Muslim identity on the North American scene and provoke thought by saying that modern Muslims being an "unreflective sort, are something of an embarassment to Islam." The value of proper education is emphasized and the role of Muslims in American politics is stressed. Of special interest is the authors' analysis and response to Huntington's theory of the "Clash of Civilizations." Amidst present image of Islam and Muslims in America, the authors opine that Muslims being a "median community," in a society of extremes, will also have to become an active, assertive, and vibrant community, working towards the benefit of the society as a whole. The authors also point out that the major organizations in North America should prepare a Muslim agenda for the millennim in order to chart the course of action for future years.

I

ISLAMIZATION OF KNOWLEDGE IN NORTH AMERICA

History of the Islamization of Knowledge and Contributions of the International Institute of Islamic Thought

Jamal Barzinji

Since the European challenge rose to confront the Muslim *Ummah*, Muslims have never given up their attempts to catch up with Europe and in trying to rebuild Muslim civilization. One early approach was "industrialization," following the example of Europe, and pursued by Sultan Mahmud II (1784-1839) throughout the entire Ottoman Sultanate. That was followed by numerous other attempts, outstanding among which, were the efforts of Mohammad Ali Pasha (1769-1849) in Egypt.

Another approach pursued was the political reform by Muslim reformers, outstanding among whom was Sheykh Mohammad Ibn Abd al-Wahab in the Arabian peninsula in the second half of the 18th century. There were also other movements in North Africa, Persia, Afghanistan, and India (e.g., The Sunusi Movement of North Africa, the Mahdi movement of Sudan, the reform movement of Midhat Pasha in Turkey, Khayri-i-Din Pasha in Tunisia, Malikum Khan in Persia, and Sayyid Ahmed Khan and Amir Ali in India).

The culmination of all these efforts was the reform movement of the late 19th century and early 20th century. This was pioneered by Sayyid Jamal Eddin al Afghani (1837-1897), his colleague and contemporary Sayyid Abd Rahman al-Kawakibi (1848-1902), Sheykh Mohammed Abdu (1849-1905), and his student Sayyid Mohammed Rashid Ridha (1865-1935). We also find the movements of leading *Ulema* in Persia, Iraq, and India, all aspired to produce the required change in the *Ummah*.

While such movements succeeded in stirring up concerns and bringing awareness to the *Ummah*, we find that, in general, they receded without bringing about the anticipated change or improvement in the condition of the Muslim *Ummah*. However, most of those reformers realized that the problem was more deeply rooted in the *Ummah* than a political crisis or a lack of industrialization to catch up with Europe. We see in writings and speeches of many Muslim reformers that they perceived the problems of the *Ummah* as related to a crisis in thinking of the Muslim intellectuals, scholars, and *Ulema*. For example, we find that Sheikh Abd al-Kadir al-Maghribi in his book "Zikrayat wa Ahadith" ("Memoire and Discourses" pp. 32) quotes Sayyid Jamal-al-Din who talked about the need for a thorough religious reform movement which is not unlike the movement of Martin Luther, the founder of Protestantism in Europe. Such a movement would deal with uprooting what has settled on the minds of intellectuals and non-intellectuals alike, in their misunderstanding of many concepts of *Aqidah* and basic Islamic beliefs and texts of *Shariah*.

Sayyid al-Afghani also presents us with a picture of the general condition of the *Ummah* as follows: "We can say that people of the East, after what they had enjoyed of a great role on earth, a formidable state and the width and breadth of dominion and might, descended from that high place and allowed the colonizers to occupy their lands because, somehow, they stopped using their brains and were morally corrupt" (*Silsilah alA'mal al-Majhulah*, 1883, pp. 91-99). Here are some examples that testify to the influence of Afghani's views on many of his students and scholars who followed in his footsteps on the way of reform of thought:

1. Sheikh Mohammed Abdu in elaborating upon the opinion of Afghani says: "I have been raising my voice calling on two major issues: (1) to liberate and free the mind from the mentality of blind imitation (*Taqlid*) and misunderstanding of Islam, so that we may approach Islam the way our forefathers did and that is to apply our reason to it." This was, of course, in addition to his discussion on the need for reform in the art and political arenas.

2. Sayyid Abdul-Rahman al-Kawakibi repeatedly insisted that the only way to reform or improve the condition of the Muslims was to achieve one thing and that is, "to make a deliberate and organized effort to eradicate the perversion (*Jahiliyyah*) of our *Ulema* and the ignorance of the masses." Another point of concern for him

is for the Arabs to assume their role in managing the Muslim *Ummah*. Kawakibi also elaborated on the functions of the famous *Jam'iyyat Um al-Qurah*, stating that, on top of the list is to educate the masses, fight illiteracy, generate interest in the arts and sciences, improve methods of teaching Arabic and Islamic disciplines, and make a concerted effort to reform the foundation of education and textbooks therein.

3. Sayyid Mohammed Rashid Ridha, was among the scholars who repeatedly called for reform in the *Ummah* based upon mastery of both religious Islamic disciplines and worldly secular disciplines (*Ulum-al-Din wa ad-Dunia*) and that the reform should be done in a contemporary manner. Sheikh Rashid Ridha comments on how he was impressed and influenced by the Afghani thought, saying that his understanding of Islam convinced him that the issue of reform has to assume a different level. "In the past, my concern used to be trying to rectify the beliefs and *Aqidah* of Muslims, exhorting them away from prohibitions and encouraging them to do worship, asking them to be humble and deny this world. Following my interaction with the thoughts of Jamal din al-Afghani, now, I understand that it is essential to preach and guide the Muslims in general to what civilization is all about and how important it is for them to maintain their states and to compete with the emerging nations in sciences, arts, industry, and all the ingredients of modern life."

Following this first generation of reformers, at the turn of the century, we find that the modern Islamic movements took over and carried the banner. These movements developed their discourse so they became a comprehensive call, benefiting and picking up from what those early reform movements had left. This was within the framework of *al-Ikhwan al-Muslimun* (the Muslim Brotherhood) established by Imam Shahid Hassan al-Banna in 1928, in addition to other reform movements like *Jama'at-I-Islami* which Abu al-A'la al-Mawdudi established in 1941 in the Indian Subcontinent.

It was only natural that these movements would develop the discourse of the early reformers and present a more general and comprehensive call addressing the masses. As such, we find a lot of compromises and maybe some shallowness in the treatment of issues of concern, which does not go to the depths of rationalization as the early reformers did. At the same time, we also find that the modern Islamic movements gained tremendous experience in dealing with the masses and making some effort to organize them and present some aspects of Islam in their midst such as economic cooperation, social counseling, and educational setup. These things were not available during the earlier generation of reformers.

As a result of this popularization of the Islamic discourse, we find that the brilliance of Imam Hassan al-Banna, which can be felt in many of his writings and speeches, does not find its match among his followers in the organization. In many cases, we see that the movement was concerned with horizontal expansion, unaware of the more serious issues relating to the crisis of its content and of thought. We can look back now and see how much the Islamic movement missed by not addressing this issue at an early stage. This resulted in major obstacles in the way those movements handled the concerns of the Muslim *Ummah* and the issue of reform. We see that despite the very active involvement of the Islamic movements in the political and social arena, it is obvious that these movements were still far from achieving the objectives that they had set for themselves. Some observers even contend that the gap between the aspirations and reality has been widening over the past several decades. This issue is further compounded by the complexity of the present day situations and challenges that we see in both the social and political fields. Today, we can confidently say that it is unfortunate that the path pursued by the contemporary Islamic movement actually, contributed to its failures, because little attention was given to the essence of the crisis: the crisis of thought. The prevailing assumption in the Islamic movement that it has total monopoly on the interpretation of Islam (whether explicitly said or implicitly assumed), did not help to develop a new vision and approaches to handle the crisis of the *Ummah*. Invariably, the Islamic movement resorted to rhetoric and emotional appeal in order to stir up the masses to secure their loyalty and following. In other cases, we find that the majority of the followers of the Islamic movement were among the young students and youths who would soon mature and fall out of the movement and settle in society. All of this deprived the Islamic movement of utilizing and capitalizing on the brilliant minds of its members and the masses, to raise their awareness and address the issue directly in better hope of its resolution.

It is interesting to note that when the *Ikhwan* movement was inflicted with the first crisis in 1948 at the hands of the monarchy, and then again in 1954, following the revolution of Abd En-Naser, we started seeing more interest in intellectual development within the ranks of the *Ikhwan* movement. Outstanding among the leaders who were concerned with the issue and crisis of thought were Shahid Abd el-Kadir Oda, Ustaz Farid abd el-Khaliq, Dr. Fathi Othman, and Sheikh Mohammed el-Ghazali.

These efforts, however, were too little and too shattered to produce the change that was desired. As a result, the Muslim *Ummah* remained far from real change and improvement in its conditions. We also note that the reawakening movement, that took place throughout that period, was unable to address the issue of seeking practical and direct guidance from the revelation in order to develop a workable model or a system that is applicable in real life situations.

Even today, we see that the reawakening movement in its latest wave, which started in the 70s, is starting to fade out in many parts of the Muslim world. And as this revival and reawakening movement recedes, we find a more aggressive approach now towards modernity, especially a secular one. The West finds itself in alliance with whatever is leftover of Marxism, Leninism, and the like, and trying to blow some life into them, and get them to battle the Islamic revival that we have been witnessing in the last two or three decades. Also, we are seeing a surge of studies and publications on the issue of modernity, why it has failed in the past, and what is needed for its survival and success. The Muslim *Ummah* is being bombarded afresh with such views in an attempt to do away with whatever is left of its vitality and the *Ummatic* bonding. The secularists are trying to convince us that this defeated *Ummah*, in backwardness, has failed to adapt to Western modernity for reasons that must be uprooted from it. Basic among those reasons is the Islamic mentality itself, which has blocked the way towards full and proper understanding of the modernizing scheme. Otherwise, modernity in itself is an excellent program and it is the only hope for the Muslim *Ummah*, a program that has proven its success in every place and time.

It is only appropriate here to ask why these Islamic reform movements have failed in achieving the desired results. And why is the *Ummah* still weak and defeated the way we see today, despite all the sacrifices and efforts made toward its reawakening. The main reason for this could be that these reform movements invariably addressed only a few issues and left others. These reform efforts also did not go the full length in order to comprehend the real crisis in the Muslim *Ummah* and to plan for its revival in a systematic and scientific manner.

As the condition of the *Ummah* continued to deteriorate, a group of Muslim youth, while attending different universities in the United States, had the opportunity for revaluation and reassessment of the various Islamic movements in the Muslim world. The resources available to the students were limited, but the enthusiasm was there to keep them going. A series of seminars were held between 1968 and 1977 focusing on such crucial questions as: What went wrong in our history, why have repeated reform movements failed, what is expected of the contemporary Islamic movements, and is there any real hope for them to achieve their objectives?

Gradually, and after much labor, it became more and more evident to the group that the crisis of the *Ummah* is primarily in its thought which has become totally stagnant, unable to come to its rescue, or to generate answers to the emerging questions and challenges. In fact, many of the problems that the *Ummah* is suffering from are no more than symptoms of the crisis of its thought.

In light of this realization, the Association of Muslim Social Scientists (AMSS) was founded under the umbrella of the MSA (The Muslim Students' Association of the US and Canada). The AMSS reached out to many movement leaders, scholars, social scientists, both within and outside the US, to debate the issue of the crisis of thought and seek their critical evaluation. It was finally decided in 1977 that the debate had matured to the point where an international conference should be called to discuss this issue. About 30 invited participants from among the top scholars, movement leaders, and intellectuals from all over the world met in Switzerland in November 1977 to discuss the issue.

The First International Conference on Islamization of Knowledge (Switzerland, 1977)

The unanimous consent of the participants was that the crisis of the *Ummah* is rooted in the thought and mind of the Muslims. The prevailing educational system in the Muslim world which is based on the Western secular world view, is making it more difficult for Muslim intellectuals to see their way out of the crisis.

It became evident that new effort is needed to reform the methodology of thought at its foundation, so the crisis and the resulting malaise in

18

the *Ummah* can be addressed critically and comprehensively. The new reform effort should present a systematic and methodological approach to rebuild Islamic knowledge on the same firm foundation that supported Islamic Civilization in its first cycle. The Muslims, being an *Ummah* of a Divine message, can only rise to civilization dominance if they carry the message in its original clarity, purity, and relevance.

The Switzerland conference further concluded that the complexity of the crisis, both in its historical and present day dimensions, make it far beyond the capability of individual efforts, no matter how dedicated or sincere one may be. It was then agreed that a collective effort is needed in the form of specialized institutions working specifically toward a resolution of the crisis.

It was in response to this call that, in 1981, the International Institute of Islamic Thought (IIIT) was founded and registered in the USA. Among the objectives that IIIT was set to achieve were the following:

1. To make the *Ummah* aware of the crisis in all its dimensions.
2. To research and understand the contemporary crisis of Islamic thought and how it may be resolved.
3. To revive Islamic thought, develop its methodology, and relate it to the objectives of *Shariah*.
4. To develop a comprehensive Islamic approach to the social sciences and the humanities in a manner that relates to the needs of contemporary society to human nature and the Islamic ideals.
5. To develop, coordinate, and direct research in different, yet related fields, resulting in the production of textbooks that clarify the vision and lay the foundation for Islamic disciplines in the Human Sciences.
6. To develop the necessary human resources capable of fulfilling these objectives.

Following the conference in 1977, the IIIT Office was set up in 1983 in the USA. An aggressive program of international conferences was adopted in order to reach out to the intellectuals, academicians, and scholars around the world.

The Second International Conference on Islamization of Knowledge - (Islamabad, Pakistan, 1983)

In 1983, the Second International Conference on Islamization of knowledge was held in cooperation with the International Islamic University, Islamabad and was attended by a number of prominent scholars and leaders who presented and discussed issues on Islamic thought and knowledge. This conference had two objectives:

- To expose the participants to the findings of the first conference, and on formulation of IIIT, addressing the crisis in the *Ummah*.
- To encourage critical evaluation of the crisis of the Muslim *Ummah* and its causes and symptoms, to enable scholars and researchers to address and treat it as a priority.

The approach of IIIT to the crisis of thought in the Muslim *Ummah* takes into consideration two main factors which contributed to the crisis:

- The Western cultural and educational onslaught, especially in the fields of human and social sciences, which resulted in leaders and intellectuals in the Muslim world looking towards the West for knowledge, unaware that the body of this secular knowledge was developed out of a world view that is totally alien to the Islamic worldview. Western knowledge reflects Western experiences and is tailored to meet its specific needs in total denial of revelation as the source of guidance and knowledge. As a result of this, we find that Muslim intellectuals are torn between Western values and precepts on the one hand, and Islamic beliefs, values and norms on the other. At IIIT, we are convinced that the crisis in the Muslim mind is aggravated in the educational system, borrowed blindly from the West and implemented all over the Muslim world, which is systematically producing graduates who are cultural misfits, indoctrinated in alien values. If we look closely at the state of affairs, we find that much of the loss of identity and conflict in thought is a result of this dichotomous duality in our educational system. The situation is so critical that the cornerstone in any effort to regain our civilizational intellectual Islamic identity has to be in the Islamization of disciplines in the social sciences.

- The big gap is now present between the intellectuals of the Muslim world and their legacy (*Turath*). The conscience and cultural memory of the Muslim *Ummah* embodied in its legacy are not accessible today to the general body of millions of university and college graduates of the Muslim world. Except for the very few who are trained in *Shariah* sciences and who have little or no say in the management of the affairs of the *Ummah*, the mass of the educated people in the Muslim countries cannot deal with traditional literature. In fact, they are not even aware of the treasures therein.

The participants of the second international conference called for a first step to be taken in the reform of Muslim thought by addressing the problem of the body of Western knowledge and Islamic heritage and legacy. The need to critique, analyze, and reformulate Western disciplines in a form that deals with revelation as a source of knowledge was heavily stressed. As for the Islamic legacy, being the crucible of the products of Islamic civilization, it has to be viewed as a human effort that reflects *Ijtihad* of our forefathers during a certain time, for their environment was limited by the ceiling of human knowledge prevailing at that time. This approach, however, should not bind us or burden our dealing with the Qur'an and *Sunnah*.

The Third International Conference on Islamization of Knowledge (Kuala Lumpur, Malaysia - 1984)

This conference was co-sponsored by the Malaysian Ministry of Youth and Culture. The call for papers was sent to an extensive list of about 10,000 individuals and organizations all over the world.

The working paper presented a summary of the earlier conferences on the condition of the Muslims and the need for Islamization of knowledge. Scholars and researchers were urged to submit their papers in the following disciplines : Economics, Sociology, Psychology, Anthropology, Political Science and International Relations, and Philosophy.

The paper called for a survey of the present state of each discipline, a critical evaluation of its achievements, and suggestions for its Islamization. Among other things, the third conference aimed at the following:

- To develop plans for the reform of the foundation of thinking in the Muslim mind, with specific reference to its methodology and future priorities.
- To critique and discuss the forty papers that were accepted for presentation (out of more than 150 papers received).
- To develop an outline for the Islamization of each of the above seven disciplines.

The Fourth International Conference on the Islamization of Knowledge (Khartoum, Sudan - 1987)

The theme of this conference was "Methodology of Islamic Thought and Islamization of the Behavioral Sciences." The deliberations in the third conference convinced everyone at IIIT, and many others, that we have a major obstacle in the issue of methodology. It was then necessary to convene a conference especially for this purpose. A total of 38 papers were accepted for presentation and some 50 scholars were selected to present and discuss.

The results of the fourth conference fell short of the aspirations and hopes of IIIT. It became evident to us that the Muslim *Ummah*, represented by its scholars and intellectuals, is not yet ready to make an original contribution to human thought, more specifically in the Behavioral Sciences, based on the *Tawhidic* paradigm, and drawing on the wealth of our heritage in *Turath*. Further, it became clear that Muslim specialists in the Western disciplines of Social and Behavioral Sciences are not able to present an in-depth evaluation and criticism of their own specialization. In all fairness, we concluded, that the Western scholars had already assessed their own fields more critically than Muslim scholars could now do. The obstacle, once again, seemed to be, persistently, a lack of Islamic methodology that will provide the tools and the frame of reference for Muslim scholars to make a substantial contribution.

The fourth international conference gave us an honest first-hand evaluation of the environment that we have to deal with, an assessment of its individuals and institutions, their strengths and weaknesses. The findings of the conference told us to put a hold on future international gatherings, and instead, emphasize on small groups for research and study, and on specialized seminars in the disciplines. Our disappointment with the contribution of the Muslim *Ummah* towards a resolution of the crisis is best measured by our initial plan of 1983, and what has materialized. We had hoped that in ten years (i.e., by 1993) a number of university level textbooks would be written, with the contents thoroughly Islamized. Although we are close to that target in a few specializations, the fact remain that none exist today, notwithstanding the hundreds of research papers and dozens of books that have been published so far.

The shift of practices in the program of IIIT made it prudent to address the obstacles in the path of Islamization of thought and knowledge. In-depth treatments are now carried out in many of our twenty or so offices by small discussion groups or specialized seminars and research committees. At the headquarters of IIIT in Washington DC, we have the group on Islamization of Economics, Finance, and Development of *Usul Al-Fiqh*; while the Jordan office is home for the groups on Education and *Shariah* disciplines. The Cairo office deals with Political Science, International Relations and Economics; whereas Morocco specializes in Philosophy. The Riyadh office handles *Tafsir* and Sciences of the Qur'an and *Sunnah*; Islamabad office - Psychology, and Canada and California have their focus on studies in the rise and fall of civilizations.

Islamization of knowledge is viewed as an epistemological and civilizational necessity not only for the Muslim *Ummah*, but also for mankind at large. There is general agreement today among the Muslim and Western scholars and philosophers, that Western thought is facing a serious crisis resulting from its separation between the divine and the mundane.

The Muslim *Ummah* is uniquely qualified to reconstruct human knowledge through an integrative approach and comprehensive reading of both books of Allah: revelation, in Qur'an and *Sunnah*, and creation in the physical world. No doubt, this approach can only be pursued by scholars who are endowed with knowledge of revelation, i.e., Qur'an and *Sunnah* and human efforts, i.e., human and social sciences as well as the Islamic legacy.

It is best to clarify this point by presenting the methodology adopted by IIIT in its workplan, along the following themes:

Developing methodology for dealing with the Qur'an:

The objective here, in dealing with the Qur'an as a source of divine guidance and knowledge, is to organize human life on earth, and shape it according to the divine norms. We seem to be trapped by classical and traditional *Tafsir*, interpretations that were expressed centuries ago by great scholars to suit their time and age. None of these great scholars ever meant their interpretations to be as eternal as the Qur'an itself, for only Allah's word is absolute and is valid for all times and places. These great scholars, with full admiration and respect for their great strides and thorough scholarship, were subject to all the human limitations of fallibility and constraints of political and social pressures. On top of that, they could only have done their best within the available human knowledge at that time. Is it not against the very nature of the Qur'an, being divine and absolute, to bind it by the relatively minute knowledge that was available to our forefathers centuries ago? Therein lies the crisis of our daily dealing with the Qur'an.

With the above in mind, it is little wonder that we have failed so miserably in attempting to find solutions to the problems of contemporary society in the Qur'an, as all we are doing, classically, is to research our *"Turath"* to see if our great *Ulema* (learned people), in the days of glory of the *Ummah,* faced an identical problem. If nothing can be found, as usually is the case, we try to stretch the meaning, force an analogy, or failing all this, take a safe approach of declaring it *"Haram"* in total contradiction to the very basics of Islam.

One example, that may be cited is the case of economics and banking. Muslim economists and scholars of *Fiqh* have, so far, been helpless in developing an outline of the theory of Islamic Economics based on the broad cardinal guidelines and principles in the Qur'an, such as: *Tawhid* and brotherhood of mankind, vicegerency (*Istikhlaf*) and trust (*Amana*) on our earth. The best we have done, so far, is to imitate Western capitalist practices and institutions, thinly veiled behind Islamic words of grace, and then stitch some verses of the Qur'an or *Hadith* to it. This is not Islamization! For, indeed, the resulting system that we are calling "Islamic Economics or Finance" is much less efficient and quite inferior to its illegitimate father, Western capitalism. This cannot be a divinely inspired Islamic system. We need only to compare a typical *"Murabaha"* deal with fixed rate financing, or our *"Albai' Be Thaman Aajil"* with the much simpler indexed installment purchase.

The crisis of dealing with the Qur'an has another major contributing factor; the Old Testament and Biblical influences. The Muslim mind has been heavily burdened with fabrications, concoctions and manipulations of the scribes and interpreters of the Bible. We seem to have ignored totally what the Qur'an has repeatedly condemned *"Ahl-Al-Kitab"* for tampering with their "Holy Books." The impact of this *"Israeliyyat"* as it is commonly referred to, has been to cloud the Muslim vision and heavily shield our minds from accessing the Divine Wisdom and appreciating the miraculous beauty of the Qur'an. Even the most authentic books of *Tafsir* are infested with queer stories copied from the Talmud or similar books which seek to interpret the Torah, as if we are filling in for Allah *Ta'ala*, Be He praised. Over the centuries, many of these narrations have been accepted, resulting in adulteration in *Aqidah* and confusion in many concepts.

There is a need today to restructure the *"Ulum-ul-Qur'an"*, i.e., to free our *Tafsir* from what has crept into it. The basic characteristic of the Qur'an, being absolute in time and place, must be upheld. We also need to break away from the linguistic treatment of the text, which fragments the meaning, reducing it to literarature and vocabulary; in variance to its comprehensive, and permeating themes.

Developing a methodology for dealing with the *Sunnah*:

Ever since the days of Prophet Muhammad, and throughout the generations that followed, the Muslim *Ummah* accepted and held the *Sunnah* as binding upon them, similar to the Qur'an, within certain guidelines and limitations contained in the prophetic traditions. No scholar or *mujtahid* of the early generations questioned this matter. Later generations, however, raised some peculiar questions and engaged in extensive debate, which is documented in volumes and volumes of our *Usul and Hadith* literature. The questions concerned the *Sunnah* in general and *"Hadith al-Aa had"* or the *Hadiths* that are narrated by one or a few, in particular. The arguments and doubts that were raised left a very negative and rather dangerous effect on the unity of the *Ummah*. It gave legitimacy to sectarian and divisive trends, and diverted the efforts of our *Ulema,* from constructive work in developing a healthy methodology, to theoretical and often irrelevant issues. Prominent among the issues raised is the hierarchy of the *Sunnah* in relation to the Qur'an, and the abrogation of the *Sunnah* by the Qur'an and vice versa. Another area of concern, was the extent to which *Hadith* disciplinarians were criticized in the field of narrations, in terms of continuity, validity, and authenticity. As a result, little effort was allocated to critical studies of the text by developing scientific methods for textual analysis and researching time-space factors therein.

The IIIT has always had a special concern for the understanding of the *Sunnah* and developing an appropriate methodology for its critical evaluation. How do we make use of the *Sunnah*, being a Divine Revelation and a source of knowledge in the rebuilding of *Ummatic* civilization and culture? Without these and many other issues, there is no hope for the Muslim mind to be reconstructed and reshaped so as to qualify for the generation of Islamic thought. In order to do justice to this crucial issue, let us dwell briefly on some major concerns:

1. Comprehension and understanding of the *Sunnah* is essential for us to deal with it. What factors have affected Muslims' understanding of a text of *Hadith* throughout our history? How did confusion arise over so many *Hadiths*? What kind of mind and what preparations are needed to qualify for a healthy understanding of the *Sunnah*?

2. The rise of different scholars and sects in our history subjected the *Sunnah* to much misuse or abuse. How did these divisions arise? What is in the *Sunnah* that made it impart legitimacy to contradicting positions? Is it the way it was collected or documented or authenticated? Invariably, we find all schools and sects have been using *Sunnah* as their best weapon to defend their position or defeat an opponent's argument. What is the major reason for the concoction and fabrication of *Hadith*?

3. The time-space factors: How does the environment of a particular *Hadith* affect our understanding of that *Hadith*? Scholars of *Usul* have always taken special interest in the time, place, and the event that occasioned the *Sunnah*. They also looked closely at specific circumstances which prevailed during different stages or phases of the Prophet's life and weighed that into reports and narrations on his actions, and acceptance or consent to others' action. The issue of the Prophet as a human has been treated extensively. Is this to be taken as relating to a certain period of history? What is general, and what is not, in the *Sunnah*? What can modern studies of *Hadith* offer to help us develop the necessary methodology?

4. *Sunnah* and the Arabic language: The Prophet spoke the plain language of his people; and as such, they needed no interpretation or explanation. His companions lived the *Sunnah* in its full dimension.

26

They also understood the Qur'an directly as it addressed them, guided by the life and practices of the Prophet. Successive generations, however, needed to refer to lexicons and dictionaries to fully understand the *Sunnah* as classical Arabic lost ground as a conversational working language. Thus, we find the role of dictionaries and linguistics increasingly created a culture of literal treatment of the *Sunnah*, until, at the end, it was reduced to little more than a narration of the personal lifestyle and behavior of the Prophet with little concern for the role of building an *Ummah* and civilization. How can contemporary *Hadith* studies help liberate the Muslim mind from this atomistic and literal mentality that has made Islam devoid of its essence of *Ummah*, culture, and civilization?

5. Biblical influence on *Sunnah*: The Prophetic *Sunnah* has been the victim of many a hypocrite or traitor or overzealous Muslim. Driven by different motives, they introduced into the *Sunnah* hundreds of thousand of *Hadiths*, some containing glaringly anti-Islamic positions or orientations, totally objectionable to our *Aqidah* or *Shariah*. Despite the superb efforts by generations of great scholars, the body of *Sunnah* is not totally bug-free. What can modern facilities of information technology offer to help continue the great efforts of our glorious *Muhaddithin*?

Dealing with the Islamic legacy (*Turath*):

There are several reasons why Muslim scholars were reluctant to review and evaluate the Islamic legacy or *Turath*:

I.   The colonial era and the need to preserve the Islamic identity by instilling a sense of pride in our history.
II.   The sensitivity and negative reaction that met scattered earlier attempts which resulted from confusing a critique of an opinion with disrespect for the scholar who expressed it.
III. Misconception of the issue of consensus, so much so that a different opinion is viewed as opening the door for disunity and division.
IV.   Historically, the emergence of *Madhabs* and sects has been associated with review and evaluation of "*Turath*".
V.   The several critical challenges that confronted the Muslims and

the need for our *Ulema* to stand united and speak in one voice.

VI.   During the last two to three centuries of decline, to *Ulema* promoted attitudes and statement that blocked Muslim minds from such evaluation; such as "our predecessors left nothing untackled" and "...it is not conceivable to excel over what had been achieved."

VII.   During the era of decline, followers of each *madhab* blindly clung to their leaders, glorifying and justifying every word they uttered.

VIII. The terrible misfortunes that met our greatest Imams in the past. Imam Malik was beaten and his hand was paralyzed, Imam Shafie was brought in chains from Yemen to Baghdad, Imam Ahmad bin Hanbal died in prison, to name a few of the great founding Imams.

IX.   Confusing issues of opinion on marginal matters with *Aqidah*, which is "untouchable."

X.   The misconception of "the one saved party," which may not allow multiplicity of opinion.

The above factors, and others not mentioned here, blocked the Muslim scholars from an objective treatment of our legacy as a rich human experience developed to meet the need of the time but never intended by those great *Mujtahids* to be for all times and places.

Dealing with the Western Thought:

What is the essence of Western achievement in the social sciences and knowledge in general? How much could Western contribution help us in understanding the "*Sunan*" of Allah and the nature of His creation in mankind and the universe? To what extent can we claim Western achievements as a credit to Islamic Civilization, whether in the experimental methods of research, rational inquiry, or in the physical and natural sciences?

As stated earlier, and in fairness to the Western scholarship, the collective efforts of Muslim philosophers and social scientists fall short of what many Western scholars have criticized and questioned in their own disciplines. In our work plan, the first step would be collecting and organizing these works in the different disciplines in the form of an "Anthology on Western Thought." The next step would be to make it available to a select group of highly qualified Western trained Muslim specialists in each field. The objective would be to challenge them in order to come up with an Islamic position vis-à-vis, evaluation. It is hoped that this effort will result in university level introductory textbooks in each discipline to prepare the young Muslims in studying these subjects critically.

Developing an Islamic Methodology

It was realized from the early days of IIIT (1983-Islamabad Conference) that the issue of methodology is probably the most obstinate obstacle in the proposed plan of Islamization of knowledge. The methodology of *Usul*, which was developed early in the history of the Muslims, served the *Ummah* wonderfully. It provided an efficient tool to access the primary sources of Qur'an and *Sunnah* in order to get answers to emerging problems in developing Muslim states. However, in our effort to develop Islamized Social Sciences, it became evident, that the traditional *Usul* falls short of the need. Much debate went on before scholars accepted the need to commit *Ijtihad* in *Usul* itself.

Researches in our *Turath* unearthed a brilliant approach which was developed by Imam Al-Shatibi as *Maqasid Al-Shariah*. Little can be found in classical works, mainly because of the position taken traditionally by our Classical *Ulema,* on the sufficiency of *Usul*. The *"Maqasidi"* approach suggests that we look into Qur'an an *Sunnah* to define or identify the higher objectives of *Shariah* in each discipline, or area of human activity. The *Sunnah* then guides us into realization of the objective within the environment of the Prophet's life. This approach, it is hoped, will start by defining the kind of society the Qur'an wants to establish on earth, and the guidance that revelation provides for each area of human interaction and activity. Major Qur'anic principles of *"Tawhid"*, *"Istiklaf"*, Trust or *"Amana"*, *"Uboodiyyah"*, propose goodness of this life and brotherhood of mankind - all have to manifest themselves in an Islamized Social Science. I am glad to tell you that, so far, the IIIT has published three titles to introduce the theory and to promote its understanding.

Achievements and Future Outlook

From the initial stages of the Islamization of knowledge movement in North America, the Muslims in America played a leading role in the process. There was an opportunity for Muslims, representing various Islamic movements from everywhere, to comparatively analyze and critically assess the success and failures of the Islamic movements globally. The intellectual atmosphere of the United States was rich with research resources, universities, and libraries. Drawn to such resources, many of the brightest students and intellectuals of the *Ummah* were in America with an opportunity to meet as a forum. This forum, while being responsive to new ideas, was able to critically assess it and develop the idea in a methodological and systematic way.

With the establishment of the School of Islamic and Social Sciences (SISS), a major new opportunity has opened for the future of Islamic studies in America. SISS will provide an opportunity for excellence in Islamic studies with the perspective of Islamization of knowledge and at the same time play a role in interacting with American universities to improve the content of their Middle Eastern, Oriental, and Arabic programs.

The issue of identity is of special concern for the new generation of American Muslims who have realized that their identity can only be that of an American Muslim. Breaking away from cultural constraints, the essence of Islam must be emphasized. And it is Islamization of knowledge that lies at the essence of Islam. And these are the reasons why America will continue to be a place where the Islamization of knowledge movement would receive an honest and objective assessment.

In the past fifteen years, probably, the most valuable achievement of IIIT is the awareness brought among the scholars and intellectuals world over. IIIT seminars and publications assured that the need for Islamization of knowledge and the dilemma of the *Ummah* in its crisis of thought is debated, discussed and researched in every serious institution of Islamic learning. After IIIT's success in bringing awareness about the crisis of thought in the *Ummah*, it is now felt that there is a need to overcome the challenge for intensification in research for the next ten to fifteen years by concentrating on projects such as those of the anthologies on Western thought. The need is to locate scholars who have the capabilities to take on such a project. After this period of intensive work, research may reach the point where higher learning institutions would be able to implement aspects of Islamization of knowledge.

While the Islamization of knowledge project has been criticized, analyzed, and condemned by opponents, others have hailed and glorified it as the most promising approach to pull the *Ummah* out of its decline. In more tangible terms, we may look at the two hundred or so titles of quality books in Arabic, English, and other languages as a significant contribution to the intellectual wealth of the *Ummah*.

The Transforming Experience of American Muslims: Islamic Education and Political Maturation

Louay M. Safi[*]

INTRODUCTION

The growth of the American Muslim community in the last three decades has been quite remarkable, and holds a promise of a bright future for Islam in America. America has i 1 many ways transformed the Muslims, and in turn stands to undergo profound transformation by their presence. American Muslims, I contend, could contribute profoundly to the restoration of the spiritual and moral core of modern civilization which has been fading away with the advancement of hardcore secularism. Indeed, American Muslims are in a position to restore the spiritual and moral dimensions of modern life while continuing to be faithful to the true spirit of liberalism.

I further contend that for American Muslims to undertake this historic mission they need first to build their moral and political strengths by paying closer attention to two interrelated processes: Islamic education and political maturation. This article, therefore, examines the progress made on these two fronts, and then outlines an overall strategy for future Islamic development.

[*] I wish to register my appreciation to Prof. Ghulam Nabi Saqeb and Prof. Saiyad Fareed Ahmad. Both have read the manuscript of this chapter and provided me with useful editing suggestions. I wish also to thank Dr. Amber Haque for motivating me to write this chapter.

33

THE GREAT LEAP

To understand the earthshaking impact of the experience of American Muslims, let us first explore briefly the dynamism of the globalization process in the last half century, a period which constitutes the postcolonial era for the bulk of Muslim countries. The postcolonial era represents, for most Muslim societies, a time of great social turmoil and political upheaval. It has been also a period of experimentation and soul searching.

Colonial powers have been fairly successful in destroying traditional social and political structures and altering Muslim consciousness by introducing new institutions and patterns of social organization and interaction, and by transplanting modern education system in Muslim societies. Colonial powers altered state boundaries, carving new smaller states out of old larger ones; changed the distribution of power; established armies led by new military elites; and introduced a new lifestyle and a modern taste among the educated elites; designed new curricula for schools modeled after European curricula. While these curricula reintroduced to Muslim societies sciences that had been neglected and omitted in traditional schools, such as mathematics, physics, chemistry, they also included subjects which brought new interpretations and meanings of human experience, such as history, philosophy, and social sciences.

In the postcolonial era most Muslim countries have witnessed varying degrees of economic deterioration, particularly experienced by social classes which lost their privileged position as a result of the change in power structures. Coup d'etat by ambitious military leaders became a frequent occurrence in most Muslim countries. Economic difficulties and political turmoil, combined with the desire of the newly independent countries of the Muslim world to upgrade their technical skills, have brought hundreds of thousands of Muslims from the four corners of the world to the United States. Muslim migration to the United States increased after World War II and peaked in the seventies and eighties. Some came as students who were sent on government scholarships or by their families to pursue higher education in American universities, and then decided to make the New World their new home. Others came in pursuit of better jobs and better life. Yet others moved to the United States to escape civil wars, military occupation, or political persecution.[1]

---

1 For more details on the history of Muslim migration to the United States see Yvonne Haddad, *A Century of Islam in America* (Washington, D.C: American Institute of

The migration of hundreds of thousands of Muslims over the last four decades, undoubtedly an act of historical proportion, may prove to be a defining moment in the history of Islam, indeed in the history of mankind. For as I argue below, the migration of Muslims to the United States has contributed to the profound transformation in the understanding and practices of Islam among Muslim immigrants, as well as among the Afro-American Muslim community.[2] The impact of this massive migration of Muslims is not limited to the growing American Muslim population alone, but is bound to transform the American society at large, and even has the potential to transform Muslim societies the world over.

IN SEARCH OF COMMUNITY

Throughout the last two centuries, America has been the land of opportunities for those who were denied equal opportunities in their homeland. Many people who aspired to a life of freedom and better opportunities chose the United States as their new adopted home. Muslims are no exception. As Muslims began to realize their dreams of freedom and better economic conditions, they soon came face to face with a question which proved to be more difficult to answer than originally thought: what to do with the newly acquired freedom and wealth? After all, freedom and wealth have meaning only insofar as they can be enjoyed and expressed in a social context. For many of the immigrant Muslims, the social context in which they lived was both alien and alienating. For one thing, many Americans who were comfortable to work with immigrants in professional settings have always found it difficult to interact with people of different cultures and lifestyles in social settings.

Similarly, most Muslims found it exceedingly difficult to relate to a lifestyle they sincerely believed to be permissive and in several ways sinful. Muslim cultures, without exception, place great emphasis on chastity and abhor self-indulgence, particularly in the drinking of alcohol and sexual promiscuity. Cultural differences, therefore, limited greatly the level of social interaction between Muslim immigrants and their non-

---

Islamic Affairs, 1986); also Fareed H. Numan, *The Muslim Population in the United States*, (Washington: American Muslim Council, 1992).

2 For a general account on the impact of Muslim migration on Afro-American Muslims see Jonah Blank, "The Muslim Mainstream," *U.S. News*, 20 July 1998.

muslim neighbors and co-workers, and forced many of them to search for a community of compatible social norms and values.

The migration of Muslims in the seventies and eighties coincided with the worldwide phenomenon of Islamic resurgence. A significant number of students pursuing university education in the United States brought with them the newly found Islamic identity and activism. The Muslim Students' Association, founded in the early sixties, became the locus of Muslim activities. Initially, meetings and activities were conducted on university campuses, using university facilities. However, Muslim students soon became involved in collective projects to build local mosques, which immediately became centers for all Muslims; students or otherwise.

Throughout the United States, the mosques served as a pole around which the Muslim community was galvanized. They gradually became true community centers where Muslims prayed, received education in the teachings of Islam, conducted their marriages, celebrated their festivals, and deliberated their common concerns. It was in America that the comprehensive role of the mosque, exemplified in the Madina Mosque built by the Prophet of Islam and his companions, was restored. In America the mosque reclaimed its true meaning and comprehensive role as the center of the Muslim community.

THE CHALLENGE OF AMERICA

Muslims who came to America found themselves in the midst of a vibrant culture and assertive society. Anyone who decides to leave his or her old society and make America their new home would surely be impressed by the sense of autonomy and equality which form the core of American culture. Americans, by and large, speak their minds freely and boldly, assert their rights against any act they deem to be unfair or representing an incident of excessive use of power, and resort to collective action in pursuit of their shared interests. Muslims slowly but surely have been learning the values of asserting one's rights and the importance of organized and collective endeavors.[3]

---

3 For an interesting news feature on Muslim self-assertion see Donna Abu-Nasr, "Muslim Learn to Speak Up Like Americans," Washington: Associated Press, August, 29 1996.

While Muslims have been impressed by the vibrant American culture, and hence willing to learn from its strengths, they have been equally alarmed by its downside. Particularly of concern to Muslims is the increasing moral laxity of the American society, reflected in sexual promiscuity, violence, pornography, drug abuse, and other social ills that have been on the increase. The perceived moral laxity has prompted many Muslim parents to search for alternative schooling and social activities for their children, and hence brought them closer to Islamic centers, and highlighted the importance of community.

Moving to America and becoming part of the American society challenged the Muslims yet in another, and even more profound, way. Living in a society that provided the individual with more freedom and autonomy revealed to many Muslims the moral and political limitations of contemporary Muslim cultures which they brought with them to the New World. The American experience of the Muslims became a constant reminder not only of the extent to which the universal teachings of Islam have been confused with parochial customs and traditions, but also of the serious deformation afflicting Muslim consciousness. America has indeed challenged the old habits of Muslim immigrants and made the need, even necessity, for cultural reform more apparent than ever.

The deformation of Muslim consciousness has been a protracted and subtle process, stretching over many generations. While factors leading to cultural distortions are varied and complicated, two stand out as central to this process: spiritual laxity and intellectual rigidity. Spiritual laxity is a historical process and has inflicted all cultures and civilizations. It has been described and dissected by eminent philosophers and historians, including Plato, Ibn Khaldun, Taynbee, and Spengler, to name just a few.

Spiritual laxity takes place when the strong commitments to the beliefs and ethos of a rising and vibrant culture are weakened by the passage of time. Intellectual rigidity, on the other hand, denotes a state of confusion whereby historically bound practices and behavioral patterns are mistaken for the universal values which gave rise to them in a particular time and place.[4]

---

4 For a detailed account on the impact of moral laxity and intellectual rigidity on cultures and civilization see our book, *Truth and Reform: Exploring the Patterns and Dynamics of Historical Change* (The Open Press: Kuala Lumpur 1998), pp. 45-72.

Spiritual laxity and intellectual rigidity were brought to the fore in America. They surfaced first when ethnic commonalities triumphed over Islamic bonds as the basis of communities. Many Muslims found it easier to work with people of similar ethnic background rather than going the extra mile to work with those who share with them their values and aspirations. The result has been a continuous fragmentation, and hence waste of human and financial resources, and the loss of power.

The parochialism of Muslim immigrants was further highlighted in the generation gap between the first generation who continued to be emotionally attached to their old cultural habits, and very often insisted on replicating the old environment and living habits in all details, and the second generation who identified themselves with America, their natural homeland and the only society they ever experienced. The gap is particularly pronounced whenever the parents insist on assigning religious significance to otherwise parochial customs and traditions.

EMERGING NEW REALITY

The limitations cited above notwithstanding, several indicators reveal signs of positive developments, and hence engender hopes for a better and more promising future for the Muslim community. Evidently, spiritual and intellectual limitations have not been equally distributed throughout the community, and the Muslim community has been blessed with countless individuals who have been able to rise above their socio-cultural limitations, and have in the process succeeded in pulling others along with them.

One outstanding feature of the Muslim immigrants who came to the United States in the last few decades is that many of them are highly educated with remarkable personal achievements. The free and well-organised American society has provided these achievers with ample challenges and opportunities to bring their talents and skills to bear on the life of their communities and the greater society around them. The outstanding achievements of the morally committed and highly skilled Muslim leadership is revealed in the mushrooming of full-time schools and national organizations committed to advancing a genuine and authentic Islamic spirit despite mounting odds. The concerted and organized efforts of the local and national Islamic organizations have made remarkable inroads in a relatively short time into the mainstream social and political American life. The list of achievements includes: the establishment of hundreds of Islamic centers and full-time schools, introduction of Muslim chaplains into the U.S. military, establishment of political action and lobbying organizations, publishing houses, small size media organizations, etc.

Also remarkable is the great enthusiasm given to Islamic education by American Muslims. In a relatively short period of time, the efforts to provide Islamic education to Muslim youths progressed from weekend schools to full-time Islamic schools. There is hardly any major city in America without an Islamic school. Metropolitan areas, such as Detroit, Los Angeles, New York, and Chicago, have over a dozen full-time Islamic schools each.[5] A number of Muslim education councils have been established to coordinate efforts to improve Islamic education, particularly in the area of curriculum development and teacher training.[6]

Another remarkable achievement has taken place in the area of political organization. Several national organizations concerned with politically mobilizing the Muslim community and defending the civil and political rights of Muslims have been established in the last decade, such as the American Muslim Alliance (AMA), the American Muslim Council (AMC), the Council on American Islamic Relations (CAIR), and the Muslim Public Affairs Council (MPAC). These political-action organizations have been quite instrumental in raising Muslim awareness regarding their civil and political rights, educating them as to how they should respond to various political events through local gatherings and national conventions. They have also been lobbying the Congress and federal agencies on their behalf. This is quite remarkable, given the fact that individuals leading these efforts belong to the first generation of Muslim immigrants.[7]

---

5 There are a little over one hundred full-time schools nationwide, over sixty percent of which are concentrated in six states: California, New Jersey, New York, Illinois, Michigan, and Texas. See the Muslim Students' Association's website for a complete list of Islamic Schools [URL:www.msa-natl.org/resources/schools.html].

6 There are over fifteen educational councils and organizations involved in promoting Islamic schooling and providing training and consultation. See ibid. for details.

7 There are over a dozen socio-political Islamic Organizations which are committed to promoting Muslim unity and encouraging collective action. These include, in addition to AMA, AMC, CAIR, and MPAC, Islamic society and North America (ISNA), Islamic circle of North America (ICNA), Islamic Assembly of North America (IANA), Human Assistance and Development International (HADI), Muslim American Society, Muslim Students' Association (MSA), and others.

The great interest in Islamic education and political action, alluded to above, though still in its infancy, holds great hope for a brighter future. But the American Muslim community will have to travel a long way before its struggle for Islamic education and effective political voice can bear fruits. More importantly, Muslim leaders must develop sharp vision and clear goals, and then proceed to plan their steps with precision and vigor. I will therefore devote the remainder of this article to addressing some of the concerns pertaining to the main foundations of the future development of the Muslim community in America: Islamic education and political maturation.

THE PREDICAMENT OF SECULARIST EDUCATION

Historically, education was viewed as a process aiming at both providing students with technical skills and inculcating a set of values and beliefs that are basic and essential for the formation of conscientious citizens and good human beings. Indeed this was the purpose of education in the United States throughout the nineteenth century and the early part of the twentieth century. Gradually, however, the inculcation of moral values was deemphasized, and schools were seen as a place for providing students with technical know-how. Many educationists thought that value inculcation amounted to indoctrination, and hence was inappropriate for secular schools. A secular school's mission, they insisted, should be limited to teaching students how to think and make decisions, and hence allow them to adopt their own values and beliefs. Others thought that since moral values are rooted in the religious experiences of the people, a secular school operating in a multi-religious society should better leave the task of moral orientation to parents and the churches. In many cases, however, neither could the children come to grips with moral issues on their own, being denied guidance by school authorities, nor could families provide proper moral orientation in a rapidly changing and exceedingly complex modern world, as they were lacking the professional training or the time needed to handle this strenuous task, or both.

Evidently, to provide logical and methodical knowledge and then expect inexperienced and fragile souls to make right choices and correct decisions was to expect too much. For one thing, making choices and decisions is never merely a procedural matter, but presupposes the presence of a set of principles and criteria that form the basis of one's decision. For another, it is quite unreasonable to expect a child, who lacks moral fortitude to begin with, to forego immediate pleasure and gratification for personal and societal interests that seem distant and elusive. This is more so when youngsters are bombarded with media programs which constantly glorify violence and thrive on erotic stimulation. Most vulnerable and susceptive to the effects of the sex-and-violence content of media programs are the children who come from poor and broken families, and who lack parental guidance and supervision.

It is quite appropriate before we turn to examine the role of Islamic education in counter-acting moral laxity to pause a bit to understand the social and cultural conditions which contributed to the moral "neutrality" of the education system in America. The current neutralistic posture of the American education system signifies an advanced stage of the project of secularism which has successfully undermined the authority of religion as an essential source of moral and ontological knowledge. The process of secularization started as an effort aiming at liberating science and scholarship from the authority of the church. Early advocates of the separation of state and church, such as Descartes, Hobbes, Locke, and Rousseau, had no intention to undermine religion, or faith in the divine, but rather predicated their reformist ideas on the notion of God and civil religion. Descartes, hence, argued "that the certainty and truth of all knowledge depends uniquely on my awareness of the true God, to such an extent that I was incapable of perfect knowledge about anything else until I became aware of him."[8] Similarly, Rousseau, while critical of the way religion was traditionally taught and practiced, recognized the need, even the necessity, of religious commitment and faith for the modern state to function properly. He, therefore identified a number of "dogmas", and argued for their inclusion in the "civil religion" he advocated: "The existence of an omnipotent, intelligent, benevolent divinity that foresees and provides; the life to come; the happiness of the just; the punishment of sinners; the sanctity of the social contract and the law – these are the positive dogmas. As for the negative dogmas, I would limit them to a single one: no intolerance."[9]

---

8 Rene Descartes, *Meditations on First Philosophy*, trans. John Cottingham (Cambridge: Cambridge University press, 1986), p. 49.

9 Jean-Jacque Rousseau, *The Social Contract*, Trans. Maurice Cranston (London: Penguin Books, 1968), p. 186.

Even Kant, who limited the notion of truth to empirical experience and labored to set morality on a rational foundation insisted that "without a God and without a world invisible to us now but hoped for, the glorious ideals of morality are indeed objects of approval and admiration, but not springs of purpose and action."[10] However, by denying the possibility of transcendental truth, and as a result of the relentless attack on the authority of revelation as a source of ethical and ontological knowledge, secularist scholars have been able to successfully marginalize religion and undermine morality. The efforts to ground morality in utility and cost-benefit calculation, rather than truth, proved to be counter intuitive and futile, and gave rise to moral relativism; which continues to undermine efforts to revive ethical teaching in schools.

Overcoming the moral crisis of education requires a solution that restores religious faith while continues to be mindful of the need to avoid any authoritarian imposition of beliefs and values particular to any specific religious group on others.

A MODEL FOR ALTERNATIVE EDUCATION: TOWARDS INTEGRATION OF KNOWLEDGE

By undermining the authority of divine revelation as a source of moral values and the overall meaning of life, secularism has contributed in a decisive way to the loss of meaning and transcendental purpose of life, and hence has precipitated the rise of the hedonistic and nihilistic tendencies of modern society. Drug abuse, teenage pregnancy, school violence, collective suicide, rampage killing, and child prostitution, are some of the more visible manifestations of modern-day hedonism and nihilism.

The loss of meaning did not happen immediately as a result of the marginalization of religious knowledge because philosophy replaced religion as provider for the overall meaning and purpose of life. Indeed, up to the late nineteenth century the various fields of knowledge were seen as branches of the study of philosophy. While the various fields of knowledge were united around a core of religious beliefs and values in medieval times, the unity of knowledge and the interconnectedness of

---

10 Immanuel Kant, *Critique of Pure Reason*, trans. Norman Kemp Smith (New York: Macmillan, 1929), p. 640.

disciplines were ensured later by a core of metaphysical beliefs and values.

However, by the mid-nineteenth century, knowledge began to experience a process of fragmentation or disintegration, as philosophy, religion, and ethics were reduced to disciplines standing on par with other disciplines. The various disciplines of knowledge have become autonomous spheres lacking any uniting core of overarching beliefs and principles. With the fragmentation of knowledge, the concept of universally valid truth and moral principles became problematic, and truth became parochial, as it became valid only to a specific discipline or community.

The new concept of truth did not only take away the total meaning of human existence, but led to the fragmentation of human consciousness and knowledge. For in the absence of a set of absolute values universally valid, the various branches of modern knowledge (i.e. sociology, economics, psychology, political science, etc.), which emerged out of the demise of modern philosophy, developed their own idiosyncratic standards. With the development of modern social sciences the unity and interdependence of the various fields of knowledge were lost. Henceforth ethics and religion were reduced into two of the various spheres of knowledge, independent of economics, politics, psychology and all other fields of social sciences. Thus morality does not figure in economic studies and is not a legitimate concern of the specialist in the field. Economic transactions are valued or devalued only in relation to the concern of utility maximization; justice, fidelity, and fairness are not legitimate concerns of the modern economist.

Because modern knowledge lacks a central core and overarching principle to keep the totality of social experience in unity, the consciousness of the modern man has been disintegrated, and modern social sciences have been fragmented. The mission of Islamic education is to reintegrate the fragmented consciousness of modern man by once again repositioning divine revelation at the core of human consciousness, the binding and nurturing core which the secular project has managed to destroy.

Methodologically speaking, restoring the divine core to the spheres of knowledge means that revelation has to be reinstated as a source of knowledge. This has to be done without bouncing to the other extreme one finds in traditional knowledge, whereby notions found in the divine text are dogmatically interpreted, without regard to the knowledge acquired through worldly experience. Both revelation and the experienced reality should form the foundation for producing a body of knowledge dealing with modern socio-temporal challenges while remaining true to the spirit, purposes, and aspiration of transcendental truth. This body of knowledge has to emerge out of a vigorous and methodical application of reasoning on the two main sources of knowledge: divine revelation and the observable world.

The above conclusion has far-reaching implications for the ongoing effort to develop an Islamic education capable of producing well-balanced personalities that combine efficacy and vigor with profound religious commitment and faith. The complete secularization of the autonomous spheres of knowledge simply means that the Islamic school curriculum that haphazardly combines subjects produced by secularist schools with Islamic subjects does not go far enough towards producing a balanced Islamic personality. For such a curriculum fails to reconcile the internal contradictions between the secularist worldview embedded in the subjects adopted from the public school system and the Islamic worldview reflected in the Islamic study subjects.

If the Islamic school project is to succeed in achieving the goal of graduating well-rounded human beings, creative energy and financial resources must be channeled to produce an alternative school curriculum capable of bringing about integration of knowledge and consciousness, so ultimately students graduate from Islamic school with (1) clear awareness of their purposes in life and responsibilities to their family, community, and humanity at large; (2) sharp vision as to what has to be accomplished for the betterment of human life; and (3) methodical thinking and substantive knowledge of the social and natural environments.

While some schools and individuals have already started moving in this direction, the resources required for achieving these goals are beyond any individual person or school.[11] The task requires concerted action on the part of the entire Muslim community. The few educational councils concerned with advancing the agenda of Islamic education, and effecting better coordination among Islamic schools and educationists, such as the Council on Islamic Education (CIE) and the Council of

---

11 Susan Douglass, in association with the Council on Islamic Education, U.S.A., has made important contribution in this area; see, for example, *Strategies and Structure for Presenting World History* (Beltsville, MD: Amana Publications, 1994). Similarly Freda Shamma, in association with the International Islamic School Project, under the auspices of the International Islamic University, Malaysia, has done some important seminal work in Islamic curricula development.

Islamic Schools of North America (CISNA), have not received the type of community support required for the arduous task they face. The lack of substantial support is due partially to the lack of awareness of the need for an alternative school curriculum based on the notion of integration of knowledge. The meager support given to educational councils is also due to the fragmentation of communities and organizations alluded to earlier, and the absence of strong and well-organized cooperation on the national level.

The above conclusion underscores the interconnectedness between the development of educational system and the political maturation of the Muslim community, and hence leads us directly to raise the question of political action. This is the focus of the following section.

POLTICAL MATURATION

Most Muslims who migrated to the United States grew up in societies that had become accustomed to political elitism and popular quietism. It was, therefore, quite natural for them to shun political activism and maintain low-key political posture.

However, beginning with the late seventies, a new wave of Islamic activists arrived in America. These were mainly young men who had come to pursue their higher education in American universities. Emboldened by the nascent Islamic resurgence in the Muslim world, and saturated with Islamic idealism, they busied themselves with political agitation and mobilization. But the political activism of these Islamists was limited to activities targeting the Muslim community in particular, and involved mainly programs that were high on rhetoric and low on action. While high-rhetoric conferences and meetings served initially as an outlet for the anger and frustration of Muslim activists with regard to moral degradation and political subjugation practised by Muslim regimes supported by major western powers, including the U.S. government, they also served as avenues for exchange of views and ideas, and the education of the American Muslim community about the plight of Muslims the world over.

The early nineties witnessed a remarkable elevation in the level of Muslim political involvement. For the first time American Muslims began to rally mainstream political leaders to their causes. The effort to use the voting power of Muslims to influence the decisions and priorities of American politicians has been led by Islamic centers and community-based organizations; some national organizations (e.g., AMC and CAIR) have been playing an important role in educating the public on Islamic causes, and providing logistical and technical support to Muslim activists. National political action groups have also been lobbying the Congress and the Administration in support of Islamic causes.

Yet the overall impact of the political action of Muslim organizations on the general public and the American political scene is hardly noticeable. While reasons for the meager impact of Muslims on American politics are multifarious, two clearly stand out: political fragmentation and political aloofness.

Political fragmentation is often the result of the lack of political experience and maturation. Many Muslims are comfortable in working with those who share with them cultural attitudes and habits, or ideological commitments. The result is a lot of reluctance and hesitation in dealing with individuals and organizations outside their group. Some self-seeking community leaders have found it convenient to play the ethnic and ideological card to maintain their grip on the community affairs. While selfishness and short-sightedness play an important role in the fragmentation of Muslims, the lack of political experience and maturity lies at the core of the problem. Many Muslims came, as has been pointed out earlier, from a socio-cultural background characterized by political quietism. People of such background often possess a negative attitude towards political action in general and tend to harbor suspicion against any individual or group projecting an assertive agenda. It is therefore imperative for the American Muslim political leadership to address the misgivings and insecurities of the American Muslim population and gradually build confidence and trust. One way to overcome this limitation is to demonstrate the uplifting effects of concerted political action by providing exemplary models and success stories. Such success stories of effective cooperation can stir the imagination and uplift the spirit of the community.

Political aloofness, on the other hand, manifests itself in the lack of serious involvement in issues of concern to the general public. By and large Muslim political action addresses questions involving the violation of the civil rights of American Muslims, or human rights and political liberties of Muslim communities worldwide. While these are legitimate concerns of American Muslims, and should naturally take priority over others, it is very vital for Muslim individuals and groups to stand for the principles of right and justice in general, and support good causes, regardless of the ethnic and religious affiliation of their beneficiaries. Muslims should also join hands with different groups, including non-Muslims, in fighting injustice and corruption; such an involvement of the Muslims is only natural as emphasis on universality of good will and intention is the hallmark of Islam itself.[12] After all this is the essence of the principle of *tawhid* which emphasizes the unity of: the divine, revelation, creation, truth, and humanity.[13] The dynamism and integrative power of Islam has been beautifully captured by Hegel when he states : "The leading features of Mohammedanism [Islam] involve this : that in actual existence nothing can become fixed, but that everything is destined to expand itself in activity and life in boundless amplitude of the world, so that the worship of the one remains the only bond by which the whole is capable of uniting. In this expansion, this active energy, all limits, all national and caste distinctions vanish, no particular race, no political claim of birth or possession is regarded ¾ only man as a believer."[14]

Yet the political mobilization of the Muslims should not center on the assertion of rights and the promotion of justice. Equally important is the question of institutional building and the development of human resources. Muslim socio-political organizations should work towards the development of educational bodies devoted for producing school curricula based on the idea of integration of knowledge, discussed in the previous section, and for the preparation and training of quality teachers. They should also channel Muslim talents to the various areas of services the community requires, including education, journalism, law, media, scholarship, etc.

Community strength does not come from sheer activism, but requires strategic planning. While it is true that numbers count in a democracy, it is equally true that spiritual and technical strengths of the individuals whose numbers add up to form the community are quite essential for the making of a critical mass. A good strategy, therefore, should enhance unity and cooperation among Muslims and ensure the

---

12 A Quranic verse (21:107) characterizes the mission of the Prophet of Islam as follow: "We have not sent you but as a mercy to humanity."

13 For more on the notion of *tawhid* see Ismail al Faruqi, *Al-Tawhid: Its Implications for Thought and Life* (Herndon, VA: International Institute of Islamic Thought, 1992).

14 G.W.F. Hegel, *Philosophy of History*, trans. T.M. Knox (New York: Dove Publications, 1956), p. 357.

diversity and sophistication of their skills; while the bulk of Muslim professionals work as physicians, engineers, and businessmen, the Muslim community is in a dire need for lawyers, educationists, journalists, novelists, and similar professions that provide direction, project the correct and true image of Islamic ethos and values, and raise the Muslim voice so that the American Muslim community can be heard loud and clear.

To sum up this discourse, the emerging Muslim Communities like their earlier counterparts of various religious communities from Europe, have lodged themselves in a free, challenging and dynamic world where all have the opportunity to express their true Islamic impact. Islam by its universalistic value system and simple, commonly understood ethical norms and practices has a natural vitality which prevails in such situations. Islamic history is full of precedents where as Islam appeared on similar crossroads of cultures and conglomerations of peoples in situations of chaos and moral confusion, it succeeded in uniting them around the central and binding core of unity of *tawheed* and led to the new vision of building the society on the divine purpose. So today in America Muslims have a role and a duty to lead the way through Islamic education, sound moral conduct and active participation in positive political movements, for the creation of a just, peaceful and righteous society. In this pursuit, Muslims should not only close ranks and combine their resources, but should also build bridges and join hands with all individuals and groups whose aim is to build a better future for the humanity.

A Critical Review of Islamization of Knowledge in the American Perspective

Shujaat A. Khan

A general awakening among Muslim men and women, searching for their Islamic roots and identity, and aspiring for the revival of the Islamic Civilization is a well-recognized social reality. Several different terms, such as Islamic Renaissance, Islamic Revivalist Movement, Islamic Reformation, have been used to capture the meaning and purpose of this 20th Century social phenomenon of immense significance to both Muslim and non-Muslim worlds. The notion of Islamic Renaissance and several other related concepts such as Islamization of knowledge, Islamic world-view etc., have been the exciting themes of discussion at various Islamic fora, during the past two decades. Even though Muslim scholars have not been able to reach a consensus over the definitions and dimensions of these thought-provoking notions, they all subscribe to the belief that the revivalist movement can be accelerated through stimulating the process of Islamization of knowledge. They show their willingness and commitment to fulfill their shared responsibility to provide momentum to the Islamic movement by making intellectual contributions to Islamic thought in their chosen fields.

Recently, Muslim organizations have shown their displeasure over the slow progress of Islamization. Rather than giving sufficient time to Muslim scholars to discuss these issues at length and to develop a standard Islamic paradigm, they have shifted the focus from theory to practice. One possible reason for this shift could be the fact that some Muslim countries, such as Saudi Arabia, Pakistan, Malaysia, Iran, and Sudan, have shown interest in putting Islamic ideals into practice. During the past two decades, these countries have introduced interest-free banking, and now they are looking for practical solutions for many of their existing problems.

An overemphasis on a purely substance-oriented practical approach at the recently held conferences and seminars, has kept theoretical discussions on the back burner, ignoring the fact that lasting solutions for complex socio-economic problems are hard to come by; of course, not without building a solid theoretical base in the first place. An intuitive grasp of the functioning of the various components of a social system expressed in the form of a theoretical model is necessary before a practical model can be produced. Putting unnecessary pressure on the social scientists to develop an all-practical model without allowing them to hypothesize causal relationship among the critical variables and without allowing them to provide a conceptual underpinning of the proposed model is a naive approach. It must be recognized that modern Western literature in the field of social science has been the outcome of cumulative efforts made by a large number of scholars and researchers during the past two centuries. Since Muslim scholars have engaged in this arduous task for only a couple of decades, they need more time for theoretical deliberations, to seek a rational basis for formulation of policies and strategies. This means that prolonged engagement of Muslim scholars in intellectual exercises seeking resolution of theoretical issues, though timeconsuming, is worth while. Rejecting theories altogether, or assuming that all theoretical issues have been extensively discussed and conclusively resolved, is deceptive thinking that leads to defeatist tendencies, undermining the great potential of the Muslim mind.

In recent years, some serious criticism has emerged against the process of Islamization as well as against the organizations which claim to be its champions. Though some of the criticism appears to have been made for the sake of criticism or for some ulterior motives, yet there is an indication that the process of Islamization has been derailed mainly because of the dysfunctioning of the organizations which were founded and designed to promote revivalist movement through Islamization of knowledge. The thrust of the forgoing discussion is to depict the real world conditions and constraints under which Muslim social scientists are carrying out their mission.

The notion of Islamization is an old concept which was revived by the efforts of the late Ismail Raji al-Faruqi in the United States, during the 1960s. This paper tries to examine the process of Islamization of knowledge in the light of new realities and new challenges, determining its potential and prospects in the context of historical experiences. Since Islamization of knowledge is assumed to be an integral part of the Islamic

Renaissance, and because it derives its meaning and purpose from the Islamic world-view, hence a brief discussion of the Islamic world-view and the Islamic Renaissance are presented for expositional purposes.

THE WORLD-VIEW:

The world-view or *Weltanschaung* is a notion that offers a comprehensive vision of life and all other creation from a philosophical or ideological point of view, defining the purpose, goal and the destiny of human life. In this section, we shall first trace the philosophical foundation of the western world-view and then delineate the ideological foundation of the Islamic world-view.

THE WESTERN WORLD-VIEW: The western world-view is based on a social philosophy rooted in the ideologies of secularism, materialism and scientism. There is no apparent denial of God in this philosophy, yet its insistence on privatization of religion keeps affairs of society out of influence of moral values. It glorifies absolute human freedom, liberal democracy and self-interest as the highest values, and trivializes the spiritual aspects of human life. It values the life of this world as an end in itself and denies the belief in life beyond the present. It considers realization of material gains under the guidance of self-interest to be the ultimate goal of all economic activity, showing little concern for social responsibility and social welfare. The sole purpose of acquiring knowledge is to seek higher monetary returns on the resources invested in education and other intellectual activities. Consequently, the pursuit of knowledge without moral and human concerns has turned into a purely secular and commercial activity, carried out for monetary gains. Since college, university, and professional education involve higher costs, therefore, low income people have neither any means nor any right to acquire higher education. This is justified on the basis of the philosophy of Social Darwinism, which is a dominant component of the social philosophy of the West. The philosophy of knowledge based on the social philosophy of the West is profoundly deficient in many respects. For example, it can be used for destructive and wasteful purposes if the monetary returns are expected to be higher than costs. For this reason, a well-known western philosopher Nicholas Maxwell insists on replacement of the philosophy of knowledge by the philosophy of wisdom. He defines wisdom as a notion that includes knowledge as well as a desire to strive for what is of value. He argues that wisdom provides the ability to judge what is of value, actually and potentially. In summary, the western world-view has only one purpose - to strive for material gains, and it has only one goal - to seek maximum enjoyment from these gains before death overtakes.

THE ISLAMIC WORLD-VIEW: The Islamic world-view, which is based on a system of beliefs, offers a distinctive outlook on the phenomena of creation, evolution, existence, and final destiny. The ideological apparatus that undergirds the Islamic world-view, consists of three basic beliefs: belief in one unique God, belief in the divine message and the messengers, and belief in the Day of Judgment and the Hereafter. Belief in one eternal God, in His attributes, will and Wisdom, which is called *Tawhid*, constitutes the core of the Islamic faith. It gives meaning, coherence and direction to human life. Through inspiration, it raises the level of human understanding to the point where the self becomes aware of its spiritual nature and its everlasting nexus with the Supreme Being. The direct relationship between human soul and the Creator is based on pure and pristine love from which the human soul derives enlightenment and vision, and a motivation to submit to the Will of God. The Divine Message was received and delivered by the messengers chosen by Almighty God. The Qur'an is the complete and final Divine Message that was revealed to the last and final messenger, Muhammad (pbuh), who completed his prophetic mission during the last 23 years of his life, delivering the Divine Message to the people, shaping their lives according to the Islamic principles and norms, and establishing an ideal Islamic society based on *Shariah*. The Qur'an, the fountainhead of all knowledge and the basic source of guidance, provides a vision and mission of life on earth, projecting its pilgrimage to the eternal abode on the Day of Judgment after resurrection, reckoning and retribution. It also defines the role of the human being on earth as God's trustee (*Khalifah*), entitled to use and enjoy the bounties and gifts available in the material world with a sense of responsibility, accountability, and gratefulness to the Lord. The strong moral force rooted in faith initiates an urge to chose the right option and to follow the right path, using rationality and seeking guidance from the teachings of Qur'an and *Sunnah*. Since freedom of choice makes every human being responsible for his/her decisions and actions in the worldly life, everyone would be rendered accountable to the Lord on the Day of Judgment. Those who chose a life of faith and righteousness shall receive a high reward, and those who reject faith and follow a way of life guided solely by their own self-interest, and who indulge in immoral and sub-human activities, shall receive a severe punishment on the Day of Judgment. According to the Islamic world-view, the sole purpose of life is to worship God; the ultimate goal is to seek His blessings, mercy and proximity, and the best way to realize this goal is to submit one's will to the will of his Lord, to follow His guidance and obey His commands in all aspects and matters of life, following the Prophet's practical model. The notion of worship has the dimensions of both material and spiritual strivings. This implies that all economic and intellectual activity undertaken for the realization of material gains is considered worship if the means and ways used in these endeavors are lawful and just, and the ultimate goal in sight is to seek God's proximity. Striving and sharing monetary rewards with others in society ensures success in the worldly life and a grand success in the life hereafter. Thus, the goals defined under the Islamic world-view include the material goal that can be measured in monetary units and the goal of spiritual well-being which cannot be subjected to measurement but its benefits, in the form of peace and tranquillity, are real and realizable. Given the purpose and goal of life as defined under the Islamic world-view, Islamization of knowledge can be defined as an intellectual advancement under inspiration and guidance of divine knowledge, revealed in the Holy Qur'an, seeking spiritual upliftment at the personal level, and fostering material well-being in the context of human society. From the Islamic outlook, the basic purpose of pursuit of knowledge is to seek Allah's proximity by discovering truths in a just and truthful manner, and appreciating the divine wisdom underlying those truths. This means that acquisition of knowledge is not an end in itself; it is a means to an end. In this perspective, any Muslim social scientist who wants to develop a theory or a model in his/her discipline of specialization needs a thorough grounding in the teachings of the Qur'an, the Prophet's *seerah* and sayings, and the history of Islamic civilization. If this basic requirement is not met, a Muslim scholar may make efforts to promote knowledge, but most likely without serving the cause of Islamization of knowledge.

THE ISLAMIZATION PROCESS:

Generally speaking, the term Islamization refers to planned and organized changes designed to improve the individual and society by conforming them to Islamic norms. Defined in this way, the term Islamization appears to be synonymous with the term Islamic Renaissance which is defined as a reform-oriented modernization movement driven by a conscious change in Muslim thought, attitude and behavior and characterized by a commitment to revive Islamic Civilization. Since the term Islamic Renaissance is more comprehensive and more popular in modern Islamic literature, I will use it in this paper. There are three major currents or forces constituting this movement:

a) Reformism
b) Activism
c) Intellectualism

a) Reformism refers to forces that tend to reform Muslim society by reforming individuals with the help of the basic social institutions such as the family, the mosque and the school. This means that the reformists try to reform society by reforming the individuals with the help of social institutions.

b) Activism refers to a political movement, seeking transformation of the existing Muslim states into true Islamic states. Political activists often chose democratic means to bring about a political change, but occasionally they use force against force to achieve their objectives.

c) Intellectualism refers to the movement of Islamization of knowledge that inspires and motivates Muslim intellectals to advance, promote and disseminate knowledge, to seek reformation of Muslim thought and to facilitate Islamic transformation of Muslim communities in Muslim as well as non-Muslim countries.

In general, these three different currents flow separately, each having its own leadership and its own following. However, these apparently different movements reinforce one another because they have the same common goal - to forge an Islamic social order and to promote truth, knowledge, justice and goodness in society. In every Muslim country and in every Muslim community, these forces, weak or strong, are actively working toward Islamic reformation, though their identification is difficult, and their potentials and their dimensions are hard to measure. Occasionally, when a single leadership unites these three streams into one single Islamic movement, only then it is possible to determine its real strength and potential. The organizers and leaders of these movements are neither rejectionists, apologetics, nor accomodationists. They are neither secularized Westernized elites nor ultra conservative *Tablighi* or *Taqlidi* demagogues.

The leadership is clearly marked by vision and wisdom and a commitment to sacrifice everything in the fulfillment of the Islamic mission. These dedicated and committed leaders morally influence people to follow that way of life. Muslim history has an excellent record of many such individuals who provided Muslim *Ummah* leadership, thought and direction in times of need. Some of them were persecuted and some laid down their lives for this noble cause. Today, the Islamic movement, in one form or the other, is making its headway everywhere in the world, but it is grossly misunderstood and strongly opposed by the West. Partly due to ignorance and partly because of bias, the Western media has been stereotyping every Muslim organization as a terrorist organization and every Muslim movement as a terrorist movement. Provocative terms such as " Islamic Fundamentalism", Islamic Fanaticism", Islamic Terrorism" are often used synonymously by the American Western media while mentioning Muslims and discussing Islam.

In the US, Muslim intellectuals are showing utmost patience towards these daily intellectual onslaughts made by the " Free Media" on Islamic culture. Moreover, they are making consistent efforts to resolve conflicts and confusion through open discussions and deliberations. They pay homage to their fallen heroes such as Malcom X and Ismail Faruqui, and show no respect and mercy for the crooked writers such as Sulman Rushdi and Taslima Nasreen, who try to disgrace Islam, using their literary skills as the cheapest means of earning honor in the West. The possibility of the emergence of Muslim power - political, economic and intellectual is not yet on the horizon. Still, Muslim civilization is seen in the West as a potential threat to its hegemony on the world and a challenge to western culture in its heartland. But this apprehension of a violent cultural confrontation is unsound and unwarranted.

Today, Islam is the fastest growing religion in the West and especially in North America, and its message is spreading because of its strong inspirational appeal to common sense, and its spiritualism as a source of peace of mind and tranquillity of heart. In Muslim lands, the pace of the Islamic movement appears to be quite slow due to many factors. Firstly, the process of awakening the Muslim masses is extremely slow because of mass illiteracy. Secondly, the forces of conservatism as well as the forces of secularism, scientism, and materialism are making roadblocks slowing down the Islamic movement. Thirdly, there is a lack of visionary and dedicated leadership capable of uniting Muslim people at one platform. Despite these serious problems, there is a ray of hope for a bright future for Muslim civilization. The younger generation is becoming increasingly aware of this heavy responsibility, and it is building reserve energy to meet the challenges. It is free from illusions and understands clearly that in the real world there is no such thing as Alladin's lamp to fix every single problem without effort. It is confidently holding the lamp of Allah's *deen*' in its hand to light its path.

i)   **ISLAMIZATION OF KNOWLEDGE**: In Section II, we defined the overall purpose and the ultimate goal of human activity on the basis of the Islamic world-view, and used this notion as a strong conceptual foundation for the purpose of defining Islamization of knowledge. In this Section, we shall give a new dimension to the meaning of this term by specifying the purpose of intellectual activity in the light of the teachings of the Qur'an and sayings of Prophet Muhammad (pbuh). Moreover, we shall also try to determine the potential and prospects of this intellectual movement, especially in the context of the American Muslim community. The Quranic teachings lay heavy emphasis on the pursuit of knowledge with wisdom, using all intellectual faculties and facilities that Allah (swt) has provided us for this purpose. The following *ayahs* and many other *ayahs* revealed in the Holy Qur'an have laid down the Islamic foundation of knowledge, emphasizing its significance in the Islamic way of life. "Read in the name of thy Lord and Cherisher, Who created man out of a clot of blood. Proclaim, and thy Lord is Most Bountiful, He Who taught by the pen, taught man that which he knew not. Nay, but man transgresses all bounds. In that he looks upon himself as self-sufficient. Verily to thy Lord is the return of all." (96:1-8) "We have indeed created man in the best of moulds" (95:4) "It is He Who has made you His vicegerent (trustee), inheritor of the earth; He has raised you in ranks, some above others that He may try you in the gifts He has given you,...." (6:165...) "Do not you see that Allah has subjected to your use all things in

56

the heavens and on the earth. And has made His bounties flow to you in exceeding measure both seen and unseen....." (31:20) "....Thus Allah makes clear His Signs to you that you may give thought" (2:266) "And he who brings the truth and he who confirms it, such are the righteous people." (39:33) "Nay, whosoever submits his whole self to Allah, and is a doer of good, he will get his reward with his Lord....." (2:112) "Those who reject faith in the Signs of Allah will suffer the severest penalty....." (3:4) "But he who is greedy miser and thinks himself self-sufficient and gives the lie to the Best, We will indeed make smooth for him the path to misery" (92:8,9). According to the Prophet's sayings: "The best form of worship is the pursuit of knowledge" (Muslim) "Acquisition of knowledge is obligatory for every Muslim man and woman." (Ibn Majah) "Knowledge is the legacy of Prophets" (Bukhari) "He who acquires knowledge whereby Allah's pleasure is sought will have a reward in the hereafter, whereas one who acquires it only to get some worldly gains, will have no such reward" (Ibn Majah, Abu Dawud). The basic theme of these messages is as follows: Solemnly proclaim faith in One Supreme God, Who out of His Will and Wisdom created a human being from a mere clot of blood and cast him into the best of molds; and Who, out of His Mercy, blessed humankind with special intellectual faculties and the ability to enhance knowledge, to be able to explore and discover the truth and exercise control over the physical world. Life and knowledge are the two best gifts, and the bounties of the physical world constitute yet another special gift from the Lord, the most Beneficient, the most Merciful. Human beings, as beneficiaries of these free gifts, and as trustees of the bounties, are obligated to make the best and most efficient use of these gifts and bounties, enjoying benefits from their use and showing gratefulness to the Lord by sharing some of these benefits with others and promoting justice, goodness and peace in society. Love for the Supreme to Whom all will ultimately return is the strongest moral force, and the pursuit of knowledge out of His love is the highest form of worship. The value of knowledge lies in discovering new realities, in understanding the wisdom underlying those truths, and in applying knowledge for the betterment of human society, seeking Allah's mercy and proximity. The essence of this message is that the Revealed Knowledge is the source of all knowledge. It inspires the human mind and enlightens the human soul, enabling it to understand those fundamental realities which cannot be understood through any other form of knowledge acquired through empirical methods or human intuition. Without seeking guidance from the Revealed Knowledge, human beings would go astray; they are likely to become violent and rebellious, misusing acquired knowledge and transgressing rational and moral limits; proclaiming self-sufficiency; and harming the larger interests of human society and its natural habitat in pursuit of their own self-interest. These messages contain the basic elements of the Islamic philosophy of knowledge which defines knowledge as a truth seeking intellectual activity, discovering wisdom, facilitating spiritual uplifting, and promoting human welfare. Given the purpose of life as defined by the Islamic world-view, and the purpose of knowledge as spelled out by the Islamic philosophy of knowledge, the overriding purpose of Islamization of knowledge is to facilitate the process of the search for truth with objectivity and wisdom, and to ensure its application with justice and humanity, strengthening faith and bringing one close to the Lord. From this perspective, Islamization of knowledge may be viewed as a comprehensive intellectual activity characterized by spiritualization, humanization and universalization of knowledge. Muhammad (pbuh) was the last and the final Messenger of God, entrusted with the responsibility of delivering the message and providing guidance to the entire humankind. This means that every Muslim man and woman is the trustee of the whole stock of knowledge - Revealed and acquired. Moreover, Muslims are morally obligated to promote advancement of knowledge and to facilitate its application, seeking common good. These teachings of Islam inspired Muslim minds and drove them to remarkable accomplishments in many fields of knowledge such as science, maths, medicine, humanities, arts, etc. The rise of Muslim Civilization in a short period of time and its domination over the world for a millennium is attributed to Islam's heavy emphasis on pursuit of knowledge and Muslims' elan and commitment to engage in intellectual pursuits as a moral obligation.

ii) **POTENTIAL AND PROSPECTS**: The true potential of Islamization of knowledge as an Islamic movement can be properly determined by examining it in its historical perspective. In a broader sense, Islamization of knowledge appears to have been started soon after the first five *ayahs* were revealed to Prophet Muhammad (pbuh). The Qur'anic revelations and the sayings and practices of the Prophet (pbuh) provided the doctrinal framework that laid the foundation of the philosophy of knowledge and a methodology of scientific investigation to establish truths through observation, experience, and wisdom (logical thinking). Prophet Muhammad (pbuh) used the revealed knowledge and all other available knowledge with wisdom in bringing about a change in thinking, attitudes and behavior of people and then built the first Islamic civilization on a spiritual foundation. Islamization of knowledge continued playing a major role in building the social super- structure of the growing and flourishing Islamic society. Historical records stand witness to the fact that Islamic civilization, which thrived and sustained growth for 1000 years, promote learning, research and publication of literature through properly organized and adequately financed educational institutions. Primarily, the success of this civilization lay in its hunger for knowledge and a commitment to establish truth and justice and to promote goodness and peace in society. *Ijma* and *Ijtehad* were frequently used as indispensable tools to meet new intellectual challenges, safeguarding the dynamism and buoyancy of the Islamic civilization, and maintaining its global domination.

In their quest for knowledge, Muslim scholars made great efforts in translating and studying the writings of the early Greek philosophers such as Socrates, Plato and Aristotle. They greatly benefited from the logical approach of the Greek philosophy, and improved and applied it in scientific investigations. Muslim scholars paid special attention to measurement of quantities and distances, and developed mathematical techniques to solve measurement problems. These new analytical techniques developed by Muslim mathematicians and scientists triggered development of empirical sciences. This was a remarkable achievement of Muslim scholars that led to the foundation of modern scientific disciplines.

However, some Muslim scholars became so impressed by the Greek philosophy that they accepted many of its speculative ideas and false notions as truths. By blindly following the Greek approach, they tried to explain every truth, including the Qur'anic truths on the basis of logical reasoning. Many such scholars were bogged down in the mysteries of Greek mythology and lost their sense of direction by abandoning the Islamic approach.

Imam al-Ghizali made an accurate assessment of this alarming situation and made tremendous efforts to clean Muslim minds from this corruption and to reform Muslim society. Ghizali's philosophy of Sufism was an attempt to bring back spirituality in Muslim life through devotion and self-improvement. During early stages, Sufism served as an effective tool of reformation, and devoted Sufis played a major role in spreading the message of Islam in distant lands, and often in inhospitable and hostile environments. But, the mystical approach (*Kashf*) to discover Absolute Knowledge was not consistent with the teachings of Islam. Generally speaking, Ghizali's intellectual efforts reflected the true spirit of Islamization of knowledge, seeking reformation of the Islamic civilization.

The beginning of the 15th Century marks the decline of the Muslim civilization and the rise of Western civilization. Among the many factors that contributed to the decline of the Muslim civilization and the rise of the Western civilization, pursuit of knowledge, especially in the fields of science and technology, has been recognized as a critical factor. Muslims lost their motivation for seeking knowledge, whereas the West started building its intellectual base from the stock of the knowledge it borrowed from the Muslim institutions. Intellectual stagnation of the Muslim world was followed by political subjugation, when Colonial powers of Western Europe occupied most of the Muslim lands. This dark period of Muslim history continued for almost five centuries, and during this long period the entire Muslim Ummah continued suffer from the devastating effects of their obscurantism. Pursuit of knowledge in various fields of science and technology was not allowed in Islamic schools of higher leaning because of the risk of penetration of Western thought and culture in Muslim society. Moreover, use of *Ijma* and *Ijtehad* was restricted to religious matters only. These introversive and backward looking tendencies produced an inertia in Muslim thought that destroyed the vibrancy and viability of the Islamic civilization. During the 19th century, when the Muslim people opened their eyes, they found themselves in a state of chaos, frustration and humiliation. Many concerned Muslim intellects, reformists, and activists responded to the call of their faith, and made their best efforts to take the *Ummah's* ship out of the stormy waters. They infused fresh ideas in Muslim minds and prepared them to overthrow foreign domination, seeking intellectual, cultural and political freedom. They also fought an uphill battle against two internal forces which had been slowing down the process of awakening and recovery. Conservatism, in the form of *Taqlidi* forces, was resisting change in Muslim thinking. Forces of secularism and materialism led by Westernized elites were promoting the idea of servile imitation of the West. Under these precarious conditions, individuals like Muhammad Abduh, Imam Shamail, Shah Wali-Ullah, Muhammad Abdul Wahab, Sir Syed Ahmad Khan, Jamaluddin Afghani, Allama Iqbal, Hasan al-Banna, Muhammad Ali Jinnah, Syed Qutb, Abul Aala Moududi, Ali Shariati, Shahbaz Malcom X, Ismail Raji al-Faruqui and many others, stimulated the process of awakening and reform with wisdom, courage and commitment. Allama Iqbal, the great Muslim philosopher and poet of the 20th Century, was in the forefront in the revivalist movement. His inspirational poetry played a great role in the awakening of the Muslim people in Indo-Pak subcontinent. He made a constructive criticism of Ghizali's philosophy of Sufism, and cleansed Muslim minds from the ruinous influences of 20th century Sufism and western secularism. His outstanding intellectual contribution "Reconstruction of Religious Thought in Islam" had a great impact on many Muslim minds during his time and afterwards, inspiring intellectual movement based on spiritualism, and motivating political activism. After the Second World War, Dr. Ismail Raji al-Faruqui emerged as an outspoken and dynamic Muslim intellect whose efforts transformed the slow process of intellectual reform into a full-fledged Islamic movement, which he termed as the Islamization of knowledge. In his writings, he insisted on modern education with proper Islamic orientation. Initially, the term Islamization of knowledge did not make much appeal even to mature Muslim minds. But, gradually, it gained currency all over the world when Faruqui's efforts became instrumental in the establishment of modern Islamic Universities in several Muslim countries. In a monograph on Islamization of knowledge, he said: "There can be no hope of a genuine revival of the *Ummah* unless the educational system is revamped and its faults are corrected. The present dualism in Muslim education, its bifurcation into an Islamic and a secular system must be abolished once and for all." Another Muslim genius, Dr. Hussain F. Nagamia says: " Many Islamic Social Scientists have subscribed to the belief that, in the modern day Islamic world, many disciplines of knowledge have veered from Islamic ideologies and developed secular or non-Islamic ideologies in imitation of the West. This has led to decadent and disastrous results in most of these disciplines." Before the assassination of Faruqui and his wife on May 17, 1986, the two great organizations which Faruqui had founded - the International Institute of Islamic Thought (IIIT), and the Association of Muslim Social Scientists (AMSS) - had been doing a great service, giving momentum to the Islamization movement not only in America but all over the Muslim world. But Faruqui's death gave a severe blow to the Islamization movement. According to some Muslim scholars, the process of Islamization had lost all its steam, making the process of awakening and recovery very difficult.. " In Quest for New Science", S. Pervez Manzoor, a noted Muslim journalist, wrote: "Much more needs to be done very soon, if the credibility of the Islamic option is not to suffer irreparably." This is an undeniable, sad reality that, since the early 1990s, the Islamization movement at the intellectual level has been progressing at snail's pace. In the last decade, a large body of literature, especially in the field of economics, has appeared proclaiming Islamization of social sciences, but with a few exceptions no real contribution in the form of solid theoretical work has been made as yet. If someone happens to read any three economics text books written by three different Muslim authors, no wonder, if he would feel reading three books on three different subjects. Some very good initiatives were taken by Dr. Nijatullah Siddiqi, Dr. Muhammad Umar Chapra, Dr. M.A. Mannan, Dr.Irfanul Huq and others, and Muslims had high expectations that some solid theoretical work will soon be added to the existing literature on Islamic Economics, but the process of Islamization in the field of economics has become all the more slower in recent years. Some scholarly work has been produced in the field of political science, but in economics, there is a need for development of a sound theoretical base and an appropriate methodology of social accounting, analysis and evaluation. Recently, some new books on the issue of interest and interest-free banking have been published, but most of these works lack scholarship, and have little academic worth. Recently, two new books on Development Economics have been published (Sadeq, 1990 and Chapra, 1993) but none of the two can be used as text books even for undergraduate classes. In the context of the United

States, one major reason for this exceedingly slow progress is the lack of strong, visionary and dedicated leadership capable of revitalizing the IIIT and the AMSS. It is disheartening to see that both organizations have started showing signs of senile decay in their youth. They are consistently and gradually becoming less effective and less efficient in promoting the cause they stand' for. Two well-known Muslim Organizations, the Islamic Society of North America (ISNA) and the Islamic Circle of North America (ICNA), who also claim to be promoting the cause of Islamization, appear to have some hidden agenda. They arrange costly and highly publicized annual conventions on a regular basis and invite some professional speakers to their forums to attract a large audience. More often than not, the purpose of the fiery speeches at these occasions is to entertain the audience rather than to influence their thought and practices. Underlying these efforts of intellectualism and activism is a plan to keep Muslims busy in non-essential activities. In a recently published book, Subverting Islam: the Role of Oriental Centers, Dr. Ahmad Ghorab points out that some of the Muslim organizations and institutions are linked to the ongoing crusade of the West against the Islamic Movements. He suggests that the concerned Muslims should not keep their eyes closed to the activities of such organizations, whose agenda is prepared by the forces behind the curtain. The apparent deficiencies and weaknesses of the IIIT and the AMSS have fostered the emergence of many new organizations, whose overall performance is marginal at best. In the conferences and seminars organized by organizations such as the Forum for Islamic Work, the Islamic Research Foundation, the Islamic Propagation Center, International, the Muslim Thinker Forum, the North American Association of Muslim Professionals and Scholars etc., only a few presentations can be found to be thought-provoking, while the rest is a routinized or recycled product, showing lack of interest and absence the spirit of Islamization. The following statement taken from the welcome address delivered by Dr. Ibrahim B. Syed at an International Conference on Islamic Renaissance in Chicago (1995), provides some food for thought as what is going on in the name of Islamization of knowledge: "Learning, knowledge and education have been emphasized in the Quran. Indeed, the first word revealed to Prophet Muhammad (pbuh) was 'Iqra' which means 'to read', and not:

Allah, *rasool, salat, saum, zakat* or *hajj.*" Presentations by ambitious but less apt minds are always likely to infuse such confusing and misleading ideas in Muslim thinking, seriously undermining the very process of Islamization of knowledge which they claim or intend to promote. This may be a reason why some serious criticism is being made against the process of Islamization of knowledge, not only by non-Muslim scholars but also by some Muslim writers. In a recently published article, "Islamic Economics and the Islamic Subeconomy", Timur Kuran has ridiculed the concept of Islamization of Economics. Even though most of his criticism is unsubstatiated, some of the points he has raised are to be taken seriously by Muslim scholars in this discipline. In their book "Islamic Economic Systems", Dr. F. Nomani and Ali Rahnema have critically examined the Islamization efforts made by the Muslim economists and scholars during the past two decades. They have seriously criticized the piece-meal approach which results in the development of half-cooked models - a bad practice which is becoming very popular among young Muslim scholars. The overall situation in the United States is not one of despair and desperation, however. Some efforts are being made here and there and some good works are being produced to keep the candle burning. The publication of the quarterly AJISS (American Journal of Islamic Social Sciences), which reflects a high standard of Muslim scholarship, is a true success story. The credit for this high intellectual and managerial performance goes to those who have been organizing and managing its timely publication, and also to those who are making intellectual contributions to its contents. This shows that there are still some active and dedicated individuals in the field to provide fresh ideas and supply new energy, keeping the movement of Islamization of knowledge alive and active. There are a large number of mosques and Islamic Centers in almost every part of the United States. The scope of the services these mosques and centers perform for the Muslim Communities in their respective areas are confined to religious education of Muslim children and Muslim youth, and performance of prayers and other religious activities. Although these mosques and centers do not have enough resources at the present time, they do have the potential to promote the mission of Islamization of knowledge in the future. In the perspective of the Muslim world, some significant achievements have been made in Pakistan, Saudi Arabia and Malaysia. At Madinatul Hikmah, Karachi, Pakistan, a cluster of educational institutions imparting education from the kindergarten to the highest level, with proper Islamic orientation and in an Islamic environment, is an excellent model that synchronizes Islamic thought and practice. Hakim Muhammad Saeed, a learned scholar, a dedicated physician and a spirited reformist, deserves much of the credit for this great achievement. The International Islamic University of Malaysia has made significant progress and invested large resources in the promotion of Islamization of knowledge through many of its educational programs and intellectual activities. The Islamic Development Bank, established in Jeddah, Saudi Arabia, has been deeply involved in initiating and promoting Islamic thought and practices through their educational and training programs, especially in the field of Islamic banking and financing.

CONCLUSION:

Reformation of Islamic civilization is an ongoing process undertaken by God-conscious, intelligent and active Muslims who take up this great moral responsibility on their shoulders willingly and voluntarily. Some prefer to do this job alone in their personal capacity while others work in association with some organization. Whether these motivated individuals are intellectuals, reformists or activists, or all three, they all have the same goal: establishing truth and justice, and promoting peace and goodness in society, seeking Allah's mercy and proximity. Islamization of knowledge, though an integral part of Islamic Renaissance, has no political overtones, however. It is a movement that drives the process of change in Muslim thought and action to help restore the dynamism of the Islamic Civilization by strengthening its intellectual and spiritual foundation.

A revolutionary change in Muslim thought is already underway, but a political will to implement *Shariah* in Muslim lands is not on the agenda of today's Muslim politicians and policy-makers as yet. There is a lot of lip service to Islamization but there is little or no commitment to concretize this good idea by those who are holding the reins of power in the Muslim countries. In the United States, Islamization movement has followed an uneven course during the past two decades. Whereas the decade of 1980s is marked by vigorous intellectual activity, the decade of 1990s has been much less eventful.

Some progress has been made in the field of Economics and other Social Sciences, but much remains to be accomplished. The task of building a theoretical base and a conceptual framework based on Islamic ideology is gigantic, challenging and time-consuming. The Muslim organizations dedicated to this task are in need of human resources capable of providing fresh ideas and human energy. They also need financing from sources willing to provide funds without strings or preconditions. What would happen if Western civilization falls apart? Are Muslims ready to fill the vacuum? These are some serious questions that provide food for thought for young Muslim minds, and serve as a reminder to older Muslims who naively believe in the infallibility of the Western system. Of course, there are signs in the Holy Qur'an, and also in the real world for those who care to ponder. Till the time westernized Muslim politicians and elites discard their hypocrisy and show willingness to establish *Deen al-Islam* as a social order, it is incumbent upon Muslim scholars, especially those who have seen both the East and the West, to double their efforts and fill the existing intellectual gap. No doubt, there is a leadership void everywhere in the Muslim *Ummah*, but this should not be a reason to withdraw our efforts from this noble mission.

There is no reason to be pessimistic because of the poor performance of our organizations in the recent years, and there is no justification for being overly optimistic on the basis of our little accomplishments in the past. *Deen al-Islam* invites us to strive with patience and perseverance in the cause of truth and offers hope of grand success. Allah (swt) guides us in the Holy Qur'an: "By the token of time through the ages, Verily man is in loss, Except those who have faith and do righteous deeds, and join together in the mutual teachings of Truth, and of patience and constancy" (103:1-3) Our Holy Prophet has left behind a perfect practical model of hard work, righteousness, truthfulness, patience and perseverance for us to follow.

II

ECONOMIC CONTRIBUTIONS

Perspectives in Islamization of the Labour Market: The Occupational Composition of Canadian Muslims

Masudul Alam Choudhury

Islamization of knowledge means several things in the literature. Of these, two broad perspectives will be covered in this chapter. First, we will critically examine the state of the arts in Islamization of knowledge as pronounced by the International Institute of Islamic Thought, the Islamic universities world-wide, and their mentor, the honorable late Professor Ismail Raji al-Faruqi. Because of the programmatic nature of this approach to Islamization, we will refer to it as such — programmatic Islamization.

The second perspective is the Islamization challenge to Western socio-scientific methodology in the wake of the new orientation toward an Islamic epistemological focus. This epistemological methodology emanating from the Qur'an and Sunnah and backed up by intensive authoritative discourse called *Ijtihad*, is seen as a strong denial of *Taqlid* to the West, that has otherwise entered Muslim thought in the garb of the first approach to Islamization and its unchallenging questioning (Choudhury 1995a). We will refer to the second approach to Islamization either as the epistemological approach or the substantive approach.

The link between the two approaches, in the light of knowledge being a continuous historical process, is the acceptance of methods but not methodology. The substantive difference between the two schools is the divergence in their methodologies. The programmatic school does not have a viable new methodology of its own to offer. It emulates the Western model with a palliative of Islamic values moulded into it. The second methodology is intrinsically epistemological.

OBJECTIVE

The principal objective of this paper is to examine the nature of Islamization of knowledge that has gone on in North America through published works and the efforts of existing Islamic institutions. Through such an examination, we will reflect on the nature of the impact that Islamization has attained and what the consequences of this may be for a truly Islamic socio-scientific change. From such a critical examination will emerge the alternative perspective toward realizing a universalizing Islamic socio-scientific transformation. In both of these parts of our study we will invoke a combination of conceptual and empirical investigation. On the conceptual front we will examine the nature of Islamization of knowledge and how this may impact upon the development of a political economy that could structure the occupational composition of the labor force toward realizing substantive Islamic change. On the empirical front, we will examine the occupational structure of Muslims in North America to infer from this the kind of Islamization at the socio-economic level that must be launched to bring about an Islamic grassroots transformation.

The divide between the above two approaches is the Islamic epistemology in the scientific and socio-economic domains, deeply rooted in the evolution of Islamic thought. Its history is well known. On the one hand, the rationalist spirit of the Greeks so strongly emulated by the Mutazzilites, Ibn Rushd, al-Farabi, Ibn Sina, Ibn Khaldun and many others in the school of Kalam, laid the way for a Hellenic conceptualization in Muslim thought. On the other hand, the Qur'anic epistemological approach of the *Mutakallimun*, such as, Imam Ghazzali, Imam Shatibi, Imam Razi, Imam Ibn Taimiyyah and Shah Waliullah, laid the foundation of *Usul* quite different from Hellenic thinking in the Habus Corpus of Islamic reawakening (Qadri 1988).

DEFINITION OF TERMS

At the outset, we will define a number of terms that may otherwise appear to be new to the reader. The intent here is not to be overly conceptual, but simply to attain a blending between concept and reality in the light of the objective of this paper.

1. The Epistemology of Unity

Epistemology and Unity are both substantive terms here. Epistemology means the theory of knowledge of an abiding framework of science and society including economy and polity. Such a foundational core of knowledge becomes the guiding principle of all subsequent theorizing and applications as an indelible reality of the system under study. Einstein said in reference to the Western perspective of science, that there can be no science without epistemology (Einstein 1954). Leibniz held the view that if a geometrical point was capable of explaining the universe, then a point could be considered as being more substantive than the universe itself. On such a microscopic scale of reality Leibniz based his theory of monadology (Leibniz 1965). Russell pointed out that abstraction was the soul of practical power: It is strange that we know so little and yet we know so much and how this small knowledge can give us such an immense power (Russell 1971). The theories of a priori epistemology by Kant and the a posteriori rationalism of Hume are well-known in terms of their dualized perspectives of deductive and inductive reality (Kant 1964, Hume 1988).

Islamic epistemology is foundationally premised on divine unity as the spring of complete and absolute knowledge (stock of knowledge) that conveys creative powers to the universe and all its systems. This precept of Unity is thus comprehended essentially by means of the cosmologically unified world view as premised on the singular foundation of the divine laws that cannot pluralize between systems of life. Thus, there is a unique methodology that pervades across all systems of life and thought. This is the foundational essence of Unity.

This foundationally unifying knowledge premise comprises the divine laws (*Sunnat al-Allah*). The practical manifestations and application of these laws to reality comprise the signs of God (*Ayath al-Allah*). The medium of comprehension and application of the divine laws and of realizing the meaning of the signs of Allah, is the Guidance of the Prophet Muhammad (*Sunnat al-Rasul*). The blending between *Sunnat al-Allah* and *Sunnat al-Rasul*, vigorously discursed by human volition to derive rules (*Ahkam*) from them (*Ijtihad*), comprise the creative and dynamic field of *Shari'ah*, Islamic laws.

The meaning of just balance, purpose, felicity, certainty and creative evolution as attributes (Choudhury 1997a) emanating from the epistemology of complete and absolute knowledge (Unity=*Tawhid*), is

71

brought to bear upon the observed and discursed epiphenomena by means of rules (*Ahkam as-Shari'ah*) and cognitive powers that generate endless complementarities among similar but diverse possibilities. The creation of the world 'in pairs' to understand divine nity among diversities, is a feature to be found both in the realities of truth and falsehood. The difference is that the creative power of truth happens to be based on endless complementarities among similar but diverse possibilities. Whereas, the domain of falsehood is determined by increasing individuation among 'the pairs' of competing anti-bodies.

Such is the Qur'anic explanation of the creation of the universe between Truth (*Haqq*) and Falsehood (*Batil*) (*Qur'an* 8, verse 29): "O ye who believe! If ye fear God, He will grant you a Criterion to judge between right and wrong..." Furthermore, the Qur'an says (51, 49): "And of every thing We have created pairs: That ye may receive instruction."

We thereby extend the epistemology of Unity on two fronts. First is the ontological conception of divine stock of knowledge as Unity. Second is the translation of this complete and absolute stock of knowledge into flows of knowledge in creation by means of the power of universal complementarities among similars. We refer to the latter power of unification of knowledge as the "Principle of Universal Complementarity."

2. Socio-Scientific Order

By the socio-scientific order we mean a field of scientific and social thoughts that is unified together by a unique methodology. This methodology is substantively epistemological in nature and is based on unification, that is complementarity among cognitive phenomena, by means of the primal epistemological invocation of divine unity. Thus for example, it is possible to formalize a socio-scientific theory of machines premised on this unique epistemological root of Unity (Choudhury 1993a). It is likewise possible to formalize a politico-economic perspective that ties the occupational composition of labor markets with the Islamizing approach.

3. Islamization of Knowledge and Thought

In recent years, the honorable late Professor Ismail Raji al-Faruqi pioneered the field of Islamization of knowledge and thought by premising it in a program of introducing Islamic values to prevailing methods and methodology of Western making (Al-Faruqi 1988). This was a reaction of Islamico-Western scholarship not particularly from Faruqi. Rather, the general Muslim intelligentsia reacted to the fervor of Western resurgence in the sciences in a similar way. They thought that a similar scientific revolution must be adopted by the Muslims. The way to adopt that path was prescribed as the acceptance of the existing scientific field, methods, methodology and models of received doctrines and then to make these amenable to Muslim countries and countries with an external garb of Islamic values (Idris 1987, Khalil 1991, Choudhury 1993b). The International Institute of Islamic Thought (IIIT) followed this plan of Islamization zealously and formulated its programs on translating existing scientific books from an Islamic viewpoint. Many scholars undertook the writing of articles and books in the scientific area by accepting the parcel of the existing scientific methods and world view while topping these up with certain Islamic values (International Institute of Islamic Thought 1989).

The programmatic approach to Islamization of knowledge nonetheless addressed the theme of *Tawhidi* episteme (Al-Fadl 1990, Al-Faruqi 1982), *Tawhid* meaning divine unity. But all such redress was not endogenous to the methodology of *Tawhid* taken up within the socio-scientific domain. The redress was rather of an exogenous nature calling for emulation of Islamic values in the perceived or some alternative framework of science and society. The Islamization approach did not emanate independently from Qur'an, *Sunnah* and *Ijtihad* to lay the foundation (*usul*) of a new wave of thinking — a new methodology. The endogenous socio-scientific methodology of *Tawhidi* epistemology was thus never clear to the programmatic school of Islamization of knowledge and thought. Rahman (1988) and Sardar (1984) criticized the programmatic approach of Islamization of knowledge and its grandiose Islamization blue-print of pedagogy on these grounds.

Thus, we are witnessing today in the intellectual scene of Islamization of knowledge and thought, the same kind of debate that once raged between the school of *Kalam* and the *Mutakallimun* in the history of Islamic scholasticism. Note that the core of the socio-scientific problematique is on the endogenizing of *Tawhidi* epistemology as opposed to an exogenous understanding of Islamic values in received socio-scientific doctrines. The endogenous world view causes the rise of an independent view of reality (Waliullah 1985, Choudhury 1995b).

73

4. The Concepts of Method versus Methodology

The place of methods is that of instrumentality. Such methods may surely be accepted for methodology, while leaving the latter as an independent body of epistemic derivation. Examples here are the use of Ptolemaic geometry and Sirhind number system by the Muslim mathematicians (Hakim 1942). Methodology on the other hand, involves an epistemological way of understanding reality and on building up a world view on its independent framework (Choudhury 1997b). Of course, such an epistemological exercise does not mean abandoning blindly all past and present scholarship; nor does it mean accepting blindly everything. The critical wisdom (*tajdid*) under the purview of Qur'an, *Sunnah* and *Ijtihad* governs the power of authority.

Thereby, if a method springs from methodology — for instance the use of first-order conditions of optimization in economic theory, which is the result of a marginalist substitution, of the assumption of complete knowledge at large, and optimal utilitarian behavior with economic rationality being at the center of social action — then such a method as well as methodology must be avoided. The methodology of *Tawhidi* epistemology cannot allow for the assumption of complete knowledge at large. Hence all optimal models are substantively replaced by simulation models of social, politico-economic and scientific validity.

Our categorization of methodology against methods is essential to liberate the original Islamic mind from blind acceptance of Western authority (*taqlid*). The Qur'an emphasizes the quest for Islamic purity as opposed to borrowed substance that has no abiding value (Qur'an 10, verse 32): "Such is God, your real Cherisher and Sustainer: Apart from Truth, what remains but error? How then are ye turned away?"

LINKING ISLAMIZATION DEBATE WITH THE LABOUR MARKET

How does the above debate between the two schools carry over to our discussions relating to the labor market and occupations? The labor market is a socio-economic system determining wages and quantities of labor between work and non-work (leisure, unemployment). Upon these determinations, there is also the interplay of markets and polity. This makes all labor market variables the result of social contracts rather than of the invisible market exchange mechanism (Choudhury 1996). Because of the polity-market interlinkages, the principle of complementarity between economic efficiency and distributive equity must prevail in an 'Islamic' labor market that is embedded in the bigger labor market of North America. The latter functions under the Western genre of labor market theory, institutions, policies and programs.

In the embedded Islamic labor market, occupations must be functionally related with the nature of complementarity between economic efficiency and distributive justice. The nature of Islamization must thereby, uniquely influence all — the scholarly, research and educational developments, and the consequential occupations and labor markets in terms of their variables as described above. Such a delineation of interrelationships among occupations, labor markets, polity, programs and underlying policies are thereby a two-way simultaneous interactions. The underlying principle of universal complementarity establishes *Shari'ah* rules (*Ahkam as -Shari'ah*) in the area of enterprise and community well-being derived epistemologically through Islamic community discourse. The increasing consensus of the Islamic community to such rules by discourse, establishes a preference transformation centered around the wage and consumption-production menus. We thereby, obtain the total consumption-production-distributional general socio-economic system of an embedded Islamic labor market (Choudhury 1992, 1985). One of the ways of affecting such a general systemic transformation is development of those occupations that promote the *Shar'iah*-led change with extensive discussions and knowledge formation at the grassroots and their interlinked social hierarchies.

Examples of such appropriate occupations are expertise in Islamic organizational behavior, labor market relations, economics and financing with well-trained human resource for the process of consultative (cooperative) decision-making (*shuratic* process) (Choudhury 1995c) involving agents, polity, enterprise and industrial relations (Tahir 1997). There would also be social and economic planners and community socio-economic development experts for achieving the same purpose. There must be development of efficient information systems for job opportunities, research and development that can be cooperatively supported by the Islamic business community and the labor markets. Educational institutions must devise similar programs. University students could specialize on relevant areas of research with functional linkages with the Islamic community.

The central points to note in all of these endeavors are first, the Islamic consciousness developed by reference to the Islamic unified orientation of life. Second is need for technical organization of the same. In this way, the first part premises the embedded Islamic community on the primal *tawhidi* epistemology. The second endogenously derives the ways and means (*ahkam*) from such an epistemological root along lines of unifying and dynamically regenerating the embedded Islamic political economy along the self-same path. This is the unification of knowledge realized in the cognitive domain of business community and the labor market. By the combination of these two central ideals, the meaning of Shuratic Process extends from institutional and entrepreneurial organization behavior to the methodology of general unified systems of complementarities.

We note now that the *tawhidi* epistemology, (Unity, unification, *shuratic* Process) endogenizes the Islamic transformation by creating and dynamically evolving simultaneous two-way cause-effect interrelationships as follows: The *Shari'ah* rules (*Ahkam as-Shari'ah*) permanently endogenizes the production of knowledge centered in a dynamic embodiment of the *Shari'ah* rules. This leads to the organization of business, economy and labor markets along a complementary trajectory of possibilities determined in a socio-economic development model of the community. Since such transformation takes place in the discursive medium of the *Shuratic* Process, therefore, along the path of development of the embedded Islamic political economy, two-way knowledge-inducing feedback is generated. Such a process is as much a learning process in *Shari'ah* rules reflecting unity in diversity, as it is also a participatory framework of creative evolution for the embedded Islamic community.

A FORMAL PICTURE OF THE EMBEDDED ISLAMIC COMMUNITY

The embedded Islamic community is a sub-nation, because of its complete sets of rules, organizational behavior and dynamics, all premised on a world view (Choudhury 1995d, Lewis & Schnapper 1994). This world view is established upon the epistemology of divine unity taken up in its extended form along the creative evolutionary path. The creative Islamic transformation in this embedded community takes place by means of the embryonic and pervasive medium of the *shuratic* process. This is characterized by pervasively interactive, integrative (consensual) and creative knowledge-induced evolutions in the perpetuity of thought and experience.

In Figure 1 we show how the interactions and integration (that is consensus through discursions = *ijma*) lead to creative evolution and repeat the *shuratic* process. The outward direction of the arrows indicates forward linkages from a generative embedded Islamic community, EIC (as sub-nation), to the immediate organization of knowledge (Q). Knowledge formation now becomes the determinant of occupational structure (OCCUP). Occupations in turn determine the structure of labor markets (LM) in terms of jobs, wages, human resource development policies, and simultaneity between economic efficiency and distributive equity. LM supplies the primal factor of production and economic activity, namely, services of labor in the specific occupational composition of the labor market. This causes consumption, production and distribution to define the general systemic structure of the economy (ECON). Now the forward linkages end. Because of the primacy of knowledge formation, each of these forwards embedding sub-systems is influenced primarily by Q-values.

The feedback now generates politico-economic interlinkages among the foregoing sub-systems. There is no specific order in this, as unity in diversity defines the creative path out of Ijtihadi discourse (*shuratic* process). We show these feedback interlinkages by the production of recursive 'Q-knowledge values at the level of any higher echelon of embedding sub-system, directed to the learning-by-doing experience at the epistemological level of EIC. Such a reverse process circularly interlinks with the forward process in diverse ways. The implication is the cause-effect interrelationship of deductive and inductive reasoning of the *shuratic* process. These are found to circularly enhance the *shuratic* process. New (Q, Q')-values are thus evolved while forming interactions, integration and continuity through creative evolution.

In the embedded Islamic community model, the reverse process of knowledge formation impacts upon occupational restructuring. For instance, the real experience of the information age when primarily induced by the epistemology of Unity in the model of information, can lead to the development of a field that may be called cyberbiology. This name is due to the interactive, integrative and evolutionary nature of systems studied by cyberspace technology (Shakun 1988). In the midst of cyberbiology, increasing diversities of production and technology will

77

suggest ways of rethinking older *Ahkam as-Shari'ah* to formulate newer authentic paths for the Islamic community. Accordingly, occupations in genetic engineering, cyberbiological processes, unified supersymmetry, large scale general socio-economic systems, finance and management, are among those that can be conceptualized according to Islamic epistemological orientations (Choudhury 1995e, Hull 1990). Established research and development, universities and institutional capacities can provide opportunities to Muslims to delve into these pioneering areas by means of the socio-scientific order of Tawhidi epistemology.

At this last stage of knowledge production in the interactive, integrative and evolutionary embedded Islamic community model of Figure 1, we must examine the role of the national superstructure (N). The national superstructure is not an Islamic one, as in North America and Europe. Hence, N remains epistemologically and hence methodologically different from EIC. From our earlier arguments, we cannot borrow from the epistemology of N to form the epistemology of Unity and the essential unification experience of EIC. But EIC can contribute to a reformulation of N by means of its socio-scientific world view. EIC in turn can gain from the technical and instrumental methods of N as distinct from the methodology of N. This last possibility of sharing between EIC and N is indicated by the extended arrow.

The dividing line between the two epistemes is the universally complementary and unified world view of EIC as premised on *Tawhid*, and the flows of knowledge from it that realizes unification pervasively. The episteme of N is based on pervasive marginalist substitution, ontological pluralism, rationalism and duality and their effects on the cognitive domain.

We show in Figure 1, that only by the permissible exchange of instrumental knowledge from N to EIC (methods) and the contributory epistemological knowledge (methodology) from EIC to N, can there come about creative evolution in N as well, just as in the earlier embedded sub-systems, as shown. Such an induction extends the domain of pervasive interactions, integration and evolution to the total political economy and the socio-scientific order as shown by the arrow.

EIC denotes embedded Islamic community; OCCUP denotes occupational structure; LM denotes labor market; ECON denotes the superstructure of the embedding economy; N denotes the non-Islamic embedding political economy of EIC at large, as in North America and Europe.

Some examples of research capacities where Islamic epistemology can contribute in developing paradigmatic shifts are as follows: Knowledge-centered unified field theory of everything (Barrow 1991), political economy as a general system of endogenous interactions, unification and creative socio-economic dynamics (Choudhury & Malik 1992, North 1981), human ecological systems (Hawley 1986), strong interactions based on Tawhidi unification of knowledge (Smith 1992, Gleick 1987), evolutionary ecological models of community socio-economics (Goulet 1995, Sauer 1997). There are many more.

It is the evolutionary capability of each of the concentric domains in Figure 1 that defines the knowledge-centered world view of Islamic political economy. Within this, the occupations are formed by their substantive development in the institutions of higher learning as in the market place and the polity. Now a cyberbiology becomes a study in social well-being that is ecologically formed and extended by means of a methodology that emanates and converges to fundamental unity, and that both substantively as well as procedurally complements diversities

Figure 1: Labor Market, Occupational and Politico-Economic Interrelationships in the Embedded Islamic community model

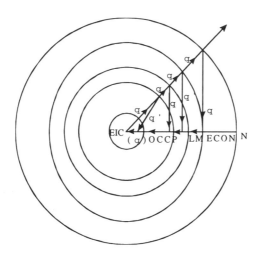

into a unified whole. Participation in the polity-market interactions is just one such example of the complementary process. Within this, occupations and the labor market become the cognitive forms.

A TRIANGULAR LOOK AT THE ISLAMIZATION OF KNOWLEDGE

The occupational model of the labor market in an embedded Islamic community model with extensive complementarities framed upon unification epistemology, leads to the following triangular understanding of the Islamization process: We will examine this triangular relationship from the viewpoint of either of the two Islamization approaches given above.

In Figure 2, we first conceptualize the Islamic epistemological impact upon occupations by knowledge formation in EIC. We note the permanent centricity of *Tawhidi* Epistemology (EP=*Tawhid*) in all of this. This primal exogeneity is shown by the one-directional arrows, causing *Shari'ah* to impact upon all changing facets of experience (unity in diversity). The relation, f_1 is a bundle of *Ahkam as-Shari'ah* impacting upon the development of instrumental knowledge flows denoted by Q_1-values. Q_1-values now become derived knowledge flows emanating from the premise of *Tawhidi* Epistemology, T. Such knowledge flows generate specific kinds of occupations through the methodology, f_2, of the Shuratic Process. The structure of labor market generated by the occupations (occup) generates new knowledge flows through the medium of discursions (interactions) leading to consensus followed by creative evolution of new knowledge, Q_2-values. The underlying inductive process is denoted by f_3. But the *Tawhidi* epistemological centricity in all of these is signified by the impacting arrows upon Q_1-values, $OCCUP_1$, Q_2-values, $OCCUP_2$, etc.

We note now that the interactive, integrative and evolutionary process is sustained in continuity by the creation of knowledge flows, Q-values. This is the direct consequence of *Tawhidi* Episteme, T. In the string denoted by,

$$P1 = \{(T \circledR_{f1} Q_1 \circledR_{f2} OCCUP_1) \subsetneq (T \circledR_{F1} OCCUP_1 \circledR_{f3} Q_2)\}$$
$$= $$
$$T \circledR_{f3 \circ f2 \circ f1} \subsetneq \{(Q_1 \circledR_{f2} OCCUP_1) \subsetneq (OCCUP_1 \circledR_{f3} Q_2)\},$$

there are two compounded sub-processes. These are as follows:

deductive reasoning denoted by, $(Q_1 {}_{f2} OCCUP_1)$;

inductive reasoning denoted by, $(OCCUP_1 \circledR_{f3} Q_2)$.

80

The same kind of compounded process can be circularly continued. This is the same as saying that revelation and reason are blended together in Islamic knowledge formation.

Such compounded processes of interactions, integration and creative evolution that structure the entire set of interrelationships between occupations and the labor market in a *Tawhidi* knowledge-centered framework, grounds the unique methodology of Islamic socio-scientific order. Here it is explained in reference to occupations and labor markets. The need for appropriateness in the organization of research and development agenda for an appropriate occupational composition of the labor markets and the politico-economic system of an embedded Islamic community, is now methodologically premised upon the implied participation, planning and transformation of the framework signified by Figure 2.

Next consider what happens in the framework of Islamization of knowledge and thought of the programmatic kind. *Tawhidi* episteme is exogenously implied. Hence, f1 does not define an endogenous methodology of *Tawhidi* episteme in the systems. f_1 is mixed up with acceptance of Western and other existing rationalist methodologies. We found this to have been the case in Islamic history with the school of *Kalam*; and today, we find it with the mainstream economic orientation of Islamic economists. The knowledge set (Q-values) is now perturbed by extraneous influences. This is shown in Figure 2 by the intersected area between Q-values (Islamic) and Q-values (non-Islamic) which are shown by the region of obfuscations.

Consequently, the OCCUP-sets are likewise perturbed by these differentiated kinds of knowledge and de-knowledge sets, their rules and arrangements. The result is that all of f_1, $F_1 = f_2 \ o \ f_1$, $F_2 = f_3 \ o \ f_2 \ o$ f_1 etc. remain obfuscated by influences extraneous to *Tawhidi* episteme. The deductive-inductive cycle of continuity is broken. Here the symbol, 'o' denotes compound mapping. The Islamic potential for transformation becomes ineffective, marginalized, and finally subsumed by the obfuscation effect of extraneous influences, by their organizations in the labor market, by the resulting kinds of occupations and the political economy.

Consequently, we find that sheer human resource development that acquires a neoclassical economic efficient labor market meaning, cannot realize distributive equity in the labor market. Unemployment remains rampant; job specification remains highly elitist in nature. The economy as a whole along with the labor market and occupations remains in the grips of dual and segmented labor markets, and marginalist substitution between price stability and unemployment rates prevails. It is well known that the goal of full employment has become an elusive one (Worswick 1989). The social welfare menu of such an economy is a misnomer in the midst of the trade-off between economic efficiency and distributive equity (Gordon 1967). Under the programmatic kind of Islamization agenda, Muslim economists have simply borrowed these ideas and tried to re-create similar terminology with an extraneous Islamic tint. The result has been a fiasco.

In the history of Islamic philosophy, Ibn al-Arabi wrote on the need for strict compliance with Unity in the formation of Islamic approach to reality. He treated all other interference in this as obfuscation (Chittick 1989). The *Mutakallimun* followed the same.

Figure 2: Occupations and Labor Market in the Triangular Interrelationships of *Tawhidi* Epistemology

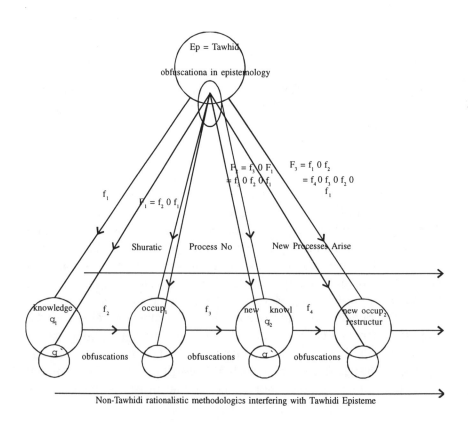

ISLAMIZATION IN CANADA: OCCUPATIONAL LABOUR FORCE ESTIMATES FOR MUSLIMS

In order to evaluate the two-way interrelationship between occupations in the labor market and the effectiveness of Islamization, we need to address the following questions: First, what has been the effect, if any, of Islamization at large among Muslims in the labor force? Second, how can the occupational composition of the labor force of Muslims be transformed to gain the benefit of an Islamization process?

It is obvious then, that if the effectiveness of an Islamization program has remained weak, then the occupational composition of the labor market of Muslims will not show up any distinct effect towards a program of Islamization. For an Islamization program to be proven effective, the occupational composition of the labor force of Muslims must be transformed in desired ways. This is a matter of policies on educational planning, human resource development and economic change.

Our empirical estimation and inferences on the above problem are based on Canadian labor force data. We had to make rough estimation because of the paucity of labor market data for Muslims. We will rely on the following approaches for estimation and inferences on the occupational composition of Muslims in the Canadian labor force.

Table 1: Distribution of Canadian Muslims Aged 24-44 Years by Educational Levels by Gender, 1981 & 1991 Canadian Census.

	Population 24-44 years of age	years of school < Gr.9	Grades 9 - 13	Some post-secondary	University degree
Canada 1981					
Total	7,156,760	835,855	2,558,980	2,783,335	978,590
Males	3,583,875	403,820	1,118,960	1,469,480	591,610
Females	3,572,885	432,035	1,440,015	1,313,855	386,980
Islam 1981					
Total	40,160	3,345	9,325	17,065	10,430
(%Can)	0.56	0.40	0.36	0.61	1.07
Males	22,960	1,100	4,620	9,910	7,735
(%Can Male)	0.64	0.27	0.40	0.67	1.31
Females	17,200	2,245	4,705	7,160	3,095
(%Can Female)	0.48	0.52	0.33	0.54	0.80
Canada 1991					
Total	9,193,915	473,920	3,213,930	3,984,905	1,521,160
Males	4,561,950	243,835	1,515,145	2,003,820	799,155
Females	4,631,960	230,085	1,698,790	1,981,085	722,005
Islam 1991					
Total	98,690	5,990	26,785	39,805	26,105
(%Can)	1.07	1.26	0.83	1.00	1.72
Males	56,180	2,320	14,000	22,560	17,295
(%Can Male)	1.23	0.95	0.92	1.13	2.16
Females	42,505	3,670	12,780	17,245	8,815
(%Can Female)	0.92	1.60	0.75	0.87	1.22

Source: Statistics Canada, 1991 Census of Population, Religions in Canada, cat. 93-319.

In Table 1, we point out the 1981 and 1991 Canadian Census distributions of Muslims aged 24-44 years by educational levels. We make the assumption that those with university degrees would be eligible to enter the professional occupations comprising "managerial, administrative and related occupations", "occupations in natural sciences, engineering and mathematics", "occupations in social sciences and related fields", "occupations in religion', 'teaching and related occupations ", "occupations in medicine and health", "artistic, literary, recreational and related occupations". These are also the potential areas for greatest Islamization impact if rightly directed. For the years 1986 and 1991, the estimates of percentage distribution of Muslims in the Canadian professional occupations are shown in Table 2.

Table 2: Estimates of the Percentage Distribution of Muslims in the Canadian Professional Labor Force, 1986 & 1991.
(thousands)

Canada Total

	1986	1991
Managerial, etc.	1,341	1,739
Natural sciences, engineering, etc.	448	573
Social sciences	247	317
Religion	34	34
Teaching	544	627
Medicine & health	614	727
Artistic, etc.	208	246
Total Professional	3,436	4,263

Source: Statistics Canada, Census of Population, Occupation, cat. 93-327.

We are using the 1981 percentage distribution of Muslims for 1986. This yields an estimate of 36 thousands Muslims with university degrees in the Canadian professional labor force in 1986. For the year 1991, the estimate is 73 thousands. Thus there was an increases of 103 per cent over the five-year period, 1986-91. This is an impressive gain as far as the usual Canadian type of the occupational composition of labor force is in the picture. It indicates that Muslims with higher education have made good head-way into the Canadian labor markets. But what can we infer from this regarding the impact of Islamization on the Muslim population and on the Canadian intellectual scene?

The Canadian labor force is highly efficiency-driven. This is evident from the tendency to favor capital-intensive, labor saving economic operations. Consequently, high unemployment rates have prevailed for a long time now. One would expect in the embedded Muslim sub-nation, that the same effect would have prevailed. Hence a bridge between the Muslims professionals and the other segments of this community, toward restructuring their own community economic development, could not have occurred. This point is empirically established.

We find that apart from those who held university degrees, the other segmented part of the Muslim labor force not holding university degrees, increased from 29,730 in 1981 to 72,585 — a 144 per cent increase between 1981 and 1991. Their Canadian labor force share also increased. Besides, in a separate work it was shown that effective discrimination against Muslims in the labor force could exist (Choudhury 1980). Now the macroeconomic employment policy of the Federal Government based on monetary and fiscal policies, do not benefit the small groups, such as the group we are considering here. The author therefore, prescribed specific manpower policies for the labor market amelioration of target groups, instead of macroeconomic policies.

In the present case too, specific socio-economic development programs and policies should be directed to the underemployed and unemployed within the Muslim community by their own intra-communal efforts. Within such an approach must also be taken up the varied interlinkages at the community level that can be generated by Islamic financial and economic institutions, programs and instruments.

Without such initiatives, as our inference goes, the gain in university degrees among Muslims in the Canadian professional labor force cannot and did not break down the usual kind of segmentation found to exist in the Canadian labor market (Smith 1976). It is expected that such an adverse effect would have carried with it all the ills of high unemployment, underemployment and low incomes for Muslims in the lower rungs of opportunities and schooling.

INFERENCE FROM THE EMPIRICAL RESULTS

The inference is then clear. The programmatic approach in Islamization of the occupations and then of the Muslim labor force, that should have restructured the Canadian Muslim community — our earlier embedded Islamic community — has not succeeded. This was despite the fact that the size of Muslim population in the professional labor force in Canada has increased substantially, only to be subsumed in the general marginalist orientation of the Canadian labor market. The significant trade-off between economic efficiency and distributive equity continues to prevail. This has reflected in the Canadian Muslims as well. In the perspective of our earlier general system model of interlinkages premised on the unification by complementarity, we cannot therefore say that Muslims have acquired any semblance of substantive Islamization in their embedded community in Canada.

POLICY CONCLUSION

1. The Inference on the Islamization Effect

Both the conceptual and empirical parts of this paper show that the Islamization agenda in North America has been put on a wrong footing. It has become much more a programmatic approach rather than a truly scientific research program premised on the Islamic epistemological roots. The consequence thus has been, that although Muslims as individuals and groups within the community have progressed economically, yet the sub-nation of the embedded Islamic community in North America, has not reaped the benefit of the progress in the more fortunate segmented part. The programmatic Islamization agenda could not realize a general systems approach toward establishing a community on grounds of the Islamic world view.

There can be only one explanation of this continuing enigma among Muslims wherever they are today scattered in the globe. Muslims have not looked seriously enough to formulate an independent methodological way of their own. Such a methodology should have been the foundation of an Islamic socio-scientific order, a politico-economic system and a constitutional framework. Be it in the disciplines, politics, institutions or social action plan, Muslims have by and large adopted the continuing occidental agenda with simply a palliative of Islamic values. On the other hand, the Qur'an says 'no' to such a piecemeal approach: "Those who reject Truth among the people of the Book, and among the polytheists, were not to depart from their ways until there should come to them Clear Evidence, — An apostle from God, rehearsing scriptures kept pure and holy" (Qur'an 98, verses 1-2). In the end therefore, we conclude that authentic Islamization has not dawned.

2. The Alternative

To counter the continuing Muslim enigma in the world scene, it is imperative that Muslims as sub-nations organize their ways of thinking and actions along the orthodox and fundamental principles of Islam. This approach would be cast in the form of a grand and interlinked discursive *Shuratic* Process spanning the Muslim research agenda and their applications in the various systems of life. Among these are the Islamic political economy, the Islamic socio-scientific order, and the social action plan.

But for such a regime to come about, Muslim countries cannot remain content simply with intellectualization of their Islamization discipline. Muslims must boldly test, discurse, apply and dynamically improve upon an on-going comprehensive model of socio-scientific order. To launch such a transformation agenda means freedom of thought, expression and actions to the protagonists. Alas! Presently these virtues are considered dreadful by prevailing Muslim political regimes. Hence, there must come about political change incorporating in it the blue-print of the general system of transformation, which we referred to in this paper as the world view.

But until that day when a better Islamic political change has dawned and a better socio-economic future has been realized by the common will of the Islamic social action program, the intermediate stages would be to mobilize the Islamic grassroots. The Muslim grassroots is the sub-nation; it is our embedded Islamic community. Such a community is to be cooperatively manned and mobilized in each and every front that otherwise would exist for a developed Islamic state, but at a smaller size. The collective of such Islamic embedded communities across the world would be able to proxy the needed scale of operation that goes with the large structure.

Thus, the engines, programs, policies and grassroots institutions of social well-being, human resource development, economic revival, the human economy and the political will and organization, must lead the future evolution of the substantive Islamization process. This is how the future *Ummah*, the world nation of Islam, can rise — from the grassroots upwards; and then continue to be circularly interlinked across hierarchies. Without such a comprehensive blue-print and the will for change, Muslims will only continue on to imitate the idle occupations of the neo-liberal Eurocentrics (Mehmet 1990), of the rationalists, of the courts of kings and rulers. Muslims will thus engage in mere esoteric pursuits against which Ghazzali cautioned us (Berggren 1992).

In North America as in Europe, this opportunity exists by virtue of the democratic will around. Besides, the interchange of scholarship between the substantive scientific research program of Islamization and the echelons of advanced learning and research, prevails. Muslims must tap these opportunities. They must abandon undertaking programs of writing articles and textbooks in a Western garb.

The occupational composition of the Muslim labor force in Canada shows that with the rapid advance in higher learning, the scope for an epistemological and resulting applied perspective of Islamization, remains potentially bright. This can come through the Islamic epistemological gift to today's spiritually dead occidental world view, regarding which Husserl lamented in his "Crisis" (Husserl 1970). So my friends, let us seek that newer world!

References

Al-Fadl, M. (1990). "Contrasting epistemics: Tawhid, the vocationist and social theory", *The American Journal of Islamic Social Sciences*, Vol. 7, No. 1, pp. 15-38.

Al-Faruqi, I. R. (1982). *Tawhid: Its Implications for Thought and Life* (Herndon, VA: International Institute of Islamic Thought)

—— (1988). "Islamization of knowledge: problems, principles and prospective", *in Islam: Source and Purpose of Knowledge* (ed.) (Herndon, VA: International Institute of Islamic Thought) pp. 13-63.

Barrow, J.D. (1991). *Theories of Everything, the Quest for Ultimate Explanation* (Oxford, Eng.: Clarendon Press)

Berggren, J.L. (1992). "Islamic acquisition of the foreign sciences: a cultural perspective", *The American Journal of Islamic Social Sciences*, Vol. 9, No. 2, pp. 310-24.

Chittick, W.C. (1989). *Sufi Path of Knowledge* (Albany, NY: State University of New York Press)

Choudhury, M.A. (1980). "An occupational distribution of Muslims in the employed labor force in Canada: Estimates for 1978", *Journal of the Institute of Muslim Minority Affairs*, Vol. 1, No. 2 1979 & Vol. 2, No. 1, 1980, pp. 63-74.

—— (1985). "Conflict between the efficiency and equity goals of manpower planning", *Forum for Social Economics*, Vol. 17, No.2, Spring, pp. 41-50.

—— (1992). "The ethical numeraire", *The International Journal of Social Economics*, Vol. 19, No. 1, pp. 60-72.

—— (1993a). *The Unicity Precept and the Socio-Scientific Order* (Lanham, MA: The University Press of America)

—— (1993b). "A critical examination of the concept of Islamization of knowledge in contemporary times", *Muslim Educational Quarterly*, Vol. 10, No. 4, pp. 3-34.

—— (1995a). *The Epistemological Foundations of Islamic Economic, Social and Scientific Order.* (Ankara, Turkey: Statistical, Economic and Social Research and Training Center for Islamic Countries, Organization of Islamic Conferences)

—— (1995b). "A mathematical formulation of the principle of ethical endogeneity", Kybernetes: *The International Journal of Systems and Cybernetics*, Vol. 24, No. 5, pp. 11-30.

—— (1995c). *"Theory and practice of Islamic political economy"*, Hamdard Islamicus, Vol. XVIII, No. 4, pp. 5-39

—— (1995d). "Muslims in Europe: a critique of occidentalist views", The International Journal of *Social Economics*, Vol. 22, No. 6, pp. 53-64.

—— (1995e). *Islamic Socio-Scientific Order and World Systems* (Penang, Malaysia: Secretariat for Islamic Philosophy and Science, Universiti Sains Malaysia)

—— (1996). "Markets as a system of social contracts", *The International Journal of Social Economics*, Vol. 23, No. 1, pp. 17-36.

—— (1997a). *Studies in Islamic Social Sciences* (London, Eng.: Macmillan & New York, NY: St. Martin's Press)

—— (1997b). *Reforming the Muslim World* (London, Eng.: Kegan Paul International)

Choudhury, M.A. & Malik, U.A. (1992). *The Foundations of Islamic Political Economy* (London, Eng.: Macmillan & New York, NY: St. Martin's Press)

Einstein, A. 1954, "The problem of space, ether, and the field in physics", in Commins, S. & Linscott, R.N. eds. **Man & the Universe**: **The Philosophers of Science** (New York, NY: The Pocket Library) pp. 473-84.

Gleick, J. (1987). Chaos: *Making a New Science* (New York, NY: Viking)

Gordon, A.R. (1967). *The Goal of Full Employment* (New York, NY: John Wiley & Sons)

Goulet, D. (1995). *Development Ethics, a Guide to Theory and Practice* (New York, NY: The Apex Press)

Hakim, A. (1942). *The Arabs and Mathematics* (Calcutta, India: Department of Mathematics, University of Calcutta, unpublished Ph.D. thesis)

Hawley, A.H. (1986). *Human Ecology* (Chicago, IL: The University of Chicago Press)

Hull, D.L. (1990). *Science as a Process* (Chicago, IL: The University of Chicago Press)

Hume, D. (1988). *An Enquiry Concerning Human Understanding* (Buffalo, NY: Prometheus Books)

Husserl, E. trans. Carr, D. (1970). *The Crisis of European Sciences and Transcendental Phenomenology* (Evanston, IL: Northwestern University Press)

Idris, J.S. (1987). "The Islamization of the sciences: its philosophy and methodology", *The American Journal of Islamic Social Sciences*, Vol. 4, No. 2, pp. 201-8.

International Institute of Islamic Thought (1989). *Islamization of Knowledge, General Principles and Work Plan* (Herndon, VA: IIIT)

Kant, I. Trans. Paton, H.J. (1964). *Groundwork of the Metaphysic of Morals* (New York, NY: Harper & Row Publishers)

Khalil, I. Al-Din (1991). *Islamization of Knowledge: A Methodology* (Herndon, VA: International Institute of Islamic Thought)

Leibniz, G. Trans. Latta, R. (1965). *The Monadology and Other Philosophical Writings* (London, Eng.: Oxford University Press)

Lewis, B. & Schnapper, D. eds. (1994). *Muslims in Europe* (London, Eng.: Pinter)

Mehmet. O. (1990). "Alternative concepts of development: a critique of Euro-centric theorizing", *Humanomics*, Vol. 6, No. 3, pp. 55-67.

North, D. C. (1981). "A theory of institutional change and the economic history of the Western world" in *Structure and Change in Economic History* (New York, NY: W.W. Norton) Chap. 15.

Qadri, C.A. (1988). *Philosophy and Science in the Islamic World* (London, Eng.: Routledge) Chapters 2-5.

Rahman, F. (1988). "Islamization of knowledge: a response", *The American Journal of Islamic Social Sciences*, Vol. 5, No. 1, pp. 3-11.

Russell, B. (1971). "Philosophical consequences", in *ABC of Relativity* (London, Eng.: George Allen & Unwin)

Sardar, Z. (1984). "Islamization of knowledge, or the westernization of Islam?" *Inquiry*, Vol. 1, No. 7.

Sauer, J.B. (1997). "Unnatural virtues for well-living: social economy, civitas, and public philosophy", in Choudhury, M.A. ed. Festschrift in Honor of Imam Ghazzali: Socioeconomics of Community Development in Global Perspectives I (West Yorkshire, Eng.: MCB University Press, being a special issue of *The International Journal of Social Economics*)

Shakun, M.F. (1988). *Evolutionary Systems Design* (Oakland, CA: Holden-Day, Inc.)

Smith, D.C. (1976). *The Dual Labor Market Theory, a Canadian Perspective* (Kingston, Ont: Queen's University Industrial Relations Center)

Smith, T.S. (1992). *Strong Interaction* (Chicago, IL: The University of Chicago Press)

Tahir, S. (1997). "Industrial relations in Islam", in Choudhury, M.A.

Abdad, M.Z. & Salleh, M.S. eds. *Islamic Political Economy in Capitalist-Globalization: An Agenda for Change* (Kuala Lumpur, Malaysia: Utusan Publications) pp. 353-77.

Waliullah, S. Trans. Jalbani, G.N. (1985). *Al-Fauz al-Kabir Fi Usul al-Tafsir* (Islamabad, Pakistan: National Hijra Council)

Worswick, G.D.N. (1989). "Full employment", in Eatwell, J. Milgate, M. & Newman, P. Eds. *The New Palgrave: Social Economics* (New York, NY: W.W. Norton) pp. 90-4.

Three Billion Dollar US 'Halal' Food Market

Muhammad Arif Zakaullah

A MARKET exists whenever and wherever the buyers are willing to buy a product and the sellers are willing to sell it, at a mutually agreeable price. The concept of market is not a geographical one; rather it is based on the idea of interaction between the preferences of buyers and the ability and willingness of suppliers to deliver the product according to the tastes and preferences of the buyers.

A successful seller is not always the one whose product is exactly like the product of others in the line, but the one who, while producing in the same product line, can cater to the special preferences, tastes and needs of the consumers, which the other producers have failed to meet.

The reality and its potential

The US car market is dominated today by Japanese automakers. But this was not the case before the 1970s. Starting in the early 70s the average American consumer was looking for a small, fuel-efficient car, but the American carmakers did not realize this particular change in the taste or preference of the American car buyers. Disappointed by the apathy of their own carmakers, they turned to the Japanese. Soon the small fuel-efficient Japanese cars were mushrooming on the highways and byways of the US.

Despite the fact that the oil glut of 1980s has resulted in low oil prices, America's love for Japanese cars remains undiminished. Having driven the small Japanese cars in a moment of great economic stress the Americans have come to think of the Japanese car as a trustworthy friend.

The moral of this story is that the American market is not unpenetrable for foreign producers.

To capture that market, foreign producers have to:

- Understand the pace and pressures of life upon the individual in the American society;
- Understand the characteristics that the American buyer is looking for in a product given these pressures;
- Identify the special tastes and preferences of different constituencies of the consumers that remain unsatisfied in the American market;
- Sell the product at a competitive price so that the consumer feels that he is not being exploited for his special needs or preferences;
- Information on the availability of the product should be spread among all potential users, through channels directly linking the source of origin (supplier) to destination (buyer) at a minimum cost; and
- Ensure that the marketing network is direct, simple, and responsive to the special needs of both buyers and sellers and the intermediaries.

Islam in the US is a reality, and a growing phenomenon. At the beginning of the decade of the 1990s the Muslim population of the US was around 5 million, and growing. It is projected to be the second largest religion after Christianity in the next millenium.

In 1987 this author conducted a survey of Muslim heads of households in New England with the help of New England Islamic Council and the Islamic Society of Greater Worcester (ISGW). It found that the average annual (non-asset) earned income of a household was above US$30,000. The size of an average Muslim household was four. Given this average household size and the 5 million population, there are nearly 1.25 million Muslim households in the US. If each household spends 30 per cent of its earned income on food, and half of that on items that ought to be "halal" in their ingredients and processing, then the annual 'halal' food demand is nearly US$ 6 billion.

If we assume that half of this "halal" food expenditure consists of items like fresh meat, beef, poultry products like: butter, milk, cheese, yogurt etc, then the total of these expenses comes to nearly US$ 3 billion. Though "halal" chicken, meat, etc, are not that easily available in the US, but they are not very difficult to obtain either. Thus we are left with nearly US$ 3 billion worth of "halal" items which are not easily available there. It is these "halal" products that offer opportunities. What then are these products?

These are usually from product lines, which are mass-produced and are processed on an assembly line pattern. These are generally the type of products which are ready to eat" kind of pre-cooked or processed edible items like hamburgers, hotdogs (i.e. frankfurters), coldcuts, TV dinners, chips, cookies, noodles, etc.

The importance of channels

Assuming that these are to be supplied to the US Muslim consumers, then the local producers or the exporters from the Muslim countries need to determine the tastes and preferences of the consumers; the marketing and networking of supplies and distribution in the US; and sources and channels of information (advertisement) to reach Muslim consumers.

A producer of pre-cooked food items faces the challenge of processing the product in such a way that a simple additional step of processing by the final consumer should bring and deliver the taste the producer has promised the consumer.

In this regard a "halal" fast food producer has two crucial dimensions to face:

(a)   In the line of product he is producing, he should know what the general characteristics are that make a product delicious and popular, e.g., should the material be well done, or should it be left raw to a great extent; or should it be a little dry or a little oily when the consumer opens the package, etc. In this regard a good idea will be to study the similar pre-cooked (or pre-processed) items popular in the US Muslim community (or conduct consumer surveys).

(b)   Generally westerners prefer less spicy food, but will it be true for Muslim consumers too? The American Muslim community comes from a wide variety of cultural and ethnic backgrounds, which reflect consumer preference for hot, mild or moderate level of spices in the food items. Thus the producers/exporters of "halal" food for the US market will have to be aware of the consumers' tastes and preferences.

Since the Muslim community in the US is relatively new and a vast majority of them earn their living in the services sector, they are rarely in the grocery business. Thus the marketing network is not well established. The lack of such a network makes the job of foreign exporters more difficult; because even if they can produce the products desired by the

American Muslim consumers, they don't have much information about or access to the marketing and distribution network.

The Muslim community in the US consists of the Arabic-speaking, the non-Arabic speaking, mainly from the Indo-Pakistan sub-continent and the indigenous (converted) Americans.

There are Lebanese/Syrian grocery stores all over the U.S., and the majority of the Arabic-speaking Muslim communities buy groceries from these stores. Lebanese/Syrian Christian immigrants or their descendants mostly own these stores. They are not chain stores but are loosely linked to each other as they are operated by those of the same ethnic origin. Getting hold of a few of them would mean having access to their network in the US.

Certification of 'halal' products and the need for a distribution network

Among the non-Arabic speaking immigrant groups the people from India, Pakistan and Bangladesh are the dominant group that operates grocery shops. Within this group the Hindu and Sikh communities from India control more than 70 per cent of the market. The Pakistanis followed by the Muslims from Bangladesh, the Caribbean islands, and Turkey, among others dominate the remaining.

Islam is fast spreading in the US and is being embraced by all, including the white and the Afro-American communities. Currently the majority of the Indigenous Muslims consist of the Afro-American Muslims. In big cities like New York, Chicago, Detroit, Houston, and Los Angeles, the Afro-American Muslims run their grocery shops. Many of them also run book stores selling Islamic literature, prayers rugs, Islamic dresses for men and women etc.

In order to market the "halal" food items produced by Muslim entrepreneurs there is a need to develop a distribution network there through existing shop owners and distributors in cities with big Muslim concentration like Chicago, New York, Los Angeles and Detroit.

The American Muslim community would like an authority, trusted by them, to vouch for the authenticity of products sold being "halal". Such an authority is the Islamic Society of North America (ISNA). Thus the "halal" products may get a quick acceptance among the American Muslim consumers if they can carry a seal of approval from ISNA. But due to its meager resources, ISNA may need support in this regard.

Thus it is appropriate to say that the American "halal" food market has a lot of potential for the Muslim business community. This potential can be utilized to the mutual advantage of the consumers and the Muslim entrepreneurs if handled professionally.

Islamic Banking in North America: Growth and Obstacles

Abdulkader Thomas

Introduction

In 1992 the American Journal of Islamic Finance (AJIF) surveyed the economic demographics of Muslim Americans. In early 1997, the United Bank of Kuwait, plc - New York Branch did the same with the same team overseeing the process. Both surveys were pursued with the intention of understanding the financial capacity, sophistication, and needs of Muslims in North America. Separated by five years, the surveys corroborate one another, as well as demonstrate specific trends within the broader community. Islam has enjoyed rapid growth In the United States through immigration, conversion and natural increase. Unfortunately, the hitherto meager efforts of Muslims to organize to overcome 'riba'[1] in their financial needs in the US have been less rapid than the growth of the domestic Islamic population.

The situation today is that Muslims are about 4% of the general population, or 10.4 million people. State agencies are increasingly aware of Islam for three critical reasons. Muslims tend to be clustered in major urban areas,[2] namely, New York, Los Angeles, Detroit, Chicago, Washington, DC, Boston and Houston. Muslims, particularly African

---

1 For a comprehensive definition of this condition see Abdulkader Thomas, *What is Permissible Now?* (Singapore: The Muslim Converts' Association of Singapore, 1994). For the purposes of this paper, we will take *riba* to mean interest in a conventional banking sense.

2 The "1992 North American Survey for Islamic Finance", by *The American Journal of Islamic Finance* (Chicago: The Muslim Journal, January 1993); Edmondson, Attitudes toward *riba*-free investing among US Muslims: A Survey Conducted by The United Bank of Kuwait, plc name (Ithaca: private paper unpublished, July 1997); and private conversation between Dr. Sabah Karam, Secretary General of the Confederation of Islamic Schools in North America and Samer Wehbe of The United Bank of Kuwait, plc - New York Branch, July 1997.

Americans are increasingly involved in local and state government, sometimes with substantial influence and public authority. And, some Muslims are actually attempting to combat *riba* in their local communities. Thus, the table is set for authorities[3] to interact with Muslim to address a wide range of community needs, including finance in a creative and meaningful manner from the point of view of Islam.

Unfortunately, the achievements of Muslims on the financial front are few. Apart from the North American Islamic Trust (NAIT) and the Islamic Cooperative Housing Corporation, Ltd. of Toronto (ICHC), both affiliated to The Islamic Society of North America (ISNA), the vast majority are small with assets of about $10 million. The typical organization is just ten years old, community based, and led by a local doctor or engineer who is frequently the *imam* for the community on Fridays, and works a regular job most of the week. On the one hand, many people fear that the organization lacks adequate structure and professionalism to manage their savings. On the other hand, not too many of their prospective constituents are certain that the services that they offer are necessarily Islamic. The net effect is that there are only about ten ongoing community based Islamic financial groups. When joined with NAIT and ICHC, they have accumulated up to $200 million in assets.

This lack of achievement has been abetted by the faux pas of two major Islamic organizations in the middle 1980's. Both attempted to seek banking licenses in the United States. When their senior executives explained their business to senior officials of both the Federal Reserve Bank and the United States Department of the Treasury, they were advised that their businesses were not banking businesses as defined under the National Banking Act. But, they were told that they were involved in the securities trade and should pursue a licensing path though the National Association of Broker Dealers and the Securities and Exchange Commission.[4] The advice and re-direction was taken as rejection and both institutions declined to develop US subsidiaries serving the domestic population. One of the two, ultimately did establish a wholesale

---

3 In 1992, Tabung Haji, (the Malaysian pilgrimage board) sponsored *The American Journal of Islamic Finance* to be sent for two years to all state and federal banking authorities. Only a very few rejected the gift subscription, and a number have explicitly maintained the subscription from their own means. This too has helped in shaping the views of local authorities in a positive manner.

4 Private conversation between Abdulkader Thomas of *The American Journal of Islamic Finance* and Charles Schotta, United States Department of the Treasury, March 1989.

presence in several American cities, and was for a short time active in a California community based company.

Even if the major foreign organizations were to have set up US subsidiaries, they would have found the going rough. Only in the 1990's has serious survey work been done relating to either the financial needs or the economic demographics of Muslim Americans. In addition to the two surveys noted above, The Arab American Anti American Discrimination Committee commissioned J. Wright formerly of Washington College in Maryland to survey the economic demographics of Arab Americans revealing interesting information about Muslim Arab Americans as well as Christians; and Dallah Albaraka and ATT have also conducted private surveys of the communities. Organizations like the American Muslim Council (AMC) and ISNA are increasingly proving to be better clearing houses for such information than in the past. In contrast to the 1980's, it is now much easier to know who, where and how much with respect to Muslims in America, and this means that logical business decisions are more easily undertaken.

Nonetheless, a knowledge gap persists. Although the major journals and periodicals of ISNA, the Islamic Circle of North America, Imam W. Deen Mohammed, and the Islamic Assembly of North America publish articles, sometimes devoting entire issues to the question of Islamic finance, there is no substantive penetration of the broad Islamic public that would truly educate them to be sophisticated Islamic financial consumers in the same way that they may be sophisticated consumers of conventional financial services. Even specialist periodicals like AJIF tend only to reach a limited audience of highly educated professionals, usually already active in the financial services.

With its population having tripled since 1980, America's Muslims are now more organized than in the past. The number of mosques is significant at 2000, and the number of schools exceeds 250.[5] The local efforts required to make communities interact with local authorities has resulted in a greater focus in several major urban areas to solve 'the next problem' which is increasingly viewed as Islamic finance. Two factors should easily welcome the endeavors of these communities and a third should abet them in a way that it could not in the past.

---

5 Abdulkader Thomas conversation with Abdul Rahman Alamoudi, Secretary General of The American Muslim Council and Dr. Sabah Karam, Secretary General of The Confederation of Islamic Schools in North America, July 1997.

103

Foremost, the US has a multi-layered financial system. This means that structuring Islamic financial entities under different acts, state or federal may suffice. Hence, several cooperatives now operate, an investment bank has been bought, and a number of alternative solutions are open.[6]

Secondly, the increasing devolution of budget obligation from the Federal to the State level requires American civil authorities to look for creative alternatives to finance local needs, or to assure that economic development takes place where desired or planned. This growing flexibility plays directly into the hands of both the growing positive contact between communities and local or state officials as well as the fact that a significant number of Muslims are the same local and state officials.

Finally, a number of overseas Islamic investors have enjoyed successful investments in the US, and several significant international banking and financial organizations are employing the ever improving statistics noted above to prepare to become active in the US Muslim consumer market.

As the following sub-sections will reveal, Muslim stand to benefit from the pluralism of American Western society, and should ultimately prove to be contributors with the result that Islamic banking and financial institutions will have successfully rooted themselves in the US by the year 2000.

Occupation of Muslims:[7]

Muslim Americans are disproportionately more highly educated than the American public, and, as a result, are more likely to enjoy well paying professional and technical positions. There is a divergence between the broader pool of Muslims and African Americans. With respect to Muslim African Americans, they tend to be employed in stable jobs, or to own their own small business. The net result is that Muslim Americans enjoy a 1996 median income of $40,000 compared to the US median income of $32,000 (both of which are slightly lower than the 1992 medians for

6 Sec Thomas, What is Permissible Now?
7 All statistics for this are taken from the following sources which are largely corroborative: The "1992 North American Survey for Islamic Finance", by *The American Journal of Islamic Finance* (Chicago: *The Muslim Journal*, January 1993); name (Ithaca: private paper unpublished Brad Edmondson, 1997); and J. Wright, The Financial Demographics of Arab Americans (Rancho Palos Verdes, California: *The American Journal of Islamic Finance*, Vol. IV, No. 6, 1994).

Muslims and all other Americans. And Muslim African Americans enjoy a median income of $30,000 compared to all other African Americans at $23,000.[8]

Edmondson discovered that a startling 70% of Muslims enjoy incomes greater than $70,000 meaning that Muslim Americans are among the most affluent sub-cultures in the United States.[9] Wright reported, however, that Arab professionals are likely to earn less than non-Arabs in the same profession. Moreover, Muslim Arab professionals are likely to earn less than Christian Arab professionals in the US. Nonetheless, in both cases, the gap is only 3%, meaning 6% for Muslim Arab professionals.[10] Although Muslim professionals who may be from Arabia or South Asia may suffer pay discrepancies, these may well relate to language skills or a lack of local market experience.

Top Professional Activities[11]

Engineers & Technicians	20%
Medical & Laboratory	14%
Business Proprietors	11%
Educational or other administration	9 %
Blue collar	5 %

Two deductions may be made from these factors. Although many Muslim immigrants may have come to the US for higher education and stayed on, the reason for that it has proven easy to stay on is that the US needs the skills of Muslim immigrants. The second is that Muslims tend to represent broadly middle class values. Hence, time and again, local communities come to feel a growing comfort with Muslim communities as Muslims are frequently found in positions of professional competence like technology, community trust like medicine, and community visibility like local trade.

---

8 See Edmondson.
9 Ibid.
10 See Wright.
11 Edmondson.

Businesses and Trade:

Referring to the above table of Muslim American occupations, we can see that conglomerations of Muslims in ethnic or religious enclaves may have a salubrious impact on local economies. Four empirical examples demonstrate the growing prominence of Muslims in America.

In technology, Muslims are proliferating in a number of areas. South Asian and Arabian software engineers are widespread in each of the major software centers. This relates to what is often superior math training in their home countries as well as a lack of opportunity to apply their skills productively at an attractive wage at home. The US suffers a substantial shortage of software engineers, and yet is the largest consumer of their services.[12] Therefore, Muslims along with other religious adherents are welcome members of the solution to a national business crisis. That is the micro level, almost invisible to the public.

On the intermediate and macro levels Muslim investors from Southeast Asia have been increasingly sophisticated investors in US high technology companies. These investors bring needed venture and intermediate stage capital to the US high technology sector. Some of this investment is connected to the development of the Multimedia Software Development Corridor in Malaysia and has the goal of achieving a successful transfer of technology to developing Muslim countries. Again, this is almost invisible and represents the intermediate level.

The macro level, which is highly visible, is when prominent and creative Muslims like Safi Qureshy are active leaders of large public technology companies. Part of what these corporate leaders bring is innovative ideas, Islamic values, and a dedication to charity. This segment is highly visible, especially on the local and regional levels. For instance, Safi Qureshy is chairman of AST Corporation headquartered in Irvine, California. AST is an important employer in Southern California, a significant contributor to local civic charities, and Mr. Qureshy is an important supporter of local Islamic charities.

For nearly twenty years, the US has relied upon foreign medical graduates to take up posts in isolated or small communities as well as inner cities. These doctors have been disproportionately from South Asia, Egypt and Syria, and the Philippines. Again, doctors from the former two regions are a plurality of Muslims. Although these postings are not

---

12 ...(New York: *BusinessWeek*, July 7, 1997).

without cultural conflict, they have done more to assist the implantation of Muslims in America and to assure that they are within areas of community trust. After all, to whom does one look to save lives but the local doctor?

Finally, Muslims communities have played an important role in regional economies. For instance, one might say that Muslims fill in the gap, reversing or halting urban decay. The first example of this is the role that Arab Americans, particularly Muslims from Lebanon and Yemen are seen to have played in preventing Detroit's urban decay from creeping south into Northern Dearborn. During the 1970's, as immigrants from Eastern Europe, often employed at Ford's Dearborn manufacturing plants sought to move away from both the borders with Detroit and African American communities, the Arabian immigrants moved in. Although many were employed at Ford, a substantial number were petty merchants. The result is that poor quality housing stock was improved. As for commercial strips like Warren Avenue near the Detroit border which were suffering many vacancies are now vibrant commercial shopping strips with a large variety of Arabian shops and restaurants.[13]

A similar impact has been achieved in part of Atlanta. The Atlanta Masjid of Al Islam purchased a largely empty convenience shopping center is southwest Atlanta, a low-income area. The empty super market space has been converted into a large mosque, and the empty shops have been taken over by Muslim merchants from the dynamic local Muslim African American community. A short distance from the shopping center, a vacant Methodist church was purchased and converted into the Sr. Clara Muhammad School (primary) and the Imam W. Deen Mohammed High School (secondary). Increasingly Muslims have settled in the area improving its quality, resuscitating a dying area. Moreover, the academic success of the schools along with their good performances in the local parochial school sports leagues has drawn increasing numbers of students to the schools and families to the neighborhood. This is truly an example of success building upon success.[14]

This process of acculturation and contribution is not without its problems. The Nation of Islam's (a non-Islamic community) leader Louis Farrakhan has correctly pointed out that a number of Muslim immigrants

---

13 Author's personal observations and interviews conducted from 1988-90 with local Arab American community leaders and Dearborn civic leaders.
14 For more details see Thomas, *What is Permissible Now?*

operate "package stores" in many of America's inner cities. These stores use the profits from alcohol sales to subsidize milk and household commodities. These drive other small vendors out of their neighborhoods, breeding pockets of resentment against some immigrant ethnicity, and in the worst case against Islam, even if the package store owner is clearly not practicing Islam.

Islamic Banking and Finance:

So what does all of this mean for Islam in America when it comes to banking and finance? We must first look at the sophistication of the Muslims, in addition to their presence, and then to the regulatory environment.

As we have seen, the Muslim American is typically more affluent than other Americans in general, or in his or her peer group. The Islamic communities of the US have begun to achieve substantial degrees of political participation, economic success, and concentration in visible areas. The first result is enhanced political recognition, which flows from skilled community leaders insinuating themselves successfully into local politics. The impact includes elected Muslims from the local level all the way to the US Senate where Spencer Abraham represents Michigan to American mosques that host delegations from state legislatures. These expanded levels and points of domestic political contact, as previously explained, have the salubrious effect of assuring that Muslims may raise a broader sphere of their personal, community, and religious interests to the nation as a whole.

On the one hand, the number of affluent Muslims who do not fully participate in the national financial systems may be disproportionately high. The gross result is that the overall economy loses. The net result is that they build up resentment, which as potential community leaders, they share with the less successful, less well educated. In our research, Muslim home ownership trailed total US home ownership by 9 percentage points - despite the greater wealth of Muslims compared to Americans as a whole.[15]

---

15 "1992 North American Survey for Islamic Finance", *The American Journal of Islamic Finance*. Latter research touched on the number who hold mortgages which is similar to the general population, but explicit ownership still appears to lag the general population in a variety of community analyses.

On the other hand, there are pockets of Muslim poverty and disaffection. Their concerns not only require the same attention as the poor and excluded of other faiths, but create an environment in which they may respond to opportunities crafted to reflect their Islamic culture or values. This very crafting is, of course, the key to ultimate success in securing their goals.

Therefore, substantial Islamic communities in America lack a full stake in their local communities, creating a risk of greater friction between Muslims and non-Muslims, The provision of appropriate financial services on a mass market basis may help to overcome these risks, generating dialogue in lieu of conflict. Serving 4% in the US can make a difference in social harmony.

Since the mid-1980s Muslims in Britain and America have made a number of attempts to serve their communities' financial needs. Boutique Islamic financial institutions have achieved no more than a 4% name recognition in any Islamic community,[16] even though several have been affiliated or inspired by major US Islamic organizations as noted above. More importantly, almost all US Islamic financial experiments have been boot strap operations, and have taken more than ten years, when successful, to amass assets greater than $10 million.

And, this begins the journey to the meat of our discussion, the regulators. US Islamic financial boutiques have typically operated in gray areas or outright outside of the law. Regulators, whether securities, banking or cooperative, are uncertain at local or national levels how to deal with Islamic financial institutions. Since substantial financial institutions have not entered the market, regulatory officials fear that Islamic financial boutiques represent fly by night operations that exist solely to defraud people on the basis of religious or ethnic affinity. Moreover, the inadequate capitalization of most boutiques means that regulatory also worry that such entities do not have the capacity to endure, and to provide the promised level of service or to return deposits or investments.

The fears of financial service regulators are exacerbated by the failure up to now of Muslim minorities to successfully articulate that their inability to obtain financing or to save and invest according to *Sharia* as a substantive problem. When one examines the fact that Islamic banking achieves about 25% market penetration in many Islamic majority

---

16 "1992 North American Survey for Islamic Finance", *The American Journal of Islamic Finance.*

societies, a like need may be extrapolated for Muslim minorities.[17] When the need cannot be fulfilled for these communities under existing regulations, then a problem exists. Herein emerges the opportunity to achieve dialogue with the regulators and elected authorities for they have, in the US at least, a mandate to assure that financial services are broadly inclusive of all segments of society.

As may be expected the ethnic distinctions among Muslim populations in the West are important because they reveal important cultural patterns relating to savings, investment, credit and social behavior - patterns which are not necessarily governed by Islam: These are discussed below. The income distinctions bear out three fundamentally different strata of financial demands.

Although African American Muslims are more successful than other African Americans, they are simply lower middle class in general American terms. Moreover, they are an urban middle class, which has not necessarily left areas that are unattractive. We grasped this example earlier in the story of the Atlanta Masjid of Al Islam. As a result, they tend to have two major financial demands. The first is for basic savings and credit product, because these are not widely available in inner cities. Hence, the African American community is keenly aware of how past US banking practice have left their urban areas under-banked.

The second demand among African American communities is for community development capital. This again ties to their location, and a broader trend among African American and other minority communities to seek to draw capital to urban inner city locations. Typically, they are seeking micro lending and investment pools similar to those developed by Dr. Ahmed Elnaggar in Egypt and Dr. Mohammad Yunus in Bangladesh. But, it also extends to a substantial demand for funding for education or debt recovery. African Americans also tend to be relatively balanced

---

17 This is more true of the Arabian Gulf than Malaysia, where the financial system is more highly developed and the current level of Islamic financial services is 5% according to Dato' Ahmad Donn, Governor of the Central Bank of Malaysia on June 18, 1997 at the Islamic Banking Summit, Labuan, Malaysia. The variation between the Arabian Gulf and Malaysia appears to reflect three substantive differences: local government policies; the degree of stratification of the local financial system; and the sophistication of the financial consumer. Arabian Gulf governments have not formally pushed Islamic finance, unlike Malaysia. Arabian Gulf financial systems are much less stratified than Malaysia, and from this it follows that the Arabian Gulf financial consumer is not always as sophisticated as his or her Malaysian peer.

in their demand for credit and saving resources. More critically, they have a healthful fear of excess leverage.

Arabian and South Asian immigrant tend to average above the overall US median in income, which means that they are significantly more affluent and may have a more sophisticated outlook on financial needs, often bifurcating their demand for Islamic services along the credit and investment lines. This means that they look to the full array of investment and deposit services available in the market and make a decision based upon goals and yield. The less certain return, or unproved track record of those Islamic financial boutiques now active in America means that they are not prepared to risk more than "charity" or "throw away" money with these companies. But, they aggressively seek home or car finance from these same institutions.

Newer Arabian and European immigrants, however, do not mirror the financial behavior of similar age and income Americans. Foremost, their financial behavior is clouded by strong suspicions of people who do not come from their ethnic group. Secondly, they tend to reflect a substantial liquidity preference, and fear of fraud. They are frequently engaged in non-conventional savings and financing schemes, some of which prove to be fraudulent, causing substantial financial loss within the communities, and further perpetrating their fears.

In contrast, the behavior of South Asian communities is more often determined by income. Lower and middle income South Asians tend to follow similar patterns to the newer Arabian and European immigrants. But, upper income South Asians reflect an exceptionally high degree of financial sophistication, frequently proving to be more alert and capable than their American peers. As a rule, upper income Muslim immigrants tend to be conspicuous consumers, which again appears to drive their relatively high demand for credit as discussed above.

The third area of demand also emerges in the more affluent immigrant communities. Instead of seeking to build mosques or Islamic schools solely from donations or grants, they seek immediate gratification. Hence, they seek credit or deferred payment structures to fund projects as soon as consensus is reached in the community to proceed.

These elements of demand are largely colored by income, but contain some cultural elements.

The basic cultural summary indicated above does not point to a high degree of financial sophistication spread evenly throughout the Islamic communities of North America. In meetings with community leaders, community groups and other, as well as based on survey results, one hears frequently about the need to provide for future needs like *Haj*, education, weddings, home acquisition, retirement, and, in some communities, burial. Common consumption goals include auto, house, major appliances, and education. The single most common demand is for home and auto finance. The savings and investment side of the equation is less frequently raised.

Under the current US banking law most Islamic financial products would be considered securities or investment and merchant banking products. Financial vehicles like *mudaraba* or *musharaka* draw strong parallels to US law concepts of limited partnerships, limited liability companies, grantor trusts, and joint stock companies. Indeed, a number of sophisticated foreign investors have used all of the above to invest in the US according to Islamic standards. Hence, they may be developed fully under existing SEC rules and delivered through the appropriately registered entities and licensed professionals to domestic populations. Other products like *murabaha* and *ijara* draw acceptable parallels to installment credit and leasing, again both have been used by a number of sophisticated Islamic investors in the US.[18] These are governed by an array of state and federal rules that are quite liberal, allowing delivery through registered, but lightly regulated finance companies or highly regulated banks. Yet another series of financial vehicles may be offered through banks under the National Banking Act, if the banks successfully demonstrate successfully that the product is "safe and sound" and a permitted banking business under the act.

Both state and Federal agencies regulate the banking sector, depending upon a bank's selection of a state of national license. The Office of the Comptroller of the Currency (OCC) and the Federal Reserve Bank (FRB) are the primary national regulators with the FRB governing state-chartered banks and the OCC governing national banks. Finance companies are not regulated by the specific Federal agencies but are subject to Federal statutes. Securities companies are governed by the SEC, self-regulated by the National Association of Securities Dealers, and further governed

---

18 For instance, The United Bank of Kuwait, plc's Islamic Investment Banking Unit in London manages a leasing fund that has nearly $200 million of equipment leases structured according to Sharia and agreed to by an impressive list of investment grade US corporations, most household names in the industrial sector.

by the states in which they do business. Unlike the banks, securities and finance companies are not regulated by the form of their business, but by the conduct.

This means that a securities or finance company is probably completely able to arrange its business according to *Sharia* and function in the US. A bank, now that the rescue of the failed thrift sector is complete, cannot be structured to operate 100% according to Sharia. But, a bank could have a substantial Islamic window with both financing and savings products. That window could even be sub-branded, so long as the bank demonstrated to its regulators that it was in control, that the products were permitted under the Banking Act, and that the practices were safe and sound.

Several banks have begun the process of dialogue with the national regulators. The result is that the FRB has permitted Citibank to own an Islamic investment bank in Bahrain and to provided murabaha for home finance to foreign vacation home buyers in the US; the OCC has permitted several Arab banks to engage in *murabaha* for off-shore clients, and the United Bank of Kuwait, plc has been approved to offer a number of one off Islamic products. There has been no similar action on the securities or finance company side by established domestic or foreign entities.

Public policy issues, even international terrorism, as well as sound banking and legal issues surround this entire regulatory process. If Muslim Americans have a lower incidence of home ownership than other Americans, despite their affluence, will they become disaffected with America and engage in unpleasant social or political behavior. If a product is offered that appeals strongly to the most religious Muslim Americans, will it give them a greater sense of participation in and commitment to America?

Another policy issue that is more clearly and substantively pertinent granted the expected removal of barriers between banking and investment banking in the US is the degree to which the success and vitality of the US banking system increasingly requires tailor made products which may bring banks either brand loyalty or higher margins than mass market vanilla fudge products. Are not Islamic products precisely that tailored products, serving a specific community's needs, and demonstrating the responsiveness of the banking system to the needs of all consumer sub-groups?

Whether dealing with the FRB, OCC, SEC or state regulators, any party working on an Islamic finance project or product must studiously avoid raising a conflict between *Sharia* and American law. US legislators and regulators do not wish to recognize a law above that which they make and enforce, and they will not approve a project or product that either takes its validity from separate legal authority, or which violates the US laws that govern the issue at hand. Moreover, they do not wish to guess which is the appropriate school of *Sharia* to be applied. Generally speaking, this is not a problem because the *Sharia* is more restrictive than US law. But, the appropriate path is to show how the *Sharia* is a moral guideline that will match up well with the consumer protection and anti-fraud segments of US law, whilst restricting the number of activities in which an Islamic entity may engage, or even tightening the US rules further.

Islamic finance is the fastest growing financial sub-sector in the World. Still small at $160 billion,[19] with a like amount is probably held in Islamic form by western banks, the sector is growing at 15% p.a.[20] This means that the Islamic institutions have aggregated no more than the assets of a single very large western bank. Nonetheless, the growth in the Islamic sector is driven by young, well-educated Muslims around the world. Only now are local markets in the Arabian Gulf, Africa, South Asia and Southeast Asia truly opening to Islamic finance. And, the results are encouraging, with a substantial out of the box market share going to the Islamic institutions, followed by rapid growth and increased competitiveness. The Islamic minority of the US should not differ substantially in their commitment to Islam from the Muslims elsewhere. Therefore, a substantial population - up to 25% of the local communities - is pre-disposed towards Islamic finance. This is potentially 520,000 households, a large market in its own right.

As instruments and delivery mechanisms are designed to serve Muslim Americans, and they prove cost efficient and user friendly, Islamic finance will prove to be competitive. This should enhance the capacity of the industry to improve its efficiencies, meaning that the "affinity" client will join the market. This will create an opportunity for

---

19 Shaykh, Samir Abid, Introductory Address, Islamic Banking and Finance Forum, Dubai, November 1996.
20 Bahar, Adnan Al-, Address at the Amiri Diwan, Kuwait, June 7, 1997.

the market to double, bringing along another half million households.[21] Clearly this means that within ten years, the Islamic market of the US could prove to be important niche market for specialized service providers.

These small markets among Muslim minorities are well suited to niche players willing to tailor products, and to learn about the specific needs of localized communities, sometimes fractured by ethnicity and dogma. Such markets in stable monetary and political environments also offer something in the way of useful products for investment by Muslim majority communities and their financial institutions.

Conclusion:

The tide has turned in the US. Financial service regulators and supervisors are taking a positive position to the efforts of banks and others to accommodate the financial service needs of Muslims. Slowly, the Muslims are becoming more sophisticated and interested with respect to Islamic finance. And, Muslims are gaining the economic and political maturity that draws the attention of banks, businesses, and governments. The timing could not be better for the success of Islamic financial institutions. Increasingly, this potential success will turn upon the prosecution of strategies that emphasize either gigantic economies sales or highly focused niche marketing.

Within this rosy scenario, there are a number of important factors to keep in mind. Foremost, the Muslim minorities of the US do not represent a monolithic whole. There are distinct ethnic and doctrinal sub-groups. Each has its own perception of financial need and style in financial management. Sometimes one product fits all, but this may not be the case when different *Sharia* interpretations result in some communities showing aversion to some products. Beyond the religious affinity aspect, there are professional and income distinctions that often follow ethnic lines. These too cause different types of financial demand. Hence, being wired to local communities, their leaders and their goals is a critical aspect of success in the delivery of successful Islamic financial products in the West.

---

21 "1992 North American Survey for Islamic Finance ": An almost equal number of people are positively inclined to Islamic finance if there is no cost or premium compared to conventional finance.

Overall, the statistics exist for the first time to understand who are the Muslims, what do they need and what do they want in the financial services. As a result, those organizations, which are keen to support the Muslims in meeting their religious obligation to transact their financial affairs free from riba, have the best opportunity and it is improving as data becomes more reliable, and is more frequently measured.

Islamic Home Financing
in North America

Syed Eqbal Hasan

ABSTRACT

Muslims in North America and other countries have been concerned about the prevailing practice of buying a house through interest-based financing. Since the beginning of 1970, concerned Muslims in North America have been looking at interest-free alternatives of home ownership. A group of Muslims in Canada, in the early 1970s, developed an idea that was based on interest-free ownership home. This initial idea ultimately culminated in a working model that was implemented in 1981. The basic concepts of interest-free home ownership involving the partnership between the housing cooperative and the renter/owner are presented and illustrated in this article. The evolution of Islamic housing, along with the main features of some of the successful housing projects in North America, are also discussed.

INTRODUCTION

Housing is a basic need of all humans. Every Muslim desires to secure a dwelling for his family in order to provide a safe Islamic environment. In North America, and in many European and other countries, the entrenched practice of paying interest to finance the purchase of a house has posed a serious problem to concerned Muslims living in these countries. This is because of the prohibitions of interest in Islam. Several verses in the Qur'an command us to avoid interest. For example, in chapter 2, verse 276, we are told Allah has permitted trade and forbidden usury." and again in verse 278 of the same chapter, we are reminded, "O you who believe, keep your duty to Allah, and relinquish what remains of your demand from usury, if you are indeed believers." There are many *ahadith*, that contain injunctions against interest. One of the

117

better known is as follows: Narrated Ibn Masud, Allah's messenger said, "Allah has cursed the receiver, the giver of the interest and also the witness and the scribe of the interest transaction, they are alike." (Muslim, Tirmizi).

In trying to live with Islamic principles, concerned Muslims in North America took upon themselves to confront the challenge and find an Islamic solution to the problem. The process began about 25 years ago when some dedicated Muslims brain stormed a nascent idea that, in 1974, culminated in a roughly-written document dealing with the issue of interest-free housing. This was like a rough gem; it was of value but had to be polished to achieve its maximum potential. So the original document went through several revisions and modifications until it became a working plan, ready for implementation. This happened in 1980, nearly a decade after the initial idea was conceived.

This article is a documentation of the evolution of Islamic housing in North America and is intended to provide a description of successful Islamic housing projects. Explanation of the concept and basic information on membership and other requirements of the Islamic housing projects are included in the article. It should be noted that whether Muslims join the co-op for owning a house or just to invest their money, everyone receives a dividend on his or her investment. In this regard, every Muslim who has some extra money should consider investing it in Islamic housing projects. There are several worthwhile reasons for doing this: (a) the money receives above-average return, (b) the Muslim is sure that his/her money is working to support an excellent Islamic cause, and (c) saving money for a major expense, such as college education, marriage, and the like.

HISTORIC DEVELOPMENT OF ISLAMIC HOUSING IN NORTH AMERICA

The aspect of interest associated with mortgage has been an unacceptable but vexing problem for concerned Muslims for a long time. Many of the young and bright Muslim students who came to North America for higher education during the 1960s and 1970s decided to live here for one reason or the other. Soon these people felt the need to have their own home, but the prevailing practice of financing the house on the basis of interest kept them away. Many preferred to rent an apartment despite the advantages and the clear need to own a home.

It was in 1974 that the seeds of the Islamic housing project that were so carefully sown by dedicated persons sprouted with a modest beginning in Halifax, Canada. Dr. Jamal Badawi was the prime mover who had put together the initial concept in the form of a crude working document. The Halifax Project was especially developed to help a Muslim brother get out of interest and own the home in an Islamic way. On June 26, 1981, the model was put to an actual test in that the brother, who had serious problems in renewal of his home mortgage, decided to use this model to pay for his home instead of going to a financial institution to secure a loan. To do this, the model had to be translated into a working legal document, which Dr. Badawi and others successfully accomplished. The original concept underwent some revisions and the new version, developed by Dr. Badawi and called the SHARED EQUITY and RENTAL (SER)model, came around in 1982. This generated considerable interest both among Muslims and non-Muslims. Timing perhaps had to do with this frenzy of interest, because in the early 1980s, interest rate had dramatically shot up in North America and annual percentage rates of 18-20 were common. The SER model which was designed as a no-interest alternative for home ownership caught people's attention, including non-Muslims. In fact, Dr. Badawi was invited to discuss this model at the evening news segment on the Atlantic Region of the Canadian Broadcasting Corporation (CBC). The news report also included an interview with the brother who had decided to rent/own his home through the housing society formed using the SER model.

Since the airing of the interview, there was a great demand for the video and audio tapes. Many communities across North America seriously began to look at this interest-free alternative as an Islamic solution to a seemingly unsolvable problem.

ISLAMIC HOUSING MODELS

The underlying principle in all models is avoidance of interest to finance the home. All models comply with the fundamental Islamic principle of interest prohibition. The difference occurs in the details that must be in compliance with local and national laws. The general outline of the model is as follows.

A potential buyer of a house becomes a member of the housing co-op by paying the membership fee and buying the required number of shares. Depending on the financial capability of the individual and decision of the co-op, the house is purchased by the co-op in the open market by paying the full price. The co-op then gives the house to the person on a rental basis. This person, already a member of the co-op, has acquired certain number of shares that are counted toward renter/ owner's equity in the home. The annual income from the rental is used to return proportionate dividends to the co-op share holders which include the renter/owner as well. The latter is required to buy a minimum number of shares every year, preferably more than the minimum, for ultimate and accelerated ownership of the home.

The model takes into account annual increase in share price, rental and appreciation of the property, repair and upkeep, and possible additions/alterations. In general, considering a 5% appreciation in property value, a person can own the house in 14 years. A hypothetical example to illustrate the basic concept is presented in the Box below.

Assumptions
1. Purchase price of the house: $100,000
2. Fair market rental: $1000/mo or $12,000 yearly
3. Taxes and insurance, to be paid by the renter/owner: $200/mo or $2,400 yearly
4. Divide the house price into 100 shares of $1,000 each
5. Renter/Owner has accumulated 10 shares worth $10,000 in the Housing Cooperative
6. The Cooperative owns 90 shares amounting to $90,000.
7. The renter/owner buys a minimum of 3 shares each year
8. Stock value, house rent, taxes & insurance increase @ 5% per year Fair Rental Determination
9. Fair annual market rent $12,000
10. Taxes and insurance paid by the
    renter/owner $2,400
11. Net yearly rental income (9-10) $9,600
    Return on Investment
12. Divide $9,600 by 100 to determine income
    generated per share $96
13. Return on investment to the Co-op which
    owns 9/10 of the house, 96x90 $8,640
14. Return on investment to renter/owner who owns 1/10 of the house, 96x10 $960

15. At the end of Year 1, the Coop received $8640 on its investment of $90000, which translates into 9.6% return.
16. Also the renter/owner, at the end of Year 1 received $960 on his investment of $10000.

Formula for Calculation of Return on Investment for the Renter/Owner

Items 12-14 can be included in the following general formula that can be used for calculating the return on investement for years 2-14:

$$PR = (NR \div SV) \times PS \times 100$$

where, PR is the annualized percent return in $,
        NR is net rental income per year in $,
        SV is the market value of shares in a given year in $, and
        PS is the percent of the total number of shares owned by the renter/owner.

With a 5% increase in the second year, the stock value increases to $1,050, rent increases to $12,600, and taxes and insurance go up to $2,520. Earlier, we assumed that the renter/owner has to buy a minimum of three shares in the second and following years. Further, let us assume that he re-invested his return of $960 to buy one additional share costing $1,000. Thus, the renter/owner holds a total of 14 shares at the beginning of the second year while the Coop's share decreases to 86 (compared to 90 in the first year). New share price, rental and the net return, etc., using the formula given in the Box, for the subsequent years are given in Table 1. This table is a simplistic illustration of how a person could build up the equity and own a home in 14 years. It is not designed to serve as an amortization chart

SUCCESSFUL ISLAMIC HOUSING PROJECTS

A discussion of successful Islamic housing projects is presented in the following paragraphs. Readers and other interested persons who wish additional details should contact the respective organization. Addresses and phone/fax numbers along with the main features of three housing organizations are provided in Table 2.

Islamic Cooperative Housing Corporation, Toronto, Canada

The Islamic Cooperative Housing Corporation (ICHC) stands out as the most successful and the longest lasting project. Drawing from the SER model, Br. Pervez Nasim together with a core of dedicated Muslims in Toronto, further refined the model and registered it as a corporation in Toronto on Nov. 16, 1980. The main difference, according to Dr. Jamal Badawi, was changing the share price to a fixed amount as opposed to variable amount in the SER model. The project is now in its 19th year of a highly successful operation.

SHARE TM   Project, MSI, U.S.A.

The Shared Home Appreciation in Rent and Equity (SHARE) project originated as a separate scheme of the MSI (Muslim Savings & Investment) of Los Angeles, CA in 1989. The offices of the MSI and SHARE are now located in Houston, Texas. Br. Masood Aijazi, along with other dedicated Muslims deserve the credit for initiating this project in California. Unlike other projects, SHARE does not restrict its housing program in a single state. It is set up to serve interest-free housing need of Muslims all over the U.S.A.

Islamic Cooperative Housing Corporation, St. Louis, Missouri, U.S.A.

This project is a textbook example of the benefit of a focused conference. In May 1988, The Islamic Society of North America (ISNA) organized the second conference on Economic Development with a focus on Financial Alternatives for Muslims in America. Along with other topics, Islamic alternatives to housing was also discussed. Experienced persons such as Dr. Jamal Badawi, Br. Pervez Nasim and others shared their knowledge and expertise on Islamic housing projects and offered to help fellow Muslims in establishing similar projects in the United States and elsewhere. Many participants felt motivated to initiate similar projects in their communities.

However, credit goes to Br. Zia Mahmood for his efforts which resulted in the formation of the Islamic Cooperative Housing Corporation in St. Louis, in 1989. This is an active project that was developed following the ICHC of Toronto, Canada, modifying the legal aspects to conform to the United States laws. Br. Pervez Nasim, President of the ICHC Toronto, extended every help and was fully involved in the development and implementation of the St. Louis project.

Qurtuba Housing Corporation, Montreal, Canada

This is yet another project modeled after the ICHC of Toronto. It was established in 1991 and is an active project serving the needs of Muslims in the province of Quebec in Canada. As of December, 1995, nine homes were purchased by the Qurtuba Housing Corporation. Br. Moin Kermani is the president and can be reached at (514) 484-2976; Fax: (514) 484-3802. Mailing address: 7445 Chester Ave., Montreal H4V1M4, Canada.

INTERNATIONAL PROJECTS

Muslims in several other countries have been actively pursuing the idea of an interest-free *Sharia* compatible alternative for home ownership. A brief description of some of these projects is given below.

Muslim Community Cooperative, Australia

This project is designed after the Toronto model and was incorporated in August, 1990 in Melbourne. It is a successful project and has been helping Muslims in Australia meet their housing needs in an Islamic way.

Islamic Housing Cooperative Society Ltd., Trinidad, South America

Another successful project, modeled after the Toronto ICHC, was established in 1994 in Trinidad, South America. The Society is in the process of acquiring its first house.

ISLAMIC HOME FINANCING INSTITUTIONS

Unlike the Housing Cooperatives, these institutions offer home financing conforming to the principles of the Sharia. According to Br. Abdulkader

Thomas (editor of the Islamic Finance Journal), after a great deal of work that involved compliance with the U.S. laws, a vehicle had been developed that will enable Muslims to finance home purchase in the United States. Basically, it involves two contracts: a lease agreement and a promise-to-purchase contract. The United Bank of Kuwait PLC, New York Branch, was about ready to test market the innovative financing program in California and Florida. Details are available from Abdulkader Thomas, United Bank of Kuwait, New York at (202) 906-8500, code CIHF. Other organizations such as the American Finance House, Pasadena, CA., Ilahi Investments, Detroit, MI., and some others have been providing Islamic financing for home purchase in the past.

ACKNOWLEDGMENTS

Numerous persons have provided information for this article. I wish to thank everyone for their time and cooperation. In particular, I would take this opportunity to express my gratitude to Dr. Jamal Badawi, Br. Pervez Nasim, Br. Abdulkader Thomas and Br. Zia Mahmood for their assistance in researching material for this article. I also wish to thank Syed Obaid Ahmed for his help in checking the accuracy and finalizing Table 1. Finally, I would like to thank Dr. Amber Haque for his interest and gentle persuasion that resulted in preparation of this article.

References

Badawi, J., Is there a *halal* mortgage? In Hasan, S.E. (editor), *Proceedings of the Second ISNA Conference on Economic Development, Financial Alternatives for Muslims in   America*, The Islamic Society of North America, Plainfield, Indiana, U.S.A., 1989., pp. 83-91.

Hasan, S.E., (editor), *Proceedings of the Second ISNA Conference on Economic Development,   Financial Alternatives for Muslims in America*, held at Kansas City, MO., May 28-30,   1989 and published by The Islamic Society of North America, Plainfield, Indiana, U.S.A., 1989, 149 p.

Nasim, P., Islamic co-operative housing project, Toronto. In Hasan, S.E. (editor), *Proceedings of the Second ISNA Conference on Economic Development, Financial Alternatives for   Muslims in America*, The Islamic Society of North America, Plainfield, Indiana, U.S.A., 1989, pp. 92-97.

Table 1.   Progressive   increase   in   renter's/owner's   equity

Year (A)	Share Price, (B)	No. of shares Renter buys/owns (C)	Coop's share (D)	Home Rental (E)	Taxes & Insurance (F)	Net Rental (G) [E-F]	Return from Rental, $/share (H) [G÷B]	Coop's income from rental, $ (I)[H×D]	Renter's income from rental, $ J [H×C]	Percent return on investment to the renter/owner
1	1000	10	90	12000	2400	9600	96	8640	960	9.6
2	1050	4/14	86	12600	2520	10080	100.80	8668.80	1411.20	9.9
3	1103	5/19	81	13230	2646	10584	105.84	8573.04	2010.96	10.2
4	1157.63	5/24	76	13892	2778	00004	111.14	8446.64	2667.36	10.5
5	1015.51	5.5/29	70.5	14586	2917	00669	116.69	8226.65	3442.35	10.7
6	1276.28	6/35.5	64.5	15315	3063	12252	122.52	7902.54	4349.46	10.9
7	1340.09	6/41.5	58.5	16081	3216	12865	128.65	7526.03	5338.97	11.2
8	1407.10	7/48.5	51.5	16885	3377	13508	135.08	6956.32	6551.38	11.4
9	1477.46	8/56.5	43.5	17729	3546	14183	141.83	6169.61	8013.39	11.5
10	1551.33	8.5/65	35	18616	3723	148936	148.93	5212.55	9680.45	11.9
11	1628.89	9/74	26	19547	3909	15638	156.38	4065.88	11572.12	12.0
12	1710.34	10/84	16	20524	4105	16419	164.19	2627.04	13791.96	12.2
13	1795.86	11/95	5	21550	4311	17239	172.39	861.95	16377.05	12.3
14	1885.65	5/100	0	22628	4526	18102	181.02	0	18102	12.7

Table 2. Main features of some Islamic housing projects in North America

Name, address, phone and fax number	Membership	Other requirements	Number of houses bought	Remarks
Islamic Cooperative Housing Corp. P.O. Box - 160, Station 'P' Toronto, M5S2S7 Canada Ph: 416-977-2057 Fax: 416-977-6058 Established 1980	a) $75 application fee b) Must buy at least 6 shares of $100 each when applying for membership c) Must buy at least 6 shares in each calendar year to maintain eligibility.	New house buyer must have purchased shares worth 20% of the house price; current owner of a house needs shares equal to 10% of the price. Shares to remain with the Coop for at least 6 months.	235 as of January, 1996	$22 million worth of shares have been sold. Shares can be sold or transferred to any member of the Coop. Non-home buyers may invest their money to receive quarterly dividends (averaging 8-10 %). Program available in Toronto area.
SHARETM Project MSI Financial Corp. 300 South Gessner, Suite 150, Houston, TX 77063 Ph: 800-872-6741 Fax: 713-974-2058 Established 1986	None	20% of the house price must be invested with MSI before applying for house purchase.	100 as of January, 1996	Program available for house purchase anywhere in the U.S.A.
Islamic Cooperative Housing Corp. 11441 Ladue Rd. St. Louis, MO 63141 Ph: 314-432-6807 or 314-997-6907 Established 1988	a) $100 application fee for membership b) Must buy 10 shares of $100 each in one calendar year to maintain eligibility.	New house buyers must have purchased shares equal to 20% of the house price., Current owner of a house needs shares equal to 10% of the price	9 as of December 1995	Shares can be sold or transferred to any member of the Coop. Non-home buyers may invest their money to receive quarterly dividends. Program available in St. Louis area.

POLITICAL
AWARENESS

Awareness and Consciousness of Muslims in Canada

Syed Serajul Islam

anada is a land of immigrants. People from various regions of the world from diverse cultures have migrated to Canada for centuries. In the last few decades a large number of Muslims also have immigrated to Canada. Although their number has increased dramatically in the last half a century they constitute a tiny minority in the total population make-up of Canada. Consequently, they are facing a variety of challenges in the new environment. Therefore, attempts have been made by the conscious Muslims to preserve Islamic values and their distinct identities as Muslims. In this paper some basic questions are raised regarding the Canadian Muslims: who are the Canadian Muslims? Are they conscious of their Islamic heritage? What factors are responsible for their consciousness? What are the areas of awareness and consciousness? How do the Canadian Muslims maintain this awareness and consciousness? What is the future of the Muslims in Canada?

In their works on ethnic studies two prominent sociologists, Max Weber and Emile Durkheim, have pointed out that in a multi-ethnic society, among many factors, religion plays a dominant role in the formation of ethnic identity. According to them "religion is necessary to a society as a vital mechanism of integration for human beings and as a means to unify symbols."[1] Subsequently, many scholars like Milton Gordon, Raymond Breton, Baha Abu-Laban, Edward Herberg, Hans Mol, Frederick Barth and some others have emphasised the importance

---

1 For detailed analysis see Leo Driedger, *The Ethnic Factor, Identity in Diversity* (Toronto: McGraw - Hill Ryerson Ltd., 1989), P. 20.

131

of religion as one of the most important forms of ethnic identity.[2] In particular, they believe that religious identity becomes the "cornerstone of ethnic groups in their adaptation to a new culture."[3] A common religion strengthens the bonds of solidarity among diverse ethnic groups. This study will examine, despite the wide diversity in their ethnic, cultural and geographical origin, how has the awareness and consciousness of Muslims in Canada helped them to keep their identity along the line of religion — Islam.

THE CANADIAN MUSLIMS : WHO ARE THEY?

Canada does not have an indigenous Muslim population. The Muslims are immigrants from the Arab World, South and Southeast Asia, Africa, East Europe, the Caribbean and the South America. The earliest record indicates that there were 13 Muslim residents in Canada in 1871, who came primarily from Syria.[4] Until the Second World War, the rate of growth in the Muslim community was very slow. In fact, by 1951 it reached a level of only 3,000 Muslims. Most of them were uneducated, unskilled and of peasant background. Lacking proficiency in English, many became peddlers and some of them found jobs in factories, mines and grocery stores. With the changes in their economic conditions many who intended to return home country felt in staying permanently in Canada.

The gradual reforms in the immigration policy of Canada in the 1960s led to a further increase in the Muslim population. Those who

---

2 Milton Gordon, *Assimilation in American Life: The Role of Race, Religion and National Origins* (New York: Oxford University Press, 1964), Raymond Breton, "Institutional Completeness of Ethnic Communities and the Personal Relations of Immigrants, *"The American Journal of Sociology: 70* (1964):193-205; Jeffrey Reitz, *The Survival of Ethnic Groups* (Toronto: Mc Graw - Hill Ryerson Ltd., 1980); Edward Herberg, *Ethnic Groups in Canada: Adaptations and Transitions* (Scarborough: Nelson, Canada, 1989); Frederick Barth, ed. *Ethnic Groups and Boundaries* (Oslow: Universities Forlaget, 1969); Hans Mol, *Identity and the Sacred: A Sketch for a New Socio-Scientific Theory of Religion* (Agin Court: The Book Society of Canada, Ltd., 1976); Baha Abu-Laban "The Canadian Muslim Community: The Need for A New Survival Strategy" in E.H. Waugh and others eds. *The Muslim Community in North America* (Edmonton: The University of Alberta Press, 1983): 75-93.
3 Ahmad F. Yousif, *Muslims in Canada: A Question of Identity* (New York: Legal, 1993), P. 19.
4 Laban, "The Canadian ...", P. 76.

132

came to Canada during the 1960s were often well-educated, fluent in English and westernized, and also came from a variety of countries, including many beyond the Middle East. Most of them came for higher education or for setting up of businesses, subsequently, however, they intended to settle permanently in Canada.[5] The immigration policy was further liberalized in the 1970s, which led to a large influx of Muslim immigrants to Canada.[6] Thus, today according to one estimate there are nearly 450,000 Muslims in Canada.[7] Most of them are found in large cities like Toronto, Montreal, and Edmonton. Nearly half of them live in Ontario province. Muslims are, of course, dispersed throughout Canada. In other words, they are nowhere concentrated in a closely-knit Muslim residential community.

What led these Muslims to leave their home country? The factors, which led them to be immigrants, vary from individual to individual, because they did not come to Canada "as corporate religious groups in search of a "sanctuary."[8] However, in general there are five factors, which are responsible for the immigration of Muslims to Canada. These are a) better economic opportunities, b) political instability in their homeland, c) children's' education, d) pull of family members and friends already in Canada, and e) the freedom of expression guaranteed by the Canadian constitution?[9] In a nutshell, they all came for a "better life."

Since Muslims came to Canada from various parts of the world they differ in their language, culture and customs. Thus, they do not have a homogeneous culture. Haddad wrote, "Different ethnic allegiances tend to go to different mosques. This is true in Montreal where the Fatima mosque seems to attract a predominantly Arab congregation, while the Quebec Islamic Center appears to draw more Indo-Pakistanis. It is also

---

5 Ibid. See also A. Rashid, *The Muslim Canadian: A Profile* (Ottawa: Statistics Canada, 1985) P. 15-19.
6 See Canada Manpower and Immigration, *The Immigration Program*, (Ottawa: 1974); Freda Hawkins, *Canada and Immigration: Public Policy and Public Concern* (Montreal: Mc Gill - Queen's University Press, 1972); and David C. Corbelt, *Canada's Immigration Policy: A Critique* (Toronto: University of Toronto Press, 1957).
7 Earle H. Waugh, "Hijra and Canadian Muslim," *New Straits Times* (Kuala Lumpur) April 16, 1997, P. 10.
8 Laban, "The Canadian..." P. 79. See also, Y. Haddad, "Muslims in Canada" in Coward and Kawamura Eds. *Religion and Ethnicity* (Waterloo; Wilfrid Laurier University Press, 1978): 71-100.
9 Yousif, *Muslims in Canada, op.cit*, P. 17.

true of the Ontario Muslim Association in Toronto, which is predominantly Caribbean and West Indian. In other cities, it has been noted that after the Sunday services, groups tend to congregate according to ethnic identity."[10] Despite their diversity, however, there is one thing common among them, that is, the bond of Islam. The basic tenets of Islam remain the same among all the Muslim immigrants. It is in this area, that Canadian Muslims have expressed their homogeneous consciousness and this awareness is getting stronger day by day due to the challenges faced by the Muslims in Canada.

FACTORS CONTRIBUTING TO AWARENESS AND CONSCIOUSNESS

Before coming to Canada, Muslim immigrants were living in countries where there were institutions and opportunities for practicing Islam. Once they arrive in Canada, they do not get the same environment and opportunities and, therefore, adapt their religious practices to the requirements of the Canadian society in varying ways. The earlier immigrants tended to settle with fellow Muslims, most likely with those of similar ethnic backgrounds. They were generally too busy with basic economic survival. More importantly, most of them considered Canadian residence as temporary and therefore did not think seriously about Islamic consciousness. Gradually, with the increase in number of permanent residents of Muslims, varieties of psychological and social challenges were felt. The awareness began to develop to face these challenges. The Muslim immigrants gradually felt the need for establishing organisations and institutions to preserve the Islamic faith. The common factors that contributed to this consciousness are crisis of identity, conflict with new generation, and discrimination and racism.

Crisis of Identity:

The initial challenge that the Muslim immigrants face in Canada is that they are losing identity. As Sulayman Nyang says, "the first challenge that faces the Muslims in the West is the question of identity. Muslims in the West in general, and in North America in particular, are now

---

10 Quoted in Laban, "The Canadian ..." P. 87.

unanimous in their self-definition as Muslims vs non-Muslims. They all agree that they share a common belief in the Qur'an and *Sunnah*."[11] Muslims, upon arrival to Canada, encounter adjustment problems in language, culture and religion since they lose the identity of their country of origin. Islam provides an opportunity of macro-identity. Muslims, whatever their origin, have a very hard time fitting into the Christian majority Canadian society. The identity crisis of the Muslims is enhanced by the hostility of the host culture. Faced with rejection Muslim immigrants seek an alternative integrating system for their lives. Under the situation, Islam is perceived to be the only integrating system. The Islamic identity guarantees the preservation of the family and protects the children from total integration into the Canadian culture. Earle Waugh comments, "the paradoxes of the first migration highlight that each must choose ultimately to stay and nature in this place. Such is the experience of God's *Ummah*. The template is migration as exile, paradox, and new identity. Such notions arise out of migration experience, where the homeland becomes idealized while the new locale is perceived as full of bitterness and change. Memory transforms home into paradise. Such conception are, of course, characteristic of much migrative narrative, but they take an added meaning when the new land is viewed as hostile. Out of this comes an emotional change of perspective, a new sense of who one is while the new identity is in the process of developing the awareness that one is now forming oneself is constructing one's own being, is liberating or empowering one now can engage in the process of building a community.[12]

Conflict Between the Old and New Generations

Another crucial challenge to the Canadian Muslims emanates from their Canadian born children. Their children are born and brought up in the Canadian culture and environment. Children are quickly assimilated into the Canadian way of life and tend to move away from the Islamic tradition and values. Gradually, the Muslim parents feel that they are losing control over their children. They find it difficult to command allegiance of the new generation. In particular, the parents face the problem of upbringing their children in the Islamic faith. At home they

---

11 Sulayman Nyang, "Using the First Amendment to Maintain Muslim Identity in North America," in *Islamic Horizons*, July August, 1996, P. 32.

12 E. Waugh, "Hijra and Canadian Muslims", P. 10.

watch T.V. programmes which are full of Western culture, and outside, they see the free mixing which are often considered unacceptable to Muslim parents. Thus, the parents feel that the only way they could keep their children in the right track is through imparting to them the Islamic values and faith. A great majority of the children do not think the same way, which obviously brings them in conflict with their parents.

Discrimination and Racism:

In their daily life Muslims also often encounter discrimination and racism, despite the fact that "the Canadian constitution makes no distinction based on the basis of race, ethnic origin, colour and creed."[13] The Canadian constitution guarantees religious and other fundamental rights. However, lack of information and general misperception about Islam has led to discrimination and racism. In particular, a pejorative attitude towards Muslims has intensified after the Islamic revolution in Iran and the gulf war in 1991-1992. Discrimination and racism are manifested at the individual as well as at the institutional levels. The media often fuels them. People see media coverage of terrorist attacks by Muslims abroad, to which Canadian express their negative reactions against Canadian Muslims. Here, Wauge describes an incident in Toronto where a Muslim is "punched up by a rabid group of young rowdies taunting 'Paki Paki'."[14]

Thus, Islam is equated with terrorism, which is perceived by the Muslims as biased and prejudicial. Individually, Muslims can smell the sense of discrimination in the schools, job market and in the shopping centres, though the Canadian government does not permit such kind of discrimination. Sheila McDonough commented in one of her studies, that, "the most serious problem Muslims suffer from in Canada is the negative stereotyping about Islam which is promoted through the Canadian media,

---

13 Daood Hamdani, "Muslims in the Canadian Mosaic," *Journal Institute of Muslim Minority Affairs*, Vol.5. No.1 (1979), Murray Hogben says, "The Muslim teenagers at summer camps organized by the CMCC often object to the segregation of the sexes for sports, swimming, and even religious instruction when they can mix to a greater or lesser degree with members of other sex at home and at school the rest of the year," See his "Socio Religious Behavior of Muslims in Canada," in *The Muslim Community in North America*, P. 116.

14 Y. Haddad, "The impact of the Islamic Revolution in Iran on the Syrian Muslims of Montreal," in *The Muslim Community in North America*, P. 176. See also Waugh, "Hijra ..." P.11.

136

and which is pervasive. Muslims may differ among themselves as to how conservative or liberal they might be on issues like the dress of women, or as the nature of their religious practice, but they all suffer greatly from this negative stereotyping. They all seek ways to combat it. It is the seriousness of this problem that distinguishes the Muslim experience from that of other ethnic groups."[15]

AREAS OF AWARENESS AND CONSCIOUSNESS

Due to the above challenges Muslims believe that one of the ways that they could preserve their strength and unity in Canada is through following the Islamic ideals. The greater the challenges the greater the sense of awareness. The major areas in which their awareness is reflected are: Prayer and Ramadhan, Marriages, Diets, Burial and Education.

Prayers and Ramadhan

Since Canada is primarily a Christian majority country there is no environment for regular five times prayers, Juma Prayer or two Eid Prayers. Also there is no environment for fasting during the month of Ramadhan. The basic obligations of performing daily five times prayer presents serious difficulties to the Muslim in practice. They need to observe these prayers regularly at prescribed intervals. The ritual of *wudu* i.e., cleaning of faces, hands, elbows, ears, head and feet are required before praying. This is often difficult in public places, in schools or at offices. The place of praying must also be clean and free from any pictures or portraits, which is hard to find in any of those places. Now, there are many mosques in Canada where the Muslims perform the Friday and mid day prayers. But, for many Muslims, this conflicts with job responsibilities. The same is true for two Eid prayers and other principal Muslim religious holidays. Due to the lack of any specific place for Eid Prayers, Muslims in Toronto, Montreal, Edmonton rent huge halls or stadium where thousands of Muslims meet twice a year. However, if the Eid does not occur on a weekend the attendance is usually low because the majority has to go to work or school. There is no Muslim

---

15 Quoted in Yousif, *Muslims in Canada*, P. 73 from a paper by Sheila Mc Donough, "Religion and Ethnicity Among the Muslim of Montreal," Presented at the Learned Societies Conference, Victoria, BC 1990. P. 6.

religious holiday, while major Christian and Jewish holidays are recognised by most employers and academic institutions in Canada.[16] During the month of Ramadhan, those who fast frequently encounter job related problems. Muslims have to meet their business and job obligations, which discourage them from fasting.

Upon arriving to Canada as immigrants the Muslims face all these problems and they become conscious of their rituals. Therefore, Muslims have urged many times the Canadian government to declare Friday Prayer legal, meaning, giving leave from work during the prayer time. In 1991, a Muslim Association of Toronto, the Canadian Society of Muslims, initiated a countrywide campaign in favour of asking the Canadian government to recognise "Muslim Family Law."[17] It stated, "as Canadian and as Muslims, we care about justice, equality and fairness, rights, freedom, order, opportunity, good government, peace and harmony. As Canadian and Muslims, we care about the importance of having the sort of framework which is going to provide a spectrum of degrees of freedom, as well as constraints, which will permit all the people of Canada to pursue their individual dream, goals and interests."[18]

Marriage

The Canadian Muslims are also concerned about many marriage-related practices. Pre-marital sex, dating practices, and the tendency toward inter-religious marriages deeply concern the great majority of Muslims. The Muslims, by no means, want their children to get married with a non-Muslim Canadian since "it is unacceptable in Islam, both legally and traditionally."[19] The problem is more serious for the girls than the boys as it is stated in the Qur'an, "This day are (all) things good and pure

---

16 Yousif, *Muslims in Canada*, P. 68. He writes, "Islamic educational institutions try to counteract this problem by educating their students on the historical background of Christmas and discussing why Muslims do not celebrate this festival."

17 See *Newsletter*, Vol. 2. No. 1 (September 1991), P.2. Published by the Canadian Society of Muslims, Toronto, Canada.

18 Ibid.

19 Yousif, *Muslims*, P. 63. See also, Murray Hogben, "The Socio-Religious Behavior of Muslims in Canada" in The *Muslim Community in North America*, P. 116. He writes, "There is a fairly high incidence of Muslim men inter marrying with non-Muslim women, because the have met and fallen in love with an outsider and somehow missed finding or accepting a bride from within their community".

made lawful unto you. The food of the People of the Book is lawful unto you and yours lawful unto them. (Lawful unto you in marriage) are (not only) chaste women who are believers, but chaste among the people of the Book revealed before your time, — when ye give them their due dowers, and desire chastity, not lewdness, nor secret intrigues. If any one rejects faith, fruitless is his work, and the Hereafter he will be in the marks of those who have lost (all spiritual good)". (Qur'an 5:6) In another verse it is written, "Let no man guilty of adultery or fornication marry any but a woman of similarly guilty or unbelievers. Nor let any but such a man or unbelievers marry such a woman: To the believers such a thing is forbidden." (Qur'an 24:2-3). Sometimes Muslim children are also involved in pre-marital sex, which is not legal in Canada but occurs frequently. In Islam, sex outside marriage is prohibited. This is called *zina* and therefore is considered to be *haram* (forbidden). Parents attempt to avoid this problem by reminding their children that this practice as *haram*. However, this warning has little effect on their children because of peer pressure. In many cases, the Muslim boys have married non-Muslim girls and converted their wives but, subsequently, conflicts have arisen in the family on the basic values, which have brought disastrous consequences for their children. Either the children have been baptized or the spouses have been divorced. Thus, "safe marriage" of the new generation is a major concern of the Canadian Muslims.[20]

Foods and Drinks

The Muslim community in Canada is also facing the problem of Islamic dietary restrictions. In Islam, certain foods and alcohol drinks are prohibited. However, in Canada there are no restrictions on food and drinks. Muslims are not allowed to eat pork or pork products and the other meats need to be *Halal*, that is, properly slaughtered with appropriate mention of the name of Allah (SWT).[21] These meats, especially cooked meats, are not easily available in Canada. It is not only meat but also bakery products can be a problem as they often contain lard (pork fat),

---

20 Ibid, P. 116.
21 Y. Haddad, "A century of Islam in America," in *The Muslim World Today*, occasional paper No. 4 (Oct. 1987), (Washington: Islamic Affairs Program, The Middle East Institute), P.8.

frequently without proper labelling. Therefore, Muslims often read the ingredients of these products before purchasing them. The avoidance of such products is especially difficult in certain places like the coffee shops of the university, hospitals or in prisons. Muslims are also according to *Shariah* law, bound to abstain from alcohol which is difficult to avoid in the Canadian society where alcohol is an integral part of the social and business cultures. Muslim parents are also struggling to keep their children away from drinking alcohol in order to keep the continuity of the Islamic commitment throughout generations. The question of restricted food and alcohol is thus one of the principal areas of concern for the Muslims.

Burial

After the death of any family member, a crucial concern for the Muslim appears on whether to bury the dead body in Canada or to send it to home country. This is due to the fact that until recently, in most cities there were hardly any separate Muslim cemeteries. However, in some major cities, especially in Toronto, Montreal, Ottawa and Edmonton, Muslims have now purchased lands for Muslim cemeteries. In most cases, the Muslims are buried in non-Muslim cemeteries. Five to ten years ago, most of the bodies used to be sent to their home cemeteries. This led the Muslims to think of having separate Muslim cemeteries in the major cities of Canada. But this has not been done in all cities of Canada and, therefore, Muslims are concerned about not burying their dead bodies in Jewish or Christian cemeteries.

Education

Education of their offspring is the most important area of awareness of the Muslims in Canada. Negative attitudes of the Canadians are evident in the educational curriculum and institutions. Most of the textbooks in the schools are full of Christian mythologies and praise of Christianity, and on the other hand, pejorative terms like "infidels, fanatics", etc. are used for Muslims.[22] One scholar has stated very clearly that biases against

---

22 Garnet Mc Diarmid and David Pratt, *Teaching Prejudice* (Toronto: The Ontario Institute for studies in Education, 1971), P. 41. They write, "Prejudice still manifests in text books, but because it has been less respectable it is more subtle.

Islam exist in Ontario school textbook. He quotes, "Islam was born among the nomads of Arabia, who were wholly illiterate and for whom caravan raiding was a cherished pastime."[23] Many Muslims, who were not very Islamic in their home countries, also become concerned after coming to Canada due to the negative bias against Islam. This leads them to a search for identity and religious roots. Even the health education program offered in the Canadian public schools at the very early stage related to the sexuality and use of contraceptive measures are often viewed by Muslim parents as a serious problem because these might "actually promote sexual promiscuity among their children."[24] It is not only the curriculum, but also extra curriculum issues have become the concerns of many Muslim parents. For example, the issues of dress, especially of the girls have recently caused serious bitterness. In 1994, a Muslim girl of the Arab origin used to go to school in Montreal wearing "hijab". One day the school authority expelled her from the school. In Montreal all the public schools are under the control of either the Catholic School Board or the Protestant School Board. After this incident parents of the girl reported to the media and appealed to the School Board. The school board gave the decision that the school has the right to decide about its own school dress. Where there is no school dress the students can dress as they like. The Muslim communities have further challenged the decision. The Muslim parents are serious about the dress of their daughters in schools.

INSTITUTIONAL MECHANISMS FOR PRESERVING CONSCIOUSNESS

By now the Muslims in Canada have understood that the Islamic faith as well as their identities cannot thrive without institutional support such as mosques, associations and organizations. This is especially important

---

Immigrants may no longer be called "Shiftless and vicious," but there are still instances where they are referred to as "a problem" or "a swarm". It may be that there have a more immediate effect on readers' attitudes than would more obvious discriminatory references".

23   L.M. Kenny, "The Middle East in Canadian Social Science Text Books" in Baha Abu Laban and F. Zeadey eds. *Arabs in America: Myths and Realities* (Wilmette, 111: Medina University Press International, 1975), P. 140.

24   Yousif, *Muslims*, P. 67.

for the second generation to perpetuate their faith and to strengthen the community. Therefore, Muslims in Canada have by now established many mosques and many organizations and educational institutions.

Mosque

The mosque is the most important institution that helps the Muslim immigrants to integrate themselves into a Muslim community. In a non-Muslim society like Canada, the mosque performs the functions of prayer, social organization and a source of education. Thus the Muslims first felt the need of building mosque in major cities of Canada as the attendance in the mosque contributes to the sense of community culture. Despite all the differences in the culture and geographical origin Muslims come to the mosque on the basis of their common religion. Mosques provide an opportunity for integrating the differences of individuals into the sense of community and collectiveness. Upon arrival to Canada many Muslims feel culture stock and the mosques help the new immigrants to establish social contacts within the Muslim community. The mosque creates an awareness of solidarity and unity among the Muslims in Canada.

Before the 1970s there were very few mosques in Canada. The first mosque that was built in Canada, in 1938, is situated in Edmonton, Alberta.[25] At that time, Edmonton had approximately 20 Muslim families. This mosque was not only the place for prayer but also the meeting place for sharing their common problems. After the 1950s, mosques were built in other major cities also like Toronto, Ottawa and Montreal. But they were very limited in number. For example, during the late 1970s, while this author was a student at McGill University there was only one mosque in Montreal, far away from the downtown. Gradually, one after another, mosques began to be built and today one can find more than ten mosques in the city of Montreal alone. The same goes for other cities as well. In these mosques, besides regular prayer, Muslims observe the Friday and the two Eid prayers. In addition, mosques play the role of a

---

25 Laban, *The Muslim Community*, P. 80.

community centre responding to the specific needs of Canadian Muslims. The Islamic mosques are now to be found even in smaller cities of Canada like St. Johns (New Foundland), Hamilton, London, Windsor, Kingston, Hespler, Thunderbary (Ontario), Winnipeg (Manitoba), Dartmouth and Halifax (Nova Scotia). St. Lawrence, and Laval (Quebec). Saskatoon and Regina (Saskatchewan); Calgary and Lacla Biche (Alberta) Vancouver and Victoria (British Columbia). All these mosques have been built by the private funds of the Muslims.

The Islamic Associations and Centers

Although the mosques provide the unity among the Muslims, the larger integration of diverse Muslims in Canada is not possible without larger institutions and centres. As Baha Abu Laban says, "the social integration of the diverse Muslim national groups,"[26] is not possible without "an integrative strategy emphasizing the commonalties of all these groups"– and for this, larger institutions are necessary. The Muslim immigrants, in response to the challenges, felt the necessity of establishing Islamic associations or Islamic centres from the beginning. But this became possible only after the Second World War when the number of Muslims increased in Canada. Thus, in 1972 the Council of Muslim Communities (CMCC) was founded in Canada. The primary objective of the CMCC was to "undertake a coherent national approach to the issues facing the Canadian Muslim community."[27] A large number of Muslim associations began to operate as it's affiliated organs. The scope of activities of the CMCC is quite wide covering education, youth, women, religious affairs, public actions and public relations. Furthermore, the CMCC publishers a major quarterly magazine, Islam Canada, which focuses on religious, educational and political matters. It also contains news regarding Muslims in Canada and around the world. It also publishes articles on Islamic views on various contemporary issues.

In addition to the CMCC, associations of Muslim communities exist in almost every city of Canada. In some major cities like Toronto or Montreal, there are more than one association and centre. Thus today, one can find St. John's Muslim Associations P.E. Muslim Group, Islamic

---

26 Ibid, P. 87.
27 Ibid. P. 81.

Association of Maritime in Nova Scotia, Muslim Association of New Brunswick, Islamic Center of Quebec, Muslim Community of Quebec, Brandford Muslim Association, Canbridge Muslim Association of Hespler, Croatian Islamic Association of Toronto, Islamic Association of Sudbury, Islamic Center of Toronto, Islamic Foundation of Toronto, Ottawa Muslim Association, Peninsula Islamic Society of Peel, Brampton, Kingston Islamic Society, Millat Community Association of Thornhill, Muslim Association of Hamilton, Muslim Society of Waterloo, Noor-E-Islam Society of Canada, North Bay Muslim Association, N.W. Ontario Muslim Association, Ontario Muslim Association, Sarnia Muslim Association, Talim-ul-Islam, Toronto and Region Islamic Congregation, Windsor Islamic Association, Manitoba Islamic Association, Islamic Association of Saskatchewan, Calgary Muslim Association, Lac La Biche Muslim Association, B.C. Muslim Association, Canadian Islamic Cultural and The Educational Foundation.

All these associations and centers constantly make the Muslims in Canada aware of their Islamic identity. They express their political support for Muslim causes throughout the world. They keep informed of Muslim celebrations, holidays, on-going activities and future plans: They collect donations for Muslim causes throughout the world.

Moreover, in almost every universities and colleges there are Muslim students associations. Especially, when the foreign students come to study in Canada, they feel the need of such associations on campuses for a variety of reasons. The MSA's organise Islamic Seminars and Friday prayers on the campuses. The Muslim students, thus, from various parts of the world are able to establish links among them on the university campuses "providing the nucleus for an international network."[28]

Educational Institutions

In response to the challenges faced by the younger generations in academic institutions, the Muslim communities in different cities have established Islamic schools. There has been a growing concern for the ethical and moral upbringing of the children. Islamic education is considered necessary to preserve Islamic values and culture and to ensure the survival of an Islamic heritage for succeeding generations."[29] Thus, there

---

28 Y. Haddad, "A Century of Islam," P. 10.
29 Yousif, Muslims, P. 104.

are Islamic schools in Montreal, Toronto, Ottawa and Alberta. All these schools have the same goal, i.e., to provide their students with an Islamic education besides the regular curriculum. In addition to the regular subjects, students are taught Arabic language and Islamic studies. The Islamic codes, ethics and dress are maintained in these schools. Students perform daily Zohor and Asar prayers in the school and celebrate Islamic occasions. Besides regular schools, there are "Sunday" schools. The Islamic schools promote the consciousness among the new generation about the Islamic culture and heritage, which is essential for maintaining a strong sense of Islamic identity in Canada. In fact, many non-Muslim parents are applying for admission of their children in Toronto, Ottawa and Montreal Muslim schools. In an interview with the Principal of Montreal Muslim School, this author came to know that the non-Muslim parents are interested in sending their kids there to keep them away from the "open" Canadian culture and to instill moral values in their minds. Their purpose is not to Islamize their children but to strengthen their moral consciousness.

CONCLUSION : THE FUTURE

It appears that despite Canada's long history of migration, Muslims are a relatively recent addition to the country's ethnic mosaic. In this multi-ethnic society, Muslims are struggling for preserving Islamic heritage against many odds. Initially, the Muslims had to face a lot of challenges from the host culture. Gradually, however, due to the awareness and consciousness of Muslims on the basic Islamic values, they have developed both academic and non-academic institutions in various cities of Canada which have helped them to overcome these challenges. Today, all the schools and colleges in Canada know when the Muslims are starting Ramadhan or when they have Eid day, which was unthinkable only ten years ago. Increasingly conscious of their own identity, Muslims are now waiting to see their recognition in legal terms as the "Muslims" of Canada.

However, the Muslims could not isolate them from their participation in public affairs of Canada. The Muslims must assert and reaffirm their active participation in the larger framework of Canadian community, which will allow others to understand the Muslims better. I agree with Nyang, that, "Muslims who refuse to assimilate without being assimilated in North American Society are not very helpful ... Muslims should be conservative enough not to bargain away their *din* but liberal enough to seize any political opportunity to form alliances with others having shared interests."[30] The future of the Muslims in Canada depends, to a large extent on the one hand, on their ability to keep Islamic consciousness throughout generations and on the other hand, on the development of institutions adaptable and suitable to Canadian environment. If the past is an indication of the future, it seems reasonable to conclude that one day Muslims will be able to reach their expected targets in Canada.

---

30 Nyang, "Using the First Amendment..." P. 33.

Collective Identity and Collective Action: The Case of Muslim Politics in America

M. A. Muqtedar Khan

Introduction

In a brief period of three decades Muslims of America have grown in numbers as well as institutionally to establish a sustainable community. However, this strength in numbers has not been translated into commensurate political influence.[1] Smaller communities, like the American Jews and Cuban Americans, have had greater impact on the economy and politics of America. Today no American president, senator or congressman can afford to ignore the influence of American Jews in order to realize his or her political ambitions. Similarly no presidential candidate can ignore the Cuban American community if he or she wishes to win Florida. However, unlike these communities, the Muslim population of America has failed to register its presence on the political map of America. Indeed, even as minarets of over two thousand Muslim mosques stand tall on the American horizon, Muslim voices remain unheard in the Congress and the White House.

Many different reasons have been advanced for this relative political failure. The most widely believed cause is an inability of the community to organize itself to deal with American politics. There is a belief that unless the community is sufficiently competent to create think tanks, political action committees, access media such as television and radio stations and establish a network for grass roots activism it will not be able to generate the necessary attributes to be able to influence

---

1 See Mohammed A. Muqtedar Khan, "The Missing Dimension: Role of American Muslims in American Policy Making", The Message, December 1995.

American politics. I believe that rather than constituting explanations for the failure of Muslim political organization, these theories are essentially excuses for the same. My contention is that on political issues Muslims in America have not been able to solve problems that are generic to any effort to institute collective action. And more fundamentally, this problem of collective action in the political arena is a manifestation of a more serious problem — that of collective identity formation.

Politics is an attribute and a function of communities, not individuals. Politics is both, a consequence of community formation and a part of the process of forming communities. Once communities are formed, they politick with other communities in competition for resources, for power and even recognition. But the process of community formation too is a political process that involves the determination of who is included and who is excluded and what are the criteria, based on which these judgements of inclusion and exclusion are made. Muslims in America have failed to realize themselves as a political community, and until they do that, they will be involved in the politics of community formation — identity politics. Politics for the sake of advancing the interests of the American Muslim community will commence only when the process of crystallizing the American Muslim community is complete.[2]

I believe that American Muslims are beset with identity politics, which is impeding their capacity to function collectively to realize political goals.[3] Indeed, the failure to resolve problems concerning identity precludes the identification and prioritization of the community's goals, which is necessary for effective activism. In this chapter, I shall demonstrate that when it comes to matters of *Ibadah* (religious worship) the community has demonstrated an admirable capacity to adapt and function successfully in America. It has developed institutions, built masajid, and launched Islamic movements that are continental in scope and systematically resisted cultural assimilation. It is only in the area of politics (*muamalath*) that they lag. Having established that, I shall argue how identity politics can be resolved through a conscious attempt to generate an American Muslim identity.

---

2 See Mohammed A. Muqtedar Khan, "What is to be Done", The Message, November 1995.

3 See Mohammed A. Muqtedar Khan, "Muslims and Identity Politics in America", paper presented at the first Islam in America Conference at University of Indiana, Indianapolis, July 4-6, 1997.

148

Collective Identity, Collective Action and Collective Good

Collective action is the process when a group of individuals come together to pursue a collective good (also referred to as common good or public good). A collective good is a benefit, which is available to every one if it is available to any one.[4] Like clean air, safe environment or crime-free neighborhoods. These common goods cannot be materialized unless a collective effort is launched. Most sociologists, prior to rational choice exponents came upon the scene, assumed that since collective goods were in the interest of all, all would contribute to realizing them since all stood to benefit from them. However, rational choice theories, particularly Mancur Olson exposed this myth. Olson argued that rational individuals would be less motivated to do their part, because their individual failure to contribute would not undermine the capacity of the group, and if the group was successful without them they would stand to benefit without incurring any cost. Positive political economist Bates argued that rational individual will not pay to create a public good; each person does better to wait for someone else to pay for it and then enjoy its benefits for free.[5] Olson's work emphasized that this problem, the problem of "free riders," was manifestly more pronounced in large groups than in smaller groups. Olsen concluded that individuals could not be motivated to participate in collective actions even if it was in their interest, unless they were coerced or some other selective incentives were offered to win their cooperation.[6]

The work of rational choice theorists may offer a clue to the failure of American Muslims to garner political influence for themselves. One and all, Muslims stand to benefit if a politically cohesive and mobilized Muslim community is able to influence American domestic and foreign policies to make the life and lifestyle of Muslims more secure and respected. It would ameliorate the hostility towards Islam, improve conditions for Dawah, and reduce social alienation of Muslims. It will

---

4   See Mancur Olson, The Logic of Collective Action: Public Goods and the Theory of Groups. Cambridge, Massachusetts: Harvard University Press, 1971, pp. 14-16.
5   See Robert H. Bates, "Macropolitical Economy in the field of Development", James E. Alt and Kenneth A. Shepsle (Eds.). Perspectives on Positive Political Economy. New York: Cambridge University Press, 1990, pp. 37-38.
6   See Olsen, The Logic of Collective Action, pp. 53-57.

eliminate the "foreignness" of Islam and make it an integral element of American social and political life. However, when we ignore the political realm and explore the religious sphere, we find that American Muslims have done a remarkable job of building Islamic institutions — mosques, Islamic schools, and Islamic movements. Apparently in this sphere there is no problem of collective action.

Thus we realize that the asymmetry of American Muslims' collective achievements challenges the efficacy of both the traditional sociological explanations of group action and contemporary rational choice theories in explaining collective action. I believe that social constructivists[7] who rely on identity as a determinant of human action, may offer a better explanation of American Muslims' successes and failures. They are critical of rational choice theorists for assuming interests to be exogenous (that is given). They argue that group interests are based upon group identities, which are socially constructed.[8] Thus what groups do depends upon how groups see themselves. Which suggests that in the religious realm, there is complete resonance in being Islamic and building mosques and so Muslims have been successful as a group in this endeavor. However, in the political realm, constructivists would argue, Muslims do not see themselves as a Muslim community and hence the failure to have the same impact in this area. In the next section I shall demonstrate how successful Muslims have been in reproducing necessary institutions for the ritual aspect of Islamic life. Subsequently I shall explore a constructivist inquiry into Muslim politics in America.

The Emergence of a Religious Muslim Community in America

Islam has witnessed rapid growth and institutional development in America in the last three decades.[9] In conjunction with the third wave of Muslim

---

7 For a rendering of constructivist approaches see Nicholas G. Onuf, World of Our Making: Rules and Rule in Social Theory and International Relations. Columbia: University of South Carolina Press, 1989.

8 See Alexander Wendt, "Collective Identity Formation and the International State", American Political Science Review, 88, 2, June 1994, pp. 384-385.

9 See Mary H. Cooper, "Muslims in America", Congressional Quarterly Researcher, April 30, 1993. Yvonne Haddad (Ed.), The Muslims of America. New York: Oxford University Press, 1991. Also see Barbara D. Metcalf (ed.), Making Muslim Space: In North America and Europe. Berkeley: University of California Press, 1996.

immigration, Islam's growth has been propelled by the reversion and conversion to Islam of millions of Americans from all religious and ethnic backgrounds.[10] The first wave of Muslim immigration to America was when thousands of Muslim slaves were imported from Africa to work on plantations in North America. The second wave was in the late nineteenth and early twentieth century. Muslims in both periods failed to establish or sustain their Islamic identity and melted away into the great melting pot of American culture. However, the third wave of immigrants, have demonstrated a remarkable resilience and have systematically resisted assimilation.[11] For reasons that are beyond the scope of this discussion, early Muslims could not sustain their identity. In spite of their endeavors to establish Muslim communal identity, they were gradually assimilated.[12]

The case of the third wave of immigrants has been different. Helped by immigration laws that facilitated family migration and importation of religious teachers, Muslims have now succeeded to a significant extent in retaining their cultural, ethnic as well as religious identity. Two things, I believe, have enabled this remarkable feat. The social depth in the nature of the new immigrants and the development of global communication and transport. The third wave of immigration allowed Muslims of various types — professionals, religious teachers, businessmen and even political activists — to come to America. This created a social depth that has helped American Muslims in reproducing a structure of communal existence that could be nourished, developed and sustained.[13]

---

10 See Mary H. Cooper, "Muslims in America", Congressional Quarterly Researcher, P. 369. Ihsan Bagby, "Islam in America Larger than most Christian Faiths", National Catholic Reporter, Feb 8, 1991, s3.

11 See Qutbi Mahdi Ahmad, "Muslim Organizations in the United States", in Yvonne Haddad (Ed.). The Muslims of America, pp. 11-24. Also see Carol Stone, "Estimate of Muslims Living in America", in Yvonne Haddad (Ed.). The Muslims of America, pp. 25-34.

12 See Ahmad, "Muslim Organizations in the United States", p. 12.

13 See Jeffery L. Sheler, "Islam in America", U.S. News and World Report, Oct. 8, 1990. See Richard Bernstein, "A Growing Islamic Presence: Balancing Sacred and Secular", New York Times, Sunday, May 2, 1993. Pristin and Dart "Muslims a Growing U.S. Force", Los Angeles Times, Thursday, January 24, 1991. Lynne Duke, "Islam is Growing in the U.S. Despite an Uneasy Image", The Washington Post, Sunday, October 24, 1993. Mary Cooper, "Muslims in America", Congressional Quarterly Researcher. June Jordan, "Islam and The U.S.A. Today", Progressive, February, 1993, 11.

Mass communication and transport technologies have facilitated the mobility of people and knowledge. The ability of immigrants to frequently communicate with relatives and friends back home, as well as in America has helped them in maintaining traditional forms of kinship and relationships. They have been able to keep in touch with their ethnic and religious brethren and establish networks and associations easily and at relatively low costs. Frequent travel to their home country has become ritualistic as airfares became increasingly competitive. The explosion of telecom-munications has resulted in the establishment of a religio-cultural umbilical cord between American Muslims and their countries of origin.

Muslim immigrants have not only imported traditional *Ulema* (religious teachers) but now increasingly send their children and new Muslims to traditional schools in the Muslim world to learn and bring back Islamic knowledge. Imam S. Wahhaj and Yusuf Hamza — a black and a white American — are prominent examples.[14] Imam Siraj Wahhaj, the first Muslim who started a session of the U.S. Congress with a Muslim prayer (June 25, 1991), went to Saudi Arabia to study and qualify as an Islamic scholar. Yusuf Hamza went to Africa. And they are both important figures in America's religious Muslim establishment. Thus the ability to keep in touch and to travel has vastly enhanced the capability of the latest Muslim immigrants to resist assimilation into American culture.

The growth of Muslims and also the growth of the Islamic spirit in America has inspired the descendants of the second wave of Muslim immigrants to return to the Islamic way of life. This rapid growth in Muslim population is also matched by a relatively significant development of Muslim institutions. By growth of Islamic spirit I am alluding to the increased adherence to Islamic practices, rituals and beliefs, that we are witnessing amongst Muslims today.[15] This growth in Islamic spirit in the West is a form of resonance accompanying the Islamic resurgence in the Muslim World. Today the community boasts national level Islamic movements such as ISNA (Islamic Society of North America), ICNA (Islamic Circle of North America), The American Muslim Mission and

---

14 See Shahid Athar, Reflections of an American Muslim. Chicago: Kazi Publications, 1994, p. 168.
15 See Richard Bernstein, "A Growing Islamic Presence: Balancing Sacred and Secular", New York Times, Sunday, May 2, 1993. Pristin and Dart "Muslims a Growing U.S. Force", Los Angeles Times, Thursday, January 24, 1991. Lynne Duke, "Islam is Growing in the U.S. Despite an Uneasy Image", The Washington Post, Sunday, October 24, 1993.

MSA (Muslim Students Association)[16]

These movements are essentially national in character and have primarily emerged in order to coordinate, centralize and unite Islamic activism in North America. Particularly to enhance Muslim unity,[17] these movements are de-ethnicized.[18] They do not distinguish between Muslim communities on sectarian, doctrinal or ethnic grounds. By ignoring such differences they encourage the crystallization of a unified Muslim identity. These are essentially identity movements, which seek to emphasize unity and underplay difference based on ethnicity or doctrine. These movements and organizations try to play the role of a religio-cultural guardian that seeks to safeguard practices, which emphasize Muslim identity, and to resist assimilation. These activities include national conventions, neighborhood networks, training camps, Muslim group picnics, Islamic education, and celebration of Muslim festivals and proliferation of Islamic publications. They essentially are structures of "Muslim identity", whose production and reproduction through various organizational practices is designed towards "reconstructing and nurturing" the sense of Muslimness of its members.[19]

The most important role in this battle against assimilation has been played by mosques or Islamic centers.[20] Traditionally the mosque has been a place of worship and limited political activity in the Muslim World. Islamic schools, *madrassahs*, are sometimes attached to mosques and play a role in providing Islamic education. But Mosques in America are also symbols of Muslim collective identity. All mosques that are built from scratch consciously portray Islamic architecture. They serve as centers for Muslims to conduct prayers, conduct weekend Islamic education, organize social activities such as weddings and seminars, and are places where Muslims go to meet other Muslims.[21] In 1969 there were only 50 mosques, today there are over 2000. Chicago alone

---

16 See Qutbi Mahdi Ahmad, "Muslim Organizations in the United States", pp. 11-24.
17 See Shahid Athar, Reflections of an American Muslim. Chicago: Kazi Publications, 1994.
18 See Qutbi Mahdi Ahmad, "Muslim Organizations in the United States", pp. 11-24.
19 See Qutbi Mahdi Ahmad, "Muslim Organizations in the United States", pp. 11-24.
20 For an interesting study of the role mosques play in America see ch. 2. "Islamic Institutions in America", in Yvonne Haddad and Adair Lummis, Islamic Values in the United States. New York: Oxford University Press, 1987, pp. 34-58.
21 Yvonne Haddad and Adair Lummis, Islamic Values in the United States, pp. 34-58.

witnesses over 70 Friday congregations. In Washington D.C. area alone, there are over 30 congregations. The number of congregations is indicative of both size and diversity of Muslim populations in these regions. The focus on mosques is the central strategy of survival that Muslims in America have employed.

The success of the traditional Islamic apolitical movement, *Tablighi Jamaat*, is extremely interesting. It is a form of internal evangelical movement that seeks to bring vagrant Muslims back within the Islamic fold. However, their definition of Islam is limited to a singular adherence to the ritualistic elements of Islam and to travelling in the name of Allah to do *Dawah*. Their annual gatherings are perhaps the largest of Muslim conventions in the U.S. with over ten thousand, usually all male, participants.[22] While *Tablighi Jamaat* does succeed in bringing many Muslims back to the mosque they often contribute to stunting the religious as well as the political personality of their members. The presence of a strong *Tablighi Jamaat* is a sure clue that the particular community is divorced from political action. In fact, I believe that the large share of committed Muslims that the *Jamaat* has cornered is detrimental to the political aspirations of American Muslims.

Understanding Muslim Successes in America

Muslim success in producing Islamic institutions to protect the religious and the spiritual dimension of Muslim existence from the scourge of America's material and consumer culture is indicative of the capacity of the American Muslim community to produce collective goods. Political activists have often expressed the concern that while Muslims are relatively quick to contribute funds for a new mosque they are often hesitant to even consider contributions for political causes.[23] It is clear that in an unorganized but apparently widespread fashion American Muslims have prioritized their goals. A consensus seems to exist that matters concerning the aspects of *Ibadah* need to get the most attention and therefore the building of Islamic institutions such as mosques and Islamic schools should be the number one priority of Muslims.

---

22 See Steve A. Johnson, "Political Activity of Muslims in America", in Haddad (Ed.). The Muslims of America. pp. 112-113.

23 A. Alamoudi, the Executive Director of the American Muslim Council and Nihad Awad the Executive Director of the Council for American and Islamic Relations have expressed this in personal interviews to the author.

Experiences in other Western countries, such as France and Britain, have established that mosques and Islamic centers play an extraordinary role in keeping the community together and in maintaining the Islamic identity of Muslims immigrants. Islam is a faith where systematic and periodic rituals, such as the five prayers, Friday congregations, annual month of fasting (*Ramadhan*) play a major role in reproducing the Muslim community. Adherence to these rituals also plays an important part in resisting cultural assimilation in the host society. The achievements of the community indicate that it is driven more by a desire to retain Islamic values and practices and resist cultural assimilation. And in pursuit of this goal the American Muslim community seems to have done relatively better than other immigrant communities.

The success of American Muslims, specially in establishing large movements such as the *Tablighi Jamaat*, Islamic Society of North America (ISNA) and Islamic Circle of North America (ICNA), challenges many of the notions that rational choice theorists maintain about the dynamics of group behavior. All these movements are basically providers of collective goods — an institutional and cultural environment that would enable a particular lifestyle (the Islamic way). Unlike many other religious organizations in the U.S., financial contributions to Islamic organizations are purely voluntary. These movements also do not provide any special benefits to different members. There is no other attraction for joining these movements other than trying to reproduce an Islamic way of life in America.

These movements deny the two necessary elements that rational choice theorists posit for the success of collective actions, namely coercion and other special benefits. While Muslim behavior in America challenges the rational choice theorists, they do not also confirm to the generally held ideas about group behavior by sociologists. The general theories of group behavior suggest that if individuals have common interests they will form groups and seek to pursue their goals. But even though Muslims have formed groups, they have not been very successful in the field of politics. They have not pursued political influence as vigorously as they have religious practice. Common sense suggests that political influence would help the community in realizing their social and cultural goals with greater comfort. Yet Muslims have not pursued it with equal vigor. Indeed, it can be suggested that many Muslim groups, individuals and leaders have actually eschewed political influence.

155

Understanding Muslim Failures in America

Why do Muslims lack political influence in a society, which takes pride in its democratic credentials? Have Muslims pursued political influence and failed or have they eschewed it? Is it something about Muslims that has politically marginalized them, or are there structural factors in American society that are discriminating against Muslims? These are questions that challenge the student of American Muslim community when one juxtaposes their successes in the religious sphere with their failures in the political arena. They have already demonstrated a capacity to achieve collective goods through collective action. But why are they successful in realizing certain kinds of collective goods but not others?

One of the major reasons for the failure in the political arena is that American Muslims have so far been unable to articulate a cohesive domestic agenda. The failure to do so has resulted in their being focussed on politics in native countries.[24] Tensions between Saudi Arabia and Iran are replayed in the form of competition, criticism and non-cooperation between Muslim groups supported by Saudi Arabia or with majority Arab populations and immigrants from Iran.[25] Muslims from India and Pakistan cooperate on Islamic issues but efforts by Indian Muslim groups, such as IMRC (Indian Muslim Relief Committee), to help victims of riots in India get little cooperation from their ethnic brethren from Pakistan or fellow Muslims from other parts of the Muslim World. Pakistani Muslims increasingly become suspicious of the Islamic character of Indian Muslims when they disagree with their agenda on Kashmir. For them Pakistani nationalism is Islamic but Indian nationalism is definitely anti-Islamic. Pakistani assumptions that Indian Muslims have been assimilated in to Hindu culture often manifests in derision that alienates Indian Muslims.[26] On the other hand, when Indian Muslims come in contact with many Pakistanis who are far removed from Islamic practices, they are shocked.

---

24 The recent annual convention of the American Muslim Council, April 26, 1997, Washington D.C., highlighted this aspect of Muslim political activism. Speakers such as Jim Zogby, Mohammed A. Muqtedar Khan and Mamoun Fandy specifically pointed to the need to develop a domestic political agenda for American Muslims activism.

25 See Steve A. Johnson, "Political Activity of Muslims in America", in Haddad (Ed.). The Muslims of America, p. 119.

26 See Athar, Reflections of an American Muslim. p. 87.

Awareness of the corruption and moral decline of Pakistan further shocks Indian Muslims who see Pakistani nationalism as a betrayal of Islam.

Differences of national origins, still strong due to involvement in politics back home, has prevented cooperation among American Muslims. Even in a classroom setting, while discussing issues of Islamic identity in America, I had great difficulty in keeping bitterness between Pakistani and Bangladeshi immigrants from distracting the discussions. Some of these immigrants had been American nationals for over three decades and had migrated to the U.S. in the early sixties.[27] Their obsession with the politics in their native countries seemed to impede their capacity to understand and relate to issues of identity and interests in the American context.

Some Muslim organizations are funded by foreign nationals and foundations and are under pressure to respect the international interests of donating states. In rare cases they are even expected to pursue the interests of donating nations in the activities of American Muslims.[28] The shadow of Arab-Israel conflict is also significantly large on the domestic politics of American Muslims. Groups break up and even undermine each others efforts based upon the foreign policy posture of their native country towards Israel.[29] American groups such as American Muslim Council (AMC) have been criticized and people have protested during their convention for supporting the Middle East peace process. This is one issue on which many Muslim and Arab American groups have been divided. Genuine common interests vaporize in the heat generated by debates about the peace process.

The growing tensions between the two Islamic states, Iran and Saudi Arabia is reflected in the relations between Iranian and Shii immigrants and Arab and Sunni Muslims in north America.[30] Muslim organizations, which are indebted to Saudi Arabia's generosity for their

---

27 Recently I offered a 8-week seminar on Islam in America through the Washington D.C. chapter of ICNA, from March 15th to May 4th 1997. This seminar had an over all enrollment of 43. The participants were, South Asians, Arabs, Whites, African Americans, English and East Asians.

28 See Steve A. Johnson, "Political Activity of Muslims in America", in Haddad (Ed.). The Muslims of America, pp. 118-119.

29 Sentiments of this nature were expressed by the executives and members of the American Muslim Council at the their first annual convention in Washington D.C., April 25-27, 1997.

30 See Steve A. Johnson, "Political Activity of Muslims in America", in Haddad (Ed.). The Muslims of America, pp. 118-119.

activities now no longer, attract Shii and Iranian Americans. Similar sectarianism is beginning to divide and render the community incoherent on many issues.[31] The politics of identity is one of the biggest barriers to the Muslim community's capacity to agree on a necessary and focussed domestic political agenda.

This pattern of sectarian and identity politics amongst Muslims in America is the most likely reason why they have failed to realize their potential for political influence. When it comes to issues of Islamic *Ibadah* (rituals) there is hardly any room for difference and disputation in interpretation significant enough to cause fissures in the community. Therefore American Muslims find it easy to identify on ritual issues. However when it comes to politics they are unable to find identification, as tribal and sectarian interests are powerful enough to preclude cooperation. American Muslims, I posit, will not be able to realize their political potential until they break away from the politics of their native states and focus on carving out an American Muslim identity which will unite them.

Theories of rational choice and group behavior cannot explain the asymmetric achievements of American Muslims because they fail to factor in issues of identity. When it comes to Islamic issues, largely understood in terms of obligatory rituals, Muslims identify easily. But in the arena of politics "other" identities, such as nationalism and ethnicity or even race, have more currency. The ability of American Muslims to create collective goods for ritual purposes emphasizes their ability to act collectively. But the failure to engender a cohesive identity in the political arena creates collective action problems for Muslims no matter how important the desired collective good. Thus Muslims are unable to garner political influence because there is a problem of "rationality", but because there is a failure of collective identity.

The American Muslim Identity

Political influence is a collective good which when available to a community benefits every member of it. In order to have such an influence requires cohesive thinking, meaning very focussed articulation of the community's interests and cohesive action in the pursuit of these interests. American

---

31 See Mohammed A. Muqtedar Khan,"Tribalism the Historical Nemesis of Islam", The Message, March, 1996.

Muslims will be able to create such a collective good only if they cease to exist as a motley group of multiple identities and transform themselves into a tightly knit unified community. This can only happen if all Muslims in America consciously rethink of themselves as American Muslims, closer to another Muslim here than those in their native countries. American Muslims have the historical opportunity to create a microcosm of a global *Ummah* in America.

The political diversity of American Muslims precludes the articulation of cohesive interests. Each community seems to be seeking political goals, which have more to do with the interests of their "former homelands" than their own. American Muslims are still preoccupied with the interests of their forefathers rather than their children. This backward orientation cannot be altered into a forward and futuristic vision unless American Muslims think more about the future of their children than the future of the states they left behind. American Muslims will have to weaken their cultural ties with their ethnic and nationalist origins and strengthen their connection with Muslims from "other" nationalities in the U.S. The trade off is clear — traditional identity versus political influence and a strong unified Muslim community in America. The benefits of a strong American Muslim community to the entire Muslim World far outweighs the usefulness of parochial linkages maintained by "diasporic Muslim ethnicities". Only when American Muslims shift their attention from back home to an American future will they be able to ignore ethnic and nationalistic differences and become an American Muslim Community that could be the vanguard of a civilizational resurgence.

Islamic Activism:
Organizing Lobbying Efforts for
Muslim Influence in America

Ejaz Akram

INTRODUCTION

The social and political process in America has certain operative ideals, which are a result of specific historical outcomes, and these ideals have transformed as result of diversity in this country. The immigrant is an important part of that scheme of thin ςs and, as we know, through successive waves of immigration, America was built. Whereas the Muslim immigrants have had to face economic difficulties and cultural adjustment, it is also they who have led successful lives and have added meaning to their *Hijrah*. Without public participation, such a goal would be difficult to achieve.

On the other hand, among the American born Muslims, as well as the immigrants, the debate of political participation in America vs. isolation from the un-Islamic political intercourse, is what will decide the quality and security of their existence on this continent. The isolationists, who make the claim that it is morally wrong and un-Islamic to participate in the political processes of the mainstream of this society are absolutely misguided and they are working with an understanding of Islam which is responsible for the present plight of Muslims all over the world. They have a defeatist attitude and neither understand Islam, which requires full activation in your immediate social surroundings to make them conducive to your existence, nor do they understand the Western political process that encourages involvement, rewards participation and penalizes isolation. In any pluralist society, a group has to vie for its rights and work for the *Islah* of the society and this is the religio-moral duty of all the Muslims in America today.

A spark is required, which will ignite the process of learning and provide a forum for the discussion of most immediate concerns of Muslims in their cities of residence as well as the safeguard of their interests overseas. The method of this process should be pedagogic, which is instrumental in providing a medium of informed, and rational discussion, to explore the most suitable policy options open to Muslims and to determine the most strategic course of action. The need for a course of action that is devised to teach American Muslims the dynamics of public, economic and foreign policy in America is most pressing, which will bring into spotlight the opportunities and threats that are out there for a Muslim activist. It will empower the Muslims through setting realistic goals and working towards them, by learning how to best utilize community resources and by exploiting the resources outside the community. This will not only result in bridging the gap with the majority of the society, but also enable them to influence the public and foreign policy to their own advantage.

Muslims who have decided to live in America and lead lives as practicing Muslims, are faced with this choice and their collective future depends very much on, which path is chosen. They are different from the Muslims elsewhere in the Muslim world due to the diversity of their cultures and the kind of Islam they choose to follow, which could very well become the reason for their fragmentation and political impotence. On the other hand, they have a higher level of learning and earning than other members of *Ummah* and no shortcoming of resources, should they decide to mobilize them for the sake of their collective betterment, which is their best choice at the present. If they choose to stay isolated and passive, not only they will become the target of all the negative criticism but also, they will give up all the material gains that could be theirs if they chose to be active and live up to the operative ideals of Qur'an and *Sunnah*.

NEED FOR ORGANIZATION

Muslims in America have a history of presence in the Americas, but, compared to many groups that migrated to America, their influence remains minimal. Current demographic data shows us that there are between five to eight million Muslims in North America,[1] and compared

---

1 Nu'man, Fareed H. *The Muslim Population in the United States: A Brief Statement.* The American Muslim Council, Dec. 1992. p. 11

to the Jewish population in the US, which is estimated to be about six million, their influence on domestic and foreign policy is next to none. There are many reasons for this: Jewish migration en masse predates Muslim arrival in the continent, especially in modern times. Familiarity with Western cultures was a plus in understanding life in America, collective memory of the holocaust and determination to prevent that from happening again was perhaps the biggest factor in motivating them. There are so many other groups and organizations that are dedicated to their respective causes, may that be the National Rifle Association, Gays and Lesbians, or the Association of Retired People. Muslims have numerical strength, sufficient belief in their cause of regaining confidence in their identity and that their values and norms are superior and viable. Yet there is lack of initiative and pessimism in making that an achievable goal.

The single most important denominator of success of these groups is organization. It is true that most groups from inside look as if they lack organization compared to others, upon which one looks as an outsider. Objectively seen, Muslims in America, in the battle over issues, have failed to act as a pressure group, a group that has a consensus stance on at least the vital issues, anywhere from the issue of girls' right to wear a head scarf to that of unquestioned US aid to Israel and discriminatory policies towards much of the Muslim world. Many such examples in the last two decades are indicative of the fact that American Muslims lack organization.

When we talk about organization, the foremost thing to remember is that in order to bring about a positive and lasting change, organizational skills should be learned and taught from very early on, and also as a part of adult education. It has been recognized by most of the social reformers that institutional change was a pre-requisite to positive outcomes in policy, which cannot be achieved without adequate level of organized effort. Organization comes from a desire for change, inspiration and techniques of mobilization. No group is easy to organize and there is no group that is impossible to organize. Successful organizations are those, which are willing to go out of their way in order to unite, fight for their rights and win. Even if they do not win most of the time as it is the case in the political arena, act of organizing itself will bring them a high level of self-assurance, self-reliance and confidence in their personal lives which will keep them empowered and make them feel that they are in control of their destiny.[2]

---

2 Kahn, Si. *Organizing: A Guide for Grassroots Leaders*. NASW Press, 1991. p. 3

Democracy is meant to empower people, not just one individual, so a single charismatic leader cannot accomplish the task of furthering a group interest, unless there is a hierarchy of leadership within institution, an organized institution. To realize a participatory democracy, interests of a large no of individuals have to translate into the collective interest, which vies to become a public interest through coalition, alliance-building and lobbying. Private interest+ private interest+ private interest+ private interest... = public interest, is the equation of pressure politics either routed from the constituency or routed to the Capitol Hill.[3] Power of many working together has more chances of making a change, as one person can do little.

In the United States today, power is concentrated in the hands of a small number of well-organized individuals and corporations. The oil corporations and many of whom control coal and hydroelectric power also have increased their profit margins up to 800 times a year.[4] What percentage of the general population even doubles their income in one year? This is an example of real power. The moribund health care reform is an example of why medical costs are superlative due to the total monopoly of doctors in the field of health care. This is how things are run in the USA. It is a society of pressure groups and factional interests.

If one looks at the social structure of revolutionary America, it becomes evident how several social classes, the former aristocracy (the new cognitive elite), the bourgeoisie (farmers, artisans, merchants), the lower class (white servants, landless laborers and Negro slaves) all came together in a strategic alliance to manifest the most radical form of organizational behavior, i.e., the revolution.[5] Through organizing they realized themselves as to who they were, defined their ideals and rediscovered themselves. Their family, gender, class, ethnic group became a source of strength than a decisive factor, it became a source of collective resistance and struggle, motivation to fight replaced complacency,

---

3 Ibid. p. 7
4 Main, Jackson Turner,. The Social Structure of Revolutionary America. Princeton University Press, Princeton, NJ. p. 272
5 Kahn, Si. *Organizing: A Guide for Grassroots Leaders*. NAS Press, 1991. P.13. Many such corrupt Muslim post-colonial states have been and are supported by Western and, particularly, American policy-makers, which should be a target of fierce criticism by American Muslims in order to bring about positive change in those Muslim societies. Egypt and Saudi Arabia are good examples.

revolt overcame passivity. The roots of the American legacy lay in organized resistance and demand for positive change, a demand in which citizens ask the government what it can do for them, instead of the Kennedyesque rhetoric of what you can do for the state. For American Muslims, who are by far the most law-abiding citizens, who have seldom imposed any demand on their government, it is time to get organized and demand than to follow blindly the rhetoric of what we can do for the country. If they sense discrimination in domestic or foreign policy, instead of just getting angry they should turn their anger into constructive action, an organized action which is focussed on a single issue at a time.

Organization is an imperative for people who have problems. It is not only a means to an end but it is also an end in itself. As people organize, they not only learn to speak for themselves but also get heard, which is immediate empowerment of the group. It should be a continuous process, proactive rather than exclusively reactive. Fortunately, reactive methods work also. If there is unfounded Muslim bashing in the news or entertainment Media, that may be a good rallying time to organize the enraged members of Ummah. In order to influence US foreign policy, for example, we should not wait for another Gulf War to happen. To secure Palestinian rights, let us not wait for more massacres and encroachments and protest Israel's blatant violations of International Law. In the case of Kashmiri Muslims, what should keep us from twisting the arm of the Indian State for gross violations of human rights?

Most of us are not organized because we assume that it is something difficult and dangerous. As a matter of fact, organizational skills are everyday skills. Most people have a tremendous capacity to work with people, assume positions of leadership and offer motivation. Most of us are discouraged somehow that organization and leadership is only for the superman types, thus robbing us of that confidence and initiative that could be our community's asset. These attitudes are especially reproduced by the immigrant community whose older members' optimism about positive change has been castrated by the oppressive state structures in their countries.

Adult education of such groups can be instrumental in bringing about change; for if these attitudes are not changed; the passivity associated with it will reproduce itself and infect the thinking of next generation. A recent seminar, titled "Islam in America", proved to be instrumental in challenging some of the archconservative attitudes about

American Muslim's participation in the public arena.[6] Such efforts are crucial to grassroots organization, community spirit and the project of Muslim empowerment in America.

Muslims do have a history of organization in America but the earlier waves of Muslim migration failed to preserve their identity because of lack of cohesion. However, the three million African-American, white Muslims and the immigrant Muslims in more recent decades have exhibited a nascent form of organized activity which manifests itself as various institutions like Islamic Society of North America, Islamic Circle of North America, Council of Muslim Communities of Canada, Federation of Islamic Associations, and a few PACs such as CAIR, AMC and MPAC. The variety of activities that these institutions specialize in will decisively be a contributing factor in the resilience of Islamic movement in America.

What is needed is a directional elite from among these groups that can help form Muslims' opinion on different issues and democratically take a stand on policy matters, domestic or foreign. Muslims in modern times have unfortunately depended upon one-man leadership; if that leader is no longer there, the movement comes to a halt. An organization in which a variety of leaders who perform different layers of tasks is a better organization, as division of labor works best in modern organizations. There is no Mr. Do-it-all in today's world. Organizational strength and power depends upon cross-sectional representation of members in a society and a variety of leaders from within them. Having different types of leadership will attract corresponding type of membership, having leaders from across social classes will keep the organization from becoming elitist keeping it more democratic. The idea of having an *Amir* of American Muslims, as put forth in the above-mentioned seminar, could potentially be the realization of one of our organizational goals.[7]

It is important to find and develop other leaders, as long-term survival of leadership is crucial to the growth of Muslim organizations.

---

6 An eight week Seminar which was organized at the American University, Washington DC, sponsored by ICNA (Islamic Circle of North America) and very successfully conducted by Muhammad Muqtedar Khan, Ph.D. fellow at Georgetown University. March 8, to May 3, 1997.

7 Muqtedar Khan proposed the idea of electing an Amir of American Muslims through an electronic ballot, from registered Muslim members using local mosques as constituent districts, in which a nominated Amir could be directly elected or nominated through the elected council of elders as a *Shura*.

Several tiers of leaders must be developed across generations to ensure continuation of organizational goals. Leadership is a difficult role indeed. It often puts unusual demands and emotional toll on the leader. What Muslims across the world need is not a surplus of leaders but the right kind of leaders: ones who can relate to members, staff and other leaders alike.

STRATEGIC DIRECTION

Any group which is not organized enough and is not actively involved in the political process will wind up isolated, marginalized and will forsake potential political gains for loss and humiliation. Thus, all politics is organization–concerned with galvanizing people on a certain issue in order to sway or influence the decision-making process to their favor. All politics is lobbying and all lobbying is organization. Lobbying is an organized activity aimed at influencing public officials and, especially, members of a legislative body on legislation. The act of swaying the congressman, senator, president or any public official towards a desired course of action is called lobbying.

Most of us, who have a surface level knowledge of this process through entertainment or news media, have the image of a lobbyist as an unethical, cigar-smoking peddler of influence who is a source of corruption in the political process. This is not the case in real life. It is true that there have been unethical uses of campaign money and pushing for selfish interests with no regard to overall societal good, but it is also true that lobbying activities which were aimed at lobbying the legislature or at the grassroots level have accomplished favorable results for many good causes, may those be for the benefit of the elderly or protection of our environment. The debate about lobbying, whether it is acceptable or not, goes back to the times of the founders of the American Republic. James Madison expressed his concern in The Federalist, No.10 over the dilemma of the selfish interests of groups and faction vs. the idea of expression of freedom.[8] He correctly realized that man has an innate nature to pursue his own interest. Curtailing that would clearly take away the political freedoms.

---

8 Berry, Jeffrey M. *The Interest Group Society.* Little Brown and Co., Boston, 1983. p.2

Since there is no middle ground between these two alternatives, the former had to be chosen. In order to achieve true pluralist society with a democratic ethos, it was acknowledged that if there is an organized body of individuals who share same goals, they have the right to push for their cause in public arena.

Before one embarks upon the task of collective action it is important to realize that we think of ourselves as a community of people who live under similar constraints, have a similar world view and sense of identity that is besides other things, rooted in Islam. Further, it is important that social and political goals are clearly defined before strategy is devised. The US is a highly mobile society and demographic shifts can alter substantially how policies and new laws come about. In that scheme of things, it should be remembered that most Americans, when relocated, usually leave their politics behind, and start a new life. These shifts are primarily due to economic reasons, while sometimes due to socio-political factors, such as the massive black population shift to the nothern U.S. cities from the South. While these shifts may or may not affect Muslims in America, it is definite that a group that is most organized free of time or space, due to the fact that the primary source of their identity is constant, will have an advantage over the ones whose sense of belonging is sub-temporal and sub-spatial. In the short run, this may have a disruptive impact upon the grassroots lobbying efforts of Muslims but should have no impact on Muslim pressure on other sectors of government, the state and Washington lobbying in the form of combating faction mischief in form of protest, as it is sometimes done presently in response to nefarious activities of malignant think tank/lobby groups like the AIPAC (American-Israel Public Affairs Committee) in Washington DC.

Becoming a citizen is as simple as picking up a pen, writing letters to legislators or local newspaper and radio/TV stations. A good Muslim is under obligation of *Dawah* (in the modern sense of institutional organization for social and political outreach) and our lobbying ethic should be informed by Islamic principles of justice and fairness. Unlike many religious traditions Muslims are simultaneously thinking and acting beings, therefore as political activists it is important for us to blend our visionary ideals with the mundane activities. In our daily course of life our ideals and policy needs should be converted into our lobbying assets.

Genuine change must be demanded for, it is never a gift. Genuine change comes from imaginative and innovative struggle by employing all the existing methods of struggle and by creating one's own tools.

American Muslims should have multiple strategies for organizing lobbying efforts. Grassroots lobbying for example is the smallest engine of the society. At this level lobbying is not only communication, awareness but also education. On the other hand lobbying at the "grasstops" (or often called "astroturf" lobbying by which it is broadly meant the Washington lobbying) is often complementary and sometimes necessary component of advocacy of any given cause.[9] Grassroots lobbying is mass communication and mass education so that people can exercise popular mandate and reflect the sentiment of constituency about the issue in question, whereas grasstops is communication with a targeted office or a public official.[10] This is special education aimed at that official by providing him/her pertinent information that reflects your point of view on the issue.[11] Grassroots is awakening your constituents about a certain policy matter and grasstops is selling your cause to the public official to sway his/her decision.[12] Both forms of lobbying require influencing, proper image and organization.[13]

Often lobbying activities are categorized as single issue or multiple issue. The reality is that all lobbying is multiple issue. Most public decisions taken will affect society in a variety of ways. Many emotional issues such as abortion rights, gun control and the environment are known as single issues but various laws and social policies are affected by their campaign. Thus, there is no such thing as a single-issue area due to the nature of political process there will always be multiplicity within issues. Multiple issue organization must be highly sophisticated in their departments of research and intelligence, legislative monitoring and in approaching executive and maintaining cordial relations even when not in need. Most lobbying organizations in Washington are, in fact, multiple issue institutions. Once a lobbying organization has been set up it can prioritize its issues and either work one at a time or handle it simultaneously.[14]

---

9 Dekeiffer, Donald E. The Citizens Guide to Lobbying Congress, Chicago Review Press, Chicago, Illinois. 1997. p.9-13
10 Ibid. p.15-17
11 Ibid. p.21
12 Ibid. p23-25
13 Berry, Jeffrey M. *The Interest Group Society.* Little Brown and Co., Boston, !985. p.119
14 Greenwald, Carol S., *Group Power: lobbying and Public Policy.* Praeger, New York. 1977. P.66-68

LOBBYING TACTICS

Foremost of all the steps is adequate research on the issue being dealt with. One must gather as much information as one can about the issue. Its genesis, proposed legislation regarding it, possible legal consequences, how federal bureaucracies are reacting to it. For example: What's the defense establishment's position on the issue in question, or, if international, then what's the leading global position on it, and, if it is a case of too much government intervention in private lives, how can it be projected as a constitutional issue?

The most important wing of a lobbying organization is its intelligence function, which performs the task of information gathering. Part of information gathering is knowing your friends and possible alliances, and also knowing who the adversaries are and expected centers of antagonism. On, the Palestinian issue it would be only sensible to solicit for the support of different Arab organizations who have a similar view of the problem. On the Kashmir issue, it would make perfect sense to invite different human rights organizations to our conferences to speak and forge alliances. Similarly, it is imperative that all information be collected about our opponents, which includes much of their propaganda in the media, books, pamphlets and any public statements and all, be reviewed by our research committee. Their rationale should be understood and a response prepared as to how their logic can be easily rebutted.

Most importantly, key players should be recognized in the decision-making process. The Legislative process has various routes, track should be kept whether it was generated from the House, the Senate or the President, and subsequently it will be dealt by a committee or a sub-committee on the Capitol Hill. A list of all possible sources of contacts must be prepared through whose hands the legislative process will pass. This may include congressional staffers, the administration agency that will be charged with enforcing the legislation. The opposition within the administrative agencies must be neutralized before it surfaces. Also, different departments of federal government must be studied as to how they interact with each other and see the existing polemics in that sphere that we can exploit. Copies of existing laws, legal memorandum prepared by our lawyers, logistical information of alliance and opponent, contact people within various congressional departments and administrative agencies should all be compartmentalized as a resource book which should be professionally prepared, and a handy source of information to be consulted and handed out.

There are a few time-tested techniques of lobbying which should be used as principles from which tactics should be derived. The most important factor upon which decision-makers will base their occasions upon is the credibility of the party addressing them and their institutional reputation. This is where the difference should be evident between mischievous lobbying and a genuine effort based on sincerity and justice. Theatrics and gimmicks for the sake of catching media attention is all fine but the heart of the message should reflect integrity and honesty. For a sustained influence and long-term benefits, institutional credibility cannot be over-emphasized.

It should be remembered that only facts count. The effective messenger will carefully isolate factual data from rhetoric. Literature that is generated, in the form of memos, newsletters, handouts, reports and commentary on laws and regulations, should be strictly based on facts. Any thing that is not tangible enough has a chance of being dismissed immediately. Emotionalism works at mobilizing grassroots support, but it may be a good way to kill your case at grasstops. Gathering the factual data, reproducing, analyzing and critique can be an educational and rewarding process for the lobbyists. The more educated the lobbyist is, more the chances of success he or she has.[15] Educating yourself and providing information needed to a congressman, senator, committee or a sub-committee can be a good favor to them and may create a dependency upon you. Such a situation can be very favorably exploited to your continuing benefit.

The outcome of most issues may be in form of a compromise. Politics is, in fact, an art of compromise and shifting alliances. The lobbyist must be a fine artist of this game. A good activist must never burn his bridges due to temporary setbacks or unleash negative criticism of the decision-making authority. This is especially true of the bureaucratic administration, Pentagon and executive branch because bureaucracies tend to outlive the elected bodies. Often compromise may actually be victory and partial recognition of any of our areas of concern is better than no recognition at all.

In lobbying Washington, a few people who serve as the contact men can sometime accomplish more in five minutes than constituents do in a few months. The need for the 'contact man' is one of the basic steps

---

15 Dekeiffer, Donald E. *The Citizens Guide to Lobbying Congress,* Chicago Review Press, Chicago, Illinois. 1997. p.54-55

in this activity, which serves as a 'door opener' because of his proximity to decision-makers. His job is not what he knows but whom he knows. A team of professionals like that has to be cultivated who can be catalysts in the efforts of the constituency lobbying efforts. Auxiliaries to this type are more commonly found in Washington, i.e. the Lawyer-Lobbyists who are considered "the stars of the lobbying profession" who not only litigate laws but help create new laws conducive to the community goals. At crucial times it may be necessary to "hire" a door opener, thus establishing and maintaining contacts with people of access is necessary to achieving this end.

All politics is local. All Muslims who are registered voters must follow closely what is happening in their constituency. In every constituency there should be a grassroots hierarchy of leadership, which keep track of all politics at a local level. Similar to the Washington type lobbying, a group of people should serve as the legislative and issue intelligence at the local level that should follow legislative developments and contact staff members occasionally. Thus collecting, evaluating and disseminating information to adequate locations of decision-making should come from a local level.

Those Muslims who are already working in various departments in establishment are instrumental in carrying on the task of legislative intelligence. From the constituencies, what catches the congressman's attention the most are letters. If the congressman is bombarded with a lot of mail he is bound to take notice of the problem. E-mail, telegrams or mailgrams are other ways of making your opinions known on a certain issue. Since information that is transmitted electronically is not 'physically' present on the staffers' desks, it may not have the same effect but surely can be used for those who have access. Generally, a postage meter is still the best way, because letters are 'weighed' not read. However the congressional mail service does a decent job of responding to a mass of form letters by a form reply. The best way to carry out an effective letter writing campaign is to write as personalized letter as you can so that staffers and congressman don't give it a ready made mass produced response and your letter soon finds its way to the trash can. An effective part of a letter writing campaign to Capitol Hill are fact sheets. Fact sheets should contain the statement of your issue, the position of your group, proposed legislation or administrative action or reasons for opposition.

Dismissal of the myth that American courts are apolitical and perform a neutral function is important for our lawyer-lobbyists to remember. By juxtaposing old constitutional standards with new disputes they make new laws. Therefore, lobbying through the courts may be another avenue of minority security. Another myth is that the courts are undemocratic because Justices are appointed for life by the President and not elected. However, they are democratically motivated because of their expected role of "justice for all" in society "...As in the Wizard of Oz, if the curtain of impartial justice and neutral law were dropped, we should see politically astute men moving levers to accommodate change without revolt. Paradoxically, the myth gives justices a flexibility to extend their 'constitutional' beneficence to aid rising minorities or assist resolution of issues that elected officials feel are too hot to handle. In doing so they can open the system to those groups that cannot or prefer not fight their battles through Congress or the executive bureaucracy". Thus, women's occupational rights, inequality, criminal's legal rights and other civil and religious rights issues can be effectively lobbied through the courts. At times litigation may be the only choice open to minorities to petition for redress of grievances.

Demonstrations, though sometimes necessary, are a less effective way of communicating a group's view to the congress. The Vietnam war might have ended sooner if the groups concerned had rallied proactively and lobbied correctly. The very nature of demonstrations is reactive communication and it is only a good idea if there's nothing else you can do at all and protest is your last resort. This is where the role of media comes in. It may be a good way of catching the media attention, but, again, not the surest way to project your point of view the way you want it because edition work and biased commentary can distort the nature of problem beyond belief. To achieve that it may be good idea to invite a well-briefed celebrity to speak at you demonstration to get press attention.

Finally, group resources should act as our lobbying resources. Institutional organization is a pre-requisite before talking about how money should be generated and how it should be spent. Organizing Muslims for access and influence is unthinkable without a coherent self-sustaining plan of how to first organize their money. I suggest it should be a simultaneous process in which people and money come together at the same time. If people are not motivated to give money, it will never come   together.   If,   somehow,   money   is   generated by soliciting a foreign government without dedicated workers and leaders, it will steer the direction of our cause and undermine the movement as an American Muslim movement. Initial fundraising for this should exclusively occur with American Muslims' money. Foreign money is also subject to more inquiry, registration requirements are different and, instead, of the clerk's office at Capitol Hill, under the FARA act one has to register with the Department of Justice, thus, more inquiry. There is no set formula in which the group resources will translate into political power. Again, I suggest that funding obligations could be tied with voting obligations and the site of mobilizing our faith, plus our money, should be an electronically connected mosque.

MEDIA AND LOBBYING FOR VALUES

An elected body in America derives legitimacy from defining the American Spirit. Things counter to that are perceived as hostile and inimical to the American soul. Everyone has an image of American values and feels that their image is the correct one. The ERA is an example of one such debate. On one hand, the women's movement is pushing for an equal, discrimination-free atmosphere and discusses serious issues like draft and divorce laws. At the same time, homemakers argue for what the ideal role of women should be in the American family.[16] Many things in American society are perceived as wrong and immoral. Jerry Falwell's group, the Moral Majority, would like this country to get rid of secular humanism which is seen responsible for rising divorce rates, crime, abortion, drugs and pornography. Television shows in this regard are involved in the debate of personal freedom vs. American values. "Cherishing religious beliefs is an American tradition; forcing them on others is not."[17] Similarly there are big corporations that constantly define what American values are in the economic sphere by spending millions of dollars to inculcate in society the idea that capitalism is a better economic system.

Individual liberty and morality are both necessary for democracy. How morality and liberty are to be defined is how we, as Muslims, live our lives as an example of perfect balance and carry the message to

---

16 Berry, Jeffrey M. *The Interest Group Society*. Little Brown and Co., Boston, 1985. p.139

17 *The New York Times*, "The Gospel According to Four Religious Leaders". May 10, 1982, in Jefferey M. Berry. P. 139.

the larger community that is in need of it. The Muslim family is perhaps the strongest in the world. It is compatible with the developmental needs of the modern society, yet governed by principles grounded by revelation. It acts as a spiritual-moral check on individual extremism and materialism. Such themes are needed by American society today and they are also part of the presidential debates.

American Muslims should preserve these social goods by living them. These goals will only be safeguarded if they become a part of our lives and if, through *Dawah*, we can project our living examples to the society and attempt to cultivate a social consensus. The mainstream local and print media is an ideal place of projection. Recently, AMC has started an excellent half-hour of radio talk relating to Muslims in America on a local AM channel in Fairfax, Virginia. More efforts like that will be the beginning of realization of our goals on this continent.

Lobbying skillfully can produce narrow shifts in minor positions that produce major changes in policy outcomes. As a party interested in positive change, we must build horizontal and vertical relationships. In the former we must have influence and for the latter, access. Grassroots lobbying should serve as our broad approach, aimed at society at large to help them build a consensus on an issue and take a warrant of their mandate to Capitol Hill, which is the most legitimate way of exercising power in a democracy. On the other hand, we must also have a specific target: the President, Congress, administrative bureaucracies or courts. All this activity is group activity, which is the heart and soul of a pluralist society. Those who are organized, win.

IV

MASS MEDIA

Hollywood's Reel Arabs and Muslims

Jack G. Shaheen

Introduction

As an important artistic and pervasive medium, television does many things on many levels. Functioning as art and entertainment, programs provide information and help shape values. Produced with extraordinary skill, programs present powerful and penetrating messages, serving to educate and helping to condition viewers toward a particular worldview. Intentionally or otherwise, TV's images teach people whom to fear, whom to hate, and whom to love.

To their credit, the positive steps taken by leaders of television networks recently to shatter myths show that they are sincerely concerned about presenting a view of the world sans stereotypes. As a result of glasnost, the writers seldom display the Communist culprit; the Mafioso component among the Italian-American has been reduced to the occasional harmless buffoon. And "greaser," "Mammy/Uncle Mose," and "Chink" images have been relegated to a video Valhalla. Aware that all Americans have characteristics, producers are embracing a fresh approach to portraying diverse peoples. They now display characters of many and distinct cultural identities complete with accents various shades of color.

In this country, cultural diversity is visible everywhere—on the streets, in shops and in offices. Such diversity is seen even on prime-time television, with one notable exception: America's Muslims and Arabs, their accomplishments and heritage, remain invisible. Although America's eight million plus Arabs and Muslims are an integral part of the American landscape, viewers almost never see accurate portraits; they do not appear as fully human heroes or heroines.

Americans of Arab heritage are not part of the television landscape. Since the beginning, programmers have presented only two Arab-American

179

characters in series. The first was Uncle Tanoose, patriarch of the Williams family, and portrayed by Hans Conried in *The Danny Thomas Show* (1953-71). The second was Corporal Maxwell Klinger, a soldier wearing women's clothing, played by Jamie Farr M*A*S*H, (1972-1983).

Given television's recent appreciation of ethnicity, Arab-Americans are both hurt and puzzled as to why programmers never present them in a remotely sympathetic manner, and why they remain invisible. Although their customs, traditions and accomplishments make America an exceptional nation, their contributions to society as doctors, grocers, home-makers, lawyers, laborers, and teachers are ignored.

This lack of presence generates wounds. Surely programmers know what happens to young people "when someone with authority"(e.g., the TV programmer) portrays our society and "you are not in it." Such experiences, writes Adrienne Rich, may be disorienting—"a moment of physic disequilibrium, as if you looked into a mirror saw nothing."[1]

As of this writing, networks fail to pattern any of their shows after ordinary Arab-Americans. Nor do any programs focus on Americans of Arab descent. For example, characters patterned after noted Arab and Muslim doctors, lawyers and journalists are not transmitted into programs such as *Chicago Hope*, *E.R.*, *Murphy Brown*, *Law and Order*, *News Radio* and *Murder One*. No TV movie reveals the realization of Danny Thomas, Arab-Americans and others, who established St. Jude's Children's Hospital, in Memphis. To date, TV has not presented characters patterned after men and women like lawyer and consumer advocate Ralph Nader, heart surgeon Dr. Michael DeBakey, UPI's White House correspondent Helen Thomas's, radio's Top-4O celebrity Casey Kasem, or government executives such as Donna Shalala and former officials such as Chief of Staff John Sununu and Chief of Protocol Selwa Roosevelt.

Ever since the late 1800's, America's Arabs and Muslims have contributed much to our country. Like most Americans, they are peaceful, hospitable people providing for the basic needs of their families, and enjoying, respecting and assisting neighbors, regardless of their race, religion, position or wealth.

Sadly, in lieu of projecting Arab and Muslim American notables as

---

1 "Blood, Bread and Poetry: Selected Prose," by Adrienne Rich, cited in Ron Takaki's, *A Different Mirror: A History of Multicultural America*, Little Brown: Boston, 1993, p. 16.

an integral part of America's ethnic rainbow, producers opt to denigrate Arabs and Muslims from "over there."

Research reveals that occasionally a few stock villains appear: Latino drug dealers, sadistic Nazis, corrupt politicians, cutthroat businesspersons. Yet, since 1974, when this writer initially began documenting the Arab and Muslim image on entertainment shows, the predominant rogues have been Arab and Muslim ones, including boisterous billionaires, bombastic bombers, backward Bedouins, belly dancers, boring harem maidens and submissive domestics.

For more than two decades, odious portraits and themes have presented both the Arab and the Muslim as a bogeyperson, the dangerously threatening Cultural Other. Image-makers ridicule their hospitality, rich culture and history, failing to understand many basic facts about Arabs and Muslims. For example, they do not know that Islam is a faith embraced by 1.2 billion people, including 250 million Arabs in 21 nations. Also, Islam is the fastest growing universal religion. By the year 2000, it is estimated that Muslims will constitute 27 percent of the world's population. Approximately 15 million Christians reside in Arab states; and the majority of America's three million Arab-Americans are Christians. Five to eight million Muslims live in the United States. "There are more than 200,000 Muslim businesses, 1,200 mosques, 165 Islamic schools, 425 Muslim associations and 85 Muslim publications."[2]

Damaging portraits are not harmless cliches. There is a dangerous cumulative effect in repeated images, especially those that remain unchallenged. And TV shows, like books, last forever. Once the Arab and Muslim surface as the quintessential other, ugly portraits assume a life of their own, communicating for generations a "hate-the-Arab/ Muslim" message.

My research work demonstrates that Arabs and Muslims are consistently portrayed in a stereotypical manner. Presented here is selective overview and analysis taken from hundreds of TV programs, including comedies, soap operas, children's cartoons, dramas, and movies of the week.

To illustrate that entertainment television is not the only medium offering Arab and Muslim caricatures, I will show how the image found on entertainment TV prowls other media, referring to occasional TV newscasts and news magazines, documentaries and motion pictures. As

---

2   Steven Barboza, *American Jihad*, Doubleday: New York, 1993, p. 9

with the TV image, more than 700 feature films, and scores of documentaries show the Arab-Muslim sans a humane face.

Television movies. Englishman John Buchan declared in his popular 1916 novel *Greenmantle*, "Islam is a fighting creed, and the *mullah* still stands in the pulpit with the Koran in one hand and a drawn sword in the other."[3] Approximately 70 years later, viewers see clones of Buchan's *mullah* in motion-pictures-made- for-television. The TV films present especially injurious portraits, narrowing our vision and blurring reality.

The TV movie genre asserts that all Arab-Muslims are terrorists. The following five TV-movies advancing images-of-sameness appeared during the mid and late 1980s. Yet, they all—*Hostage Flight* (NBC, 1985), *Sword of Gideon* (HBO, 1986), *Under Seige* (NBC, 1986), *The Taking of Flight* 847 (NBC, 1980, *and Terrorist On Trial: The United States vs. Salim Ajami* (CBS, 1988)—regularly emerge as re-runs on cable and network systems.

Screen Arabs and Muslims resemble yesterday's images of Hitler's SS and Attila's hordes. Throughout each of these TV movies, the Arab Muslim lurks in the shadows. Armed with an AK 47, dagger or bomb, he proceeds to rape, beat and murder innocent Americans. In *Hostage Flight*, a passenger aboard an airplane hijacked by "terrorists" says: "These (Arab) bastards shot those in cold blood. They think it's open season on Americans." In *Under Siege*, Muslim fanatics invade the United States, blowing over 200 soldiers. A White House oracle says: "They're Shiite terrorists . . . we all knew they would hit us at home." Several scenes show the "terrorists" killing innocents on street corners, restaurants and at airports. Finally, with the assistance of Arab-Americans in Dearborn, Michigan, they proceed to blow up White House.

A FBI official orders his men to check out "every Middle East community" (in the United States). He adds, "There's a large Shiite community in the Detroit area." Superimposed on the screen we see: "Dearborn, Michigan." This is followed by shots of stores with Arab names and signs with Arabic lettering.

The producers of this fiction film should have employed a fictitious city, or a place where few or no American Muslims and reside. When they state that Arab and Muslim terrorists are operating out of the Detroit/ Dearborn area, the largest American-Arab and Muslim community in the

---

3 *Greenmantle*, John Buchan, 1916, Grosset & Dunlap, p. 16, Also in 1993, Oxford University Press published *Greenmantle*.

U.S., the producers not only cross the line between fictional images and real portraits, they endanger innocents. Although in reality, Detroit/ Dearborn is home to more than half-million peace-loving and law-biding Arab-Americans, some viewers could easily believe the opposite.

Even the dialogue is racist. The U.S. Secretary tells Iran's Ambassador: "People in your country are barbarians." The FBI Director jumps in, telling his colleague: "Those people (Arabs) are different from us. It's a whole different ball game. I mean the East and the Middle East. These people have their own mentality. They have their own notion of what's right and what's wrong, what's worth living for and dying for. But we insist on dealing with them as if they're the same as us. We'd better wake up."

Finally, *Siege's* two writers, one of whom is Pulitzer Prizewinner Bob Woodward, mistakenly inform viewers that Iranians are Arabs. Woodward does not know that Iranians are Persians, a people speaking Farsi, and not Arabs speaking Arabic.

Terrorist On Trial focuses on Ajami, a Palestinian Arab who is a heartless fanatic opposed to peace. He is captured in the Middle East and brought to trail in the U.S. Ajami has no regrets about ordering the deaths of American women and children, and admits that he would even use nuclear weapons. "We will strike at them in their home country as well as overseas. Long live Palestine!"

One protagonist explains that Palestinian Arabs, not just Ajami, "prefer to walk up to unarmed people and shoot them." A noted journalist says Arabs and Muslims are more violent, than others. "They appeal to our sympathy by calling themselves 'guerrillas or freedom fighters.' They're not." And Ajami's defense attorney requests that the jury view the Palestinian as "someone who might as well have been from another planet." Finally, ignoring the contributions of Ralph Nader and other prominent Arab-American lawyers who contribute much to our country, the writers have a Justice Department official say: "A fact is a fact. There are no qualified American-Arab attorneys to defend Ajami."

What is so disquieting about these TV movies is that they effectively show all Arabs, Muslims and Arab-Americans as being at war with the United States. Nicholas Kadi, an Arab-American performer who earns a living playing mostly Arab terrorists, is uneasy about his craft. Relegated to playing an Arab terrorist in short-lived series, *The Last Precinct*, Kadi says he "did little talking and a lot of threatening looks, threatening gestures threatening actions. Every time we (he and others playing Arab heavies) said 'America,' we'd spit." Explains Kadi, "There are other kinds of Arabs in the world besides terrorists. I'd like to think that some day there will be an Arab role out there for me that would be an honest portrayal."[4] Yet, a decade after Kadi's plea for balance, the situation on television remains static.

As with all groups, a small minority within a minority are heavies. Although terrorism is a legitimate screen theme, this writer argues that to paint all members of any group of people, in this case, Arabs, with the same negative brush is morally and ethically wrong. Over the years television's monochromatic images have wrongly perpetuated the myth that all Arabs possess a violent gene, that they are not human like us and deserve to die. The terrorism theme has only been exploited, never seriously addressed.

No TV movie remotely approaches the complexity of the terrorist bombings in *The Battle of Algiers* or the kidnapping execution in *State of Siege*. Here, the characters are portrayed with subtlety and precision.

Producers permit viewers to only see Arabs and Muslims as perpetrators of violence, never as victims. TV movies and specials never show images of Palestinians struggling to live under Israeli occupation. The camera does reveal Palestinian homes being destroyed, families coping with poor living conditions in refugee camps. Nor do viewers see Palestinian arms being broken, demonstrators tortured or shot dead. Nor are apolitical images projected. Viewers do not see the Arab mother singing to her child. They do not see a doctor tending the ill, a teacher giving a lesson in biology, a programmer working with computer software. An Arab man never embraces his wife. Families do not picnic or go to mosque or church. To paraphrase journalist Edward R. Murrow, what we do not see is as important, if not more important, than what we do see.

What do writers intend to accomplish by singling out one group of people for humiliation? Appropriately, the TV terrorist movies of the 1980s did not vilify the Campolongos, Goldsteins, O'Reillys, or Yammamotos. To do so would invite charges of racism, engendering an onslaught of critical media coverage and protests.

Although network officials may boast that they do not unfavorably stereotype individuals of any ethnic origin, when it comes to Arabs, Muslims and Americans of Arab heritage, that is exactly what the industry

---

4 Kadi appearing on *48 Hours*, CBS-TV, January 30, 1991.

has done. Consider NBC-TV's Broadcast Standard manual which states, "Television programs should reflect a wide range of roles for all people ... and should endeavor to depict men, women, and children in a positive manner, keeping in mind the importance of dignity in every human being."[5] To date, network practice has yet to follow network policy! The sins of omission and commission continue.

Dramas. Talented Arab-American performers such as Nicholas Kadi are obliged to demean their heritage. Although Kadi is a highly competent character actor, producers cast him primarily as a *kuffieh*-clad heavy. As Kadi explained on CBS-TV's *48 Hours*,[6] if he wants to work, he is obliged to portray evil Arabs in films such as *Navy Seals* (1990), and in TV shows such as NBC's *JAG* episode, "Scimitar."[7]

In "Scimitar" the Iraqi-born Kadi impersonates a Saddam-like Colonel holding an innocent U.S. Marine hostage. The lusting Kadi tries forcing himself on Meg, an attractive blond U.S. Naval officer. And why not? One TV myth maintains that Arabs consider "date rape" to be "an acceptable social practice." The camera shows drooling Kadi using a "Damascus scimitar" to slowly remove Meg's uniform.

JAG producers and others demean today's Arab as television and filmmakers once demonized American Indians. Clad in strange garb, both Arabs and Indians speak muddled dialogue and lust after blonde heroines. Screen protagonists called Indians "savages" and Arabs "terrorists." The following sequence denotes the stereotypical commonalties. "Scimitar" concludes with Kadi being killed. Watching an Iraqi helicopter pursuing them go down in flames, the American protagonists cheer. "Yahoo. It's just like *Stagecoach*,"says a U.S. Marine, "with John Wayne." The puzzled Meg asks: "John Wayne was killed by Iraqis?" The reply, "Indians!"

Even Hulk Hogan clobbers Arabs. In a *Thunder In Paradise* two-part program, set in the mythical kingdom of Mogador, Arabs imprison Hogan and friends.[8] Meanwhile, gobs of clad-in-black rogues try to force Kelly, the heroine, to marry a fierce-looking giant. Our heroes escape by duping the dense guard, convincing that his food is camel dung. Hogan and his party proceed to rescue Kelly, beat up the Arab giant.

---

5   NBC-TV Broadcast Standards and Practices Manual, 1982.
6   Op. Cit, *48 Hours*
7   *JAG*, December 7 1995, Channel 3, Savannah, NBC-TV series.
8   *Thunder in Paradise*, a two-part program, TNT, January 29 and February 5, 1996.

185

As the new champion, Hogan is given scores of mute ladies-in-waiting. The only catch is this: Hogan must have an operation, meaning he will become a eunuch. Opting to depart, our hero punches out the King's son, "a royal wimp," and he and his pals escape. In the process, they blow scores of Arab heavies to smithereens.

Comedies. Arabs are degraded on two *Married With Children* segments. In one, a couple clad in Arab garb inquires about a car for sale. One carries a homemade bomb in his hand; he threatens the vehicle's owner.[9] In the other, Al Bundy questions Peg, his wife, about her reckless spending. Asks Al: "How about the kids, Peg? Did they really go to your mother's house or do they belong to the Arabs now?" The audience howled![10] A *Small Wonder* segment features Akeem, a 13-year-old rich Arab sheikh complete with harem, who is tagged a "camel jockey."[11] Akeem is out to acquire Vickie Lawson as his bride. He gives her a diamond ring the size of "a large grape." Vickie shouts "Camel breath," at Moustafa, Akeem's rotund guardian. No one counters the slur. Mr. and Mrs. Lawson associate with Akeem only because Mr. Lawson wants to secure a "multimillion (dollar) contract." In exchange for Vickie, Akeem offers to give the mute Araba, one of his maidens, to Jamie, Vickie's brother.

Akeem wants Vickie for two reasons. One, she is an American; the other, Vickie seems "obedient." He tells her, "You must do as I say and fluff my pillows." Barks Vickie: "You can fluff your own pillows, turkey." She adds: "You clap your hands one more time at me, Buster, and I'll fluff your mouth."

The Arab-mocking dialogue and scenes continue until the show's closing minutes. During the final scenes, Arabs and Americans separate. Akeem does not wed Vickie and Jamie returns to Araba. But the Lawsons get the contract.

Soap Operas. This writer never watched the soaps, until a few years ago, when, as I was conducting a workshop for secondary school teachers in Madison, Wisconsin, I asked whether anyone was aware of stereotypical Arabs and Muslims. "I think so," said one teacher, "There are some strange types on *Santa Barbara*."[12]

---

9 *Married With Children*, July 17, 1994, Channel 2, Savannah, Fox-TV series.
10 *Married With Children*, August 24, 1993, KMOV-TV, St., Missouri.
11 *Small Wonder,* March 3, 1989, Channel 5, Washington D.C.
12 Teacher's Workshop, University of Wisconsin, Madison, Aug. 6, 1990.

Since then, I have studied Arab images in *Santa Barbara*, *Loving*, and *The Bold and the Beautiful*. As some of *Santa Barbara's* and Arab characters are similar to those in *Loving* and *Beautiful*, I will limit my comments to this soap. Daily, for several weeks during the summer of 1990, I taped and studied *Santa Barbara's* two shady sheikhs at war with each other. The story shows both potentates holding Americans hostage and fighting each other. The Sheikh of Kabir is intent on invading the neighboring "two-bit country" called Khareef. Kabir's ruler executed the Pasha of Khareef's "mother and father and two sisters" right before his "very eyes."

The Pasha has "sacred ways," including "a harem." None of his wives please him; he lusts for Eden, the American blond. And he intends to execute a wife because she dared run off. Not to do so would mean, "losing face." He boasts that "to take advice from a woman is equal to a bubble floating on air." In the end, the American hostages are released, Kabir's evil ruler is toppled, and the Pasha promises Eden he will eliminate his "prejudice" against women.

Soaps such as NBC-TV's *Santa Barbara*, CBS-TV's *The Bold and the Beautiful*, and ABC-TV's *Loving* teach viewers that Arabs live in tents, hold Americans hostage, have harems, dislike and/or torment their own women and act in a humane manner only when accompanied by an American women.

Children's cartoons. Ever since the 1926 cartoon "Felix the Cat Shatters the Sheik," America's cartoon champions have denigrated Arabs and Muslims. Beginning in 1975, I have randomly monitored and studied TV cartoon shows. Though incomplete, my research reveals that 60-plus animated cartoons feature heroes—Mr. Gadget, Popeye, Bugs Bunny, the Pink Panther, Porky Pig and others—trouncing and ridiculing Arabs. Animators paint Arabs as swine, rats, dogs, magpies, vultures and monkeys. Posing as Arab women, animated woodpeckers and rabbits don harem outfits and feign belly dancing. Selected to be a lecherous sheikh's "75th bride," even Popeye dons harem garb. As for Olive Oyl, she would "rather starve to death than marry" the Arab.

Writers tag cartoon Arabs "Sheikh Ha-Mean-Ie," "Ali Boo-Boo," "The Phoney Pharaoh," "Hajji Baba and the Forty Thieves," "Fast Abdul, the Sneakiest Thief in Town," "A Wolf in Sheikh's Clothing," "Ali Baba, the Mad Dog of the Desert," "Ali Ben Schemer," "Hassan the Assassin," "The Desert Rat" and "Desert Rat Hordes." These animal names and images that producers attribute to Arabs are not benign. Some adults may be able to separate fact from the animal stereotype. But for most children the animated world of cartoons is simple, good people versus bad people: Batman versus Arabs.

The animated Bedouin and sheikh caricatures are variations of yesterday's hateful portraits of the stereotypical dense African-American and savage Native American. Resembling the brutal "Buck" and the fierce "Injun," the unkempt Bedouin brigand appears as an uncivilized caricature, a cultural other. By cultural other, I mean someone who appears, speaks and acts differently than the typical white westerner, someone of a different race, class, gender and/or national origin.

Wearing different garb, the cultural other possesses an unusual set of characteristics and looks unlike the typical westerner. Like the painted face of the animated "Chief Ugh-A-Mug, the Bedouin in bed sheet speaks broken English. Representing evil, both the Bedouin and Indian attack innocents in forts. Symbolizing the forces of goodness, characters such as Porky Pig and Bugs Bunny repel the charging villains.

When viewing such scenarios, especially those in which sheikhs resemble buck-toothed "Japs" and Shylocks with burnooses, some families are reminded of identical messages from which Jewish mothers in Europe of the '30s and '40s, and Japanese mothers in the United States of the same time period, tried so hard to shield their children.

When focusing on Islam, especially offensive are *Inspector Gadget* and *Heathcliff*, cartoons showing animated Muslims not glorifying God, but idolizing Westerners. In Heathcliff, Egyptians believe the cat to be their ancient ruler and continually prostrate themselves. When Gadget discovers an ancient relic, Muslims repeatedly bow, mumbling "the chosen one, the chosen one."

Even Hollywood trade publications such as *Variety* bash cartoon Arab and Muslims. In his October 1995 *Variety* story, writer Peter Warg is very critical of Kuwait's Muslims because, instead of purchasing and telecasting U.S. cartoons that demean Arabs, they want to begin producing and projecting Islamic animated cartoons, featuring Arab champions.[13]

The fact that Kuwaiti Muslims are expressing legitimate concerns about the effect American cartoon images have on Arab children is ridiculed. Also, *Variety* adds injury to the essay by displaying a color

---

13 *Variety*, "Censors Changing Their Toons," Peter Warg, 2-8, 1995 p. 95.

illustration resembling TV's cartoon Muslims. The picture shows several militant desert Arabs, saber and rifles raised, about to mow down Tom and Jerry, who are tied to the stake. What prompted *Variety* to brandish such a color sketch, mocking Arabs? Consider this: Had some Asians or Africans expressed similar concerns about the impact of U.S. cartoons being telecast in their nations, would *Variety* have published a stereotypical sketch, demeaning peoples?

Missing from Warg's story is that Americans are never disgraced in Arab children's cartoons. In fact, eighty percent of the programs telecast by Kuwait TV's English Channel are American imports. Although U.S. distributors earn millions from these syndicated TV shows, profits flow in only one direction: From Arab to U.S. pockets. Our networks never import and telecast Arab cartoons or other TV entertainment programs.

Feature films telecast on TV. The focus of this essay concerns television, but it is significant to understand that soon after Hollywood's features depart from movie theaters, they are transmitted onto TV screens. Beginning in 1986, I began tracking features that were being telecast on cable and network channels in. Louis, Missouri. The research reveals that each week 15 to 20 movies ridicule and/or denigrate Arabs. TV viewer witness scores of motion pictures such as *Navy Seals* (1990), *Killing Streets* (1991), *The Human Shield* (1992) *The Son of the Pink Panther* (1993) and *Bloodfist V: Human Target* (1994) and *True Lies* (1994), a film showing Arab-Muslim villains igniting an Atomic bomb in the Florida Keys. These movies and others show U.S. agents and military personnel, as well as Inspector Clouseau's son, massacring pesky Arabs.

Especially disturbing is the fact that unsightly Arabs are implanted in movies shown on television which have nothing to do with Arabs or the Middle East, films such as *Network* (1976), *Reds* (1981), *Cloak & Dagger* (1984), *Power* (1986), *Puppet Master II* (1990), *Patriot Games* (1992) and others. Surprising Arab caricatures are fastened into the viewer's consciousness at unwarranted times, like insistent unforeseen phantoms.

These movies have absolutely nothing to do with story lines. Yet, to date, Hollywood studios have released more than 200, many of which are telecast. Infusions began with Universal's *The Rage of Paris* (1921). Here, the western heroine's husband "is killed in a sandstorm by an Arab." Currently, Libyans are a target. In *Back to the Future* (1985),

Broadcast News (1987) and *Patriot Games* (1992), Libyan "bastards" shelter Irish villains, bomb U.S. military installations Italy, and shoot our heroic scientist in a mall parking lot!

Columbia's, *The American President* (1995), is an agreeable romantic comedy about a widowed president falling for a lovely environmental lobbyist. Yet, the Libyans are referred to as culprits who bomb a U.S. weapons system. It should be noted that writer Aaron Sorkin does soften the anti-Libyan dialogue by extending sympathy for the Arab janitor and other innocents about to be bombed.

History illustrates that although the industry is trying to curb biases, even family feel-good films denigrate Arabs. In 1995, Touchstone Pictures, a subsidiary of the Walt Disney Company, released yet another screen rendition of Edward Streeter's 1948 book, *Father of the Bride*. The Disney film, *Father of the Bride-Part II*, which is the fourth film based on Streeter's work, was listed for months among the top ten weekly money-makers. According to "Entertainment Weekly," the sixteenth ranked *Bride II* has become a booming moneymaker, grossing more than $80 million for the studio.[14]

American-Arabs and Muslims, however, do not share Disney's enthusiasm. They are troubled by the unwarranted appearance of *Bride II's* disagreeable Arab-Americans. Beginning with the original 1950 Spencer Tracy, Elizabeth Taylor film, all *Father of the Bride* movies have focused on marriage and love. *Bride II* is a sequel to the 1991 Steve Martin remake. Muslims and Americans of Arab heritage do not appear in any of the earlier versions. So, what prompted Disney to inject stereotypes in its 1995 *Bride II*?

Consider the plot. Martin and Diane Keaton appear as the happily married Bankses; they have everything, including a "Brady Bunch" home. When George convinces Nina to sell it, an Arab-American couple surfaces: the crass Habibs. The film's ferocious Doberman pinchers behave better than this disagreeable duo.

The rich, unfeeling and unkempt Habib (Eugene Levy) smokes, need a shave, and talks with a weighty accent. When his wife attempts to speak, Habib barks mumbo-jumbo at her, supposedly exemplifying Arabic. Heeling as a wounded puppy, Mrs. Habib shrinks and becomes mute, perpetuating Hollywood's stale image of the Arab woman as a mute, submissive nonentity.

---

14 *Entertainment Weekly* "Top Grossers," February 2, 1996, p. 28.

Blurts Habib to George: "When can you move? You sell, we pay top dollar!" Habib purchases the house, insisting the Banks' "be out in 10 days." George and daughter Annie (Kimberly Williams) rush back to their Maple Drive residence to rekindle memories. Music underscores sentiments as father and daughter recall the times when they carved their initials on a tree and played basketball.

Abruptly, the music changes. Habib enters the frame, commanding, "You got a key, George? The key!" As George and Annie fondly view the house, Habib tosses his cigarette and crushes it on the immaculate walkway. The message is clear: there goes the neighborhood.

Not if George can help it! When Habib steers a huge yellow wrecking ball toward the house, George flings himself in front of the driving ball. Pleads George, "I built this fence; I planted this grass. Don't bulldoze my memories, man! I'm begging you."

Habib proceeds to rip-off George. Though Habib owned the house for just "one day," he will return it, provided there is "profit." Only after extorting $100,000 from George does Habib halt the wrecking ball.

As "Entertainment Weekly's" Ken Tucker writes, "The caricature of a cold, rich . . . (Habib) amounts to a glaring slur."[15]

Regrettably, no screen professionals affiliated with *Bride II* denounced the stereotypes. Nor did protests emanate from members of the ScreenWriters', Actors', and Directors' Guilds of America. *Bride II* could easily have projected the Habibs as a regular Arab or Muslim-American couple with likable children. Featuring the Habibs as helpful acquaintances, whom the Bankses befriend, would be a more accurate image. Unlike Disney's stereotypical Habibs, most of America's Arabs and Muslims here (as well as those over there) spend many hours helping their neighbors solve real problems. They attend the sick, champion legal services for the poor, petition for better schools and improved shelters for the homeless, work for a better environment, and strive to improve the status of women and minorities as well as help curtail domestic crime and violence. They and their neighbors embrace the words freedom, liberty and justice. Working together, they are the foot soldiers that make our democracy a reality.

Sadly, *Bride II's* tainted writing ignores this reality, bringing to mind other narrow-minded authors, such as *Club Paradise's* (1986) screenplay.

---

15 *Entertainment Weekly*, Review of *Father of the Bride, Part II*, Ken Tucker, December 15, 1995, p. 50.

This script, too, displays an Arab cur. Like *Bride's* Habib, *Paradise's* mute white-robed sheikh cares only about money. Not concerned about the environment or people, the sheikh seeks to destroy a Caribbean paradise, threatening to build factories, high-rise condos, and even a hideous Arabian palace.

In *Earthbound* (1980), the opinionated scenario focuses on adorable Americans, much like the Bankses. Here, rural Americans befriend an outer space family. Although the film has nothing to do with the Middle East, the producers inject a mute burnoose sheikh, threatening to ruin our environment. This Arab wants to buy a picturesque hotel and replace it with "a twenty-story monstrosity." The American owner laments that the sheikh is trying to "sell my hotel right from under me" so he "can build condominiums . . ." But he insists that "not on this land" will such construction occur. All ends well, as the plot to snatch the hotel is foiled.

There are numerous similarities in the three previously discussed movies. Armed with gobs of money, those Arabs from over there come here to destroy our cherished landscapes. Viewers see *Earthbound's* scheming sheikh trying to ravage the environment by erecting American condos. And *Paradise's* covetous sheikh attempts to demolish the Caribbean landscape. Finally, *Bride II's* conniving American-Arab not only wrings $100,000 from Steve Martin, but he nearly demolishes Martin's quaint Los Angeles home.

Disney is the same studio that demeaned Arabs in Aladdin (1992), the second most successful animated picture ever. Disturbingly, although Arab-Americans, including this writer, believed the sensitivity meetings with executives in Los Angeles were constructive, that Disney would honor its promise not to demean peoples of the region, the studio went ahead and trounced Arabs, again, by projecting several hook-nosed, buck-toothed Arab "desert skunks" in its home video release, *The Return of Jafar* (1994). Disturbingly, in lieu of honoring their commitment to eradicate the stereotype, Disney continued to vilify Arabs and Muslims.

In June 1993, the studio tossed a scrawny bone to concerned Arab-American watchdogs, deleting only two offensive lines from Aladdin's opening lyric from home videos. That was it! The line "It's barbaric, but hey, it's home," remains. As a July 14, 1993 *New York Times* editorial, "It's Racist, but Hey, It's Disney," points out, "That's progress, but still unacceptable. To characterize an entire region with this sort of tongue-in-cheek bigotry, especially at a movie aimed at children, borders on barbaric."

Those acquiring the Aladdin video still hear the region being tagged a "barbaric" place, still see all the unsightly stereotypes. Disney could easily have edited the video's opening scenes and present viewers with distinguished storyteller such as Damascus' Abu Shadi, a poet and expert teller of tales. Instead, Disney's *Aladdin* presents viewers with a shifty, disreputable storyteller. Also, throughout, viewers still see dastardly saber-wielding trying to cut off the hands of needy maidens, ugly shopkeepers and guards and the wicked vizier getting his kicks by "slicing a few throats." For generations, such scenes will teach children that Aladdin's home is, indeed, "barbaric."

If the studio intends to create a harmonious American, they do so at the expense of others. For example, though Disney executives possessed ample understanding to excise offensive black centaurettes from their animated classic *Fantasia* (1940), the studio has empowered *Aladdin's* injurious Arab images to remain intact.

Effect. Image-makers engaged in defaming peoples should heed Bill Watterson's insights. In his *Calvin and Hobbes Tenth Anniversary Book*, Watterson writes, that like TV shows, "Comic strips have historically been full of ugly stereotypes, the hallmark of writers too lazy to honestly observe the world. Declares Watterson, "The cartoonist who resorts to stereotypes reveals his (or her) bigotry."[16]

Should not writers be held accountable for their caricatures? How much longer will professionals are able to present repulsive images of Arabs and Muslims and get away with it? Haven't they learned that damaging words and pictures have a telling effect that images serve as ritualistic glue, instructing peoples whom to despise?

Not so long ago, television images advised viewers that the Asian was "sneaky"; the black, "Sambo"; the Italian, "a Mafia member"; the Irishman, "a drunk"; and the Hispanic, "greasy." Fortunately, such offensive labeling is no longer tolerated.

So why continue painting Arabs as cultural others? Explains Sam Keen, author of *Faces of the Enemy* (1986), "You can hit an Arab free; they're free enemies, free villains—where you couldn't do it to a Jew or you can't do it to a black anymore."[17]

---

16 *Calvin and Hobbes Tenth Anniversary Book*, Bill Watterson, p.202, Andrews and McMeel: Kansas City, 1995.

17 Citation is from Sam Keen's speech, presented at the annual meeting of the Association of American Editorial Cartoonists, San Diego, California, May 15, 1986. For additional

The time is long overdue for image-makers to begin eradicating portraits that cause harm. Television's caricatures afflict innocents. Cliches do not exist in a vacuum. They engender among America's Arabs and Muslims feelings of insecurity, vulnerability and alienation, and can even lead to denial of one's heritage. As scholar Alfred C. Richard, Jr. points out, media systems provide "an excellent reflection of a nation's collective mentality, (and) its national consciousness."[18]

Make no mistake. The "bad Arab-Muslim stereotype" is firmly embedded in America's "collective mentality." For example, consider the aftermath of the April 19, 1995 bombing of the Alfred Murray Federal Building in Oklahoma City. The two American-born men indicted for the crime, Timothy J. McVeigh and Terry L. Nichols, are not Muslims; nor possess Arab roots. They are considered to have been driven by political beliefs. Appropriately so, journalists do not discuss the suspects' faith or heritage. Immediately after the Oklahoma City bombing reporters initially and wrongly speculated for 60-plus hours that the tragedy was brought about by "Middle East" terrorism, by people who looked "Middle Eastern." As documented by the Council on American-Islamic Relations (CAIR) special report, "A Rush to Judgment," such speculation resulted in more than 200 hate crimes being committed against Arab and Muslim-Americans. Eight mosques were vandalized or burnt to the ground; innocents beaten, harassed and humiliated at work. Fearing violence, some closed their businesses. Finally, hours after the suspects looked "Middle Eastern" reports, an angry mob began stoning a pregnant American-Muslim woman's Oklahoma City home. During the unwarranted attack, she lost her child.[19]

Many Americans who believed those journalists who incorrectly reported that the bomber was someone who looked "Middle Eastern" did so because of pre-conditioning. For decades, TV entertainment programs as well as TV news specials have demonized Arabs and Muslims, tagging them as "terrorists," "radicals," "militants" and "fanatics."

---

information on stereotypical portraits in cartoons, see Keen's text, *Faces of the Enemy,* Harper & Row: New York, 1986.

18 *The Hispanic Image on the Silver Screen*, Alfred C. Richard, p. 192, Greenwood Press: New York, 1992.

19 *A Rush To Judgment*, a special report on Anti-Muslim/Arab Stereotyping, Harassment and Hate Crimes Following the Bombing of the Oklahoma City's Alfred Murrah Federal Building, April 19, 1995. Published by the Council on American-Islamic Relations (CAIR), 1511 K Street, NW Washington, D.C. 20005, September 1995.

This writer, like most Americans, regards a news program as an honest attempt to take an unbiased examination of important issues, explore them fairly and provide credible information to viewers. But even television newsmagazine shows and specials contain diatribes against Muslims. Almost no effort is made to ensure accuracy, depth, fairness, or objectivity. Some journalists, like some illusion inventors, perpetuate the myth that Muslims hate "civilized" peoples, notably Americans and Israelis.

Several weeks prior to the November 1994 telecast of his PBS news special, *Jihad In America*,[20] journalist Steven Emerson appeared on CBS TV's *Eye On America*,[21] and began slandering Muslims. He asserted that money is being raised by America's Arabs and Muslims for a "holy war" here, and in the Middle East. On Nov.13, 1994, CBS TV's *60 Minutes* displayed Emerson preaching a similar gospel. Finally, on November 27, Emerson's *Jihad!* featured the journalist telling Americans that it seemed "inevitable" they would be attacked by "Muslim radicals."

Monolithic Muslim portraits in *Jihad!* and other documentaries presented on the Public Broadcasting Service (PBS) such as *The Islamic Bomb*[22] and PBS's *The Sword of Islam*[23] fester alongside those of today. Documentary images of Muslims as fanatics are analogous to portraits in entertainment shows. *Sword* was telecast on PBS, January 10, 1994, only two days after CBS-TV presented its Muslim-As-Bogeyman TV-Movie, *Terrorist On Trial*.[24]

Continuously pounded into psyches, abhorrent words and images in news show help ignite the fires of bigotry. What journalists say and project can have grave consequences. These portrayals are not without their consequences. As a result of poisonous images peace-loving Muslims who love and genuinely respect the United States may be victimized by vicious slurs and/or hate crimes. For example, on March 23, 1996, employees of a Denver radio station burst into a Denver mosque and began harassing worshippers. The station broadcast the incident live. One DJ played the national anthem on a trumpet; another donned a mock

---

20 PBS-TV, *Jihad in America!* , November 27.
21 CBS-TV, *Eye On America*, October 3, 1994.
22 PBS-TV, *The Islamic Bomb*, November 1982, Channel 9, St. Louis, Missouri. Bomb was first telecast in England on the BBC, Aug. 2, 1981.
23 PBS-TV, The *Sword of Islam*, January 12, 1988, Channel 9, St. Louis, Missouri, A Grenada TV production.
24 CBS TV-Movie Special, *Terrorist On Trial*, January 10, 1994.

turban and a Mahmoud Abdul Rauf T-shirt. The assaults launched against Muslims by Denver's DJ's affirms that there is a commanding link between reel images and reality.[25]

Producers fail to take into account that in all groups there are some rotten apples, a tiny minority of destructive, violent people, representing perhaps one-half of one percent of the total. Prejudice thrives on defaming stereotypes; as a *New York Times* editorial pointed out in July 1993, "Most Americans now know better than to use nasty generalizations about ethnic or religious groups." Yet, "one form of ethnic bigotry remains an aura of respectability in the United States" prejudice against Arabs and Muslims.[26]

Ultimately, it is the continual stain of indelible portraits that hurts most. The images are permanent. They will never be erased. The accumulated resonance of these pictures in the minds of Arabs and Muslims takes its toll over time. This may explain why many firmly believe all TV producers not only hate them, but also despise their religion and heritage. During the May 1995 annual American-Arab Anti-Discrimination Committee conference (ADC) in Washington, D.C., an Arab-American girl approached the guest speaker, ABC TV's Sam Donaldson, and asked the journalist, "Why do you hate us?"

In 1980, the editors of *The New Republic* wrote: "Arabs (and Muslims) have been the victims of ugly racial stereotypes in recent years . . . (and) the widespread casual violation of such standards threatens all potential victims of racial slurs. It ought to stop.[27] It hasn't stopped. The Arab remains a favorite target, repeatedly framed as yesterday's Teutonic hordes, Nazis and/or the yellow peril.

In the *Jon Stewart Show*[28] "Talk Show Jon" displays U.S. soldier puppets killing white-robed Arab puppets. Waving the American flag, one soldier boasts: "I killed many of them." Brags another: "I decapitated quite a few of them myself." Immediately, Stewart's live audience applauded!

In *Twisted Puppet Theater*, Ali, the Arab puppet sporting a black beard and turban, shouts: "There is only one God and Mohammed is

---

25 CAIR "Action Alert: Denver Mosque Violated," March 24, 1996

26 *The New York Times*, Editorial entitled, "It's Racist, but Hey, It's Disney," July 14, 1993.

27 *The New Republic*, Editorial, "The Other Anti-Semitism," March 1, 1980, p.5-7.

28 The *Jon Stewart Show*, February 25, 1995, KMOV-TV, St. Louis, MO.

his prophet." Then Ali shoots Kukla, the good clown puppet dead.[29]

In an *X Files* episode a mute Muslim agent and "Mohammad," his associate, appear and are immediately killed after they attack Lauren, the show's heroine. Viewers are told that the two dead Muslims belonged to an "exiled extremist group operating in the U.S.," that they are responsible for "a July bombing of a navy transport van," and that they "killed a couple of sailors in Florida.[30]

During July 1994, a *TimeTrax* segment entitled "The Gravity of it All," features inept Arab kidnappers/assassins out to steal advanced U.S. tactical weapons. Operating in Malibu, they are punched out and killed by the American protagonist.[31]

Dispelling a stereotype. Negative stereotypes take a long time to wither away. For example, consider the criticism leveled at Laila Lalami, a doctoral degree candidate in linguistics at the University of Southern California. Ms. Lalami wrote an Op-Ed essay for the **Los Angeles Times** critical of **Bride II**.[32] One week later **Times** published an essay by actor Terrence Beasor, who dismissed the effect of Arab caricatures. Beasor advised Ms. Lalami to "cheer up." He writes that stereotypes are a "time-honored tradition" and "not based on racial or gender bias.[33]

Countered Casey Kasem in his letter to the *Times*, "Historically that's exactly what such slurs are based on. It's the thoughtless dismissal of the consequences that allows the practice of slurring to continue doing its harm." Kasem concluded with this sentence, which the *Times* did not publish: "Perhaps if everyone named Beasor had been the target of negative stereotyping for the past 75 years, the writer might have had some small idea what it's like to grow up on the receiving end of dehumanizing prejudice."[34]

In time, prejudices may evaporate, provided one keeps in mind the basic law of physics: Nothing percolates unless you apply heat. One way to provide sufficient heat would be if the prestigious Disney Channel and Disney Studios lead the way in debunking harmful myths. By inserting

---

29 ShowTime's *Twisted Puppet Theater*, July 23, 1995.
30 FOX-TV, *X-Files*, May 26, 1995 Channel 2, Savannah, Ga.
31 FOX-TV *Time Trax*, July 15, 1994.
32. Laila Lalami, "'Bride' Walks Down the Aisle of Stereotyping", Counterpunch, *the Los Angeles Times*, January 1, 1996.
33 Terrence Beasor, "Stereotypes: A Time Honored Tradition," *the Los Angeles Times*, January 8, 1996.
34 Casey Kasem, letter to Counterpunch, *the Los Angeles Times*, 29, 1996.

ordinary Arabs and Muslims in their programs, Disney could lead the way, encouraging other image-makers not to "do it" to an Arab or Muslim "anymore."

To their credit, Disney's weekly TV series, *Aladdin*, offers, in lieu of stereotypes, mostly balanced and heroic Arab portraits. And during 1995, Disney executives per-mitted Arab-Americans to peruse the screenplay of its upcoming home video, *Aladdin and the King of Thieves*. One reader of *Thieves* was Media Coalition President Don Bustany who told this writer the teleplay was devoid of stereotypes.

Yet, Disney has not employed any American-Arabs or Muslims to do voice-overs for *Thieves*. Nor are American-Arabs on the scene, regularly consulting with writers and animators. Their presence certainly would sensitize image-makers, and surely lead to more faithful and diverse portraits of the peoples and their cultures on television entertainment programs.

For example, to insure hurtful images would not appear in its successful *Pocahontas*, Disney went to great lengths to try and win the endorsement of Native Americans. Not wishing to repeat its experiences with *Aladdin*, the studio was resolved to avoid caricatures. This time it sought out and hired Native American leaders to work on the film and to act as consultants.

The studio cast American Indian performers such as actress Irene Bedard to be the voice of Pocahontas, and Russell Means as the voice of Pocahontas's father, Chief Powhatan. Means, a well-known American Indian (a term he prefers), praised the Disney film: "Looking at it as an American Indian, I cannot find anything wrong with this movie. I love the treatment of everything, because it's all done with respect."[35]

"**Respect**." This is what Americans of Arab origin want—to be projected on TV screens, as others are, no worse, no better. Image-makers seeking to eradicate images of enmity should seriously contemplate the following conversation between *Earthbound's* alien father and son.

"Why do they (the police) hate us, so?" asks the boy.

"I guess because we're . . . different," says the father. "Just because somebody's different doesn't mean they have to hate 'em. It's stupid!" contests the boy.

---

35 "Disney did its homework on 'Pocahontas.'" Frank Bruni, *Island Packet*, June 11, 1995, p. 9D

"It's been stupid for a long time," concedes the father. No one knows when the producers of fantasies will begin to understand that just because someone may be perceived as different; they should not prompt viewers to "hate 'em." After all, "it's stupid " to denigrate peoples because of religion, color, ancestry, or country of birth. The ultimate quest should be an image of the Arab as neither saint nor devil, but as a fellow human being, with all the potential and frailty that condition implies.

As Jeffrey Katzenberg, former Disney Chairman, says: "Each of us in Hollywood has the opportunity to assume individual responsibility for creating films (and TV shows, too, for that matter) that elevate rather than denigrate . . ., that shed light rather than dwell in darkness, that aim for the common highest denominator rather than the lowest."[36]

Disney Chairman Michael Eisner echoes Katzenberg's commitment to quality. "I'm very responsible, he told critic Ken Auletta. "And I think our company is very responsible. I would never make a movie that I would not allow my ten year old son to go to." [37]

Eisner's and Katzenberg's rhetoric notwithstanding, Professor Joanne Brown of Drake University believes *Aladdin* is "racist." She explains that the Arab villains display "dark-hooded eyes and large hooked noses. Perhaps I am sensitive to this business about noses because I am Jewish," she writes. Brown wonders how she "would feel if Disney Studios created a cartoon based on a Jewish folk tale that portrayed" Jews as "Shylocks," and her "culture so unsympathetically."[38]

The Arab and Muslim stereotype will be canceled provided screen executives put into practice Katzenberg's philosophy and begin striving for the "highest common denominator." Discrimination and cinematic "hate" may be erased from screens when producers and industry officials present scenarios that "elevate" and "shed" on all people.

36 *Modern Maturity*, "Reflections On the Silver Screen," Charles Champlin, p. 23.

37 *The New Yorker*, "What They Won't Do?" Ken Auletta, May 17, p. 48.

38 *The Des Moines Register*, "Stereotypes ruin the fun of Aladdin," Joanne Brown, December 22, 1922, p. 12.

Conclusion

Openness to change is an American tradition and the strength of our society. As Benjamin Franklin advised, "To get the bad Customs of a Country changed and new ones, though better, introduced, it is necessary first to remove the Prejudices of the People, enlighten their ignorance, and convince them that their interest will be promoted by the proposed Changes; and this is not the work of a Day.[39]

Franklin's words take on added meaning when contemplating the Arab and Muslim stereotype. History teaches us that no one benefits when people are continuously denigrated. Regrettably, we fail to comprehend that when one ethnic or minority group is degraded, we all suffer.

Industry professionals have a Promethean role, as they possess the ability to crush damaging caricatures, to shape sensibilities, and to constructively ignite hearts and minds. One such who has spoken out is writer-producer Ted Flicker. In his 1988 letter published in the newsletters of the Writers' Guild and Screen Actors' Guild, Flicker, identifying himself as a Jew, writes: "Arabs are portrayed as crazy billionaires, terrorists, devious voluptuaries, barbaric white slavers, etc., ad nauseam. Dear fellow writers, on behalf of my Arab cousins, I say to you, think before you write that Arab." Adds Flicker, "I think honor requires that we, the makers of our nation's myths, consider the plight of these people . . . and help get rid of the Arab stereotype."[40]

Flicker is not the only television insider to speak out against bigotry. Other TV professionals are concerned about the Arab Muslim stereotype. In 1980, while being interviewed for my book, *The TV Arab*, the producer Alan Rafkin told me: "When I see a Jew portrayed as Shylock, I want to cry. So I know how an Arab feels when he is described as a killer."[41]

---

39 Franklin citation *from Not the Work of a Day: The Story of Anti-Defamation League of the B'nai B'rith*, ADL: New York, 1965. p. 1.

40 Prior to addressing Guilds, Ted Flicker gave this writer a copy of his speech. See Shaheen's *Los Angeles Times* essay, "Television Chose to Make the Palestinian America's Bogeyman, January 10, 1998, p. 5

41 See Rafkina's comments in *The TV Arab*, Jack G. Shaheen, The Popular Press: Bowling Green, Ohio, 1984, p. 64

Recently, in a personal note to this writer, critic Jeffrey Wells expressed some optimism. He wrote that most writers he knows "feel that towel-head villains are a tired cliche." During the summer of 1994 screenwriter J.F. Lawton told him that "the wild eye Arab villains in *True Lies* felt like a joke. They'd already been the villains in Hot Shots. The whole thing has gotten stale."[42]

And in "Entertainment Weekly," Wells and Pat H. Broeske pointed out that several upcoming terrorist movies displayed a variety of baddies: a non-Muslim psycho, North Koreans, and effete Europeans curs. Only one film, *Executive Decision*, which made its way to movie screens in March 1996, featured Arab terrorists. "Finding workable, hissable villains," attests Wells, "has been a tough chore since the fall of Communism."[43]

This writer contends that finding "hissable villains" is a simple "chore." All producers and writers need do is present accurate portraits and offer generic culprits. No one benefits when rouges are repeatedly projected according to race, religion, ethnicity and/or color.

In spite of Wells' assurances about features and Flicker's compassionate plea for equity on television, I remain apprehensive as to whether television entertainment programs will soon cease blemishing Arabs and Muslims. After all, the caricatures have served the industry's selfish interests for nearly half a century.

As one who has addressed the TV Arab and Muslim for more than 20 years, I know one thing for certain: image-makers promoting the stereotype can no longer use "ignorance" as an excuse for perpetuating enmity. When slandering Arabs and Muslims, some know exactly what they are doing.

Observing the bullheaded image-maker cling to his stereotypes reminds me of *Peanuts'* Linus, stubbornly clinging onto his security blanket. Both Linus and the producer know exactly what they are doing. They know their behavior is totally wrong. Yet, they remain adamant, refusing to alter their actions.

Perhaps I am too cynical; perhaps the day will come when TV writers and producers will use dialogue and images that heal emotional

---

42 Jeffrey Wells letter to the author, December 2, 1995.
43 *Entertainment Weekly*, "The 'Hard' Stuff," Jeffrey Wells and Pat H. Broeske, December 1, 1995, p. 8, 9.

wounds, not those that inflict them. Perhaps in lieu of US ("good" Americans) beating up THEM reel ("bad" Arabs), image-makers will one day project honest-to-goodness, true-to-life Arabs and Muslims that viewers cheer for, not against. Perhaps biases will eventually be shattered.

The impact of the stereotype and the continued absence of realistic portrayals of America's Arabs and Muslims on TV screens has a telling effect on viewers, especially on children with Arab roots and those embracing Islam. Programmers do not project adequate role models; children are denied opportunities to increase their self-esteem, as they are unable to positively identify with their heritage.

The counsels of common sense and fair play should prevail; no one should be excluded from our rich, cultural mosaic. The time is long overdue for the real Arab-American to cease being invisible. He/she should be presented in TV programs honestly and accurately, as a vital part of our country's cultural mainstream.

During the early days of television, comedian Milton Berle eloquently addressed the theme of this research. I recall still, Berle's sensitivity and insights. During 1951, when he was at the height of his television career as host of the *Texaco Star Theater*, he told fellow comedian Danny Thomas, "There is no room in our profession for prejudice." No room indeed!

Islam, Muslims
and the American Media

Ahmadullah Siddiqi

Images are very important to a civilization, culture and religion. People generally wish to have a good image. There is nothing essentially good or bad in images themselves, but only in what they portray, evoke or justify. Image, as Fox (1994) describes, refers to "any form of mental, pictorial representation, however generic or fleeting." For most people, in most cultures, major source of information about other people, cultures and religions is mainly the media; it is what we read or see that we believe; especially what we see, we believe. Seeing is believing refers in particular to what we see on television.

The new information technologies are capable of creating instant history and provide live images from distant locations to our living rooms. Desert Storm, the Persian Gulf War, was an unprecedented event reflecting the triumph of orchestrated imagery by the media. As Gerbner (1994) observes, "image-driven and violence-laden, compelling as it is contrived, instant history robs us of reflection time, critical distance, political space, and access to alternatives."

A community of approximately six million (Husain, 1996), Muslims in America are growing in number as well as in their strength. Their interaction and frustration with the American media is also growing. They want themselves and their religion to be portrayed fairly and objectively. Both Muslims and the media practitioners ask questions such as, "Does the American media deliberately distort the images of Muslims and Islam? Are they the champion of presenting Islam as a threat in the post cold war era? Why is there so much Muslim and Islam bashing in the media? Are most Muslims fundamentalist by the very nature of their religion? Does Islam preach violence against those who do not adhere to its teachings? Do Muslims in the U.S. support terrorists in the Middle East and elsewhere? Unfortunately, these questions have not been answered to the satisfaction of any one. Muslims see the media as the greatest conspirator against them and Islam. The media examine Muslims and Islam within their own perspectives – secular/Christian/Capitalist. Sometimes these perspective lack facts, accuracy, and the right context, and at other, the media are deliberately involved in propaganda. It is therefore, important to study this subject in detail and analyze as well understand the nature of media coverage of Islam and Muslims in North America.

Historical overview

Historians, sociologists and anthropologists, among others, have been challenged for centuries in their attempts to classify and define different civilizations and cultures. Spengler (1926), Berdyaev (1936), Northrop (1946), Sorokin (1950), Cowell (1952), Malinowski (1955), Daniel (1975), and Huntington (1993, 1996) among others, have attempted to classify and define cultures and civilizations. Some of these scholars have been very optimistic in their analyses. Analyzing Huntington's thesis, Braibanti (1995), states that "Northrop emphasizes the mutuability of cultures and attempts to discover the ideological bases for their compatibility. He classifies cultures into two broad categories: East and West. 'It should be eventually possible,' he concludes, 'to achieve a society for mankind generally in which the higher standard of living of the most scientifically advanced and theoretically guided Western nations is combined with the compassion, the universal sensitivity to the beautiful, and the abiding equanimity and calm joy of the spirit which characterizes the sages and many of the humblest people of the orient.'" Huntington, however, sees Islam as the most probable enemy of the West. In his book, *The Clash of Civilization* (1996), Huntington warns that Islam poses the most serious security threat for the West. It is between these two extreme contexts – the highly optimistic and mostly pessimistic – that most studies have examined the portrayal of Islam and Muslims in the American media.

Before the Iranian revolution in 1979, most of the media portrayal of Muslims and Islam was limited to Arab images in the media. In one of the earliest studies of Middle East news in the American media, Sulieman (1965) found that Arabs were portrayed in American news magazines as backward and nomads. "Fairness is sacrificed," notes Jack Shaheen (1984), "when producers and writers go into a series with preconceived ideas about people. As we know, notorious Arabs do not appear in a single series, but they are scattered among numerous programs." After analyzing numerous television documentaries portraying stereotypical images of Arabs, Shaheen concludes, "when one ethnic or minority group is degraded, for whatever reason, we all (Americans) suffer." As for the Arab images, he wonders, "how would Jewish-Americans react if they witnesses a host of TV Shylocks posing as nuclear terrorists? Would the blacks welcome being portrayed as white-slavers? Would Hispanics be chagrined if they were shown, along with Orientals, as crude foreigners buying up America?" Shaheen (1990) further notes that most often Westerners have tried to understood the Image of Islam through a distorted picture of the Arab nations and Western media have played a significant role in this distortion. In a recent article, analyzing the 1995 Disney movie "Father of the Bride II," Shaheen (1996) notes, "The prejudice in Disney's Bride II and other films engender among America's Muslims and Arabs feelings of insecurity, vulnerability, alienation and even denial of heritage."

Many recent studies have analyzed the movies and television documentaries' portrayal of Muslims and Islam in general. The images presented in these have been much more dramatic, powerful and negative. *Lawrence of Arabia* (1962), *Black Sunday* (1977), *The Formula* (1980), *Rollover* (1981), *Jewel of the Nile* (1985), and *Delta Force* (1986) are among such movies and television documentaries portraying a negative and violent image of Muslims. After conducting a qualitative and quantitative analysis of two movies – *Lawrence of Arabia* and *The Message* depicting Muslim and Arab culture and civilization, Rehman (1992 (a) concludes that "Hollywood, with few exceptions, has viewed the Muslim world as an exotic, strange, and violent place." He notes that the film directors and writers rely on negative stereotypes and inflame the international misunderstanding and unrest. Most such movies, according to Rehman, are successful in creating myths such as 1) all Muslims are Arabs and all Arabs are Muslims; 2) the Arab families are self destructive; and 3) all Palestinians are terrorists. In another study, Rehman (1992 (b)) have analyzed two other movies, *Cannonball Run* (1979) and *Protocol* (1983). He observes that the portrayal of Arabs and Muslims is too offending and negative. Al-Zahrani (1988), in his study of the U.S. television and press coverage of Islam and Muslims, suggests that the television news in general report Arab and Muslim issues mostly in a negative manner lacking balance and objectivity. Most other studies of television coverage of Muslims and Islam [Adams (1981); Altheide (1976); Asi (1981); Atwater (1986); Ghareeb (1983); Heumann (1980); Kern (1981); Paraschos (1985); Said (1981); and Woll and Miller (1987)] have also concluded that the portrayal lacks objectivity and fairness.

Print media has been studied more extensively for they provide more Muslim and Islamic images on a daily basis. Studies of the print media suggest that the print media portrayal of Islam and Muslims are even more distorted. Shaheen (1985) notes that the American Press presents Islam and Muslims negatively, and as terrorists. A common trend, among American reporters, is to stereotype the act of an individual or a group as being representative of the case of other groups such as Christians, Jews, Blacks, or Hispanics. Allen (1990 agrees with this observation of taking stereotypes a step further to place all people of one color, race, or origin in one category and treat them as a homogeneous group. Said (1981 and 1987), in his studies of the Western and American media and Islam, suggests that the media portray Islam and Muslims as being responsible for all the ills of this century every where in the world. Gahreeb (1984) notes that even the prestigious newspapers such as The Washington Post portray Muslims as terrorist. Oxtoby (1980) finds Arabs being depicted as religious fanatics whose religion embraces such concepts as "assassin" and "*jihad*." While analyzing the media coverage of the Middle East, Said (1987) notes the presence of six major themes:

(1) Arab or Islamic terrorism and Arab or Islamic terrorists states or groups;
(2) Revival of Islamic movements and the Muslim awakening associated with a phrase, "the return of Islam";
(3) Middle East as the origin of violence and terrorism;
(4) Middle East as backward excepting Israel and sometimes Turkey;
(5) Middle East as place for the re-emergence of so called anti-semitism;
(6) Middle East as the home of PLO.

Another recurring theme, according to Mughees-uddin (1993), that has become more popular in recent times, is that of the so-called "Islamic Fundamentalism," and its links to violence and terrorism. "Islam," according to Mugheesuddin "will be the next threat candidate for the U.S. media after the end of the Cold War." Afzal (1991) notes that the American media portray Muslims and Islam as anti-modern, anti-progress, uncivil and anti-West. He argues that the media portrayal is designed to dehumanize the Arabs and Muslims so that their destruction can be made palatable. In a more cecent study Afzal (1993) suggests that the main focus of media in the remaining years of this century will be on the so called "Islamic terrorism" which has become almost synonymous to "Islamic fundamentalism." Zaidi (1991) in an article titled "Medium is the Mischief" presents two cases, one representing a series of articles in the New York Times and the other is that of the Washington Post. He points to the extreme bias of these two newspapers as they present a very distorted image of his home country – Pakistan. *The Message International*, a Muslim magazine published by a New York based Muslim organization compares the overall treatment of Muslims by the mass Media to that of the mental tyranny. A number of studies [Ali (1984); Al-Marayati (1994); Brewda (1990); Badran (1985); Belkaoui (1978); Dart and Allen (1994); Gerbner (198); Ghandour (1985); Haynes (1983); Mortimer (1981); Mousa (1984); Mughees-uddin (1992); Parenti (1986); Sheler (1990); Terry and Menderhall (1974); and Wagner (1973)] have also looked into the portrayal of Arabs, Muslims, and Islam in the U.S. print media, and have arrived at conclusions similar to those discussed above. In Suleiman's (1993) words, "The term Arab, Arabism, Arab nationalism, and the religion associated with them i.e. Islam (and Muslims) have been given an extremely negative connotation in the United States."

Many scholars have traced the roots of the conflict between Islam and the West. Esposito (1992) observes that, "despite common theological roots and centuries-long interaction, Islam's relationship to the West has often been marked by mutual ignorance, stereotyping, contempt, and conflict." Islam's early history of expansions and victories has always posed a challenge to the followers of other faiths. In recent times, the Iranian revolution in 1979, the resurgence of Islam throughout the Muslim and non-Muslim countries, and the situation in the Middle East have inculcated a sense of fear and antagonism among many of the non-Muslim historians, theologians, politicians and the policy makers. Perlmutter (1993) reflects this fear and antagonism by warning about "a general Islamic war waged against the West, Christianity, modern capitalism, Zionism and communism all at one." He argues for an all out "war against Muslim populism" to be the top priority of the West. Professor Bernard Lewis (1990) in his Thomas Jafferson Memorial lecture, which was later published in the *Atlantic Monthly* under the title, "The Roots of Muslim Rage," tries to isolate Islam by presenting it as a threat to the "Judeo-Christian heritage." The provocative term "rage" has earlier been used by the Los Angeles Times journalist, Robin Wright (1979) in her book, Sacred Rage: The Wrath of Militant Islam. However, both the media and the scholars ignore that part of history, which is filled with stark confrontation between Judaism and Christianity and cooperation and co-existence among Jews, Christians and Muslims. American's images of Muslims and Islam would be different if they knew that Muslims, Christians and Jews share much in their monotheistic traditions and the much talked about Judeo-Christian heritage is, in fact, a Judeo-Christian-Islamic heritage. Islam is the last and the latest of the three faiths. It is unfortunate that the media focuses more on highlighting the tensions and conflicts among people than the roots of understanding and cooperation that is at the core of people's survival as human beings.

American Media and Islam

A large number of the so called experts on Islam, the Middle East and terrorism give the impression that their interpretation of Islam beliefs, practices and events is fair, balanced and responsible. However, what the consumers of news get from these experts is a distorted and inflated image of Islam. Islam appears to be a racially biased and culturally uncivilized religion perpetuating violence and hatred against people of other faiths. Often, Islam is dumped with underdevelopment, thereby creating a feeling of economic insecurity among people and forcing them to remain at a distance from Islam. As the following examples suggest, the media continuously remind the American people about the dangers and ills of Islam, sometimes in a threatening way, and at other times in a subtle way, creating myths and stereotypes.

Islam is a communal way of life and the vast majority of emigrants and their European-born children live together isolated form, and hostile to, the society around them... The Muslim communities demand to be allowed to retain all aspects of Islam, including laws unacceptable to the West (such as blood vengeance and killing of females in revenge for the desecration of family honor, to name but a few), and argue for making Islamic law superior to the civil law of the land (Pipes, 1992).

The above is a good example of making erroneous association between "blood vengeance and the killing of females" with Islam. The author relies on isolated incidents of male members of a family attacking daughters or siblings based on personal indignation and not a community's desire to implement Islamic law. In another article appeared in Chicago Tribute (1981), Professor Raphael Patai implicates Islam with violence:

> In the West, assassination has become typically a political act, while in Moslem world it was, and remained, primarily a religious deed.

The claim that assassination is primarily a religious deed is totally unfounded in Qur'an and other sources of Islamic knowledge. One neither finds the same treatment given to violent acts committed by the followers of other faiths, nor are Christian or Judaic ethics blamed for a violent act committed by a follower of either of these religions.

Islamic fundamentalism has been a major concern to many among the media scholars and experts. It is viewed as a major threat to the West. It is often associated with any form of Islamic resistance against the existing dictatorial and unrepresentative governments in the Middle East. It is considered to be a force that is out to destroy any modern culture and civilization. It is proven to be against the Judeo-Christian heritage. It is presented as a violent, radical and extreme form of Islamic behavior. The following examples are but a small sample of such representation of Islam by the media:

> If communism has often been described as a disease, Islamic fundamentalism is a plague now infecting the entire Islamic world from Morocco to India... [It is] a very real representation of the anti-Western, anti-modern forces in the Arab and Islamic World (Perlmutter, 1993).
>
> Ultimately, the struggle of the fundamentalists is against two enemies, secularism and modernism... This is no less than a clash of the civilization perhaps irrational, but surely historic reaction of an ancient rival against our Judeo-Christian heritage, our secular presence and our world wide expansion of both (Lewis, 1990).

> This generation of Islamic fundamentalists have embraced the concept of "jihad" or struggle and emphasized its meaning as violent warfare. (Steinfles, 1993).

> This is the dark side of Islam, which shows its face in violence

and terrorism intended to overthrow modernizing, more secular regimes and harm the Western nations that support them (Nelan, 1993).

Islam is a religion conceived in hell. It was and is determined to destroy all Jews and Christians. Again I refer to the fundamentalist extremists. They are the one who claim "holy war" upon an "unbelieving" world. Their "holy war" is inspired by Satan himself. (Woods, 1996).

In order to understand the inaccuracy of the above assertions and the extent of misrepresentation of Islam, it is important to understand the meaning of the central term that has been used in the above examples. Fundamentalists have been traditionally meant to be those Christians, especially Protestants who believed that the Bible should be followed literally. This definition qualifies all Muslims, practicing or non-practicing, to be fundamentalists because the Qur'an is viewed by all Muslims as the literal word of God. The Qur'an's purity and divine nature of its text was never been an issue among Muslims, Sunnis and Shias alike. No theological doctrine separates the fundamentalists from the non-fundamentalists. Most media practitioners do not understand the above context and indiscriminately use the term "Islamic fundamentalism" which was coined as an aftermath of the Iranian revolution in 1979. Bodansky and Vaughn (1990 and 1992) authored several reports on behalf of the House Republican's Task Force on Terrorism and Unconventional Warfare. In these reports they purportedly uncover a global conspiracy by Muslim fundamentalists to incite violence and terrorism in order to weaken or eliminate the Western powers. According to this report, Muslim fundamentalists are devious, self-centered, power-hungry, and war mongers. Although the authors provide "facts," there is no attribution, and no one can verify the accusations.

Over the past several years, a number of publications have published special reports and columns on Islam implicating Islam as the most significant threat to the liberal democracies of the West. These include, among others, *Time* (1993), *The Economist* (1992), the *New York Times* (1993), *U.S. News & World Report* (1993), and the *Chicago Tribune* (1995). Some of these reports are so inflammatory that if seriously taken, it will lead to a great misunderstanding between Muslims and other people in Western societies. For example, Zuckerman, M.B. Editor-in-Chief of the *U.S. News & World Report* and publisher of the *Atlantic Monthly* writes:

> Islam's militant strain is on the verge of replacing communism as the principal opponent of Western liberal democracy and the values it enshrines... The Gulf War was just one paragraph in the long conflict between the West and radical Islam; the World Trade Center bombing, just a sentence. We are in for a long struggle not amenable to reasoned dialogue (Zuckerman, 1993).

Muslims and the American Media

The American media pundits never let go off an opportunity to tell their audiences that the Muslims are anti-modern, uncivil and anti-West. While media have always pointed out that "Muslim men" were implicated in the World Trade Center bombing, never did the media say that the suspects in Oklahoma City bombing were Christians. The media completely failed to take note when a million-dollar newly-built mosque in California was burnt and completely destroyed on September 1, 1994. Similarly the media failed to report the arson of a New York City mosque. Daniel Pipes, director of the Foreign Policy Institute in Philadelphia, expresses concern (1990) about the stubborn record of Muslims' illiteracy. He notes that, "the key issue is whether Muslims will modernize ... should they fail to modernize, their stubborn record of illiteracy, poverty, intolerance, and autocracy will continue, or perhaps worsen." It is not clear in what way Muslims have failed to modernize. Does "modern" mean acceptance and practice of the culture and values of the West, or is it meant to say that as long as Muslims follow Islam they can not modernize? The statement of Pipes also suggest that Muslims are intolerant and autocratic. Muslims are in power in more than forty countries in Asia, Africa and Europe. Is it fair to generalize their behavior based on the example of one or two Muslim governments? Muslims have welcomed, cooperated, interacted and worked with people of other faiths during the climax of their civilizational power in Spain and the Middle East. Muslims, Jews and Christians have lived peacefully for centuries in the Middle East, especially in the Palestine-Israel region (Chacour and Hazard, 1984). It is true that there have been wars among Muslims, Christians and Jews, and it is also true that there are some basic differences in religious thoughts and practices between Muslims and non-Muslims. However, let us not forget that there have been wars among many people and many nations through out the human history. From the ancient wars to the holocaust, and from the American-Japanese conflict to the war in Vietnam, human history is filled with conflict and confrontation based on religious, political, and cultural differences. We will better serve ourselves and the world if we focus on points of similarity rather than picking on points of differences, conflicts, and confrontation.

As a result of the media stereotyping, Muslims are the first suspect in a crisis situation. The bombing of the Murrah Federal Building in Oklahoma City on April 19, 1995 is a good example. Immediately after the bomb blast, radio and television started reporting that people of Middle Eastern origin were the prime suspects. Expert after expert including one Congressman, appeared on television and radio talk shows supporting the idea that suspects were of Middle Eastern origin. Chicago Tribune Columnist Mike Royko joined the bandwagon and wrote on April 21, 1995, "President Clinton says we should be cautious about placing blames or taking action. O.K., but when the time comes for punishment, it wouldn't be an eye for eye. That's just a swap. We should take both eyes, ears, nose, the entire anatomy. That's how to make a lasting impression." Looking at Royko's columns after the suspects were arrested and they were found to be white, Christians, and from the Midwest, not from the Middle East, one could not find any impatient appeal for a swift action. Royko obviously calmed down after finding out that the suspects were one of his own.

In 1991 alone, 119 hate crimes against Arabs and Muslims were reported in the U.S., even though the Gulf war occurred during this period. In three days, immediately following the Oklahoma City blast, more than 227 hate crimes against Muslims were reported by the U.S. Department of Justice in 1993. A hate crime is a criminal offense committed against a person or property which is motivated, in whole or in part, by the offender's bias against a race, religion, ethnic/national origin group, or sexual orientation. What Muslims experienced after the Oklahoma City bombing may well be categorized as "hate crimes". Included in this were hate calls to individual Muslims as well as Islamic Centers, stalking, false arrests, police harassment, verbal threats, death and bomb threats, beating and physical assaults, and shootings. The environment of hate and suspicion significantly affected the daily life of Muslims. Many Muslim businesses experienced a substantial decrease in the number of customers. Muslim women wearing Islamic dress and school-going children suffered most as they were afraid to go out during the first few days after the bombing. A Muslim women in her mid 20s miscarried her near-term baby after an attack on her house in Oklahoma City on April 20th, 1995. The Islamic Center at High Point, North Carolina was burnt to ground on the early morning of April 26, 1995. A seventh grade Muslim student at the Richardson Middle School in Torrence, California was slandered with words such as "camel jockey" and assaulted physically after her English teacher included the word "bomb" in students' vocabulary and used it in a sentence, "Muslims bombed Oklahoma City because Allah told them to do so." (CAIR, 1995).

"We were held hostage for 72 hours," said the leader of Momin Mosque in Oklahoma City. The media played a significant role in spreading the rumor, and consequently, provoking Americans to think that after the World Trade Center bombing Muslim terrorists have struck in the American heartland. Within minutes of the bombing, a local TV station started broadcasting that the Nation of Islam was responsible for this attack. A couple of hours later, they reported that the FBI was looking for three men of Middle Eastern origin (Impact: May 1995). CNN was the first network to broadcast an interview with former Congressman David McCurdy on April 19, 1995. McCurdy noted that, "there could be a very real connection to some of the Islamic fundamentalist groups that have actually been operating out of Oklahoma City." On the same day Steven Emerson, producer of the PBS documentary, "Jihad in American," declared on the CBS Evening News: "Oklahoma City, I can tell you, is probably considered as one of the largest centers of Islamic radical activity outside the Middle East." A former Congressman and a so-called expert on terrorism were the most widely quoted sources of allegation that the bombing was done by Muslim terrorists. John McWeathy reported on ABC World News, April 19: "Sources say that FBI has been watching dozens of suspicious Islamic groups in cities in the Southwest and several in Oklahoma City." Jim Cumins on NBC Nightly News, April 19 compared the bombing to that in "Beirut". On April 20, Larry Johnson, identified as an international security expert, said in an interview with Robert MacNeil of PBS, "The threat [of terrorism] has narrowed – in that it is focused more on Islamic groups."

Radio talk shows took upon themselves to inflame the hatred against Muslims. Here is an excerpt from the Bob Grant Show on WABC, New York, April 20: "A Caller: "Well, I'd like to say that it's very amazing that... they're talking about Muslims and Mr. Salameh and all this, this is what you are saying, and no one ever saw anything. That's just as worse—; Grant: Now – yeah—we did see a lot of things.. In the Oklahoma case... the indications are that those people who did it were some Muslim terrorists. But, a skunk like you, what I'd like to do is put you up against the wall with the rest of them, and now you down along with them. Execute you with them."

Looking at newspapers, one finds that most newspapers, including *The New York Times*, *USA Today*, *The Washington Post*, and *The Chicago Tribune* were instrumental in adding to the confusion. The Post wrote on April 20, "The FBI has been aware of the activity of Islamic groups meeting recently in Oklahoma City, Dallas, and Kansas". *USA Today* quoted, on April 20, Daniel Pipes, editor of Middle East Quarterly. Pipes said, "People need to understand that this is just the beginning. The fundamentalists are on the upsurge, and they make it very clear that they are targeting us. They are absolutely obsessed with us." After an Arab-Muslim was detained at London's Heathrow Airport and sent back to the U.S. for questioning, *The Daily Telegraph* ran this front page headline.: "Oklahoma bomb suspect seized at Heathrow".

It is evident from above examples that it was not merely a criticism of "Muslim extremists" or "Muslim fundamentalists," rather it was an outright defamation of the entire Muslim community. Was it sufficient to infer criminality, as *The New York Times* (April 20, 1995) did, from the mere presence of Islamic religious institutions in Oklahoma City. Even after the possibility of Muslim or Arab involvement was ruled out by the authorities, some media sources insisted on maintaining Muslims' link to the bombing. CNN's Wolf Blitzer, on April 20, insisted that, "there is still a possibility that there could have been some sort of connection to Middle East terrorism." Wolf Blitzer was quoted on April 21 in *The Cincinnati Post* which went a step further in quoting an unidentified law enforcement source that a Muslim cab driver from New York, Asad R. Siddiqy, arrived in Oklahoma City an hour before the blast, is considered a suspect. The paper even published a photograph of Siddiqy.

In a journalism class of mostly seniors, when this author asked about who are the terrorists, students had only one answer: "they are the Muslims from the Middle East." This mythical image of Muslim terrorism is perpetuated by the media which relies on a number of terrorism experts who seem to have their own political agenda.

According to a 1993 FBI report on domestic terrorist acts (FBI:

1995), radicals from Muslim background carried out only one terrorist attack in the United States - The World Trade Center Bombing. In contrast, 77 terrorist attacks involved Puerto Ricans, 23 attacks involved left-wing groups, 16 attacks involved Jewish groups, 12 attacks involved anti-Castro Cubans and six terrorist attacks involved right-wing groups. Similarly with regard to the terrorist attacks against the United States overseas, the Department of State (1995) inits report, "Pattern of Global Terrorism" noted that a majority of the anti-U.S. attacks in 199 took place in Latin America, whereas 8 were carried out in the Middle East, 5 in Asia, 5 in Western Europe, and in Africa. In a story on Sudan, a country in Africa which the U.S. has categorized as a terrorist state, the *Time* magazine (August 30, 1993) has used a picture of the Muslims while they were praying. The caption on this picture reads: "At Prayer: Sudanese in Alliance of Ideology and Convenience with Iran." The Time reporter have created a new symbol for the world to hate: The Muslims performing their obligatory five daily prayers in congregation. Millions of *Time's* readers will now associate this image with terrorists and scofflaws. In the World Trade Center (WTC) Bombing 15 Muslims were indicted in August of 1993. American Muslims' response was quick, and clear. On March , 1993, at news conferences in Washington, D.C., New York, and Los Angeles, Muslim leaders condemned the bombing. In a statement published in *Los Angeles Times* (March 5, 1993) Muslim leaders of the United States and Canada made it clear that, "Any practicing Muslim would definitely be against any acts of terrorism against anyone—Jews, Christians or Muslims... It is quite honest to admit that among Muslims, just like among Christians and Jews, there are elements that are extremists. They are elements of the fringe." The 15 persons indicted in the WTC bombing were not a part of any well knitted organization. The blind Muslim cleric, Sheikh Omar Abdul Rahman, was not even known to most Muslims in the United States. He was never invited to speak at any of the national Islamic conventions in the U.S. or Canada, yet many media outlets portrayed the entire Muslim community to be part of a "grand Islamic conspiracy". Headlines such as "Islam: Terror Strikes Again..." and "Bombs in the Name of Allah," were published associating Islam and Allah (Islamic equivalent of God) with terror, violence and bomb.

Muslims were shocked and surprised to note that in one of the most popular Disney movies for children, *The Lion King*, when the evil-natured hyenas were shown, a crescent appears on the horizon. Crescent has been used as an Islamic symbol in many of the Muslim arts and paintings. Equating darkness and evil with Islam is yet another way to dehumanize Muslims and portray them as enemies.

Reasons for Negative Portrayal

Many researchers, [Ghareeb (1993), Haddad (1991), Said (1987), and Lee (1991), Wood (1996) among others], have analyzed the reasons for biased coverage. These include:

Cultural bias.
The conflict between Arabs and Israel.
The media's lack of information about the history of the conflict between Arabs and Israel.
The political power of the pro-Israel lobby and its influence over the American media.
The secular bias of the media.
The new technological capabilities of the media.

Cultural, religious, or other civilizational differences are some of the many factors responsible for prejudice and conflict. It is natural to have different cultures at different times and space. However, it is not natural to develop cultural arrogance and a sense of civilizational superiority and hegemony. Arrogance, prejudice and hatred are mostly a product of ignorance. If many of us think that the world begins and ends within the United States of America, we will tend to look down at others, especially to those others whom we perceive as being hostile to us. In one of my classes on international press and foreign media, students were surprised to learn that some of the so called Third World Countries also publish newspapers with comparable size, quality, and circulation to U.S. newspapers. For some students it was difficult to believe. Islam, with 1400 years of history, has its own cultural traditions. Lack of the Islamic cultural perspectives leads people to perceive some Islamic traditions as being hostile to the West or Western traditions. Lee (1991) describes the basis of this hostility by suggesting that "Western nations live in a culture of war. How can the media play a role which is constructively critical of the State and which contributes directly to a culture of peace?" Media play a constant and illusory role in people's lives, argues Lee. Newspapers, television, magazines, comics, videos, and computer games reinforce only those images that fit the culture of war at a given time. There was a time when "Cold War" rhetoric was so powerful that millions of Americans firmly believed that USSR was capable and ready to over-run Europe and America. Now it is the turn of Islam and the Muslims. If it is true that Americans can not live without having a major enemy or a major global threat, then perhaps Islamic fundamentalism or Islam is the easy, natural and the only choice after the fall of communism in USSR and Eastern Europe. Suleiman (1983) supports this argument by contending that an important reason for negative portrayal of Muslims and Islam in the media is the fear of Islam and the Muslims by the West. This fear is unfortunately reinforced by Western scholars and so called experts of Arabs and Islam in the West. Immediately after the arrest of Mohammad Salmeh, the World Trade Center Bombing suspect, a University of Miami expert on Middle East and terrorism remarked during a CNN newscast that the real issue in the Middle East is not the Arab-Israeli conflict, but it is the threat of Islamic fundamentalism. This and many similar discourses, on American radio and television, by the so called experts and analysts show a deliberate attempt to present Islam as the enemy of the West, especially America. Most media rely on such uninformed or prejudiced sources.

Arab-Israeli conflict plays an important role in shaping the Islamic images. The way media portray Arabs and the policies of the U.S. administration make Israel the most trusted friend and the Arabs and consequently Islam as the most hated enemy.

After analysing the impact of American foreign policy in the Middle East on the identity of Arab Muslims in the United States, Haddad (1991) notes, "… A major element in the experience of the Muslim community in the United States during the last forty years has been a rising sense of hypocrisy of succeeding presidential administrations. Muslims feel they are living in a country that is hostile not only to their ethnic origins, but increasingly to Islam and Muslims in general (p.223)." Many reporters follow the approach adopted by the administration. Mugheesuddin (1993), after analyzing the *New York Times*, the *Washington Post*, and the *Los Angeles Times*, has concluded that most media follow and support the administration's approach in foreign policy issues related to the Muslims and Islam.

The secular bias of the media is yet another important factor. Muslims suffer more than any other religious group because of Islam's emphasis on the unity of religion and state. The secular bias combined with the market-oriented goals of media industry and political and corporate pressures on the media often make it very difficult for the media to exercise self restraint and adhere to the notion of social responsibility. Most media practitioners are unable to understand and appreciate why Muslims see things in a holistic world view of Islam, rather than a compartmentalized and fragmented "World Order." Clifford Christians (1987) advocates moral reasoning to minimize the secular bias and profit motives. He contends that the social responsibility of the media, does not just lie in placing the ethnic of truth telling, human dignity and solidarity with the weak above the need to make a profit. It is also a matter of acting independently of social and political restraints which are contrary to universal human values such as justice and peace. Christians observes that, "in a frenzied world, how can 'obligation to truth' or 'comprehensive coverage of minority groups' hope to hold on its own against ;get the quote' and shoot the 'tear-jerking photo'? How can truth-telling be allowed to give a competitor an advertising edge? How can respect for the elderly be written into television comedy? Somewhere in the sorting out of these media imperatives, a practitioner must begin to assign priorities and then live by them. That process is called moral reasoning. We contend that journalists, advertising executives, and entertainment programmers should be among the best trained moral thinkers in the land."

Another factor which is mostly ignored by many researchers is the technological capability of media to manipulate and create pseudo-contexts in which events can be easily removed from their real contexts and presented in any manner that is dictated either by the competitive necessity or by the profit motive. The Pentagon production "Operation Desert Storm," and the mid-air shooting of the Iranian jetliner are among the best examples of a pseudo-context in a technological order detached from democratic accountability and set free from moral restraints [Phelon (1991)].

The treatment of Muslims by the media is due mainly to the perception of many Americans, including media practitioners, that Islam is anti-West and in particular, anti-American. It is true that many events, especially the revolution in Iran in 1979, the World Trade Center Bombing in 1993, and the bombing in Riyadh, Saudi Arabia in November 1995, encourage one to think that it is Islamic to be anti-American. However, more than anti-Americanism these events reflect the political instability, deprivation of basic human rights in many of the Muslim countries supported by the U.S. administration, and an exploitation of these countries' resources to the advantage of a royal family of kings, amirs, presidents, and dictators. "Muslims can not be anti-Western because Islam is pro, not anti-any religion or its people," noted Hasan Turabi, Secretary General of the Popular Arab and Islamic Conference (*Impact*, May 1995).

Another reason of the prejudice and unfair treatment of Muslims by the media is, as some researchers and analysts (Abuljobain, 1993) believe, the presence of a strong anti-Muslim Zionist lobby that controls most of the media and influence the legislators at state capitols and in Washington, D.C. These researchers assert that the majority of the American media practitioners adopt the line of argument advanced by powerful interest groups who support the government of Israel. A series of reports published by the House Republicans Task Force in 1990, 1992 and 1993 ferociously attack Muslims and hold them responsible for terrorist attacks against U.S. (Bodansky, Yossef and Vaughan Forrest, 1990, 1992). Many Muslims see the 1995 Omnibus Counter Terrorism Act as an attempt by the above-mentioned groups to undermine Muslims' religious freedom in America. The legislation, signed by President Clinton in April 1996, has been widely condemned by Muslim organizations all across America. Twenty major Muslim organizations issued a signed statement asking the members of Congress and Senate to oppose measures that will presumably violate basic rights to free speech and religious practices. While some have compared it with the principle of guilt by association that defined the McCarthy era (David Cole, 1995), others have looked at it as the mockery of democracy in America where "Rule number one is that every one is equal under the law; and rule number two is that the government will determine to whom Rule number one applies." (*Impact*: May 1995).

Last, but not least, an important reason of the negative media coverage of Islam and Muslims is Muslims' own lack of interaction with and participation in the media. Muslims have long seen the media as an arch enemy, a conspirator and a blasphemer, and rarely tried to establish a mutually beneficial relationship with the media. Consequently, neither the Muslims nor the media are comfortable with each other. "If Islam is put into an American context," said Salam Al-Marayati, Director of the Lost Angeles based Muslim Public Affairs Council, "then it will emerge as a valuable element of American pluralism... Being Muslim does make one different, but there is so much that Muslims can share with other Americans." (Al-Marayati, 1995). Muslims need to understand the nature of American pluralism as well as the power dynamics in America, then only they will be able to get a more positive coverage from the media. "Any group that projects itself as a threatening group is humiliated," said Maher Hathout, a cardiologist and President of the Islamic Centre of Southern California in Los Angeles. He asserted that, "there is a part played by media and others, but a great part of the fear in this society's mind comes from what we say and what we do. If we continue to allow ourselves to be projected as a frightening group, it will be very detrimental for the future of Islam in America. American society does not mind if you are liberal or conservative, but they do not like when they feel scared. The experience of the Black Panther or Waco group is very relevant." (Hathout, 1995). Emphasizing Muslims' active interaction with media, Hathout (1993) observed that, "ignorance is the breeding home of fear, anxieties and prejudice. People are always afraid of things they don't know." "Blaming others, the media, and living under the conspiracy theory are very detrimental to Muslims' growth in American society," said Fayyaz Khan, former editor of a New York based Muslim monthly magazine, *The Message International*. "The victim syndrome is the loser syndrome," noted Khan (1995). He summarized Muslims' future strategy in dealing with the media by reading an anonymous quotation: "The best defense is no defense. The best defense is compassion and confidence."

During the last five years American Muslims have become more proactive. Organizations such as the American Muslim Council (AMC) and the Muslim Public Affairs Council (MPAC) have been educating Muslims to play an effective role in American politics, and, at the same time, exerting pressure and influence upon U.S. law makers to recognize the strength of the fast growing Muslim community in America. The Council of American Islamic Relations (CAIR) has been successful in their campaign to monitor the media for distorting Muslim images. Recently, they have successfully persuaded a number of corporations and organizations to withdraw commercial messages stereotypical of Muslims. The North American Association of Muslim Professionals and Scholars (NAAMPS), among others, has been organizing media workshops to educate and train Muslims in media skills and media relations. National organizations such as Islamic Society of North America (ISNA) and Islamic Circle of North America (ICNA) are trying to develop their own radio and television networks. A number of Muslim magazines and newspapers including The Minaret, The Message, Islamic Horizon, and the Muslim Journal have significantly grown in size and circulation. They are serving Muslims as well as reaching into the Americans in general. Muslims have also ventured into the internet and web sites. Many news groups and discussion forums are interacting with Americans and providing them with a better opportunity for dialogue and interaction.

Let us hope that American's view of Islam becomes more complex and comprehensive as they learn more about Muslims and Islam. Let us hope, as John Spayde (1994) observes, "A faith that is professed by the fundamentalist misogynists in Iran and Egypt, feminists in Morocco and England, taxi drivers and kings in Ghana, Nigeria and Kenya, office workers in Malaysia, nuclear scientists in Kazakhstan, martyrs in Bosnia – and more than six million Americans – is as far beyond stereotyping as humanity itself."

"The word Islam," as noted by Haddad, "comes from the three letter root word in Arabic "slm," which stands for peace." (USA Today, 1993, March 10). "Islam," she says, "is the religion of peace. That's the way Qur'an talks about it – the religion of peace. When you become a Muslim, you become at peace with God. And, that's what Islam means, to surrender to God, to stop fighting God... People should know that Islam, in a sense, urges people to worship the same God that Christianity and Judaism do."

References

AbulJobain, Ahmad (1993). *Radical Islamic Terrorism or Political Islam?* Annandale, VA: United Association for Studies and Research, Occasional Paper Series No. 1.

Adams, W.C. (1981). *Television Coverage of the Middle East.* Norwood, N.J.: Ablex.

Afzal, Omar (1991, January). The American Media's Middle East War. *The Message International:* 19-20.

Afzal, Omar (1993, March). "Media's new Shooting Targets." *The Message International:* 17-18.

Al-Marayati, Salam (1994, June). "The Rising Tide of Hostile Stereotyping of Islam." *The Washington Report on Middle East Affairs:* 27.

_____ (1995). Quotation from personal interview given to this author, (January 21).

Al-Zahrani, Abdul Aziz A. (1988). *U.S. Television and Press Coverage of Islam and Muslims.* Doctoral dissertation, Norma, Oklahoma: University of Oklahoma.

Ali, M. (1984). Western Media and the Muslim World. The Concept, 4 (2): 13-19.

Allen, Irving Lewis (1990). *Unkind Words: Ethnic Labeling from Redskins to WASP.* New York: Bergin & Garvey.

Altheidi, D (1976). *Creating Reality: How TV News Distorts Events.* Beverly Hills, CA: Sage.

Asi, M.O. (1981). *Arabs, Israelis and U.S. Television Networks: A Content Analysis of How ABC, CBS, and NBC Reported the News Between 1970 - 1979.* Doctoral dissertation, Ohio University. Dissertation Abstract International, 42: 893A.

Atwater, T. (1986, August). *Terrorism on the Evening News: An Analysis of Coverage of the TWA Hostage Crisis on "NBC Nightly News."* Paper presented to the Radio-Television Journalism Division, AEJMC 1986 Convention, Norman, Oklahoma.

Badran, A.B. (1985). *Editorial Treatment of the Arab-Israeli Conflict in U.S. and European Newspapers: 1980 - 1982.* Doctoral dissertation, University of Massachusetts. Dissertation Abstract International, 45: 3021A.

Belkaoui, J. M. (1978). "Images of Arabs and Israelis in the Prestige Press: 1966 - 1974." Journalism Quarterly, 55: 732-733 & 799.

Berdyaev, Nicholas (1936). *The Meaning of History.* London: The Centenary Press, 1936: 207-224.

Bodansky, Yossef and Vaughan Forrest (1990, March). *A Question of Trust.* U.S. House of Representatives House Republicans Task Force on Terrorism and Unconventional Warfare, Washington, D.C.

_____ (1992, September). *Iran's European Spring Board.* U.S. House of Representatives House Republicans Task Force on Terrorism and Unconventional Warfare, Washington, D.C.

Braibanti, Ralph (1995). *The Nature and Structure of the Islamic World.* Chicago: International Policy and Strategy Institute: 16-22, 90.

Brewada, Joseph (1990, July 20). "Super Powers Prepare Middle East War: Final Solution to Arab Problems." Executive Intelligence Review: 28-30.

CAIR (1995). "A Rush to Judgment." (A Special Report on Anti-Muslim Stereotyping, Harassment and Hate Crimes Following the Bombing of Oklahoma City's Murrah Federal Building, April 19, 1995). Washington, D.C.: Council on American Islamic Relations (CAIR).

Chacour, Elias and Hazard David (1984). *Blood Brothers.* Grand Rapids, Michigan: Chosen Books.

Christians, G.G., Kim, B.R. & Mark F. (1986). *Media Ethics: Cases and Moral Reasoning.* New York: Longman: 131.

Cole, David (1995). As quoted by Rafique Mirza in *Impact*, May 1995: 8-9.

Costanzo, William V. (1994). "Reading Ollie North," in Roy F. Fox (ed.), *Images in Language, Media, and Mind.* Urbana, Illinois: National Council of Teachers of English: 108-122.

Cowell, F.R. (1952). *History, Civilization and Culture.* Boston: Beacon Press: 9.

Daniel, Norman (1975). *The Cultural Barrier: Problems in the Exchange of Ideas.* Edinburgh: Edinburgh University Press: 13-14.

Dart, John and Allen Jimmy, (1994). *Bridging the Gap: Religion and the News Media.* Nashville: The Freedom Forum First Amendment Center at Vanderbilt University.

Esposito, John L. (1992). *The Islamic Threat: Myth or Reality?* New York: Oxford University Press.

Federal Bureau of Investigation (1995). *Terrorist Research and Analytical Section's Report.*

Fox, Roy F. (1994). *Images in language, Media, and Mind.* Urbana, Illinois: National Council of Teachers of English: x.

Gerbner, G. (1995). "Forward: What's Wrong With This Picture, in Kamalipour," Yahya R. (ed.) *The U. S. Media and the Middle East: Image and Perception.* Westport, Connecticut: Greenwood Press: xv.

_____ (1994). "Instant History: Lessons from the Persian Gulf War," in Roy F. Fox (ed.), *op. cit.*: 123-140.

Gerbner, G. and Marvanx, G. (1984). "The Many Worlds of the World's Press, in G. Gerbner & M. Siefert (eds.)" *World Communication: A Handbook.* New York: Longman: 92-102.

Ghandour, N. H. (1985). *Coverage of the Arab World and Israel in American News Magazines Between 1975 and 1981: A Comparative Content Analysis. Doctoral dissertation*, Teachers College of Columbia University. Dissertation Abstract International, 45: 2476A.

Ghareeb, E. (1984). "The Middle East in the U.S. Media." *The Middle East Annual Issues and Events*, 3: 185-210.

Ghareeb, E. (1983). "A Renewed Look at the American Coverage of the Arabs": Toward a Better Understanding, in E. Ghareeb (ed.) *Split Vision, the American Media*. Washington, D. C.: American Arab Affairs Council: 157-194.

Grant, Bob (1995). Bob Grant Show on WABC, New York, April 20, as quoted by the CAIR: op. Cit.,:6.

Haddadh, Yvonne Yazbeck (1991). *The Muslims of America*. New York: Oxford University Press.

Hathout, Maher (1995). Quotation from interview given to this author (January 21, 1995).

Haynes, J. E. (1983). "Keeping Cool about Kabul: The Washington Post and The New York Times Cover the Communist Seizure of Afghanistan." *World Affairs*, 145: 369-383.

Heumann, J. (1980). "U.S. Network Television: Melodrama and the Iranian Crisis." *Middle East Review*, 13: 51-55.

Huntington, Samuel P. (1993). "The Clash of Civilization?", *Foreign Affairs*, 72, #3: 22-49.

_____ (1996). *The Clash of Civilization and the Remaking of the World Order*. New York: Simon and Schuster.

Husain, Asad and Imran Husain (1996). "A Brief History and Demographics of Muslims in the United States," in Asad Husain, John Woods and Javeed Akhtar (eds.) *Muslims in America: Opportunities and Challenges*. Chicago: International Strategy and Policy Institute: 29.

Impact (May 1995). "Targeting Islam, targeting America": 8-9.

Impact (May 1995). "Polite Engagement is an Unilateral Islamic Obligatioin": 14-15.

Keen, Sam (1986). *Faces of the Enemy: Reflections of the Hostile Imagination.* New York: Harper and Row.

Kern, M. (1981). "The Invasion of Afghanistan: Domestic Vs. Foreign Stories," in W. C. Adams (ed.), *op. Cit.*: 106-127.

Khan, Fayyas (1995). Quotation from an interview given to this author (November 21, 1994).

Lee, Philip (1991). "Images of a Culture of War." *Media Development,* 4: 12-15.

Lewis, Bernard (1990, September). "The Roots of Muslim Rage." *The Atlantic Monthly*: 47-60.

Los Angeles Times (March 5, 1993). "U. S. Islamic Leaders Condemn Bombing, Brace for Backlash": A20.

Malinowski, Bronislaw (1955). *The Dynamics of Culture Change.* New Haven: Yale University Press: 17-40.

Mortimer, E. (1981). "Islam and the Western Journalist." *Middle East Journal,* 35: 492-505.

Mousa, I. S. (1984). *The Arab Images in the U. S. Press.* New York: Peter Lang.

Mughees-uddin (1993). "Many Voices One Chorus": Framing Islam and Islamic Movements (FIS and Hamas) in the U.S. Elite Press (The New York Times, The Washingon Post and The Los Angeles Times). Paper presented at the First Conference of the North American Association of Muslim Professionals and Scholars, Chicago, April 9-11.

_____ (1992). *Editorial Treatment of U. S. Foreign*

Policy in The New York Times: The Case of Pakistan (1980-90). Paper presented to the International Communication Division of the AEJMC Convention, Montreal, Canada, August 7.

Nelan, Bruce W. (1993, October 4). "The Dark Side of Islam." *Time*: 62-63.

Northrop, F. S. C. (1946). *The Meeting of East and West.* New York: Macmillan: 296.

Oxtoby, W. G. 91980). "Western Perception of Islam and the Arabs," in M. C. Hudson & R. G. Wolf (eds.) *The American Media and the Arabs.* Washington, D. C.: Georgetown University Press: 3-12.

Paraschos, M. Rutherford B. (1985). "Network News Coverage of Invasion of Lebanon by Israel in 1982." *Journalism Quarterly*, 62: 457-464.

Parenti, M. (1986). *Inventing Reality: The Politics of Mass Media.* New York: St. Martin's Press.

Patai, Raphael. (1981, December 6). "Violence, The Islamic Curse," *Chicago Tribune.*

Perlmutter, Amos (1993, January 22). "Islamic Fundamentalist Network." *The Washington Times.*

Phelon, J. M. (1991), "Image Industry Erodes Political Space," *Media Development*, Vol 37 (4): 6-8.

Pipes, Daniel (1990). "The Muslims are Coming, The Muslims are Coming." *National Review*, November 19: 28-31.

Pipes, Daniel (1992, October 30). "Fundamental Questions About Muslims." *The Wall Street Journal.*

Rehman, Sharaf N. (1992.a, January/February). "Muslim Images in American Cinema." *The Minaret*: 39-42.

_____ (1992.b). "Portrayal of the Arabs in the Western Mass Media" (pp. 153-162), in Dilnawaz A. Siddiqui and Abbas F. Allkhafaji. *The Gulf War: Implications for the Global Business and Media.* Apollo, Pensylvania: Closson Press.

Royko, Mike (1995). "Time to up the ante against terrorism." *Chicago Tribune,* April 21.

Said E. W. (1981). *Covering Islam: How the Media and the Experts Determine How We See Rest of the World.* New York: Pantheon Books.

_____ (1987). "The MESA Debate: The Scholars, the Media and the Middle East." *Journal of Palestine Studies,* 16 (2): 85-104.

Shaheen, J. G. (1984). *The TV Arab.* Bowling Green, Ohio: Bowling Green State University Popular Press.

_____ (1985, November), "Media Coverage of the Middle East: Perception and Foreign Policy." *Annals,* 482: 160-174.

_____ (1990, August 25). "Our Cultural Demon: The Ugly Arab." *Des Moines Register*: 7 A.

_____ (1996, March/April). "Disney Has Done It Again." *Islamic Horizon*: 38-39.

Sheler, Jeffery L. (1990, August 8). "Islam in America." *U. S. News & World Report*: 69-71.
Sorokin, Pitirim A. (1950). *Social Philosophies in an Age of Crisis.* Boston: Beacon Press: 279.

Spayde, Jon (1994, March/April). "Islam." *Utne Reader*: 76.

Spengler, Oswald (1926). *The Decline of the West.* New York: Alfred Knopf, 1:32.

Steinfles, Peter (1993, March 8). "Like Islam, Its Fundamentalism has many Forums." *New York Times*: A11.

Suleiman, M. W. (1965). "An Evaluation of the Middle East News Coverage in Seven American News Magazines, July-December, 1965." *Middle East Forum*, 41: 9-30.

_____ (1993). "American Views of Arabs and the Impact of These Views on Arabs in the United States," paper presented at the Arab Sociological Association Conference, 29 March - 1 April: 6.

Terry, J. & Mendenhall, G. (1974). 1973 "U. S. Press Coverage on Middle East. Journal of Palestine Studies," 4 (1): 120-133.

The Cincinnati Post (April 21, 1995). "Face of Terrorist?" Pages 1A, 3A, 6A, and 9A.

The U. S. Department of State (1950). *Pattern of Global Terrorism.* Washington, D. C.: U. S. Government Printing Office.

Time (August 30, 1993). "Is Sudan Terrorism's New Best Friend": 30-31.

Utne Reader (March April 1994). "Terror and Tolerance, Muslims rage at the West is justified-but it is not Islamic": 81-84.

Woods, J. E. (1996). "Imagining and Stereotyping Muslims," in Azad Husain, John E. Woods, and Javed Akhtar (eds.) *Muslims in America: Opportunities and Challenges.*

Media Relations Tips for Muslim Activists

Ibrahim Hooper

INTRODUCTION

As the Muslim community in America grows and develops, it is very important that its members help shape the public perception of Islam and Muslims. This image has suffered most when its development is left to those who are either ignorant of or hostile to Islamic beliefs and traditions.

This chapter is designed to provide community activists with the tools necessary to coordinate an efficient and effective local media relations effort. Using the practical steps and concepts detailed in this chapter, almost anyone should be able to build positive relationships with local editors and reporters.

MEDIA RELATIONS OVERVIEW

Rule #1 - The news business is a bottomless pit that can never be filled. Corollary to Rule #1 - A journalist will thank you for helping to shovel.

Media relations are a long-term effort. It does not happen overnight. To be an effective resource for media professionals, you must exhibit the following attributes:

Always be truthful and accurate. You can get a media outlet to use inaccurate information one time, but they will never use you as a news resource again.

Be available when needed. If a journalist cannot reach you, he or she will call someone else and that source may offer inaccurate information.

Have a "legitimizing" title or position. This means you should form a media relations group within an existing organization, or better yet, form an organization or committee exclusively for this purpose.

Be willing to do the legwork for a journalist. If you do the work and provide the information, you shape the story without having to write it.

Be willing to offer information about those who oppose your views. You will gain credibility from providing a journalist with spokespeople from opposing viewpoints. The journalist will probably find these people anyway. Why not control this aspect of the story as well?

Become a one-stop-shopping source for information about the local Muslim community. Your name should be in every media gatekeeper's rolodex. You should be the first one called when a story impacts the Muslim community.

Your Goal: Becoming a "News Resource"

STARTING A MEDIA WATCH COMMITTEE

A media watch committee will carry out the following functions in the local Muslim community:

Monitoring the local media. This means making sure that all the local papers are read each day, most of the local news broadcasts are monitored, etc.

Responding to negative coverage. The response may include letters to the editor, editorials, calls to reporters, and/or meetings with editors. Pro-active activities such as media luncheons and conferences should also be organized.

Training community leaders in media relations. Many leaders in the Muslim community are inexperienced in this area. The media watch committee should handle the administrative aspects of media relations for these leaders (media databases, news releases, etc.) and offer practical training in the form of seminars and role-playing.

Organizing local responses to national and international events. Committees will coordinate protests, rallies, issuing statements, etc.

Steps to Forming a Media Watch Committee

1) Pick a name. Names such as "Islamic Information Service," "Minnesota Muslim Media Watch," "Concerned Muslims of Iowa," are good in that they offer members legitimizing titles of "coordinator," etc.

2) Pick a coordinator. This person should be someone who would do this kind of work even if the committee did not exist. The coordinator is not necessarily a "leader" in the community, but that person should have the trust of the local leadership.
3) Create a media database. Consult the "Media Gatekeepers" section of this handbook. Call all the local media outlets to find out contact information for these people.

Important note - Members of the media watch committee should also express and represent consensus views in the Muslim community. They must always stay within broad Islamic guidelines on any particular issue and avoid references to differences within the Muslim community. When dealing with the media, never offer sectarian views. It will confuse the media and the non-Muslim public. Always seek out and include each segment of the Muslim community in your efforts.

Example #1 - If you are asking the local food editor to do a story on "Recipes of Ramadan," supply recipes from India-Pakistan, the Middle East, America, Malaysia-Indonesia, etc.

Example #2 - If your committee organizes a news conference, try to include speakers from all segments of the community, including sisters.

CREATING A COMMUNITY ACTION ALERT NETWORK

There are two factors in any successful media event:

1) Media interest
2) Community involvement

You can be the best media relations person in the world, but if you cannot show support in the local community, your efforts will be wasted. Each time your committee organizes an event, a reaction to negative coverage or a meeting with the media, the turnout must demonstrate your credibility.

To make community members active participants in your activities, they must be informed and motivated. To inform the community, you must set up an "Action Alert" network similar to your news release distribution system. In fact, both of these audiences, the media and members of the Muslim community, can be reached using the ACT/ WinFax Pro software combination described in the "Media Gatekeepers" section of this handbook and the phone tree described in the following section.

Faxed action alerts cut down on expenses, increase enthusiasm and decrease response time. Those with computers can also take advantage of Internet opportunities. (SEE - "The Internet") Consider setting up an Internet email mailing list for local Muslim activists.

ORGANIZING A PHONE TREE

Steps to Organizing a Phone Tree:

1) Contact potential members of the phone tree.
2) Each person on the tree should receive a copy of that tree.
3) Limit the tree to four tiers for a total of 15 members.
4) Keep messages sent through the tree short and simple.
5) Have those at the bottom of the tree confirm receipt of the message by calling the coordinator.

MEDIA RELATIONS GUIDELINES

You are responsible for what is said about Islam in your local media. If a story is inaccurate or biased, do not blame the news media's "conspiracy." View it as a challenge to correct and educate.

Be a pro-active "news resource," not a reactive complainer. Your goal is to build long-term relationships with media outlets. Building trust and credibility comes from repeated contacts and demonstrated reliability.

Think visuals. All media, including newspapers, rely on visuals. In television, the video determines what goes in the story. If there is no video, there is no story. Use your creativity to provide built-in visuals for any story.

If you do not control the flow of information, someone else will. If you listen to those who say it is no use interacting with the media, you give an open invitation to those who would defame Islam.

Initiate contact with the media. Pitch stories. Don't just wait for a call. Remember that journalists must fill newspapers, radio programs and television broadcasts every day. They need and appreciate the help of people like you.

"Piggyback" on larger stories or trends. National and international news outlets will provide coverage of events outside your community. Local media must provide a local angle to these events. That is where you come in.

Act quickly to exploit opportunities. You must work within the journalist's work and news cycle, not yours. The best information is useless if offered too late.

Call during off-hours, not when a journalist is likely to be on deadline. Journalists are under extreme deadline pressure. They will ignore information that comes when they are "on deadline."

Do not complain unless there is evidence of actual malice. Education is the key. It is actually quite rare (at least on the local level) for journalists to defame Islam and Muslims out of conscious bias. They are most often ignorant of the basics of Islamic beliefs.

MEDIA GATEKEEPERS

Gatekeeper Rule #1 - Never stiff a gatekeeper.

Media "gatekeepers" are those behind-the-scenes people who determine what news you see, read or hear. They are not necessarily the people you read about in the newspaper, see on television or hear on the radio. For example, a television news anchor does not normally write the news stories or determine what will go in a particular broadcast. The news is written by a news producer and selected by an assignment editor.

Gatekeepers for the various media include:

TV

    News Assignment Editor - Selects stories to be covered and assigns reporters and/or photographers to those stories.

    Show Producer - Coordinates production of the entire news program

Radio

    News Directors - Similar to TV assignment editors

    Public Service Directors - Schedule and produce public service announcements

    Talk Show Producers/Hosts

Print

    City/Metro Editor

    Photo Editor

    Religion Writers/Calendar Editors

Feature Editors
Foreign Desk Editors
Letters Editor/Editorial Page Editor

Wire Services
Daybook Editor
News Editor
Bureau Chief

To find out who these people are in your area, just call the particular media outlet and ask. Keep a computer database of all these names, addresses and phone/fax numbers. Be able to fax pre-selected lists or produce mailing labels quickly.

NOTE - Computer software useful for maintaining media contacts and distributing media relations materials: ACT contact management software and WinFax Pro fax software. ACT interfaces with WinFax as a "phonebook," thereby allowing easy customization of fax distribution lists. These are the two most popular pieces of software in their categories and are available in computer stores and by mail.

LOCAL WIRE SERVICE BUREAUS

A "wire service" is a company organized to gather and distribute news and information in more than one area, region or country. The most important wire services are Associated Press (AP), United Press International (UPI) and Reuters. Most large cities will have an Associated Press, or "AP" bureau.

(SEE - "Wire Service Contact List") These bureaus feed news in two directions. They receive national and international news for distribution to local subscribers and they send local news gathered from these subscribers to national outlets.

The local wire services are a very important factor in your media relations effort. Each day, the local bureau distributes what is called a "DAYBOOK. " This daybook lists all the events the wire service editors believe might be worthy of coverage on that particular day. A listing on the daybook does not mean that your event will be covered. It just means that all media gatekeepers will know about the event and know that the wire service believes it is a newsworthy event.

To have your event listed on a wire service daybook in your area, just send a news release addressed to the "Daybook Editor" at your local bureau.

NOTE - The local wire service "Daybook Editor" is your most important media contact.

RESPONDING TO AN ANTI-MUSLIM INCIDENT

Rule #1 - Use facts, not emotion.

American Muslims are faced with unique challenges that sometimes result in anti-Muslim incidents in the workplace, in schools or in government agencies. Bias against Muslims is also expressed through the news media, both local and national. There are a number of steps that should be taken to deal with these incidents:

Determine the FACTS of the case. Too often, we rush into action without learning what really happened. That means acting like a news reporter. Get the WHO, WHAT, WHEN, WHERE, and WHY of the situation before deciding on a course of action. Make sure to get a response from the other side, whether it is a media outlet, a police department, an employer, or a school.

Decide on the appropriate action to be taken. There are several techniques for dealing with anti-Muslim incidents, including: 1) Issuing a statement from community leaders, 2) Holding a news conference to call for specific actions, 3) Organizing a protest, 4) Meeting with appropriate officials, or 5) Organizing a grass roots campaign of letter writing, etc.

Ask for attainable results. If someone were fired from their job for wearing hijab, a reasonable result would be getting the job back; an apology from the employer and a promise of reimbursement for lost wages. An unreasonable demand might be a request for one million dollars in damages for emotional distress.

Act quickly. Each incident must be dealt with when it happens, not when it is convenient. Actions that will have a decisive impact today may be worthless next week.

Go to the top. If an employee is discriminated against, don't bother with the low-level manager. Go right to the president of the company. If it is a chain store, contact the corporate headquarters, even if it is in another state. In cases of police abuse, go to the chief of police, the mayor, the state attorney general, etc. At a university, contact the dean's office.

Mobilize community support. There should be an established mechanism for letting the community know about these types of incidents. Community members must be given simple, specific actions they can take to support the leadership's effort. This can include making phone calls, writing letters, sending e-mail messages, and taking part in protests.

Stay on top of the situation. You must push (politely) for action to be taken to resolve the incident. Employers, the media, school officials, law enforcement agencies will respond if approached in the right way.

Announce results. When the incident is resolved, make an announcement to the same people and organizations contacted when the effort began.

RESPONDING TO MEDIA BIAS CHECKLIST

Who are the sources of information? Are Muslim representatives quoted? Are only hostile sources used?

From whose point of view is the news reported? Are all points of view considered?

What are the double standards? Are Muslims "fanatics" while others are "orthodox?"

What stereotypes are being used?

What are the unchallenged assumptions?

Is "loaded" language used?

Is there a lack of context?

Do the headlines and stories match?

LOCAL MEDIA OPPORTUNITIES

Community Newspapers

Community newspapers offer an excellent media opportunity for Muslims. If there are Muslims in a particular area of the city, write an article about those Muslims and their impact on the community's welfare. Remember, community papers are mainly interested in information that deals with the local neighborhood.

Very often, community newspaper editors will take an article submitted by a member of the community and run it "as is." They may even print a photograph supplied by the writer. Community newspaper editors are more or less forced to do this because they do not have the resources to research and write about all the news happening in their area. These papers are typically run by one or two people, who sell ads, write articles, paste up the newspaper, and even deliver it to newsstands. They appreciate any help they can get.

Local Cable Access

Most local cable companies offer low or no-cost training in video production. There are also opportunities to become part of a production crew on local programming. Take advantage of these opportunities to gain experience and to learn to produce Islamic programming.

Cable companies are also required by law to accept pre-produced programming for "local access." You can supply Islamic videos to be broadcast free of charge.

Public or University Radio

Most urban areas have opportunities to work as a volunteer at the local public radio station. Universities, and sometimes even high schools, also have radio studios. Those who have an interest in media production can gain valuable experience by volunteering their time.

CHARACTERISTICS OF A JOURNALIST

Rule #1 for Working with Journalists - They will expect you to do their work. Let them.

Do a little primary research. This gives you the opportunity to provide accurate and timely information. This is information that shapes the story in the way you want it shaped.

Under extreme deadline pressure. This pressure means a journalist must rely on you to help him or her meet the deadline.

Fears charges of inaccuracy. Will respond to criticism of information presented in any story. If the criticism is constructive, the journalist will generally do better "next time."

MEDIA RELATIONS BLUNDERS TO AVOID

Becoming hostile or threatening. The journalist will merely hang up and ignore what you have said.

Overuse of rhetoric. Rhetoric prevents the journalist from using your materials.

Trying to "overtly" manipulate coverage. Journalists do not mind working with groups that have a particular viewpoint and will include that viewpoint in their stories. They do resent open attempts to dictate content.

Example - A journalist will sometimes appreciate an offer to check foreign terms in an article. Just tell the journalist you are available to make sure he or she "doesn't get any angry calls" about terminology from Muslims after the story runs. Journalists recognize that they are unfamiliar with Islamic terminology.

Providing inaccurate information. You will be crossed off the "news resource" list.

MEDIA RELATIONS WRITING

Write in "AP" Style
Write with nouns and verbs
Avoid foreign words or jargon
Be clear and concise
Rewrite, rewrite, rewrite
Use short sentences and paragraphs
Give facts, not opinions
Put opinions in quotes with attribution
Use an active, not passive voice
Triple check for accuracy

The Inverted Pyramid

Schools of journalism teach a particular writing style called the "inverted pyramid." This name is derived from the image of an upside-down pyramid formed when the most important information is placed at the beginning of a story and the least important being used at the end of the story.

An EXAMPLE of the "who, what, when, where, and why" of a story being included in the lead sentence of a news release:

(NOTE the use of the "pronouncer" for Ramadan. This helps television and radio anchors hosts and reporters say it right. Spell out the words phonetically and underline syllables to be emphasized.)

WASHINGTON, D.C. - On February 1, the Muslim community in America and around the world will begin the month-long fast of Ramadan (rom-a-don). Ramadan is the month on the Islamic lunar calendar during which Muslims abstain from food, drink and other sensual pleasures from dawn to sunset. The fast of Ramadan is performed in order to learn discipline, self-restraint and generosity while obeying God's commandments.

News Releases

News Release Rule #1 - Without a news release, any coverage you receive will be by accident.

Corollary to Rule #1 - A good news release only increases your chances of coverage. It cannot guarantee coverage.

How a News Release is Used

A news release is the basic means of communication between any Muslim community and the news media. A good news release reads like a good story or at least the framework for a good story. The less re-writing it takes to use your release, the greater its chance of being used. Its use "as is" also decreases the likelihood of inaccuracy or bias in any story about the Muslim community.

Different media professionals use news releases in different ways. For example, a religion editor may use your release to write an item for the religion calendar. That same person may also use the release as the basis for a story. The news editor may use the release to assign a photographer to the story. A public service director might use the release to make a pre-event announcement.

Every day, media outlets receive hundreds of news releases from organizations seeking coverage. Most get just a 10-second scan.

What Editors look for in a News Release?

"Give a Rip" factor - The news release must offer an interesting story.
Cultural diversity - Media outlets are under pressure to include more "multicultural" news.
Local angles
Contrariness - Editors look for stories that go "against the grain."
Tie-ins to national of international events or trends
Famous people/Human interest
Kickers and other niches
Visual appeal

Good Reasons to Send out a Release

Tie-in with news of the day
Staged media events
Social service efforts such as food drives, blood donations, etc.
Protests
Release of survey results, position statements, etc.
Building a new masjid
Achievements of local Muslims
Lectures and conferences

Types of News Releases

Media Advisory
Short and to the point
Lists photo/sound opportunities
Contains notes to media outlets
Time sensitive

Public Service Announcement

Conversational style/Written to be heard
Light on facts
Timed
ALL CAPS
Repeats important information
Use "pronouncers" - phonetic spellings of foreign or uncommon words

Feature

Can be longer than one page
Focused on trend or broad issue
Not as time sensitive

News Release Components

Contact Listing - The release should be directed to a particular person.
Letterhead - You can create your own letterhead using a computer.
Typeface - Use common typefaces such as "Times" and "Helvetica."
Release Date and Contact Information - Indicate when the release was issued and who may be contacted for more information. Be sure to list pager and cellular phone numbers.
Headline/Sub-Head
Must summarize "angle" of the story
Must grab attention
Lead Paragraph
Spacing/Length - Try to double space. Keep to one page if possible.
Conclusion - State standard facts that can be used in an intro or tag.
- END-, - 30 -, or ### - Indicates the end of the news release.

Press Kits

News Release
Backgrounder
Q&A
Reprints of articles
List of event participants

NEWS RELEASE CHECK LIST

Rhetorical phrases have been eliminated or placed in quotes and attributed to a spokesperson.
"END," "-30-" or "###" is included at the end of the release.
The release has been triple-checked for accuracy and the facts have been verified.

The release is printed on plain white, letter-sized paper. Paper clips are used instead of staples.

The release is double-spaced, or single-spaced with room on the margins.

"Media Advisory," "News Release" or "Public Service Announcement" is at the top of the release.

The phrase "FOR IMMEDIATE RELEASE" is included on the release.

Contact information, including phone, fax, pager, cellular, World Wide Web site and e-mail is indicated.

A summary headline is used.

Editorials/Opinion Pieces

Opinion pieces and editorials can have quite an impact on the public debate about any issue. To make effective use of the editorial pages, a media relations committee should:

Contact the editorial board of the newspaper to get a clear understanding of the editorial guidelines for that newspaper. For example, some newspapers will not consider an article that has also been submitted to another publication.

Arrange a meeting with the editorial page editor or editorial board. (SEE - "Meeting With Editorial Boards and Station Officials")

Read the opinion pages every day and be prepared to react quickly to offending articles.

Keep articles to between 800 and 1200 words.

Stress local impact.

Address humanitarian concerns.

Take a contrary stance on major issues.

Keep trying. A high rejection rate is normal.

Other tips:

Double-space text.

Use statistics or a quotation from a legitimate source.

If you are not a native speaker, have one check for style and usage.

STAGING MEDIA EVENTS

Media Event Rule #1 - Remember the "kicker."
Key Points to Remember

News about your community should not just "happen." You should make it happen. Much of the news that you read, see or hear is the result of so-called "media events." These are pre-arranged activities designed to attract the media and convey a particular message to the public. As Muslims we have several ready-made media events:

Ramadan
Jumah prayers
Eid ul-Fitr/Eid ul-Adha
Hajj
Activities which tie-in to national and international news (Bosnia, the Middle East, etc.)

Points to remember when organizing a media event:

Make sure to build visuals into the event. For example, the media are bored with ordinary protests. Why not stage "street theater" that highlights your issue (Young men dressed in "Serbian" army uniforms attacking Muslim women, etc.) Make sure to describe these "photo opportunities" in your news release.

Timing is important. Never schedule media events in the late afternoon. Events held at this time will not fit into the newsgathering work cycle. (SEE - "Media Event Scheduling")

Designate one or two people as media contacts for the event. Make sure all those who are participating in the event know to direct media inquiries to these people.

Send out a news release about the event as early as possible.

Follow up with phone calls to key media gatekeepers. (SEE - "Media Gatekeepers")

Types of Media Events

Good Deeds Tied to Issues
News Conferences

Protests
Informational Leafleting
Open Houses
Conferences/Lectures
Inter-Faith Dialogues
Media Luncheons

Media Event Scheduling
Journalist's Daily Work Cycle

9 a.m.	arrive at station
10 a.m.	attend morning news meeting
10:30 a.m.	make calls to sources
11 a.m.	on the road
11 a.m.-2 p.m.	do interviews/shoot video
2:30-5 p.m.	pull sound bites/log video/write and voice script
5-6 p.m.	report on air

Best and Worst Times to Hold Media Events

Best	Worst	Never
10 a.m. - 1 p.m.	2-6 p.m.	4-5 p.m.
7 - 8:30 p.m.		

MEDIA EVENT CHECK LIST

A news release has been delivered to all local media "gatekeepers."
The local wire service "Daybook" editor has been notified.
A media kit has been prepared containing a statement, a copy of the news release and relevant backgrounders and fact sheets.
An articulate, knowledgeable spokesperson has been selected.
Representatives from all major groupings within the community have been invited to take part.
Sisters will be represented at the event.
Spokespeople have met and decided on appropriate "talking points."
All participants have agreed to stick to the talking points.
A suitable site has been selected.
If the event will be held in a mosque or Islamic center, approval

has been obtained and relevant parties notified.

A table or podium has been arranged.

If the event is outside, a microphone stand has been obtained (available from Radio Shack).

Room at the site has been made for television cameras.

Signs directing media to the site have been put up.

Steps to Holding a News Conference

Determine the location. A mosque is the easiest and cheapest place to hold a news conference. It also provides other visuals (people praying, exterior shots) to be included in any story and shows the non-Muslim public that there are Muslims in their community. An alternative is a hotel conference room. These rooms may cost $100-200 for one or two hours. Also, most major cities will have a "Press Club" that offers rooms for this purpose.

REMEMBER - It is better to book a room that is too small than one that is too large.

Contact those who will be attending the news conference to get their approval on the broad outline of the format and statement. They must trust the coordinator to come up with final language.

Fax out the news release. Remember to send one to the local wire service "Daybook Editor."

Arrange to have the conference participants arrive early to discuss the format, etc.

After the media are set up, introduce the participants and give their organizational affiliations.

Read a SHORT statement. (SEE - "Statements") Offer other participants an opportunity to say a few words (1 minute) and then take questions.

BEING INTERVIEWED BY THE MEDIA

Interviewing Tips

What to Do before Being Interviewed

Write down likely questions.

Practice with someone.

Gather statistics to support your views.

What to Do When You Receive a Call Asking for an Interview

Clarify who is calling

Find out "angle" of story

Ad Libbing vs. "Talking Points"

"Talking points" are the 3-4 pre-planned messaged that you want to put forward during any interview. These points should be worked out and memorized well in advance of any interview. They should be:

Positive - "Islam is a faith of peace and forbids harming innocent people."

Challenging - "The media must adopt one standard when dealing with religiously oriented violence."

Truthful - "The Muslim community is also in need of development in terms of social and political activism."

What to Remember during an Interview

You are in control of the interview.

You can ask that a question be re-stated.

You can give your answer a second time - and that answer should be used.

Begin with your talking points.

Summarize at end of interview.

It is a dialogue, not a conversation.

When you finish your answer, stop talking.

It is in a reporter's best interest to make you sound articulate.

Deflecting Statements

"Let's look at this issue from a broader perspective."

"There is an equally important concern."

"Let's not lose sight of the underlying problem."

TALK SHOWS

Talk Show Rule # 1 - If you look good, they look good.

There are many opportunities to appear on local radio and television talk shows. Talk show producers and hosts look for guests, who are knowledgeable, articulate and legitimate. Take stock of the people in your community who might project a favorable image of Islam and Muslims. These potential guests may not be the leaders of the community, but to be effective they must be given the support of the community's leadership.

Who Runs the Show?
Producer
Public Service Director
News Director
Program Director

Things Producers look for in a Guest
Available and punctual
Articulate
Authoritative/Legitimate
Ability to translate complex topics into digestible form

Steps Necessary for Any Booking

1) Pre-call - Call to gauge interest and get contact information.
2) Pitch letter - Send information as to why your issue would be of interest to audience.
3) Follow-up - Call back to press for an answer.
4) Pre-interview - A phone dialogue in which the host/producer will probe for guest suitability and information.
5) Confirming letter - A courtesy
6) Re-confirming call - The day before the interview

On-Air Etiquette

Let the technical people do their job.
Don't be wishy-washy.
Use interviewer's first name.
Never question interviewer's knowledge.
If you must correct, do so lightly.
Don't read responses.
No notes (TV).

3x5 card notes allowed on radio.

Learn to take cues.

Remember all mikes are "hot."

Don't look at the camera or the monitor.

Sample Script for Phone Conversations with the Media

You speaking to receptionist at radio station:

"HELLO...COULD I HAVE THE NAME AND DIRECT PHONE NUMBER OF PERSON WHO PRODUCES THE "GOOD MORNING SEATTLE" SHOW?

Operator:

"YES THE HER NAME IS MARY SMITH...HER DIRECT LINE IS 543-1234...WOULD YOU LIKE ME TO CONNECT YOU?

You:

"YES"

Producer:

"THIS IS MARY SMITH...

You:

"YES...MY NAME IS ANISA ABDULLAH...I AM A MEMBER OF THE SEATTLE RAMADAN INFORMATION COMMITTEE...OUR COMMITTEE THOUGHT YOU MIGHT BE INTERESTED IN DOING A PROGRAM ABOUT THE UPCOMING MONTH OF RAMADAN...ARE YOU AWARE OF WHAT RAMADAN IS?

Producer:

"YES...I KNOW A LITTLE ABOUT THE FAST OF RAMADAN AND MIGHT BE INTERESTED IN DOING SOMETHING WITH IT...CAN YOU SEND ME SOME INFORMATION?"

You:

"YES...I HAVE FACT SHEETS AND BACKGROUND MATERIAL DEALING WITH RAMADAN.

Producer:

"THAT'S GREAT...SEND ME THE MATERIAL AND I'LL SEE WHAT I CAN DO"

You:

"I'll SEND IT OUT TODAY...OR I COULD FAX IT TO YOU IF YOU WOULD PREFER...I'LL ALSO CALL BACK IN ABOUT A WEEK TO SEE WHAT YOU THINK OF THE MATERIALS...

Taking Cues

One minute - The producer or floor director raises an index finger to indicate one minute remaining in the program.

30 seconds - An index finger is held up but is now bent in half.

Wrap - The index finger is circled in the air. This cue tells the host to end the program quickly but with a natural flow of dialogue.

Cut - The index finger is drawn across the neck. This cue indicated the need for an urgent end to the program without the need for a natural end to dialogue.

Stretch - A sign similar to someone pulling taffy. It indicates that the host needs to fill more time with dialogue.

Dealing with Tough Questions

Answer the question you would have liked them to ask.

Return to your talking points.

Laugh. This indicates you do not feel threatened by the question. It also gives you a little time to think up a response.

Say: "I will research the subject and get back to you in person after the show. Please leave your number with the station reception desk."

If you do not know, say so.

Use deflecting statements.

"Let's look at this issue from a broader perspective."

"There is an equally important concern."

"Let's not lose sight of the underlying problem."

Blunders to Avoid

Use of rhetoric

Defamatory language

Attacking other faiths

Inaccurate information

Use of foreign words

Being late for an interview

"Missionary" tone

Summarizing Sound Bites

Summarize key points in no more than 15 seconds.

Use no more than two sentences.

Use colorful language in points you want to be sound bites.

Why was CAIR established?

The Council on American-Islamic Relations (CAIR) is a nonprofit, grassroots membership organization. We have headquarters in Washington, D.C., and chapters exist or are being formed in most major cities across America. CAIR was established to promote a positive image of Islam and Muslims in America. We believe misrepresentations of Islam are most often the result of ignorance on the part of non-Muslims and reluctance on the part of Muslims to articulate their cause.

What is CAIR's mission?

CAIR is dedicated to presenting an Islamic perspective on issues of importance to the American public. In offering that perspective, we seek to empower the Muslim community in America through political and social activism.

How does CAIR carry out its mission?

Media Relations
We work with media professionals around America to help shape a positive image of Islam. CAIR activists also monitor the local, national and international media to challenge negative stereotypes of Islam and Muslims.

Conferences and Seminars
We organize conferences and seminars for media professionals, government officials and the academic community. These events are designed to present otherwise unavailable information about Islam and Muslims.

Publications
A variety of publications addressing the needs of Muslims in America are offered to opinion leaders and the public. We also publish a quarterly newsletter CAIR News. CAIR also produces practical handbooks, such as "Hajj and Ramadan Publicity Resource Kits," for use by Muslim leaders and activists.

Action Alerts

CAIR issues action alerts to local communities as a means of promoting local activism and generating a grassroots response on important issues. We believe local response is a key factor in making our voices heard.

Research

CAIR undertakes research on subjects relevant to the American Muslim community, including gathering data for an annual report on the status of Muslim civil rights. This report details anti-Muslim bias and violence. Position papers on a variety of issues relating to Muslims in America are produced as required.

Anti-Discrimination Work

CAIR works through its legal advisors and local activists in fighting discrimination of any type directed against Muslims in America. This discrimination often relates to misuse of Islamic symbols or the violation of civil rights in the workplace.

Lobbying

We lobby American political leaders on issues related to Islam and Muslims in America. Issues of particular interest include freedom of expression and religious practice for Muslims in America.

Training/Outreach

CAIR trains American Muslim community activists and leaders in techniques of effective media and public relations, lobbying and public speaking. Experts are available to offer seminars in local communities.

Internships

CAIR offers internships to students and other interested individuals who wish to gain experience in media relations, political activism and anti-discrimination work.

Inter-Faith Relations

Islam places much stress on promoting mutual respect and good relations between followers of the Abrahamic faiths. CAIR works toward this goal through public education and inter-faith cooperation.

EDUCATIONAL
CONCERNS

Islamic Studies
in America

Seyyed Hossein Nasr

The name of Islam appears in the news nearly every day and several million Muslims constitute an element of American society, which can no longer be ignored. The thought of Islamic philosophers and the contribution of Islamic scientists is embedded in one way or another in the background of the philosophy and science being cultivated in the Western world including America; and words of Arabic and Persian origin are used in American English more than Japanese, Chinese or Hindi words. The adobe architecture of the American Southwest reflects clearly its Islamic influence through both its forms and its building techniques as well as the word adobe itself; and the poetry of the Islamic people is read and the music heard to an ever greater degree in this land. Yet, despite all these and many other similar facts, the state of Islamic studies in America is far from satisfactory.

In this essay, which is confined to Islamic studies in American colleges and universities, we wish to consider some of the factors which prevent Islamic studies from occupying the position one would expect for a field which embraces the culture and history of a billion people stretching across the Afro-Asian land mass with important extensions into Europe and now to an ever greater degree the Americas. One must ask why it is that whole areas of the Islamic world, such as Southeast Asia, fail even to be considered in most centers of Islamic studies; and why, despite so many universities where Islamic studies is taught, America has produced so few outstanding scholars in this field who can be compared to such European Islamicists as Louis Massignon, Sir Hamilton Gibb or Henry Corbin. One must, of course, also ask why much of the fruit of scholarship in Islamic studies in America is so strongly opposed by Muslims despite the attempt by a number of American scholars to cultivate a more sympathetic view of Islam than that which was developed by classical European orientalism.

Some of the causes for the existing state of affairs are related to the history of the development of Islamic studies as a discipline in this country. The early American scholars of Islam were mostly missionaries with an often open and vocal opposition to Islam. A number of the early scholars, however, came from the background of Rabbinical studies and, since they belonged to the era preceding the partition of Palestine in 1948, did not feel the need to produce the polarized and "motivated" scholarship associated with Zionism which has affected Islamic studies so greatly since the decade of the 50s. There appeared among them, therefore, some outstanding figures who contributed greatly to Islamic studies, such scholars as Harry A. Wolfson, who although primarily a scholar of Jewish thought, made notable contributions to the history of Islamic theology (*Kalam*) and philosophy. Among the pioneers of Islamic studies there were also a number of Maronites like Phillip Hitti, who, while being outstanding scholars of Arabic, were not Muslims although they were seen by many in America as authentic voices of Islamic scholarship since most people almost naturally equated Muslim and Arab. Many of these early scholars, however, had little love for the specifically Islamic dimension of the subject, which they were studying, although they helped to advance the cause of Arabic studies.

Despite the appearance of a number of scholars of distinction, there existed from the beginning a trait in Islamic studies in America which distinguished it from, let us say, Chinese, Japanese or Indian studies, this trait being an opposition to or even disdain for Islam and its culture among many scholars in this field. Usually, when an American went into the field of Far Eastern studies, a few missionaries being the exception, he was attracted to some aspect of that civilization or religion which he loved and defended as can be seen by the attitude of Langdon Warner of Harvard University, who played such an important role in saving Kyoto from being bombed during the Second World War. This attitude of love and empathy has manifested itself much less frequently in Islamic studies, not that of course it was or is totally absent.

After the Second World War, with America entering the international scene in an active way, a new phase opened in the history of Islamic studies, which caused the field to expand, but at the expense of depth and concern for the historical and religious dimension. Centers of regional studies began to be developed in many universities throughout the country from Harvard to UCLA, usually under the name of Middle Eastern but also, occasionally, Near Eastern studies. Oriented mostly toward the present day period and based upon the social sciences rather than theology, religion or the humanities, these centers taught many subjects concerning the Islamic world but with the minimum of reference to Islam itself. A whole generation of scholars was trained, some of whom became decision makers in America, who affected the history of the Islamic world itself, usually in an adverse manner, while the majority became experts and scholars of the central regions of the Islamic world. With a number of notable exceptions, however, few of these scholars made any outstanding contributions to Islamic studies or could predict any of the major transformations which came about in the region of their specialization, transformations such as the revival of Islam in various forms in the decade of the 70s. It is only the events of the past ten years in the Islamic world that have forced many of these centers to pay more attention to Islam in the Middle East.

Even to this day, however, in many of the major centers of Middle Eastern studies everything is taught seriously except Islam itself. One sees often in such centers numerous courses on history, anthropology, languages, sociology, political science and similar subjects pertaining to the Islamic world but little study in-depth of Islam as the religion which forms the heart and arteries of the body of the society and civilization being considered.

There are, in fact, in America only a handful of institutions of higher learning, like the University of Chicago and Temple University, where Islam is studied seriously in the religion department as religion and not as something else. Moreover, despite the rapid expansion of religious studies in this continent during the past four decades to include "non-Western" religions and the establishment of centers for the study of religion on a world wide scale such as those at Harvard, Colgate and Claremont, Islam has not at all fared as well as Hinduism, Buddhism or the Chinese religions. The discipline of comparative religion, in fact, has produced very few Islamicists of note. Besides the historical opposition to Islam in the Christian West, going back to the Crusades and the Reconquest in Spain, which affects almost unconsciously the attitude of many modern Westerners, including those who do not even consider themselves to be Christian, there is the question of the way religious studies has evolved.

During the 19th century, there developed in the field of "the science of religions", or *Religionwissenschaft*, the idea of the evolution of religion from so-called "primitive" to higher forms, reaching its peak with Christianity. Such a conception of religious history, which continued into this century, obviously had great difficulty coming to terms with such a major postscript as Islam. As a reaction to this historicism, there developed the school of phenomenology which had its most influential representative in America in the person of M. Eliade, who himself made major contributions to nearly every field of religious studies except Islam. With its emphasis upon myths and symbols, this school was much more attracted to such traditions as Hinduism, whose truths are, for the most part, expressed in mythological language, than to Islam, whose metaphysical and theological teachings are couched mostly in "abstract" language and whose teachings include a Sacred Law which is central to the understanding of the religion.

To these factors were added the age-old distortions of Islam as the "religion of the sword" or the "dry" religion of the desert, whose blindingly clear spirituality was supposedly somehow borrowed from foreign sources and grafted upon the body of Islam. As a result of this preference for myths in teaching Hinduism, for example, usually such sublime texts as the Baghawad-Gita were taught and not laws of inheritance in various castes and sub-castes, and Hindu art is taught rather than social and commercial conflicts. In the case of Islam, only the most external aspects of the religion were taught along with a distorted portrayal of a religion in constant conflict and at war.

The result of all these factors has been that Islamic studies has not fared well as religious studies even when compared to Hindu, Buddhist or Chinese religious studies, despite, or perhaps because of, the fact that Islam is theologically much closer to Judaism and Christianity and that Islam has shared so much more common history with the Christian West than the Indian and Far Eastern religions. It is interesting to note that the incredible synthesis created in Muslim Spain, where, under Muslim rule, Muslims, Jews and Christian lived together in peace for several centuries, contributing to a glittering civilization in which they all played a role, is passed over more or less in silence. Almost no one refers to the Judeo/Christian/Islamic tradition, but on the contrary, in forgetfulness of the reality of Abrahamic monotheism and to abet the cause of passing political goals, most scholars juxtapose the Judeo-Christian heritage to the Islamic.

Not only has Islamic studies fared poorly by and large poorly in the field of religion, it has been also neglected in the field of the humanities. Whether it be in philosophy or history, literature or the arts,

Islamic studies in America has not succeeded in flowering in any notable manner in comparison with, let us say, Japanese studies. Not only in medieval European universities did the Islamic humanities play a greater role than they do today in America, but even during the Romantic movement in England and Germany there was greater interest, at least in the literature of the Islamic peoples, than one finds today.

It is only in the field of the social sciences that Islamic studies or, rather, subjects related to the Islamic world have been treated fairly extensively in America. Here, however, there stands the major question of whether Western models apply to the Islamic world. Is it possible to study Islamic society on the basis of the theories of Durkheim, or to carry out an anthropological study of a part of the Islamic world on the basis of the theories of Levi-Strauss? These are major questions, which are now being debated, and one hopes that, as a result, more serious contributions will be made to Islamic studies in those fields which, in the West, are called the social sciences. Until that is done, however, even in this domain where so much effort is being spent, the results will usually not have much to do with the social and religious reality of the Islamic world.

As for law, which plays such an important role in Islam, it is only during the past decade that certain American law schools have begun to teach Islamic Law and that, mostly, for practical reasons. The teaching of the Divine Law, or Shari'ah, however, has not become part and parcel of Islamic studies and few American scholars have made notable contributions to this field.

At the heart of Islamic studies stands not only the religion of Islam, but also the languages involved in the study of that religion and the civilization it brought into being. Arabic is the most important of Islamic languages and has been taught in America since the 18th century. In recent decades, however, despite the appearance of several eminent Arabists who either themselves or their families migrated from the Islamic world, such as George Makdisi and Irfan Shahid, and the appearance of a number of fine American Arabists, such as Jamies Bellamy, William Brenner, Victor Danner, Richard Frank and Nicholas Heer, the teaching of Arabic has still suffered as far as Islamic studies is concerned. The main reason has been the emphasis upon "modern" Arabic at the expense of the classical language. Until recently, in most centers of Arabic studies, Qur'anic Arabic was made subservient to the prose of al-Ahram, and little attention was paid to the fact that, among literate Arabs themselves, the Qur'an is read and understood first, and only later is modern literary Arabic mastered. During the past decade some changes have been made in the direction of classical Arabic and more students are now being trained who can read classical texts. The state of the training is far from complete because too few students with advanced degrees are actually able to read classical Arabic texts with full in-depth comprehension of their meaning.

The situation of the second major Islamic language, Persian, is much more deplorable. First of all, even the name of the language is now used incorrectly, it frequently being called "Farsi" as if in English one calls French "Francais" or German "Deutsch". Second, it is usually forgotten that not only is Persian (by whatever name it is called) still the spoken and written language of Iraq, Afghanistan and Tajikistan as well as that of many people in Iraq the Persian Gulf and Pakistan, but that for a thousand years it was the lingua franca of Asia. Quranic commentaries in China were written in Persian, while even after the Second World War, just before Albania became Communist, Persian books continued to be printed in this Western outpost of the Islamic world. Without knowledge of Persian, the Muslim culture of India and most of its medieval history, both Hindu and Muslim, is a closed book, and later Islamic thought, as it developed in the eastern lands of Islam, a forbidden territory. The remarkable indifference to the teaching of Persian in many American universities has done much to weaken Islamic studies and to prevent well-rounded students from being trained. Persian is essential not only for those studying eastern history, literature and the arts, but also Islamic studies itself where some of the most important figures such as Ghazzali wrote in both Arabic and Persian.

The other major Islamic languages, such as Turkish, Urdu, Bengali and Malay, are taught here and there but rarely as an integral part of Islamic studies. This is partly due to an unfortunate classification of religions, which is detrimental to Islamic studies, the division in question being the one between Eastern religions and Western religions. In many universities Islam is taught as a Western religion despite being "non-Western." This is correct to the extent that Islam is an integral part of Abrahamic monotheism of which Judaism and Christianity are the other two branches. But whereas these branches were to grow primarily in the West, Islam was destined to spread as much in the East as the West. There are more Muslims in Southeast Asia today than in the whole of the Arab world. The religious life and culture of several hundred million Muslims in South Asia, Bangladesh, Indonesia, Malaysia and China is hardly ever mentioned in general courses on Islam and not even known to any appreciable degree by advanced students in the field.

Likewise, African Islam is rarely treated as part of Islamic studies. General courses on Islam and its history deal only accidentally and tangentially with Africa south of the Sahara, and courses on Africa rarely relate the advent and history of Islam in Africa to the rest of the Islamic world. It is possible to attain the highest degree in Islamic studies and not know anything about either the great Islamic empires of Mali nor of the millions of Muslims living in Xinjiang (Sinkiang). A work such as the *Venture of Islam* by Marshall Hodgson, who was one of the most gifted American scholars of Islam, covers the whole of the Islamic world in time as well as geographically in a manner that is quite exceptional and far from the usual treatment that is given to the subject.

The criticism made of Islamic studies in America should not detract from the achievement made in this domain by a number of American scholars in so many fields such as Islamic history, anthropology, sociology, the history of art and archaeology, music, literature, philosophy, the history of science and several aspects of the religion of Islam itself. But considering the importance of the subjects, the existing distortions and the price in terms of practical matters which the Islamic world is as well as America have paid and continue to pay as a result the misunderstanding of Islam and the Islamic world in America, it is necessary to investigate a means whereby the situation can improved. It must, therefore, be asked what can be done to improve the condition of Islamic studies while benefiting from achievements of the past few decades and learning from mistakes. This question must, moreover, be asked in light of the fact that Islamic studies in America involves, to great degree, the Islamic world itself, as a result of the presence of a large number of Muslim students in America, as well as a number of Muslim scholars and teachers whose works have an external influence not only upon these students but also within Islamic countries.

The first and most important step which must be taken in Islamic studies, is to study this field within the framework of religion rather than a discipline, which, no matter how significant in itself, is not concerned with religion as such. As already mentioned, in the vast majority of institutions of learning in America, Islam is studied as history, language, culture, a political system and the like but not as a religion. The heart of Islamic studies must be moved from all these other disciplines or regional centers and placed in religion departments where the religious significance of all things Islamic can be brought outside the Islamic world.

Not only theology and ethics should be taught, but also economics and politics, not to speak of the arts and sciences which possess a much greater religious significance than their counterparts in post-medieval European civilization. The greatest source of distortion is the application of the secular perspective of the past few centuries in the West to a religious civilization where it does not apply. The activity in the bazaar a Muslim city is economic activity but it is not just economic activity. It possesses a religious dimension which is crucial to its understanding and without which any study of it will be superficial, to say the least.

In stating that Islamic studies should be placed in religion departments, however, it is not meant that the contemporary Western religious categories should be applied blindly to Islam. For example, in Christianity, theology is much more central than law, whereas in Islam, law is more central. In Christianity, mysticism was never organized into orders independent of the authority of the Church, whereas in Islam, Sufi orders have always been independent of the exoteric "ulama". In fact, the whole question of religious authority is posed in a different way in the two traditions. There is need to make use of a theology and, in fact, metaphysics of comparative religion which is able to deal with Islam in a manner that does justice to the nature of that tradition and yet is comprehensible to the Western world view. The prejudices which have marred the study of Islam in the West since the time of Peter the Venerable, when the Qur'an was first rendered into Latin and even before that important event, must finally be overcome if understanding in-depth is to be achieved. Unfortunately, despite so many claims to objectivity, much of Western scholarship concerning Islam remains distorted as a result of many old prejudices to which new ones, resulting from the Arab-Israeli conflict and the rise of so-called fundamentalism, have been added.

Despite this fact, however, Islam must be first and foremost studied as a religion and not simply a social force or historical event. This task is made easier by the appearance of a number of works in European languages, during the past few decades, which speak, with both sympathy and authority about Islam. Most of these works have been written by Westerners who have developed an understanding of the Islamic tradition or who speak from within that tradition. A number of books in this category of writings have also been written by Muslims themselves but in European languages, primarily English and French. Although some of these works do not address the Western mind and the questions usually posed by a Westerner in quest of understanding Islam, others do succeed in creating a bridge between the Islamic world and the West. In any case, the in-depth, thorough and sympathetic yet objective study of the Islamic religion and the placing of this study at the heart of Islamic studies is a necessary task which is already facilitated by the research, study and writings of those Western and Muslim scholars who speak with the voice of authority in such a manner that they are accepted by Muslims themselves, and at the same time, are comprehensible to the Western audience.

There is, in any case, no excuse for the large number of Middle Eastern, Near Eastern or Islamic studies programs in which Islam is relegated to a single introductory course and everything else Islamic, whether it be history, art, sociology or economics is taught in almost complete detachment from the Islamic tradition which in reality is the lifeblood of all those other domains. Nor is there any excuse for the remarkably weak representation of Islam in so many comparative religious studies programs throughout the country where there are often several professors in Hindu, Buddhist and Far Eastern religious studies but hardly anyone in Islam. Of all the major religions of the worlds, Islam fares worst in most religious studies programs in America. Until that weakness is solved, there is little hope for a serious improvement in the situation of Islamic studies.

Once Islamic studies is constituted in such a manner that at its heart stands the religion and its study, then it is possible and even necessary to relate this central concern to a number of fields such as sociology, economics, international relations, political science as well as the humanities for those students who wish to have such an interdisciplinary education. This is particularly true of Muslim students coming to America for advanced education. To an even greater degree, such students are interested in studying not only economics, sociology, anthropology or, for that matter, the history of art or the history of science. They are primarily interested in Islam in relation to those fields. In light of the present day interest within the Islamic world in the process that has become known as "the Islamization of Knowledge", this type of interdisciplinary approach could become one of the most fruitful developments in Islamic studies in America with far-reaching consequences for the Islamic world itself. But the condition of success in this program remains a carefully prepared core Islamic studies program grounded in religious studies.

The second important consideration in improving Islamic studies is the proper teaching of the Islamic languages. As far as Arabic is concerned, fortunately, much attention is being paid to the subject, but still not enough to classical Arabic. As already stated, emphasis should be placed upon classical Arabic, which must serve as the basis for modern Arabic and not vice versa. Also, greater attention should be paid to the reading of classical texts and being able to interpret these texts according to the traditional methods of hermeneutics. Earlier orientalism, despite its numerous prejudices, rendered much service to Islamic studies by editing critically many important texts. Even this art, however, is being lost especially in America where so many young scholars prefer to write about texts without being able to read them carefully, not to speak of editing them. The fault in this matter lies most of all in the manner in which Arabic is taught.

As for Persian, the whole philosophy of teaching it must be changed. Persian must first of all be recognized for what it is, namely the lingua franca of what Toynbee called the "Iranic zone" of Islamic civilization stretching from Iraq to China. After Arabic, Persian is the most important Islamic language and the only language other than Arabic, which became global within Islamic civilization. No program of Islamic studies can be considered serious without the teaching of Persian. Arabic is, of course, very important for Semitic linguistic studies where it is studied along with Hebrew, Aramaic, Syriac and other Semitic languages. But this relationship has little to do with the relationship of Arabic to Persian and, through Persian, to other major Islamic languages such as Turkish and Urdu. Islamic studies, in contrast to Semitic studies, must emphasize this latter relationship and teach both Arabic and Persian to students seriously interested in Islamic studies, especially as far as Islamic thought is concerned.

As for the other Islamic languages, they must also be offered in major centers. A number of centers will, naturally specialize in a particular region of the Islamic world such as North Africa, South Asia or Southeast Asia in which case, Berber, Hindi or Malay must be taught. But the role of such languages, and even such a major languages as Turkish, is that of a vernacular language while Arabic and Persian constitute the classical and universal languages of the Islamic world. These languages, because of their immense richness and long history, must be mastered in depth and on the basis of a program, which would enable at least a small number of students to gain full mastery of them. American institutions of learning have not as yet been as successful in this endeavor as the amount of effort spent would lead one to expect. There has, however, been more success in the field of Arabic than Persian where there are very few American scholars who possess complete mastery over the classical literature. But the flowering of Islamic studies requires a deepening of language teaching in such a manner that at least a number of young scholars are trained every year who can read and translate with precision the texts with which Islamic studies is concerned.

As for different aspects of Islamic studies, the situation varies from one field to another. In the field history, a number of gifted young scholars have been trained, but there is a shortage of competent scholars in the field to the extent that many of the works written around the turn of the century continue to be reprinted and taught despite many important new discoveries which have been made since they were written. It is necessary to encourage a greater number of students with a real flair for history to turn to the subject of Islamic history by emphasizing not only the significance of the field itself, but also its relation to other major fields of history such as medieval European history, Indian history and the like.

In the field of philosophy, Islamic studies in America suffers particularly from the fact that the prevalent philosophical trend in America since the Second World War is particularly opposed to the religious and metaphysical concerns of Islamic philosophy. This fact, added to the lack of attention paid to the study of philosophy in secondary schools, has prevented Islamic philosophy from attracting as many gifted students as one finds in Europe. There are very few centers in America, even major ones, where Islamic philosophy is taught seriously, and where it is, rarely is it related to the Islamic tradition to which it is inalienably linked.

The situation of Islamic science is not much better. There are a small number of scholars in the field teaching in several centers but, in most cases, the study of Islamic science is cut off from the rest of Islamic studies and taught more as a chapter in the history of Western science. Rarely are the Islamic sciences seen as the fruit of the tree of Islamic civilization, nurtured and developed within a world view which has its roots in the Islamic tradition.

The field of Islamic art, however, has come into its own during the past decade and there is a greater degree of interest in both Islamic art and architecture than ever before. The Aga Khan program in Islamic art and architecture, at Harvard and MIT, has been in its own way a catalyst in this domain and has caused a number of young Muslim architects, urban designers and the like to come to America to pursue their studies in Islamic art and architecture. This very active domain of Islamic studies can be further developed by strengthening its link with the study of Islam itself and not losing sight of the nexus between Islamic art and the religion which made the creation of this art possible.

The non-plastic arts, however, have not fared as well. The literature of the Islamic peoples has attracted a number of scholars and a few, like Herbert Mason, have created literary works based on Islamic themes. But the situation is very far from that of Persian literature in Victorian and Edwardian England. There is a need to study anew the great masterpieces of Islamic literature, particularly Sufi poetry. Classical Persian Sufi poetry remains to this day a subject which attracts many who are drawn to mystical and spiritual subjects. Much more needs to be done along the line of works by A.M. Schimmel, William Chittick, Omar Pound and others to make this poetry as well as the literary masterpiece of Arabic, Turkish, Urdu and other Islamic languages known and made part and parcel of Islamic studies.

As for the social sciences in relation to Islam, the works of American scholars are numerous and American centers remain very active in various social sciences such as sociology, anthropology, political sciences and more recently economics. In some fields, such as, anthropology, American scholars such as Clifford Geertz have produced works of great influence. But by and large, these fields suffer from the imposition of alien models upon the Islamic world with often catastrophic results as witnessed by the predictions made by so many American political scientists concerning the Islamic world during the past few decades. These disciplines need to sink their roots more in the Islamic religion, its theology and philosophy, its Sacred Law and the politico-social and economic teachings which issue from it and the history and culture of the Islamic peoples. Today, in most American centers of Islamic studies, Western social, economic or political models are used for the study of the Islamic world and there is little interaction between the social sciences and Islamic studies. The walls drawn around each discipline are so high and thick that it is difficult to either mount them or pierce through them. If Islamic studies is to be strengthened in this domain, there is no choice but to remove some of these obstacles; otherwise studies whose results are usually contradicted by events will remain the order of the day.

It must be added that in order for Islamic studies to flourish in America to the benefit of both America and the Islamic world, it should also be taught as part and parcel of the general education and liberal arts programs in American universities. The experience of Muslim Spain where Christians and Jews lived in harmony with Muslims, and where all the communities interacted and collaborated with each other to create one of the most glorious episodes of human history, must be recalled and studied carefully rather than purposefully forgotten because of current political or ideological interests. The Western humanities must be taught as related both historically and morphologically to those of Islam. It is not sufficient to simply mention the "Arab philosophers" in an intermediate chapter linking late antiquity to the scholastics in the history of philosophy. The Muslims philosophers must be taught fully, not only as one of the pillars of the foundation of medieval Western thought, but also as philosophers who, while sharing the same Graeco-Hellenistic intellectual heritage and Abrahamic religious background as Western philosophers, developed their thought in a direction different from that of the post-medieval West. Islamic philosophy must be seen as not only a chapter in the history of Western thought, but also an independent school of philosophy close to, yet different from Western philosophy and having its own history which continues to the present day. Islamic philosophy, moreover, should be taught in philosophy departments as philosophy and not only in Middle East departments where neither the teachers nor the students are necessarily trained to understand philosophical discourse.

The same could be said for other disciplines. Islamic literature should be taught not only to students specializing in Islamic studies, but to all students of world literature who should see Arabic literature in relation to Provincial poetry, to the Divine Comedy of Dante, to the treatises of Raymond Lull, to the introduction of rhyme into European poetry, t the Fables of La Fontaine. They should read Persian poetry along with their study of Goethe and Ruckert or English romantic poetry or the American Transcendentalists and come to understand something of the significance of the influence of the literature of these languages upon the European literary tradition. They should also study the literature of the Islamic peoples as literature.

In music, the origin of many European instruments should be

made clear as should the interaction between Spanish and Arabic music. The introduction of the Turkish military bands, not to speak to works of Mozart and Haydn with purported Turkish themes, should be combined with familiarity with some Turkish music and the study of Bartok and Kodaly should be accompanied by some acquaintance with Arabic and other forms of music of the Muslim peoples in which they were so interested.

As for art, rarely is the history of Western art taught with reference to the significance of the Cordova mosque for medieval Gothic arching or Arabic illuminations for the art of illumination, or for that matter, the Persian miniature for certain aspects of the art of Matisse. Without denying the very different nature of European art from Islamic art, various forms of Islamic art, which over the centuries have fecundated or influenced European or American art, can be taught as a part of those subjects in the same way that Greek or Roman influences, which were influential on a much wider scale, are studied. Although Islam was not simply the foundation of Western civilization as was Rome once Christianized, it was one of the elements, which played a great role in the formative period of Western civilization. Islamic studies should therefore be taught in the light of that role as well as independently of Western studies.

Finally, it must be mentioned that every intellectual endeavor flowers and develops through the quality of the thought of those who lead and not through the quantity of those who happen to study in the particular field in question. Islamic studies is no exception. In American centers until now, there has not been in general enough emphasis upon a hierarchical concept of a program which would begin with many students and end with very few who would, however, be highly qualified. There is a tendency to offer too many courses, which move in a parallel and horizontal direction rather than a vertical one. Too much emphasis is placed upon the quantity of teachers and students, as if the greatest Islamicists that the West has produced were not products of universities where one or two outstanding scholars trained a very small number of gifted students over the years in a manner which did not simply widen their horizon but also deepened their scholarship and enabled them to penetrate more profoundly into the subject with which they were dealing. No excellence in Islamic studies, or for that matter practically any other field of intellectual endeavor, is possible without emphasis upon quality and hierarchy in the sense of building an ever higher intellectual edifice on a firm and broad foundation and not only expanding the foundation horizontally.

The future of Islamic studies in America is not only a matter of theoretical or academic concern. Upon the knowledge or ignorance of the Islamic world in America depends the future of both the Islamic world and America. The incredible distortions of the image of Islam in the American mass media complements the lack of understanding of many facets of Islam by the "experts" upon whose views depend the decisions which affect the life of millions of human beings. The Islamic world is too large and Islam too strong a force to be relegated to the status it possesses in the West and, especially, America today. The development of Islamic studies upon a more solid foundation, with greater depth and on the basis of more vigorous scholarship and intellectual honesty, cannot but be of the greatest benefit to both America and the Islamic world.

The destinies of the Islamic world and the West are intertwined in such a way that ignorance of one world by the other cannot but result in calamitous results for both worlds. It is hoped that the bitter fruits of the past decade will help usher in a period in which Islamic studies can both provide a greater understanding of that world and enrich to the extent possible the religious, cultural, artistic and educational life of America itself.

The Curriculum Challenge
for Islamic Schools in America

Freda Shamma

INTRODUCTION

Muslims in America

The history of Islam in America can be summarized as first, one of loss and, now, one of commitment. From the seventeenth to the nineteenth century, as many as one-fifth of the African slaves brought into the country were Muslim. Due to intense persecution, and forced conversion to Christianity, Islam almost disappeared among the descendants of these people. Islam was also lost among the majority of the immigrants, primarily Arab, from the Ottoman Empire who started emigrating in the nineteenth century. They were mainly unskilled and uneducated and came hoping for financial success. At least partially because of their lack of knowledge about their religion, they either totally and voluntarily assimilated into mainstream America; or they chose to fight to maintain their Arab culture, which increasingly lost out as their children grew up feeling culturally more American than Arab. As Islam was seen as only an aspect of the Arab culture, it too was lost.[1]

The early part of the twentieth century has seen a decided shift in commitment to Islam by both new immigrants and African Americans who have, in part, rediscovered their Islamic roots. Although there were small success stories of committed Muslims among African Americans before, it was not until the establishment of the Nation of Islam in the 1930s that African Americans began to commit themselves in large numbers to Islam. At first, the preaching of this group differed in significant ways from mainstream Islam, but over the years, and thanks

---

1 For an excellent discussion of these Arab Muslim immigrants, see *The Arab Moslems in the United States: Religion and Assimilation* by Abdo A. Elkholy, New Haven: College and University Press Publishers, 1966.

in great part to Malik Shabazz (Malcolm X) and Warith Deen Muhammad, the greater number of Muslims in this group have integrated into mainstream Sunni Islam. These African Americans who have chosen Islam, "are constantly aware of their choice of Islam versus the choice of a more mainstream religion, and they must struggle to nourish spirituality on a daily basis in a largely hostile environment."[2] They have chosen not to assimilate into mainstream America, and they have chosen to divorce themselves from undesirable aspects of American culture.

The mid-1940s saw the arrival of better educated Muslim immigrants, while the 1960s brought significant numbers of Muslim university students, and professional people, primarily from Arab countries and the Indian subcontinent.[3] The majority of them had no desire to assimilate completely. They preferred to retain their own nationalistic cultural identity, complete with its Islamic religion. However, as a group, they were more knowledgable about Islam and could better separate it from culture. As their children increasingly prefer the American culture, the parents have increasingly stressed the importance of religion over culture. Besides forming cultural groups, they have joined Islamic organizations composed of multiple nationalities, and encouraged the teaching of Islam.

The Rise of Islamic Schools.

The Nation of Islam instituted a nationwide system of education known as Sister Clara Muhammad Schools, which today includes more than fifty academically certified institutions across the country. From its earliest days, the Nation of Islam felt the vital importance of full-time Islamic schools. A series of issues and concerns arose over the years with respect to public education. African American Muslims generally view the public school system as hostile toward differences and often violent.[4] It is primarily due to lack of funds that there are not more of these schools.

Having been raised in the system, it is apparent to these indigenous Muslims that both the moral environment and the subject matter being

---

2 *African American Islam* by Aminah Beverly McCloud, New York: Routledge, p 117.

3 For a more complete summary of the history of Muslims in America, see "United States of America" by Yvonne Haddad and Jane Smith in *The Oxford Encyclopedia of the Modern Islamic World*, vol. 4. 1995, PP 277-284

4 *African American Islam.* p. 118.

taught are rife with concerns for Muslims. Their first concern is to have their children in a physically and morally safe environment. Primarily living in large urban areas, this is a very real concern as violence and sexual misconduct are increasing at an alarming rate. The second concern is the curriculum taught. As a noted African American Muslim scholar points out, "Western approaches to history and the social sciences are also regarded as highly problematic by Muslims. The Prophet Muhammad and Islamic civilization are seldom mentioned, and when they are it is usually in a denigrating context. In general, Muslim children in public schools across America are educated to believe that they have no place in the scope of world history and that Islam has made no significant contributions to world history."[5] Other issues of concern are the inclusion of amoral sex education courses and inclusion of Judeo-Christian and secular holidays with a decided exclusion of Islamic holidays.

Immigrant Muslims have been much slower to identify problems in the public schools. They immigrated here in part due to their respect for the American educational system, and have been firmly committed to educating their children in this American institution. Although they are much more conscious of the need to educate their children about Islam than earlier immigrants, they generally fail to see any relationship between the curriculum of the American schools and the level of Islamic commitment of their children. Instead they tend to rely on home and/ or weekend Islamic instruction. Physical safety is not as often a concern as many of these professional people live in the suburbs or smaller communities where violence is not so apparent. It is quite often only as their girls become teenagers that they discover the conflict between Islamic values and those found in the public school environment. Those with sufficient income tend to switch these youth to single sex private schools. Even if there is an Islamic school in the area, many of these immigrant parents place a higher priority on a "quality education" that will enable their children to attend ivy league universities than they do on an Islamic environment in a school which may be staffed by underpaid, less qualified teachers.

One generation of Muslim children going through the public school system has illuminated the problems of Muslims in mainstream American institutions. For African American Muslims, it is seeing many of their

---

5   Ibid., p. 119.

children reject Islam because it is too hard to fight their peers, their teachers, their school administrators and the school's curriculum that denies them a culture and a history. For immigrant Muslims, it is their grown children who don't wish to subject their own children to the problems they had growing up Muslim in America. Unlike their parents, they know exactly what is going on in American classrooms. With this illumination has come a new determination to provide Muslim children with safe and positive schooling. There are now more than 200 Islamic full time schools in America. They range from the long established and multiple campus Sister Clara Muhammad Schools to makeshift one-room schools with 3 or 4 children. They range from schools with totally African American staff and students to totally Arab staff and students to truly mixed schools with different races, nationalities and Islamic theologies interacting.

CURRICULUM QUESTIONS OF CONCERN

Current status of curriculums

The written curriculums in Islamic schools in the United States range from the voluminous to the non existent, but interestingly enough, they are mostly homogeneous. With the exception of the rare curriculum which takes as its premise that all necessary knowledge is found in the Qur'an and therefore the only factual information to be taught is from that source, the remaining curriculums modify an existing state curriculum, and add classes in Arabic, and/or Qur'an, and Religion. Why would these schools use the very same curriculum which has forced many Muslims to remove their children from public schools? Generally speaking, it is partially a matter of necessity, and partially a case of adopting what is familiar.

Advantages of secular curriculum

There are several important reasons why secular curriculums are followed.
1.   These curriculums are easily available. There is no comparable curriculum developed by Muslims. Either the secular curriculum is used, or the school must spend years, and money and scholarly energy (all of which are in short supply) to develop their own. Since it is probably accurate to say that each school has been started due

to the immediate needs of its community, none have had the benefit of time in which to start from scratch.

2. The public school curriculums are well researched in terms of what skills need to be taught, and how they can be most effectively taught. Most Muslims approve of the way in which mainstream students are taught. Adequate and attractive textbooks and additional teaching materials, which follow these secular curriculums, are readily available. There is no parallel line of Islamically oriented textbooks. Muslims have been hard put to develop a series of textbooks for even the Religion class.[6]

3. Parents often demand the use of such curriculums. Many of the immigrant Muslims came to North America precisely because of the excellence of its educational system, and they are most concerned that their children receive this quality of education which will enable them to continue in prestigious universities.

4. At the end of the Ottoman administration of the Muslim, the Muslims' educational systems became secular. The schools were designed by the western colonial regimes, supported by government money, and led to government jobs. The colonial governments "put their own interest first. They usually intended for secondary and higher schools to turn out docile government clerks and technicians."[7] They adapted their own Western, secular education system for this purpose. Islamic education, which originally had included all branches of knowledge, became confused with the subject matter of religion. When Muslims regained control of their educational systems, they kept the secular system and added the subject "Islamic education." It was logical therefore for the Muslim schools in America to follow the same system, using the public school textbooks for the other subjects and adding courses in religion and Arabic to make it an "Islamic School."

---

6 To date, the only easily available, grade appropriate, attractive series for teaching religion in the full-time school is that produced by IQRA' International Educational Foundation and that is limited to pre-school and primary education. In order to help compensate for the lack of reference to Muslim contributions in the secular history textbooks, Susan Douglas has written one unit for each of the primary grades, that offers excellent text, aids and teaching notes to help balance the secular texts. These units are designed to supplement rather than take the place of the secular text. (published by IIIT: fax: 703-709-5305)

7 "Educational Methods" by Joseph S. Szyliowicz, *Oxford Encyclopedia of the Modern Islamic World*, Vol. 1, 1995, p. 418.

Serious Areas of Concern

Before adopting any curriculum, there are some serious areas of concern that need to be taken into consideration. Among the assumptions of the typical Islamic school curriculum that need to be looked at are the following:

1 – The Islamic school is required by law to teach certain content in certain subjects in a certain order.
2 – Students cannot pass end of schooling exams like the SAT, or AP or California Achievement Tests, if they do not have the exact secular school curriculum and texts.
3 – There is no fundamental and/or philosophical difference in the foundation of the secular versus an Islamic curriculum.
4 – There is no conflict between the content of the secular textbooks and the life of the child in terms of his social and emotional development as a Muslim American.
5 – There is no conflict between the moral standards of conduct implied in the secular textbooks and those taught in the Islamic Studies class which has been added to the secular curriculum

The first two assumptions are in acknowledgment that employment, financial security and social acceptance in this country are primarily based on a recognized secondary school diploma, which can lead to a tertiary degree from a secular university. Therefore, the issues raised in the first two assumptions cannot be ignored.

A. What is required by law?

What exactly does the law require be taught in school? It is not as much or as detailed as is commonly assumed. The important 'accreditation' that schools so fervently seek, is based more on facilities than it is on curriculum. What most accreditation requires in terms of curriculum is stated as general courses. The subjects taught must include math, English, science and so on. Seldom are any details given as to what should be taught within each subject. American law requires only that a certain amount of American history and government be taught, but that is given in terms of one semester or one year's worth of time. It is common practice to teach American government in the eighth grade, and because most schools do this, the required state examinations that are appearing include that subject at that time. Now that these state exams are required at the end of eighth grade, for example, it will be necessary for Islamic schools in that state to include a study of American government before that exam. Nevertheless, the requirements are minimal, and do not necessitate using any secular curriculum or secular textbooks, except for limited courses.

B. Students cannot pass end of schooling exams

All the required examinations cover general concepts and general material, rather than specific orientation to that material. Science exams for example cover the area of biology, but they do not test whether the student believes that God or coincidence produced the plants. Where there is a major difference, as with Darwin's theory, as long as the student understands what is being said in the theory, the test makers do not question whether the theory is believed to be true or not. Examinations on such subjects as math, science, computers, etc. therefore are cause for little concern.

Culturally loaded subjects like language arts and social studies could be a different matter. However, when one looks at achievement tests and the SAT, one finds that the actual content studied is not important. Whether the student reads American authors, or European authors, or Asian authors, the tests are designed to find out whether the material read is understood, and can be analyzed. To test these reading skills, the test itself includes passages to be read and questions on those passages. There is no reason why Islamic schools cannot include Muslim authors, and/or Islamic literature, and still prepare their students well for these exams.

The exceptions to these exams are special exams for specified areas. The AP (Advanced Placement) exams are based on a particular content, as are the IB (International Baccalaureate). However the subject matter for these exams is based on one to two year courses taught in the final year or two of secondary school. They do not refer to previous years content in terms of what material is to be read in the English class, or what countries' history is to be taught.

Therefore, it is not necessary for the Islamic schools to teach the entire secular curriculum in order for their students to do well on any exam. It is necessary for the Islamic schools to teach the same concepts, (cause and effect for example) and skills as the secular curriculums. However they do not need to teach the same historical subjects or the same titles or authors as the other curriculums. Whether the Islamic schools wish to include American and European writers and history will depend on the following assumptions.

C. There are no fundamental and/or philosophical differences

The most serious conflict between the secular and Islamic curriculum is that the secular curriculum is not God centered. Not only is all knowledge in the Islamic world view based on the realization that God created everything, but it is acknowledged that everything operates according to the laws which God set into motion. The natural law of 'survival of the fittest,' if it is true, is a law which God made and set into effect. Furthermore God created the human being and his mind according to certain other laws, one of which is that he/she is to use his/her mind to discover the laws of God and to use that knowledge for the benefit of all humanity and the environment.

On the other hand, the secular content is written on the basis that the human being is supreme. There is no implied or stated acknowledgment that God is the Creator, or that all knowledge comes from Him, or that there is any moral imperative connected to knowledge. Science, for example, is taught from the perspective that the human being is capable of understanding everything through the use of his five senses, and the basic motivation for studying science is self-satisfaction. Art is encouraged as self-expression and "art for art's sake," and even pornographic material is labeled 'art' if it involves 'self expression'. The same is true for literature and music. Because science is studied for its own sake, or self satisfaction, then it becomes amoral and the destructive aspects may be developed while the constructive aspects may be ignored, according to what suits some people. The polarization of God and the universe divorces moral behavior from academic endeavors.

Islamic schools generally try to offset this by stating God-consciousness and/or Tawhid as a major goal of the school. There are also minor adjustments to particular courses, like in science where a lesson is added to teach that God created everything. Unfortunately, having a desirable goal does not assure its implementation, especially in this instance, and adding small units does not deal with any of the internal shortcomings. Mentioning Muslim mathematicians, or anecdotal stories about how Muslims use mathematics to determine the location of Mecca for prayers, does not offset the principle of mathematics as implied throughout secular texts, that mathematics is completely independent of metaphysics. Similarly, biographical information about Muslim scientists, and a lesson about God the Creator, is no cure for a secular science based on random acts, coincidences and the supremacy of the five human senses.

Another area in which the principle of *Tawhid* conflicts with the secular curriculum is that crriculums extremely nationalistic and/or western orientation. Although it is important for students to have an understanding and appreciation of the place they live in, it is hard to justify spending nearly all twelve years of schooling teaching American history. Not only does this leave the students ignorant of their own Islamic history, and ignorant of most of the world's history, it preaches American superiority. It stands to follow that if only America's history is emphasized and mostly (white) American scientists, inventors, writers, humanitarians, and other notables are taught, then the inescapable conclusion is that Americans, by virtue of being (white) Americans, are better than everyone else.

The *Tawhidic* principle on the other hand, insists that God created "you from a single male and female and made you into nations and tribes that you may know each other. Verily the most honored of you in the sight of God is the most righteous of you."(*Surah* 49:13).

Islamic schools try to balance history by teaching the history of Muslims as part of the Islamic Studies class, but spending as much as four to five times on American history (three to five full class periods of American history per week as opposed to less than once a week in the religion class) is not effective.

D. Conflict in the life of the child

Eleven years of American history, taught in chronological order after the third or fourth grade, versus part of one class, religion, where the lives of various prophets are taught, definitely teaches the lesson that Muslims played no real role in history. The prophets mentioned are taught without real reference to their historical time. It is doubtful whether any Muslim pupil connects the Egypt of Musa (Moses) with the Egypt of the Pyramids and heirographics that they study in their world history class. Prophet Muhammad, peace be upon him, does not have any place in 'real' history as the histories of the Roman and the Persian Empires are not studied in the religion class, and Muhammad is not mentioned in the histories of either of those two empires studied in the history class.

Although there is a current, laudable attempt to be more multi-cultural, that multi-culturalism is itself western-oriented. American reading textbooks, for example, now include more stories about Asian, African, and Hispanic people. However the majority of these stories are about Asian Americans, African Americans, and Hispanic Americans within the American setting but definitely outside any Muslim/Islamic reference. World literature books contain more writings of these same groups, but most of the new material is from Spanish speaking peoples of the Americas which is, of course, also western, and either secular or Christian oriented. A careful examination of two of the most popular reading series[8] revealed zero references to Muslims. (One story was about two boys in Pakistan but there was no textual or illustrative reference to any religion.)

Not only does the secular curriculum place undue emphasis on western culture; it totally ignores Muslim culture. If we look more closely at the Language Arts syllabus to see what the pupils are reading, we find three types of reading material.

Types of reading material

1. The emphasis is on stories that appeal to the pupils' belonging to the main cultural group(s) of America. The environment therefore is American with the activities of the children in the stories reflect local sports, local food, local clothing and so on. Although there is an attempt to be more multicultural, it is notable that the text material does not include any reference to Muslims, neither African American Muslims nor Muslims from other lands, nor reference to any Muslim culture. The point to be made is not that American textbooks should not emphasize American culture, but that the Muslim subculture is never acknowledged. Although African American Muslims like Malik Shabazz (Malcolm X), boxer Mohammed Ali, and basketball's Karim Abdul Jabar (Lew Alcindor) are positive role models well known by even non-Muslim Americans,

---

8 *Invitations to Literacy*, Houghton Mifflin Publisher, Boston, 1996, and *Signatures* by Harcourt Brace, Orlando, 1997.

they are not ever mentioned in American textbooks.

2. Material used to teach 'good literature' is generally or completely devoted to the writings of white English people or white Americans. An occasional token Hispanic, Vietnamese or African American writer is added to the newer texts, but none are Muslims, nor do they write about Muslims.

3. World literature is an increasingly common subject in secondary education. However an examination of the contents of such literature shows that only six percent is from Muslim cultures. The American World Literature text published by Holt Rinehart in 1993 contains more than 1300 pages, of which about two thirds is from Christian/ European/ American cultures. The other third of approximately 350 pages is from all the rest of the world. This third contains about 175 pages from the Muslim areas of the world including Israel and the ancient world of Egypt and Mesopotamia, but only about 74 pages are of material written by writers living in predominantly Muslim areas after the coming of Islam. That amounts to 5.6 percent of the total book. Even within these 74 pages, one does not notice any positive reference to anything Islamic. It is therefore misleading to think that the inclusion of a World Literature course will have anything of particular relevance for the Muslim student.

Averaging that course in with the other ten or eleven years of non world literature indicates that at best only 1 percent of what the Muslim pupils read in their Islamic schools' English/ literature classes has any relevance at all to Muslim culture.

It is not only in the English class that the western, European bias is felt. Art is taught as though American/European art is the litmus test for real art. In music only western notions of music are taught. In both these subjects, any reference to another culture is minimal, and by the amount of attention to it, designated as lesser of importance.

The cultural heritage being taught in secular schools is totally western. It is not fair or wise to discount literature or art or music solely because they reflect the majority culture. After all, the point of teaching cultural heritage is to produce a majority culture. Except for international schools, the vast majority of the pupils in the Islamic schools in America are also natives and citizens of America and they should feel comfortable with their American cultural heritage. However the fact that non-Muslims select this material for the needs of non-Muslims necessitates that the material be examined critically before it is adopted for use in Islamic schools. Muslims in America have both an American and a Muslim culture that they should be familiar with. In the same way that the American curriculum includes Christian oriented writings such as Charles Dickens' *A Christmas Carol*, and John Milton's *Paradise Lost*, and Shakespeare's plays which are British rather than American, but all part of the white Christian Americans cultural identity, Muslim children have their own Muslim identity which needs to be acknowledged and provided for.

A cultural heritage provides pupils with a sense of identity and belonging to a cultural group. Although all Muslim American children are American, they are not generally from a European background. Americans of European descent are happy to know that their ancestors wrote Hamlet and Cinderella, painted the Sistine Chapel and built the Eiffel Tower. It gives them a sense of who they are. It does not help the child whose descendants came from Africa or Asia or the Arabian Peninsula.

This very real impact of cultural material helps explain why Muslim children who spend their entire schooling in Islamic schools still turn out to feel more American than they feel like Muslims. It helps to explain why they choose non-Muslim friends in the university, rather than join Muslim groups where they find non-American Muslim students. It helps to explain why so many Muslims use non-Islamic thought processes and arguments to refute problematic areas of Islam. It helps explain why so many Muslim youths are torn between what they find in school and what they find at home.

E. Conflict between moral standards of conduct

Not only does the national curriculum encourage a non-Islamic cultural affinity; it has the potential to teach against the values of Islam. Many Muslim English-medium school graduates will claim that 'there is nothing wrong with English literature' and that western art and music belong in Muslim schools. This assumption needs to be given careful assessment. Consider, for example the subject matter of the stories found in typical, current, and well-written American textbook series.

Story subject matter

A short perusal of American reading texts[9] widely used in Islamic schools finds, for example, the following concepts and ideas in the reading material:

a. Boyfriend-girlfriend: Starting with stories for pre-school children, and included in almost every year's reading material is the idea that boys and girls should be best friends, and/or romantic pairs. It may not be the focal point of the story, but it is ever present.

b. Lying is an accepted aspect of growing up: The story is usually humorous, relating the funny after-effects of a lie. At times, the teacher may be able to point out the bad consequences of lying, but usually the story does not imply in any way that lying is wrong.

c. There are usually several stories where children are celebrating religious holidays, but never is it a Muslim holiday.

d. Stories that take place in the home country are in clean, technological advanced, western garbed environments. Stories that take place in Africa, Asia or the Middle East are either non-existent, or reflect "quaint" villages or wilderness areas like jungles, or fairy tale lands.

e. Man is able to live alone: Stating that the purpose is to teach courage or adaptability, or independence, the story generally centers about a youth or adult who is by accident or design on his/her own in the wilderness. Inevitably the hero/heroine is able to function well without the aid of family or society.

f. A pet is better than parents or siblings: Every year's reading material contains at least one story where no matter how troublesome the pet is, the owner is patient, loving, attentive, etc. On the other hand, there is seldom even one story where a sibling or parent gets or deserves to get similar loving attention.

g. The value of the family is generally ignored. Out of 22 stories to be read in one grade level in one American textbook, only 12 contain some mention or inclusion of family. In 7 of these the family is present but contributes nothing, neither advice nor support nor comfort; 2 contain negative family relationships; and only 5 mention family, or any member of the family, in a positive manner. That means that less than 25 percent of the stories contains the concept that family is important. What is more significant is that almost half

---

9   Ibid.

of the stories contain the idea that families are irrelevant, or unsupportive. The majority of these stories are not about family at all, and they don't need to be, but overall the message given is that children do not need to seek advice or support from their parents, and in turn have no obligation to help or respect their parents or siblings.

Any one of the above mentioned stories is harmless, but when the overall message is that a person is an independent unit who needs nobody, then the message becomes an active force against the concept introduced in the religion class that the family is the basic unit of society, that everyone benefits from the family and has a responsibility to the family. If the Islamic concept of family is mentioned once, but the unimportance of the family is introduced every year, is it any surprise that Muslim children raised in this environment are most influenced by the secular view?

Not all of the stories used in the Language Arts classes are inappropriate, and some contain positive statements about the concepts Muslim value. However, by the time the pupil has, in his eleven or twelve years of schooling read thirty stories about the close relationship between a child and his pet, and one or less about the close relationship between a child and his siblings, the unspoken lesson has been learned. Every year people in the United States make their wills, leaving all their worldly goods to their pets. People are outraged to hear about someone mistreating an animal or abandoning it, but pass without comment the aged parent abandoned in a wretched 'home' for the elderly, and they would live in abject poverty before asking financial aid from their wealthier brother or sister, who in turn, would not consider volunteering any aid.

NEED FOR NEW CURRICULUM

Once Muslims are convinced of the need for a different curriculum they generally try to fix the secular system. They assume that the American curriculum is basically sound, needing only a bit of infusion of Islamic ideas here and there. These attempts are often apologetic, saying that Muslims haven't really contributed that much, but we did do at least something. In history, for example, the unit on the Islamic world in the social studies class is always out of chronological order, and none of the currently available history textbooks manage to admit, in their chapters on the Renaissance, that Europeans actually adopted the learning of their Muslim neighbors, and added to it; that in fact there was no renaissance, or rebirth, at all. The lesson of world history, as found in the secular textbooks, remains that Europe and the West invented and developed alone all branches of learning with very minor exceptions like paper making from China and a numbering system known as Arabic numerals.

A curriculum based on a coincidental creation, which stresses that a people, by virtue of their place of origin, or color of skin are better than any other peoples, and which advocates a social system based on the supremacy of the individual, can never be modified enough to teach a world view based on the oneness, and unity of the divine Creator.

Earlier Muslim intellectuals "transformed the form, content and intent of sciences, education and arts into Islamic disciplines by integrating intellectual and cultural development within the Islamic worldview."[10]

It in the nature of children, or perhaps it is the nature of us all, to accept whatever they first learn as the real truth, and to judge all future 'truths' by the first. The child who first sees the story of Cinderella as cartooned by Disney will tell you that the written version is not the correct or true one. No matter that you explain that it is an ancient folk tale, written down by the Grimm brothers hundreds of years ago and that Disney changed it when he made it a cartoon movie. No, the child 'knows' that the real story is the cartoon one. On a test in a Muslim weekend school, the teenage youth gave the details of the life of Prophet Musa exactly as they are portrayed in the movie, "*The Ten Commandments*," with no awareness that they were deviating at all from the Qur'anic version. They had first 'learned' the story of Musa from the movie.

Furthermore, if this first 'truth' is written in a glossy, attractive textbook, then it is obvious to the child that it is 'the truth'. And if the media entertainment surrounding the child adds its approval of this 'truth', then it is the rare individual who can judge otherwise.

It is therefore necessary that the first 'truths' the child receives at school, are in fact, real truths. The fortunate student who learns that everything comes from his Creator, and that this Creator has made a creation based on certain rules, which serve to unify this creation, and that man himself is part of this same unified creation, and subject to

---

10 "Religious Education" by Nimat Barzangi in *Oxford Encyclopedia of the Modern Islamic World*. vol. 4, pg. 406.

these same unifying rules, will have a real truth on which he can safely trust his whole being.

The concept of unity or *Tawhid* has been, and will continue to be the object of study by Muslim scholars throughout the world and throughout time. It is not the object of this paper to delve into it, except to point out that this must be the basis of an Islamic school curriculum. It is immediately apparent that every subject will have to be based on this concept of *Tawhid*. How can science or mathematics operate outside the system of rules, which Allah has created for this world? How can one study the history, or literature or sociology or psychology of humans, outside the realm of Allah's creation, when humankind itself is a part of that divine creation?

Agreeing that the concept of *Tawhid* should be central is the easy part of developing the curriculum. Figuring out how to teach any subject according to the concept is the hard part. Following are some examples from several subjects to illustrate how the *Tawhidic* principle can be integral to the subject matter.

A Sampling of Tawhidic curriculum materials

Math:

"The development of algebra was a crucial step taken by al-Khwarizmi, one of the greatest scientific minds of the 9th century. In algebra the symbols are capable of infinite potential or possibilities. Here, at the heart of this Arab achievement, is a reflection of the Islamic Faith...a mathematical concept of a universe whose creation by God is an unending or infinitely living process."[11]

Science:

"In observing and mapping the movements of the sun, planets and stars so comprehensively, Islamic astronomers were expressing fundamental aims of their Faith, which urged a never-ending attempt to understand the visible cloak, or outer appearance, of God. Through observing the material universe they were coming to understand better the nature and works of God. Nothing man could investigate on Earth or in the skies was alien to these scientists. Thus, throughout the Islamic

---

11 *The Islamic Heritage*, PP 16-17

world, an astronomer was usually also a mathematician, a geographer, a physician, something of a philosopher, and certainly, to some degree, a theologian!"

In other words, it is not sufficient to mention the names and accomplishments of the Muslim mathematicians and scientists. More importantly, what was their *Tawhidic* understanding of the world? How did they use their Islamic worldview to discover scientific truths?

History:

The guiding principle of the Qur'anic view of history is *tawhid*, the unity of Allah, and the unity of all He created. Allah created all of humankind, and He sent prophets to all of humankind. Therefore the history of all humankind, from the Americas to Asia, from Australia to Siberia, and from Prophet Adam to the present time must be studied. The Qur'an says that Allah created people in tribes that they might get to know each other. Therefore goodness and knowledge are found in all areas of the world and need to be known. The Qur'an further points out that pursuit of wealth and power with an accompanying avoidance of ethics and morality leads to the downfall of civilizations, and that God consciousness is a necessary attribute of real success in this world, and in the hereafter. Allah says to look at those from the past, at what they created, at what they had done, and at what became of them. It is a duty for Muslims to study the past, for the purpose of learning what ultimately happens to those who believe and those who don't.

Furthermore we do not study just for its own sake, but learn in order to be of benefit to humankind.

A proper study of history includes other social sciences, like geography and sociology. According to the Muslim fourth century Hijrah historian Masudi, history includes the creation of the universe, earth regions (i.e. geography), biographies of eminent people, the emergence of kingdoms, the history of people, their social life, calendars and economic life.

If this is what a *Tawhidic* view of history includes, then it is necessary to stop using textbooks that teach that the greatest civilizations were those that ruthlessly conquered the most peoples, that one people are vastly more important than another people, and that history is divorced from morality and ethics. Instead of one year of world history, there should be nine or more years, with the history of Muslims being taught in its proper chronological, historical place. The history of

289

humankind should be taught, not as a straight line from primitive to civilized, but as cyclical, rightly guided to misguided to rightly guided.

Language Arts: (English)

One of the goals of Islamic language arts is an understanding that language is a gift from Allah that should be used to express truth and advance the cause of good.

A second is to instill Allah-consciousness in pupils via written and spoken communication and literature.

There is merit in teaching some western literature, but if the *Tawhidic* principle is kept in mind, then most of the material used to teach students how to read, and why to read will need to be written from an Islamic perspective. There are four areas of reading content to be considered in an Islamic school. Following is an explanation of how the principle of *Tawhid* can be apparent in each.

a. Representative material taken from the literature of the English speaking world. It is not necessary or desirable to prevent Muslim children from studying Shakespeare or other English literature. However, that literature needs to be understood from an Islamic perspective. One must ask if the work has literary merit from the western perspective and literary and moral merit from an Islamic perspective. Everyone agrees that Shakespeare should be read, but which of his dramas are most reflective of Islamic values? Then the literature should be discussed in terms of Islamic values as well as style of writing. The inclusion of any particular drama, or other literary work, should not be solely on the basis that it is offered by the local secular curriculum.

b. Literature of a decidedly Islamic character, particularly by well-known Islamic leaders and/or scholars. The writing of Ali ibn Abu Talib, for example, is known not only for its religious content, but also for its excellence in style and presentation. His writings can be studied as literature in the Language Arts class as well as being used in reference to specific religious content, in the religion class. This Islamic literature will also demonstrate both subtly and through class discussion how writing can be used to express truth and further the good.

c. Representative literature from at least the classical Islamic language groups of Arabic, Persian (and its cousin, Urdu), Turkish, Malay and Swahili should be included. While presenting literature that at least has a *Tawhidic* undercurrent (rather than the secular undercurrent of much western literature), this literature can also help to produce Muslims who feel their emotional and cultural affiliations to be first to the worldwide Muslim ummah, and secondly to whatever ethnic or national group they are living among. This concept of ummah is also part of the concept of *Tawhid*. It will of course be necessary to teach this material translated into English.

d. Culturally oriented reading material should be included in order to encourage multicultural understanding and tolerance, which agrees with the *Tawhidic* principle. This differs from the third category in that it does not necessarily have to be 'literature'. It can be simple children's stories both from the Muslim world, and from other areas of the world, but these stories should include at least a moral undercurrent. It may be worth noting here that this aim does not imply a lack of humor or enjoyable story line. Consider the vast amount of truth and wisdom in the animal tales of Aesop, and the humorous stories of that beloved folk character of the entire Muslim realm, known as Nasruddin Hodja or Goha or Joha.

Balance and Integration

Two other important concepts should permeate the curriculum. These are balance and integration of subject matter. It is important that the students get a certain amount of history and culture of the America they are living in. However, there should be a balance between the American culture, though it is secular, Eurocentric, and nationalistic, and Islam and Muslim culture. Students need to be immersed in the literary cultural heritage of Islam. How can we expect these students to feel like Muslims when none of their cultural experiences at school reflect this culture? Consider for example what would happen if you gathered some children from several Islamic schools who had also lived for some time in one of the Muslim countries of Egypt, Iran, Turkey, Tanzania, Pakistan or Indonesia and had some knowledge of the literature of that country. If they were asked to make a list of all the stories/literature that was common to them, what would be the result? They would have only English literature in common. There would probably not be one author from any Muslim country that would have been read by all these Muslims, including writers like Ali ibn Abu Talib, and Al-Ghazzali. From their English medium Islamic school, they likely will not have read a single selection in their Language arts classes from a Muslim writer, with the notable exception of something by Prophet Muhammad (peace be upon him).

Muslims talk about a Muslim *ummah*, and wonder why the Muslims are so divided. Why do Muslims group themselves together according to nationality and culture rather than by Islamic piety? Is it any wonder that this happens when we have no common Islamic heritage beyond the Qur'an and *Sunnah*, and even those two are rarely taught well?

An Islamic school should aim at immersing the pupils in an Islamic culture, and maintain a balance between the majority national culture in which the pupils live, and an Islamic culture which may or may not be present in the national culture.

Not only has the west separated the Divine from His creation, it has divided all of knowledge into neat, separate packages. Mathematics is a subject all of its own. Science is its own subject and so on. This idea is the opposite of *Tawhid*, but it is the basis of the curriculum in most of our Islamic schools. Interesting enough, the west has recently discovered that the world cannot be divided that easily, and the modern trend in education as well as in other fields, is to integrate previously divided fields. Physicians are now expected to know about psychology, psychologists need to know about nutrition, and so on. The most modern of secular curriculums now teach a 'holistic' education, and the students learn math in their reading class and reading in their history class. This is a welcome trend for Muslims, leading as it does back to the idea of the unity of knowledge, and it should be implemented in all Islamic schools. This includes the integration of religion into all other subjects. As has been mentioned above, much Islamic literature can be used in both the Language Arts class and the Religion class. Biographies of historians like Ibn Khaldoun and some of their actual writings can also be included in the reading material of the Language Arts class, and Muslims authors, scientists, and Islamic scholars should be included in the history classes at the chronologically appropriate time.

There must also be a balance between academics and religion. Originally it was those most infused with religious knowledge and fervor who contributed to science, literature and medicine. It is unfortunate that today it must be spelled out that a truly Islamic school will, by definition, also include the best of what is found in secular academic schools. Including literature written by Muslims does not negate the necessity of using critical reading skills to analyze it, nor does the presence of certain truths found in the Qur'an negate the necessity of using the scientific method (which incidentally was first developed by Muslims) and the five human senses to discover other truths. Studying Qur'an and Sunnah should not imply that it is not necessary to also study science and history.

The Religion Class

To this point, we have discussed the problems associated with using a secular curriculum. Unfortunately, even the course of Religion is problematic for the Islamic Schools. One principal made the comment that they had used teachers and curriculums from both the Indian subcontinent and the Arab world, and "it didn't make any difference. They were equally bad." They were bad, he went on to explain because the materials were not sensitive to the needs of children, and the methods of teaching led to boring classes and rebellious attitudes from the students. At best the classes produced factually knowledgeable youth who were not committed to Islam, and at worst, the classes were turning the students away from Islam. This seems to be the rule, rather than the exception, in our Islamic schools.

Many of the problems associated with the religion class could be eliminated by a teacher who is a practicing Muslim, knowledgeable about the religion, and knowledgeable about how to teach effectively. However this paper is limited to a discussion of the curriculum, so we must ignore the immensely important aspect of teachers and teacher training and concentrate on developing a curriculum and material that will help the less qualified teachers.

A careful examination of the syllabus or curriculum for the Religion class discloses an over emphasis on *fiqh*, and in particular the *fiqh* of *ibadat*. That is, an over emphasis on the rules of religion, and especially the rules associated with the five pillars. One syllabus, for example, included instruction about ablution (*wudu*) for four years, but did not include even one lesson on backbiting and gossip. Consider the ramifications of a curriculum which spends four years on something which if done wrong out of ignorance, will not have any effect on whether you enjoy the afterlife, but does not even contain one lesson about something which is considered one of the greatest sins, and one which can certainly lead to hell. Somewhere we have gotten our priorities out of kilter.

The religion curriculum needs to be redesigned from the beginning.

293

What are the major Qur'anic concepts that should be emphasized every year? What should be the role of the Qur'an? In too many curriculums, there is a topic titled 'Qur'an'. Recitation, memorization and *tafsir* are included in this topic. Then the Qur'an is laid to rest, respectfully of course, on the highest shelf. The textbook, if there is one, or the teacher, if there isn't, simply tells the students whatever else they need to know, but not why. For example, Muslim should be truthful because his religion says so; or Muslim should not eat pork, because the religion textbook or teacher says so, and there is only one way to pray because the *imam* or teacher says so, and so on.

Among the questions to be answered in developing the religion curriculum are these:

1. What are the major Islamic concepts, which need to be developed throughout the twelve years of schooling?
2. How can we structure the lessons so that students will see clearly the relevance of Islam to their real life? It is not enough to have stories of what the sahaba did so long ago. How should today's Muslim act toward ridicule, toward the concept of honesty when it is so easy to cheat, and everyone else is already cheating? If we do not make Islam relevant to the students, the class will be another academic subject to be learned for the exam and forgotten immediately after.
3. What is the life long benefit to the student in learning particular parts of the Qur'an? Is it more beneficial to learn the ayahs in reverse order according to their arrangement in the Qur'an, or would it be more beneficial to teach specific ayahs, or specific surah according to the needs of the students?
4. What is the benefit of memorizing without understanding the meaning?
5. What is the point of learning about the life of Prophet Muhammad? Is the benefit 'because it's part of your religion', or is it that he is a role model of behavior? If it is the latter, then should our lessons about the life of the Prophet emphasize the names of his ancestors, children, and/or close associates? Should the students be memorizing the names of all the battles, and how many soldiers there were on each side? Or should they be learning how the Prophet acted as a wise leader; what he did when he was with his friends; how he treated people who ridiculed him, or tried to harm him; or how the Prophet acted toward his wives, or toward his children? Our

emphasis should come from our priorities and our goals.

6. How can we structure the curriculum so that we cultivate thinking Muslims? What needs to be included so that the students understand that part of what they need to do is based on information found in the Qur'an for which immediate and unquestioned response is necessary, and part of what they need to do is based on other criteria which may be changed if circumstances change? How can we teach our students to be critical thinkers, to know when and how they can make their own judgments and when they should turn to the scholars; and to know what questions to ask to make sure the scholars' answers are Islamically sound?

7. How can we structure the curriculum so that we cultivate active, practicing Muslims, who learn in order to do Allah's Will, who act in order to do Allah's Will, and who are strong enough to battle the odds in order to act as Allah's vicegerent on earth?

Conclusion

The curriculum challenge is there. It is time for Muslims to reach beyond their own immediate needs, and their own immediate communities, to join together to design and develop a curriculum that will truly meet the needs of the larger Muslim *Ummah*.

Toward An Integrated Program
of Islamic Studies:
A Systematic Approach

*Abidullah Ghazi**

Introduction

In September 1968, my first child, Bushra Ghazi was
admitted to a Nursery class of Central School in
Cambridge, Massachusetts. We thought that the first day would be
rather difficult for her so we decided to stay longer with her until she
felt more comfortable. She had eagerly looked forward to the day and
had no hesitation to bid us good bye. We however, had another small
problem at hand; my two years old son who had accompanied us to the
school would not agree to come back with us and demanded equal rights
with his sister to be at the school. We had similar experience with all
of our children who looked forward to go to the school and felt sad when
it was closed. We also saw the enthusiasm of our children for their
schools increased with age. They loved to read and enjoyed completing
their homework. Visiting the local library several times a week is their
favorite activity. Our children by no means are any exception; we have
seen this scenario repeated with children of our friends and neighbors.
In fact, one of the punishments I threatened them with was to stop them
from going to school. The threat usually worked. This attitude of
children in the West is in contrast to the one I had been used to in my
home country, India, where many times children were dragged to school.
    In September 1968, the month my first child went to school,
we saw a beautiful TV documentary of North Africa. I invited my

---

* This paper is based on a presentation given by the author in a conference on Muslim
Education held in Saudia Arabia, several years ago. Since that time, IQRA' has met many
of its objectives in developing a comprehensive program of Islamic studies for children.

children to watch the program with me to educate them about an Islamic society which I had not visited myself but to which I, being a Muslim, somehow felt related. The documentary presented a scene of an Islamic *Madrasah* of *Tahfeezul Qur'an* (memorization of the Holy Qur'an) where young children chanted in unison the verses from the Qur'an and the teacher cracked his whip on his desk and sometimes at the back of the little children. My children were unable to understand the whipping and asked me "who is this bad 'guy' beating the children?" I did not have the courage to tell them that the 'bad guy' was the good Islamic teacher who was concerned with the Qur'anic education of the children. The scene of this *Madrasah* was not unfamiliar to my Indian background.

This methodology of teaching the Holy Qur'an was not the invention of the poor *Muqri* but was a tradition handed down for centuries which has acquired the sanctity of a sacred tradition. Both, teaching and learning in *Madrasah* are still an ordeal and modern school systems in Muslim societies have not succeeded in evolving an integrated system of education where the need of an Islamic training are met with demands of modern education.

The reasons for the enthusiasm of children for their schools in the West are due to some obvious reasons. The schools provide a friendly and creative environment for the development and growth of child's total personality. The child is respected as an individual. The school offers a well-planned and balanced program of education, recreation and sports. The curriculum is designed with children's ages, abilities, interests and environment as the guides. The educational system offers children well-equipped libraries and activity centers to satisfy their inquisitiveness and interests. There is plenty of audiovisual material available for them to further their knowledge and expand their horizons. Most schools have special facilities for both educationally handicapped and gifted children. The curriculum is not designed to frighten them away from learning but to challenge them to achieve. Besides, the teachers are, in most cases, well-trained and well-paid, who chose training as a career because of their interest in the field and not for monetary gains only.

Goals of Education

The plan of education in the advanced societies of the West is conceived around some socio-political philosophy of the country to develop a particular kind of citizen. With that objective in mind an integrated

298

curriculum is prepared and modern educational methodology is applied to raise a generation of young citizens who will shoulder the responsibilities for the future of that society.

Literature, especially children's literature and material, are produced with specific aims and objectives. A nation, a people or a community develop an entire system of education and training with a specific vision of the future. They use education as a tool to shape the course of future and train the younger generation in a particular direction. Literature is the most important means to achieve this goal.

Muslims should work together in developing not only Islamic literature for children but an Islamic system of education with the goals of developing an Islamic personality of our children and youth who will be at the helms of affairs in a society whose major source of guidance would be the Qur'an and *Sunnah*. In order to achieve this goal we need to set up an entire system of Islamic education and training with clearly defined behavioral objectives and set up a plan of action with the Qur'an and the *Sunnah* of our Prophet (s) as our guide and ideal.

The child is the center of any educational program, that is, the child should always be the center of educational planning. The child should be the focal point of educational institutions, and the curriculum, literature and educational material, methods of teaching and the teachers should cater to his growth and development being fully aware of his age, ability, interests and attention span, etc. In an ideal system of education, there is a harmony among the four, for example, while developing the tools of pedagogy, that is literature and the materials, one is always aware of the curriculum the syllabus and the teachers' background.

Perspective of Islamic Education

Here, in this paper, we will limit our discussion to educational material and children's literature. As soon as we begin to think about educational material we realize that two different types of such material are needed, viz.:

A.   Islamic educational literature and material produced for the children in Muslim countries.

B.   Islamic educational literature and material produced for the children living in Muslim minority areas.

For the former, we need to develop an integrated curriculum where various subjects are integrated with Islamic teachings and practices. The central theme through all the subjects should be Islamic teachings and the Islamic point of view. Whether we are teaching the history of Spain or India, or we are giving a lesson in physical science on Darwin's theory of evolution, or the lesson is about the theories and practices of modern banking, the Islamic point of view should be discussed clearly and emphatically. However, most of teachers and administrators in Muslim schools find it difficult to achieve this goal due to the lack of appropriate literature and material. We need training programs in our universities, which will train scholars and writers to produce children's literature from an Islamic educational perspective. If we have a serious commitment to Islam and believe in its implementation in our practical lives, we need a systematic scheme, which would work at an international level.

We need:

1. A clear statement of the philosophy at national and international levels.
2. Development of a pilot curriculum based on the philosophy.
3. Adaptation and adoption of the curriculum at national level.
4. Establishment of research institutions to prepare textbooks and other educational material in accordance with the designed curriculum.
5. Establishment of special teachers' training program to provide special training for the teachers in the implementation of the integrated Islamic curriculum.

Alhamdu li'l Allah some of the Muslim countries have enormous financial resources and most of them have a commitment to Islam. The development and implementation of such a program should not be a problem. However, we have to make a beginning.

The Case of Muslim Minority Areas

This paper is primarily concerned with Muslim minority areas, where the Muslims, being a religious and cultural minority, face a serious threat and challenge. Here the minority is concerned not only with the preservation of its own beliefs and traditions, but also, to a great extent, busy in counter-attacking the misconceptions and false propaganda against its religious values by an antagonistic majority community. Muslim minorities residing in different geographical areas share much in common, yet the problems faced by each differ from the other.

The Muslim minorities living in the secular and liberal regimes of the West have both tremendous opportunities and great challenges to their Islamic existence, and the need for a comprehensive program of Islamic education and training is especially acute in these areas. In many countries of the West, two decades of immigration and conversion has created a sizable *Ummah*. A generation of Muslim youth has struggled in relative solitude in these alien societies, which paradoxically disturb and entice them. It offers us an opportunity and presents us with unique challenges.

The Western society is a 'free society'; governed by the laws which offer equal opportunities to all religious and interest groups. In this society, the rising tides of secularism, liberalism and nationalism challenge all religious beliefs and practices and question the validity of traditional practices. Islam faces this challenge like other religions that have been facing this onslaught for the last four hundred years. Religious communites in the West have no alternative but either to accept the challenge and respond to it creatively and rationally or lose ground and become extinct. Thus we see that 1) the Western societies present the greatest challenge to the existence of religions in general and Islam in particular; 2) they offer Islam an opportunity for *Da'wah*; 3) in Muslim societies Islamic beliefs are practiced as a norm but in Western societies these are considered exotic innovations, thus, in order to believe and practice, younger Muslim generation in the West needs a rational explanation of Islam's beliefs and a coherent interpretation of its practices; 4) Islam has to be able to contend with the 'attractive' philosophies of secularization, liberalization, socialism, existentialism and rationalism in order to be accepted by a questioning generation; 5) Islam has an equal opportunity with all other philosophies to present its case and accept its course, and here lies its great opportunity; 6) Muslims living in the West need a philosophical and ideological basis to co-exist with other religious communities and act with them for the development of the society.

Muslims in the West can learn from the experiences of other religious communities, and they can also give an Islamic response to the ideas of the West and offer solutions to some of the problems of that society. If we avail ourselves of the existing opportunities, we can certainly achieve success and develop true Islamic leadership there. From Sydney to San Francisco, Muslim communities have availed themselves of this opportunity for creative engagement, developing curricula for Sunday schools, making Islamic puzzles, transliterating the *surahs* for their children at home, and establishing religious and cultural centers. The time is ripe now to prepare a pilot project of a comprehensive and systematic program of Islamic education in one language to be translated and adapted in other languages. Islamic education is not a critical problem but rather a critical challenge for contemporary Muslims.

The Role of IQRA' International

IQRA' International Educational Foundation has been established to move us into a second stage. It is concerned, first and foremost, with assessing and fulfilling the changing needs of Islamic education worldwide, and offering a coherent and comprehensive approach where, thus far, there has been fragmentation.

Our initial projects include the preparation of an educational pilot program covering the critical dimensions of Islamic studies, which will be adapted and translated for numerous Muslim societies. IQRA' represents an international movement for the dynamic application of modern methodology to the teaching of Islamic studies at all levels. We believe that such an effort must be a continuous process in harmony with the changing needs of Muslim society, and that the unity achieved in the process, carries even more *barakah* than the actual materials produced.

As English is an international language and the language spoken and understood by many Muslim minorities around the world, the Program must initially be produced in English. It is hoped that the program will benefit, in its present form, the following groups:
1. Muslim children living in English-speaking countries such as the U.S.A., UK, South Africa, Australia, etc.
2. Muslim children in other countries which have English medium schools.
3. Muslim children, in general, through translation and adaptation.
4. Muslim and non-Muslim adults with books written at an adult level which will provide easy reading for everyone wanting to learn about Islam. This literature will also be useful in *da'wah* work in the Western world.

Some Basic Difficulties

The program is a unique effort to develop a comprehensive curriculum of Islamic studies. We have had many difficulties: writing, production, and ultimate distribution. Just to highlight a few of these difficulties:

1. There are not many Muslim scholars of Islam who are trained to write books for children.
2. Unfortunately, children's literature is not recognized as a serious field of research and study in Islamic academic circles. It does not offer much chances of promotion and recognition.
3. Writing is a rare gift and we lack good writers.
4. Literature for children is a specialized and technical field and we have few experts in the field.
5. The Muslim educationists have not seriously concerned themselves with the production of Islamic literature for children.
6. Encouragement from publishers and compensation to the writers has been very disappointing. In fact, many writers have to pay the publishers in order to get their books published.
7. An unhealthy rivalry exists between the few institutions and the handful of individuals who are engaged in this task.
8. Major Islamic organizations and educational institutions have not supported this effort with needed vigor and generosity.
9. Any work dealing with Islam invites more criticism.

Unless we understand the above-mentioned difficulties, we cannot succeed in our plan. Therefore, I suggest that in order to develop the program we must establish one or more permanent institutions with the following objectives:

1. To establish educational endowments to finance Islamic educational efforts.
2. To establish an institutional base to carry out this work on a permanent basis.
3. To discover and train the best Muslims and direct their talents and energies toward developing a systematic program of Islamic studies.
4. To establish a Resource Center for education which should be well equipped with literature and educational aids to function as ready reference for such efforts.
5. To acquire expertise in the development, production and distribution

of educational materials.

6. To promote and supervise the translation and adaptation of materials in other languages.
7. To establish an Open University to administer and supervise the program internationally.

Iqra's Systematic and Comprehensive Program of Islamic Studies

I take this opportunity to present before you Iqra's systematic and comprehensive program of Islamic Studies which has been in progress for more than ten years, and has managed to progress in spite of grave financial difficulties. The program covers the needs in textbooks, skillbooks, teacher/parent guides, enrichment literature and educational aids for the Islamic education of Muslim children. This is intended to be the first phase covering the essential needs of Islamic education in a variety of school settings (such as full time schools, weekend schools, evening schools and summer schools or even at home).

This program will, *Insha Allah*, provide proper Islamic education of Muslim children through well written, appropriately illustrated and beautifully produced materials. It will also provide much needed guidance to the teachers and parents through teacher/parent manuals. This is a pilot program, which should be translated and adapted for other languages. It is hoped that it will serve for developing such programs in English and other languages.

Educational Material:
This program defines the following categories of books and educational materials:
1. Textbooks,
2. Skillbooks,
3. Teacher/Parent guides,
4. Enrichment books and
5. Educational Aids.

Textbooks:
A textbook is the basic book used by students in classrooms for the study of a subject. Each textbook will have an accompanying skillbook and

a teacher/parent guide. The information in each of the textbooks will be related to a subject or theme and will be comprehensive and relevant to the children of a particular age/ability group. It will also have a controlled vocabulary for each appropriate subject matter in a very systematic way. The textbooks will be properly illustrated with pictures, sketches and diagrams.

Skillbooks:

A skillbook follows the textbook and contains exercises for reinforcement and practice. The students can work on their own, in the classrooms or at home.

Teacher/Parent Guides:

The Teacher/Parent guide will provide ideas and guidance to teachers and parents related to the subject matter of the textbooks and general teaching methodology. It will also contain helpful ideas for the use of educational material relating to the subject matter and ways to integrate the lesson with other subjects in the comprehensive program of Islamic studies.

Enrichment Materials:

Enrichment material will consist of independent reading material, educational games, puzzles, charts, slides, filmstrips, etc. It will provide practice and reinforcement, of skills and materials covered, while making learning an enjoyable activity.

Enrichment literature books are intended to illustrate other related aspects of the subject and provide independent readings for children. They will read these books at home in their free time for pleasure and knowledge. Teachers may also assign these enrichment books for extra reading.

Educational Aids:

The use of educational aids is very important in facilitating the process of learning. Since the inception of the project ten years ago, computers and video films have flooded the market. There is an urgent need to make use of these tools.

Age Groups:

In view of the fact that these books will be studied in various educational settings where the level of comprehension of English and background in Islamic education would differ, no strict age limit could be set on any grade level. Therefore, this scheme recommends a combination of age plus ability/achievement groupings. In preparation of the material, age and ability have been proposed as the criteria for the vocabulary usage. The introduction of concepts is based on American school settings. For Islamic schools, the teacher's judgment is recommended in selecting the children's level in the particular course work.

The levels generally adopted are shown below. They are flexible and can be adjusted.

Pre-school	Level I	4-5 years
Elementary	Level II	6-11 years
Junior	Level III	11-14 years
Senior	Level IV	14 and over

Subjects:

In the first phase, the program will deal with seven subjects:
1.   Arabic and Qur'anic Studies
2.   Sirah of Rasulullah (S)
3.   'Aqa'id and Fiqh
4.   Islamic Akhlaq
5.   Islamic Social Studies
6.   Islamic Education and Da'wah
7.   Islamic Literature

Iqra's Pilot Program of the *Sirah* of Rasulullah (S)

The pilot program of *Sirah* is produced as a model for the development of other subjects. The *Sirah* program is initially prepared at three levels:

Elementary	ages 6-11 years
Junior	ages 11-14 years
Senior	ages 14 and over

The program incorporates modern educational ideas and techniques to facilitate learning. Certain characteristics of the *Sirah* program are:

1. The vocabulary is chosen with grade level and readability in mind.
2. In spite of the fact that vocabulary is controlled, Islamic vocabulary is introduced to enable our children to learn Islamic terminology and use it in every day life.
3. New and difficult words are repeated, especially at elementary levels to provide sufficient opportunity for learning.
4. New words, both English and Arabic, are given at the end of each lesson. The teacher should provide extra practice in teaching them.
5. Each lesson is summed up under three important points. This provides an opportunity to focus on the main ideas and to help comprehension. Further comprehension exercises are provided in skill books.
6. The textbooks contain basic information about the life of *Rasulullah* (S) that a child should know. The Stories of *Sirah* are separated from the biographical information.
7. The text integrates the basic message of the Qur'an and other aspects of Islamic education with Sirah. This Islamic curricular integration gradually develops through two levels, elementary and junior and finally presented in a comprehensive manner at senior level.
8. At the Elementary level we have discussed the Makkah period in more detail than at the junior level. This was warranted due to the necessity of keeping the conceptual development in children's mind as a concern and tying it with the events of the life of *Rasulullah* (S) in Makkah and Madinah. At the senior level, both periods receive equal attention and various aspects of *Sirah* are explained.
9. The Messenger of Allah, senior level, integrates *Sirah* with Qur'anic studies by offering relevant readings from the Qur'an in the text and the study questions. Thus, through these textbooks a student will grasp the central message of the Qur'an and see its relationship to the *Sirah*.
10. Islamic scholars have carefully reviewed the contents of the books. The books have also been edited professionally.

Progress in other Subjects Areas:

The success of the pilot program of *Sirah* has encouraged Iqra' to expand the program and efforts. Eleven committees have been constituted to develop the program, which follows:

1. Islamic education and curriculum development
2. The Qur'anic and Arabic studies
3. *Sirah* of Rasulullah (S)
4. *Aqa'id* and *Fiqh*
5. Islamic *Akhlaq*
6. Islamic Social Sciences
7. Islamic Education and *Da'wah*
8. Islamic Literature
9. Educational Aids
10. Publication and distribution
11. Finance and Investment

The following two committees were established to study the feasibility of and develop a program of action in the following areas:

1. Iqra' International Open University
2. Children's Islamic Magazines

Each committee will be responsible for a specific task to initiate the program of writing, researching, supervising and reviewing the draft proposal. Many authors should be identified and approached to write books in their(s) of specialization and interests.

Whether Allah has blessed us with verbal or artistic talents, with managerial skills or financial means, our cooperation in the development of Islamic education purifies our blessings through *sadaqa jariyah* (charity that endures past our lifetime).

Iqra' cherishes Muslim writers and artists as valuable resources. The community must be willing to support them in order that they may devote their energies to Islam without sacrificing the needs of their families. Those writers who have been blessed with affluence may choose not to accept monetary compensation, but we recognize that many of our potential contributors do not fall into that category.

Whatever our individual gifts, Iqra' offers new opportunity, the opportunity to give what we once held back, to give of ourselves with the confidence that our offerings will be accepted, nurtures and refined and that they will blossom as the wellspring of a new generation.

VI

SOCIAL ISSUES
AND CONCERNS

Islamic Fundamentalism

Ahmad H. Sakr

As you are aware, there are more than one billion Muslims in different parts of the world; eight million are in North America. Muslims are from different nationalities, ethnic, national and linguistic backgrounds. 20% are Arabs and the others are non-Arabs. 6-8% of the Arabs are non-Muslims. There are an average of 50 sovereign Muslim states and 23 Arab sovereign states. Muslim minorities are more than 400 million, scattered in different parts of the world such as the U.S.A., Canada, Latin America, Europe, India, Burma, the Philippines, China, Vietnam, etc.

It should be stated here that there is no clergy in Islam, and there is no pope either. There is not one single Muslim State that represents Islam or Muslims of the World. Each and every one of them represents themselves. The final authority and the legislator is only Allah.

Islam is not simply a religion, as is the case with Western religions. It is a total way of life, and it has complete systems of living for mankind. This means that there is no separation between the state and religion. They are both embodied together under the umbrella of Islam. The state and all those in power are under the domain of Allah, the Creator.

The main sources of Islamic teachings are the Qur'an and *sunnah*. Qur'an is the direct revelation of Allah to Muhammad. The Message in the Qur'an is meant for all mankind and especially for those who claim themselves to be Christians and Jews. The original Bible and Torah are found in pure form in the Qur'an. The language of the Qur'an is Arabic. Its originality, totality, and authenticity are all proved to be true.

The one who received the Qur'an was Prophet Muhammad. His sayings are called "*hadith.*" However, he lived the teachings of the Qur'an, he taught it to his people and he explained it to them. Therefore, his sayings, his living habits, his traditions and customs, are all combined in what is called "*Sunnah.*"

Is Islam a myth, a religion of a cult, or a true, and a divine religion from Almighty God? Are Muslims a group of fundamentalists, terrorists, fanatics, or radicals? Are they a group of people who are nomads, camel riders, and uncivlized? Are they unacceptable in any society? Are they a bunch of individuals who wander here and there, or are they those who go out of their way to make *jihad* and kill any and everyone who is not a Muslim so that they may enter Paradise? Many more questions have been raised and may be raised about Islam and Muslims.

If Islam were a myth, then how did it originate, and who founded this religion? It is a surprising phenomenon: how in the world are there hundreds of millions of people across the Planet Earth who profess to be Muslims? With all the stereotypes mentioned about Islam and Muslims, still Islam is the fastest growing religion in the world. With all the exploitation and with all the killings, which is taking place, the number of Muslims, is still increasing. The more Islam and the Muslims are attacked, blamed and accused by the mass media, the more innocent and educated non-Muslims are accepting Islam. It is really a strange phenomenon that needs to be studied.

TERMINOLOGIES RECOGNIZED

"Fundamentalism," as is explained by Webster's Dictionary, has nothing to do with Islam or Muslims. It has to do with Christianity!

> Fundamentalism: A movement in American Protestantism that arose in the early part of the 20th Century in reaction to modernism and that stresses the inerrancy of the Bible not only in matters of faith and morals but also as a literal historical record, holding as essential to Christian Faith, belief in such doctrines as the virgin birth, physical resurrection, atonement by the sacrificial death of Christ, and the Second Coming.

"Fundamentalism" as explained by the American Heritage Dictionary of the English Language is as follows:

1. Belief in the Bible as factual historical record and incontrovertible prophecy, including such doctrines as the Genesis, the Virgin Birth, the Second Advent, and Armageddon.
2. A movement among U.S. Protestants of the 19th century based upon this belief.

"Holy War" and the idea of the "infidels" are two terminologies that have to do with the Crusaders. Islam has nothing to do with these words. On the contrary, Islam condemns such concepts completely.

"*Jihad*" does Not mean Holy War, but means to excel and to do

312

the best to achieve the best. It is struggle against the self: to control one's lust and ego while he is trying to perform his duties to the best.

ISLAM VS. FUNDAMENTALISM

If fundamentalism means to follow the fundamental teachings of Islam, then every Muslim is a Fundamentalist. However, to be fanatic, to be dogmatic, and to be radical is against the teachings of Islam. Prophet Muhammad (pbuh) said:

Ibn Masood narrated that the Prophet said:
"They are the losers, those who are fanatics." He repeated it three times.

Islam condemns any person who is fanatic, or extremist. Islam insists on moderation and tolerance towards one another and especially towards non-Muslims. In *Surah Al-Baqarah* (The Cow), Allah made Muslims a community of moderation. The Qur'an states the following:

Thus have We made of you an Ummah justly balanced. That you might be witnesses over the nations, and the Messenger a witness over yourselves; And We appointed the *Qibla* to which thou was'nt used, Only to test those who followed the Messenger from those who would turn on their heels (from the Faith). Indeed, it was (a change) momentous, except to those guided by Allah. And never would Allah make your faith of no effect. For Allah is to all people most surely full of Kindness, Most Merciful. (2:143)

Also, in *Surah Al-Hajj* (Pilgrimage), Allah informs mankind that it is He Who controls us regularly and directs us regularly. Otherwise, people would have killed one another, and would destroy everything, including their worship places. The Qur'an states the following:
(They are) those who have been expelled from their homes in defiance of right, - (For no cause) except that they say, "Our Lord is Allah." Did not Allah check one set of people by means of another, there would surely have been pulled down monasteries, churches, synagogues, and mosques, in which the name of Allah is commemorated in abundant measure.

Allah will certainly aid those who aid His (cause);- for verily Allah is full of strength, exalted in Might, (able to enforce His Will). (22:40)

Islam instructed Muslims to call upon People of the Book to come together and live peacefully with the Muslims. The Qur'an is very explicit in inviting the non-Muslims to commonalties. In *Surah Al-Imran*, Allah says the following.

Say: "O People of the Book! Come to common terms as between us and you: that we worship none but Allah; that we associate no partners with Him; that we erect not, from among ourselves, Lords and patrons other than Allah." If then they turn back, say you: "Bear witness that we (at least) are Muslims (bowing to Allah's Will)."

In case of disputes, Muslims are to use wisdom in their dialogue with non-Muslims. In *Surah Al-Ankabut* (the Spider), Allah says the following:

And dispute you not with the People of the Book, except in the best way, unless it be with those of them who do wrong but say, "We believe in the Revelation which has come down to us and in that which came down to you; Our God and your God is One; and it is to Him we submit (in Islam). (29:46)

Islam praised those People of the Book who are honest, sincere, faithful, and God-fearing. In *Surah Al-Imran*, Allah says the following:

Not all of them are alike; of the People of the Book are a portion that stand (for the right); they rehearse the Signs of Allah all night long. And they prostrate themselves in adoration. They believe in Allah and the Last Day; they enjoin what is right, and forbid what is wrong; and they haten (in emulation) in (all) good works: they are in the ranks of the righteous. (3:113-114)

Muslims are to respect the People of the Book, to honor them, to protect them, and to encourage them to live with moral teachings of their books.

314

In some Muslim countries, we see groups, movements and individuals committing acts of terrorism or acts of fanaticism. Such acts have nothing to do with Islam. They are to blamed, condemned and penalized. However, these acts are being done as reactions to the injustices that were committed against them by state terrorism, and protected by the superpowers.

In some Muslim countries, certain individuals, organizations, and/ or movements stood for freedom of speech and freedom of religion, and they were denied. Some have gone through extreme approaches to get their freedom. Therefore, they committed serious mistakes. Some are Muslims, while others are Christians. It should be stated here that such activities were done as a reaction to the severe penalties, deprivation, hunger, lack of freedom of speech, and other actions arbitrarily imposed by the leaders against their citizens.

It is understood that Muslims in some parts of the world do not have the chance to practice a democratic way of lie. They have self-imposed leaders who are either dictators… monarchs… feudal or tyrant military rulers… They were self-imposed or were imposed by outside powers. Some of them committed crimes, killings, imprisonments, and they did not respect the rights of their local citizens. Some of them denied freedom of speech and freedom of practising the religious teachings of Islam in its purest form.

A PARTIAL LIST OF "MUSLIM" GOVERNMENTS

NAME OF THE COUNTRY–TYPE OF GOVERNMENT
1. Afghanistan–Unstable Military Anarchy
2. Algeria–Military Dictatorship
3. Bangladesh–Empowerment of a country with Pseudo-Democracy
4. Brunei–Sultan - Monarchy
5. Egypt–Military Dictatorship
6. Gulf–Sultan - Monarchy
7. Indonesia–Anarchy of Dictatorship
8. Iraq–Military Dictatorship
9. Jordan–King - Monarchy
10. Kuwait–Amir - Monarchy
11. Lebanon–Anarchy of Democracy
12. Libya–Military Dictatorship
13. Malaysia–King by Turns - Monarchy

14. Morocco–King - Monarchy
21. Nigeria–Regular Fighting between Military Dictatorship & Democratic Politicians
22. Pakistan–Unstable Balance between Pseudo-Democracy & Anarchy
23. Saudi Arabia–King - Monarchy
24. Somalia–Feudalism
25. Syria–Military Dictatorship
26. Tunisia–Military Dictatorship
27. Turkey–Secularism Against Islam

FEAR OF ISLAM AND/OR MUSLIMS

Non-Muslims are afraid of Islam and Muslims. They have the right to be afraid. There are many reasons; some of them are included in the following list:

GENERAL REASONS

1. Ignorance of the majority of non-Muslims about Islam and Muslims. (The latter group is to blame for not explaining the teachings of Islam to the non-Muslims.)
2. Non-Muslims may hate Muslims due to ignorance and isolation.
3. Jealousy – for having the Prophet Muhammad from the progeny of Ishmael and not the progeny of Ishaq and Yacoub.
4. Phobia towards Islam and Muslims for no reason at all.
5. Lack of confidence in themselves by those non-Muslims who are afraid of Islam.
6. An erroneous notion has been spread that Muslims are a superpower; and NOT part of the Third World countries.
7. The leaders of the U.S.A. are afraid because they do know that Islam offers a better way of life than democracy and capitalism.
8. The leaders here in the U.S.A. have failed their mission and they want to cover their mistakes by putting blame on others, such as Islam and Muslims. Accordingly, they keep their people busy with the imaginary issues rather than with the realities. Democrats and Republicans have failed their missions in solving the problems in America. Instead of solving their problems, they increase the economic and socio-political problems. Accordingly, they put the blame for such problems on Islam and the Muslims.

316

Isolation

Muslims have isolated themselves in their houses, masajids and jobs. They did not interact with their non-Muslim neighbours, friends, and colleagues.

They also did not interact enough with the official people of the local and federal governments.

EXTERNAL REASONS
1. Crusaders
2. Inquisition
3. Colonialism and imperialism: past and present
4. Missionaries
5. Peace Corp
6. Orientalists
7. Politicians
8. The veto power of the Security Council
9. Double standard of the superpowers in exporting Democracy to all except the Muslims.

In the past, the demolition of the Islamic Caliphate and the division of the Muslims Ummah; and to what we see now, the generous aid to the self-imposed dictators, monarchs, and military rulers, against their own people.

INTERNAL REASONS

Secular
Some Muslim countries have tried to be independent from outside control and they have established political systems such as:
1. Arab Nationalism
2. Socialism
3. Communism
4. Ba'th parties
5. Secularism with hatred towards religion
6. Dictatorship... Monarch... Sultanate... , etc.

Religious

Some Muslims tried the other route, i.e., the religious teachings of Islam.
Therefore, movements were established such as:
1. Sufism
2. Wahhabys
3. Revivalist Movements
4. Muslim Brotherhood
5. Jama'at Islami
6. Jama'at Tabliqh
7. Salafi Movements
8. and many more

Psychological

Most of the Muslims who come to the U.S. from the Muslim World are
passive. They don't get involved in politics and they are not vocal. They
have lived in America for a number of years and still are afraid to express
their views to non-Muslims. They are afraid to be known as activists.
Either they are afraid of losing their jobs or their citizenship. Therefore,
they are not in the mainstream of American politics. On the other hand,
they came from a totalitarian system and they learned not to express
their views to anyone. Otherwise they would be in trouble.

RELATIONSHIPS & COMMONALITIES

Early Muslims and Arabs were excellent friends to the West. People in
Muslim Countries were, and still are, good to the people of Europe and
America.

Europeans and Americans were, and are still welcomed in Muslim
lands at most levels: Education, Religious Missionaries, Health, Economics
and in other areas too.

Religiously: Muslims consider Jews and Christians as People of the
Book. There are tremendous amount of commonalties in terms of values,
family ties, respect, obedience, and belief in God, the Creator.

Historically: Muslims, Christians, and Jews lived together peacefully
so many times except for a few incident.

Non-Muslims were, and are, still holding the ranks of political
ministers, administrative positions, and membership in Government

Executive Councils. They also held the position of Advisors in the Cabinets of the Caliphs themselves.

Muslims living in the West have brought with them their values and their intellect. They have added to and enriched the West with their knowledge and their spiritual values. They brought financial help to build their community centers, and their educational institutions.

RELIGIOUS GROUPS:

The Religious leaders of America have a moral obligation to build bridges of understanding among all the faithful and God-fearing people.

The National Council of Christians and Jews (NCCJ) of the U.S.A. should include other religious groups, especially the American Muslims. Instead of being called NCCJ, it should be called the American Interfaith Council (AIC).

In as much as Christian and Jewish religious leaders are invited for invocations, Muslim religious leaders should be invited for the same.

The religious leaders should stop accusing Islam and Muslims during their sermons. They should bring the commonalties among all the religious people in the world, and especially those who are living in America.

Dialogues and trialogues should be initiated among the leaders of the Abrahamic religious.

Field trips should be conducted among the religious groups to visit other religious centers to observe and to learn about others. Workshops, and training programs should be conducted as well.

BUILDING A BETTER FUTURE

The White House should recruit a group of American Muslims to act as a council of Advisors to the White House concerning Muslim affairs in America, as well as the affairs of the Muslim world.

The State Department should recruit some American Muslims and appoint them as ambassadors, counsel generals, or other echelons to be sent to some Muslim countries.

The Department of Education should recruit American Muslim intellectuals to help in writing those chapters about Islam in textbooks for the public schools systems.

The Presidential Press Secretary should inform the mass media to be fair with all Americans, and treat them equally. They should not correlate American Muslims with any Muslim country. Muslims of America are Americans, and they have already demonstrated their love and respect to America. They have already contributed to the success of America, and have improved its image nationally, and internationally.

American Muslims have reacted nobly even when a crisis took place in any Muslim country. They are "shock absorbers". If the American leadership does not absorb them, they may lose them. Some Muslims may react negatively and then become extremists, as we have seen in some Muslim countries.

The Department of Education should recognize that there are more than ½ million Muslim students from different foreign countries. They are at different academic institutions. If they are welcomed, absorbed, and treated with fairness, they will become the best spokesmen for America in their home countries.

Since freedom of religion is one of the main cardinals of the American Constitution, and since Christians and Jews have acquired their religious freedom on Saturdays and Sundays, Muslims who wish to observe their Friday congregational prayer, should be given the freedom to do so without being penalized.

American Foreign Policy makers should recognize that Democracy of the West is a man-made system. There is no uniformity among those who believe that democracy is the best for the welfare of humanity.

American leaders, and the West, should recognize that capitalism is not the best solution to the betterment of humanity. It is a system whereby the rich exploit the destiny of the people. Through the economic system of capitalism, many people become jobless and homeless. The rate of crime, drug abuse, vandalism, and family breakdown have increased tremendously, while family values have almost been wiped out.

American leaders should stop helping Israel and the Arab leaders. They should be left to solve their own problems by themselves. American leadership should concentrate on their local problems, and try to solve them before it is too late, for the existence of America as a superpower.

FINAL REMARKS

It is easy to accuse Islam and Muslims these days. There is no proof of such criminality in the religion of Islam or to the people who adhere to, and practice, the tenets of Islam. It is also easy to correlate one incident by one individual who may have a "Muslim" name, to all Muslims throughout the world. Moreover, it is easy to orchestrate such an incidence through T.V., radio, and other mass media to convince the viewers that such an accusation is true. It is also easy to dramatize such as incident on a daily basis so that people are superficially convinced of what they see and hear.

It seems that the best proof against such allegations is Islam itself: its creed, its doctrine, its teachings, its applications, and its universal values. The other proof is in the Muslim community in the world today, and throughout history. Those who accuse Muslims forget that it was the Muslims who brought Europeans from the decay of the Dark Ages to the Renaissance. It was also the Muslims who freed the Africans from slav ?ry and gave them equal rights with all other people of the world - over 1400 years ago. It was the Muslims who freed the people in Asia from their primitive beliefs so that they could worship the one God, the Creator of the Universe. It was the Muslims who brought to the world Freedom of Speech... Freedom of Religion... and Freedom from exploitation. Some types of exploitation which people were freed from were: economic, political, social, cultural, and educational. It was the Muslims who practised the teachings of Islam and influenced people in different parts of the world to accept Islam.

Islam means peace to all. Whoever wants to live in peace, harmony, and happiness, has to accept the Universal Teachings of Islam which came to all human beings irrespective of color, race, gender, nationality, ethnic background, language, religion, social status, or economic status.

People in America and the West will continue to suffer from their incorrect social, political, economic and moral values until they recognize Islam. They will never improve their values and standards until they follow Islamic teachings. It is only after they benefit from Islam that they will solve many of their contemporary problems.

The people in the West should read what other Western philosophers have said about Islam, so as to benefit from the Islamic teachings. George Bernard Shaw, a Western thinker and philosopher said:

"Europe shall declare the Islam Creed innocent of what men of Europe of the Middle Ages accused it of in evil tales. The religion of Muhammad shall be the system on which the bases of the world peace and happiness shall be established. The solution of the world problems will depend on its philosophy. Many of my compatriots and other Europeans follow the principles of Islam. Therefore, I can prophesy that the European Islamic era is undoubtedly very near."

Muslim Youth of North America: Issues and Concerns

Riyad Shamma

The story is. . . "The future is with our youth", "Our youth are taking over after we're gone", "The youth are the most important aspect of our community"—These are some of the many comments about youth that are heard repeatedly at conferences, *khutbas* and dinner discussions. The question that must arise, but seldom does, is just who are these mysterious "youth" and what is being done about/to/for/by them that addresses the future that is in their hands? Is it all rhetoric? Do we just trust that Allah will work it all out?

The youth that are referred to are generally those under the age eighteen; the ones that are usually ignored because they've been instructed to simply 'study' for the all-important secular education. They are the ones whose parents turn a generally blind eye, hoping that that's all they are doing (studying) and not getting into trouble or being tempted by all the evil out in society. Of course, *Shaytan* is not one to let a golden opportunity pass by, and many youth are involved in many *haram* areas, under the cover of good grades. These youth are much more common than parents are willing to admit. Most parents struggle with and feel that their hands are tied in trying to control their children. These same youth are the ones who are our future. However, it is such general statements as were just made above that mislead so many parents. When the threat is a vague "evil society", it never applies to their children, who are all angels and model Muslims. Many parents believe that the evil in society is only in the "bad" parts of town, and that by living in the "good" / rich area of town they won't be touched. Since they don't see at their workplace much of what is actually threatening their children, they tend to disbelieve it. Of course when confronted on the issue, they will vaguely acknowledge that their children aren't completely safe even in the good area of town, but in their hearts they don't see / realize / accept the threat that is really there.

The threats

(1) Conform or else! Specifically then, what is that threat? First and foremost is the desire to conform. This is responsible for 80% of the problems youth have. Two of the leading contributors to this problem are that parents don't credit how strong this desire is and tend to disregard it. Secondly, many parents are unintentionally teaching their children that they should conform. They do this by not wearing hijab/beard/ Islamically acceptable dress to work because "it's not professional" or by going to the company party or giving their children American or Americanized names (Moe instead of Mohammed, Dave instead of Dawood, etc.). One of the most common responses given by teenage youth as to why they don't fulfill certain Islamic requirements, or engage in certain *haram* activities, is "this is what my parents do." The desire to conform ranges substantially from person to person. The parent's desire, or lack thereof doesn't affect how a child will react. Within a given family, one child might be indifferent to what others think, while the next child is terrified that his/her peers won't like what they wore that day. The danger in conforming goes well beyond clothes however. Dating is probably the number one issue where (older - 13+) youth feel the pressure to conform. Not only are hormones beginning to flow, but all of their friends are asking them if they are interested in such-an-such a boy/girl and if they'd like to go out. When they say no, then their friends look at them funny and may call them homosexual or otherwise harass them. Many youth find it easier not to stand out and have a girl/boyfriend. However, even from a young age the desire to follow the crowd is strong - to participate in making fun of another child, doing 'adult' things in the playground when the teacher isn't watching (smoking, sipping a stolen beer, making out like in the movies). Dress is another issue where there is a lot of pressure to conform and blend in. So the girls don't want to wear a scarf and the boys want to wear shorts during gym and are afraid to ask to have a private shower. (Most schools have shower rooms where 15 shower heads all point into one big room and everyone stands around naked showering together.) Going out to parties for dancing and drinking, disrespecting your parents, smoking, not taking

time out to pray and many other habits are all formed because of the desire to "fit in" with their friends and fear of being alone or ridiculed.

Another major problem is the duality/split-personality that is developed when the youth feels equally this need to please parents and peers. At home, they are the model Indo-Pak/Arab/Asian child who obey their parents and dutifully study. After they walk out the door to go to school, however, they become as much like their non-Muslim American friends as possible. They change into clothes they brought in their school bags; they put on make-up, their language changes and their attitudes change. Unless they have a different ethnic background, you wouldn't be able to tell them apart from the other non-Muslims, even if you watched for days! Confusion also arises when parents blur the line between culture and religion - usually because they are ignorant, stubborn or both. Culture is generally given more weight than religion by the parents, and so the youth are given a mixed signal because Allah and culture inevitably disagree. With regards to issues of marriage, this issue is seen most clearly. By the pro-culture parents, it is better to marry someone from your particular ethnic background who is successful by secular standards (i.e. rich & a doctor) than to marry someone based on Allah's standards (i.e. piety first). The irony is plain, but parents continue take into account culture first.

(2) Sow your wild oats! The second threat is from the temptation of natural desires. This applies mostly to the older youth who have reached puberty. The society freely accepts and encourages men and women to dress in a way that reflects the ideology if you've got, "flaunt it." It is not uncommon to see women wearing shirts that show their bellies, shorts, tight fitting clothes that very clearly define every curve of thier bodies; men wearing shorts, going shirtless, wearing tight, form fitting pants, etc. Not only are these people walking around, they are also seen on just about every television show, commercial, billboard advertisement, magazine, movie and Internet. Of course, the peers of the Muslim youth are dressing like they see their elders dressing, and so the muslim youth are forced to interact with these people eight hours a day at school at a minimum. Although schools have a certain "dress code" it becomes less strict each year. Needless to say, it can be very difficult to maintain control when a beautiful girl, scantily clad covered in makeup comes up to your son and asks him out on a date—and vice-versa. The unspoken message that sex between willing partners is not only acceptable but good is yet another difficult battle to fight. After

all, your body is telling you that it would be fun, your mind is being told by ads, movies, TV, etc. that it is fun and you have a willing partner who's asking you. The only weapon you have is your *iman*, and if that hasn't been properly trained it becomes easy for *Shaytan* to convince you to do what is so "natural". After all, everybody is doing it and they all seem fine.

(3) School ranks higher than God! Finally is 'negative' teaching. Your children receive a subliminal message from parents when they are sent to school. That message is that school is important and they go there to learn. However, not only do they learn math and how to read, they are also learning evolution without God, sex is OK as long as it's safe, education has nothing to do with religion, and that human beings are the ultimate lawmakers. It's the unspoken lessons that persuade the children not to attend the mosque and to trivialize religion. After all, parents send them to school 8 hours a day, five days a week and only take them to the mosque 2 hours, one time per week.

What's the message?

And so the story ends. . . Above all, it is important to realize that these threats are carried through the television, radio, movies, magazines and ANY public, private, Catholic or non-Islamic school. You can't move into an area of town and thereby keep your children 'safe,' and ignore the threats or simply tell your children to avoid them. The real issue, then, is how to ensure that youth are properly educated and motivated in the path of Allah. How can we bring up the type of youth that Allah speaks about in *Surah Al-Kahf*, "And they were youth who believed in their Lord, and We advanced them in guidance." In the face of global efforts of a New World Order, which orders self indulgence, self centerism and self worship, how do we influence the youth away from their peers, television, misinformation from the public schools, and the plethora of bad examples that other "Muslims" set? How can we bring up our children to be youth who believe in their lord? How can we raise our children as true Muslims, whose character is a shining example to everyone around them and in who's hands we feel relief to place ourselves as we grow old?

326

What's the answer?

Youth need some support group if they are going to be able to withstand the assault that faces them when they go to school. Without the support, it is easy to capitulate and conform to the non-Muslim standard. The key is to educate the youth and have them realize that there are other youth out there with the exact problems that they have. To know why it is better to conform to the Muslim standard than otherwise, even if it is difficult. Stop wanting to fit in with others, and, instead, be the model so they want to fit in with you. Ultimately, give the youth an Islamic alternative to what they are being offered at school and outside of school. Specifically, education is the number one answer. The youth need to be taught much more than just the mechanics of prayer and to memorize the life of the prophet as a list of facts. They need to be taught to understand the inner dimensions of prayer, the lessons from the prophet's example. They must understand the reasons why we do things, including why we pray, why we don't drink, why we don't date, why we should obey our parents, etc. etc. etc. This education has to start from the home and finish at the home. It is a lifelong process. It shouldn't start at age 15 or stop at age 10. It can't be taught in 2 hours per week at Sunday school or in a weekly Muslim summer camp. Parents need to participate in activities in which they want their children to participate; to help their children meet and keep in touch with other good Muslim children. Parents need to set the example in all aspects of their lives, that Allah is most important, not society. Communication has to be opened with the children. The children should feel comfortable talking to their parents, knowing that they will not be condemned or punished, or worse, ignored and treated as being ignorant. Youth need to learn that they must obey and respect their parents, as long as they aren't ordered to do something against Allah. They have to keep the lines of communication open, even if it is difficult for the parents to do so. Time should be set aside for Muslim activities that arise. Most importantly, the youth have to want to be Muslim. What forums are available to solve the problem? What youth groups, Muslim organizations and Islamic schools are available? What is being done?

Muslim Youth of North America

Several organizations have youth activities of some kind. However, one clearly stands out as being in the forefront of addressing the challenges faced by the Muslim community: MYNA (Muslim Youth of North America). MYNA works to develop youth at two levels. The first is to provide knowledge. The second is to put that knowledge to work by having the youth learn organizational and teaching skills. One of the major reasons youth have difficulty in being different and not conforming is that they don't truly understand why in fact they are different. Nine out of ten youth cannot explain the reasons why Muslims don't date. "It's against my religion" is not a reason why, and yet it's one of the most common answers given. Other answers include, "I'm busy", "My parents won't let me" or "I already have a girl/boyfriend"—mostly lies of course. Knowledge and understanding are critical. When the youth know why dating is prohibited, they are able to explain to their questioning peers, and thereby earn the respect of the peers and gain self-confidence in what they believe. Teaching the understanding of Islam so that youth know what they need to know, to answer the questions their peers will put to them, and how to turn down the offers of haram is critical and hence one of the objectives of MYNA.

This type of education is provided through several channels. At the local level, youth groups are formed and engage in study circles. Community leaders are also brought in to assist in the education process, as well as local university students. Regionally and nationally there are seminars, camps and conferences that bring in knowledgeable leaders, international Islamic scholars and others who are able to assist the youth in their learning and understanding process.

The second level is to provide alternative activities for youth. By nature, youth want to be active, to be doing something. Whereas adults are happy to sit around talking and drinking tea all day, every evening, the youth are quickly bored. As the saying goes, "Idle hands are the devil's workshop," and this is especially so with youth. Most mischief starts when the conversation turns to "Let's do something, I'm bored." MYNA treats these youth like the adults they are. It provides a structure to give them responsibility and teach them how to use it. It is expected that they will live up to their duty and do it well. The aforementioned seminars, camps and conferences are almost entirely organized and presented by youth ages twelve to eighteen; from the publicity to the program, the food to the fundraising. The youth are challenged to develop fun activities for their local youth group as well as educational. After all, who knows better what the youth want to do for fun than the youth? When given the responsibility and the trust, they rise to meet the challenge.

What are the future plans?

Most organizations realize that they are limited in what they can accomplish. Ultimately, the work must be done on the grass roots level, with each community providing the bulk of its own solution. Toward this aim, the goal is to develop stronger youth groups, more Islamic schools, and stronger/more active community support for the youth. Specifically, parents need to be educated that they must take time out of their regular schedules and give it freely to the youth. Parents can be wonderful educators, provide transportation for youth too young to drive, be chaperones at different events, support activities financially, and otherwise perform many vital services for their own children and other youth. Parents need to be taught that it is not acceptable to assume someone else will do the job. They cannot depend on their children's friends' parents to provide transportation, money or chaperoning for their own children. The youth need to find inexpensive halal activities they like to do. They need to keep in touch with each other, especially across cultural barriers. They need to actively pursue their Islamic education and be unabashed to ask questions. Finally, the youth need tell their non-Muslim friends what a great time they are having, so that their non-Muslim friends will beg them to come along. The non-Muslim will treasure halal fun over haram "fun" because they will start to see and understand what true brotherhood is all about.

What support is needed?

Time and money. Time can be contributed by adults toward camps and conferences in areas such as being speakers, counselors, providing transportation, helping in the kitchen. Adult help is also needed in terms of expertise in various areas the youth may work in, local transportation and chaperoning, as advisors and role models. Donating money helps pay for youth who can't otherwise afford to attend various events. It reduces the youth cost of activities that are more expensive, like skiing or providing camping equipment. Financial help also can be used to defer travel costs, so youth can meet other Muslims around the country, and then keep in touch over the phone and email. So what's it for you? It all comes down to individual effort. Yours. Allah will question you on the Day of Judgment about your ability, time and money and how you used them. Everybody can fill some niche. Think about what was mentioned above and decide in what areas you can improve and participate. We all look forward to seeing you in the forefront of getting the job done.

Islamic Estate Planning Using Wills and Living Trusts

Kareem M. Irfan and M. Nasrul Huq

Muslims well recognize the Qur'anic injunctions making it highly recommended that every Muslim have a Will, or like instrument, bequeathing his/her estate upon death, in accordance with the Islamic system prescribed by the Qur'an and *Sunnah* of the Prophet. However, a common misconception among Muslims is that this requirement may be satisfied only by way of a traditional Will. Contrary to this popular "myth", an alternative approach to estate planning is available, particularly to Muslims in North America, whereby the Qur'anic injunctions may be adequately satisfied while, at the same time, efficiently addressing critical concerns regarding provisions of necessary support and care for loved ones and patronage of Islamic community centers, Masjids, and like organizations.

This alternative is the use of a revocable "Living Trust" which provides an extremely advantageous means for precisely controlling one's property and financial rights both during life and following death. There exists an outstanding need to educate the Muslim populace at large as to the availability of the Living Trust approach as an alternative—generally, a remarkable advantageous one—to the traditional Will route toward estate planning which comports with the Islamic *Shariah*.

This article presents key concepts of Wills and Living Trusts, related terminology and their advantages and disadvantages. We wish to increase awareness of Muslims all over so they may at least consider the Living Trust as a viable alternative in estate planning according to the Islamic *Shariah*.

Inheritance with No Will:

In the event that neither a Will nor Trust has been established, disposition of the estate of a deceased is governed by State laws (which clearly disobey the Qur'anic injunctions). This situation is called intestacy or inheritance with no will and the intestate death of a married spouse with children results in the entire property passing to the surviving spouse. However, if the property was in the name of the deceased person only, the state distributes the wealth between the surviving spouse and children. Depending on the number of surviving children, the surviving spouse may be left with a substantially small portion of the estate. The situation is further complicated if the children are minors and the court gets involved in placing the children's share under a Trust and supervising the surviving spouse in the use of the children's funds.

Wills:

The problems associated with intestacy are easily avoided by the use of a properly written Will, in which explicit directions may be included directing who gets what, as well as when the designated heirs or beneficiaries get their assigned portions of their estate. Basically, a Will is a legal document establishing the intent of a Testator (the maker of the Will) to transfer or distribute his/her estate upon the Testator's death according to specific instructions.

Although Wills represent a convenient way for distribution of one's property upon death, there are numerous disadvantages which should be considered in any estate-planning project:

Complexity: Wills are based upon and subject to scrutiny under a complex set of legal rules which can vary substantially from state to state. In order to have a valid Will, stringent rules and requirements must be fulfilled including the form in which the Testator executes the document, the presence and scope of responsibility of witness, the execution of multiple Wills, and the amendment of original Wills. Even technical violations of these complex legalities can be used as grounds for contesting a Will and possibly invalidation of it in probate court.

Probate: Contrary to the popular misconception, a Will does not avoid court. In fact, a Will guarantees court and must be scrutinized by and be admitted to the probate court in order to be legal and enforceable. Any transfer of ownership of property and other assets covered by a Will can only be realized after the Will has been validated by a probate court.

The probate process is a public proceeding and all family and

332

personal records, including those specifying the property by a testator, details on whom property is being given to, and information on debts and creditors, become open to public scrutiny. The probate process is expensive since attorney's fees and court costs are often substantial. Finally, probate is time-consuming and can involve exasperating delays before bequeathed property and assets are in fact delivered to designated beneficiaries.

Provision for Loved Ones: Wills seldom accomplish the very purpose for their existence, i.e., the efficient distribution of property and other assets to loved ones. Particularly in the case where surviving children are minors, for instance, it is difficult to craft Wills capable of avoiding court supervision or guardianship and maintain timely, yet efficient control over the children's assets until actual need arises.

THE LIVING TRUST ALTERNATIVE

In general, Trusts are legal documents by which a person setting up a trust (the "settlor") designates a trustee who will hold or otherwise control specified property or assets in trust for the present or future benefit of designated beneficiaries.

Testamentary Trust: This has similarities to a traditional Will and is not in effect during a person's lifetime. None of the designated assets are placed in the trust until the death of the settlor. Accordingly, all assets in the deceased estate must go through probate before they can be placed in the Trust. While the testamentary trust may serve as a means for avoiding unnecessary estate taxes, the testamentary trust clearly cannot avoid probate and, like a Will suffers from potential changes based on events occurring in a settlor's life after the original trust has been executed.

THE LIVING TRUST

The Living Trust is decidedly one of the best alternatives to be considered in estate planning and essentially constitutes a legal document which becomes active during the life of the settlor and remains active thereafter. A Living Trust permits a settlor to transfer ownership of titled and personal property from his individual name into a trust controlled by him.

Thus, no property of the settlor remains in his or her name and, when the settlor dies or is otherwise disabled; there is no property to undergo probate court. However, during his/her lifetime the settlor retains complete control over all property defined within the Trust.

The Living trust is a revocable entrustment whereby the settlor retains the option to add or change the conditions defined in the Trust document anytime after the original Trust has been set up. According to an illustrative approach, a married couple who would set up a Living trust whereby both spouses are listed as joint trustees upon the death of the other. Consequently, the surviving spouse has instant control over all the trust property without any court involvement whatsoever. A back-up trustee is also defined in the Trust document and is authorized to step in and perform the trust directives upon death or disability of the original trustees. At that time, the surviving joint trustee or back-up trustee acts as an administrator for paying all final bills out of the trust property and then following instructions defined by the settlor for distributing assets within the estate. Transfer, disposal, or management of Trust property is extremely simple since all property is titled in the name of the Trust. Since the Living trust is settled without court proceeding, the process is fast, relatively inexpensive, and private. Since the trust assets are never frozen, it becomes possible for the trustee to almost immediately carry out distribution of the trust popery, thus, the Trust beneficiaries gain access expeditiously to their assigned portions.

A Living trust is set up based on the settlor's decisions and specific instructions as to the manner in which he/she wants property distributed at death. It, accordingly, becomes a simple matter to incorporate Islamic inheritance rules in accordance with the Shariah. Subsequently, all property, which is to be eventually distributed, is "put" into the Trust by effectively transferring ownership from the individual to the name of the trust. While the Trust document outlines instructions for managing a settlor's assets and distributing them at death or disability, the settlor still retains all control over the property and can sell Trust property, change designated beneficiaries, or even cancel the entire Trust at any time, for any reason. Distribution of property at death can usually be done within a few weeks.

When compared to the court, the cost of setting up a Living Trust is minimal. Also, tax aspects can conveniently be taken into account in setting up the Living Trust provisions in such a way as to minimize estate taxes. In addition to providing for loved ones, the Trust can be used as a vehicle foe supporting Islamic centers and organizations by designating them as charitable beneficiaries or creating separate sub-trusts within the main Trust document.

CONCLUSION:

The advantages of Living Trusts over Wills are considerable and include the avoidance of probate proceedings, excessive attorney fees and court costs, as well as unnecessary delays. The relatively few disadvantages associated with revocable Living Trusts include the inconvenience of transferring the titles to homes and other property, bank accounts, etc. into the name of the Trust. Also, the legal fees for initially setting up a Living Trust maybe somewhat expensive, although the long-term savings in fees and court costs more than offset this up-front expenditure.

In view of the foregoing, it is strongly recommended that all Muslims seriously consider the use of a Living Trust as a viable alternative in estate planning in accordance with the Islamic *Shariah*. An excellent resource to learn more about Living rusts is the book Understanding Living Trusts by Vickie and Jim Schumaker, published by Schumaker Publishing, CA (1-800-728-2665). Questions could also be directed to Dr. Nasrul Huq at (314) 581-3054.

Muslim Women in Dialogue: Breaking Walls, Building Bridges

Ghazala Munir

Women all over the world, have served as backbones of families, communities, and societies for centuries. They have nourished relationships, cultivated friendships, healed wounded souls, and restored lives. It is not surprising then, that in North America today women are engaged in dialogue, interreligious and intercultural. We are out in the trenches of academia, suburbia, large cities, and small towns in large numbers seeking to promote understanding among peoples of all colors and creeds. Like women the world over, North American women, whatever their faith, are engaged in passionate conversations with the Muslim, the Jew, the Christian, and the Bahai.

Muslim women continue to play an important role in this sacred enterprise. Women moved by their own innate desires to cultivate peace and understanding at the community level work independently and in organizations. Most importantly, we seek to bolster attempts, at all levels, to portray an honest and realistic picture of Islam and the people who practice the faith.

Islam is one of the great spiritual and social forces in North America today; its influence will extend into the twenty-first century. In order for the intrinsic meaning and significance of Islam to be understood there is an urgent need for Muslims to understand other faiths as well. The fact that this part of our world represents an extraordinary amount of religious diversity, creates the need for this mutual understanding. Interreligious dialogue, free of attempts to proselytize, is imperative to our survival as a community on this continent and the world at large.

Dialogue is not a debate. Dialogue is a sincere attempt to exchange information: to compare the ideals of the Islamic faith with the ideals of other faiths, our practice with the practice of those faiths.[1] Dialogue can only take place on the basis of mutual trust, the primary purpose of which is to learn, to change, and to heighten our sensitivity to others.[2] We have to be well grounded in our ideology if we are to engage in such endeavors, so that we do not see the other as a threat to our belief system. The switching of faith allegiance is not a precondition but a possibility of personal transformation, of a broadening of our own spiritual vision. History cannot be ignored in these conversations, but history should not be employed to shame the others for the deeds of their ancestors. Just as the horrors of Reconquista and the Crusades cannot be denied, neither can the imperial expansion of Islam in the Arab conquests of Syria, North Africa, and Spain.[3] The emphasis on the scriptural and juristic is of value only if the "experiential and salvific" is also stressed for a coherent comparison.[4]

Muslims have a calling from God to establish a moral and just social order on this earth. The *Shahada*, the five daily prayers, the concept of *Zakat*, the rigors of *Ramadan*, the passion of Pilgrimage are all but rituals in piety and self- sacrifice illuminating our path to *sira't ul mustaqeem*. The Holy Qur'an does not concern itself with historical details of the sake of history; its major concern is to uphold justice and guide human beings to live their lives for the service of God and God's creation. The only way to build and establish such societies is to work in solidarity with people of other faiths inspired by a similar calling. Muslims are commanded by God to invite Jews and Christians to engage in this pursuit of higher purpose, to seek God in our daily lives. Say: "O People of the Book! Come to common terms as between us and you: That we worship None but Allah; That we associate no partners with Him; that we elect not from among ourselves Lords and patrons other than Allah. If then they turn back, say ye: Bear witness that we are Muslims (bowing to Allah's will)." (The Holy Qur'an 3:64)[5]

Muslim women have heard this call from Quebec to Alberta, from California to Michigan, and New York to Texas. We are ambassadors

---

1 Leonard Swidler, "The Dialogue Decalogue, "Journal of Ecumenical Studies 20:1 (Winter 1983, April, 1984 revision), 1-3.
2 Ibid., 1
3 C. M. Nai, "Getting Real about Christian-Muslim Dialogue", Word and World Spring 1996: 180.
4 Ibid., 180.
5 Abdullah Yusuf Ali, The Meaning of the Holy Qur'an (Amana Corporation: 1992).

without portfolios, we are diplomats with or without the blessings of the powers that be in our established religious institutions. Is this a blessing or do we fear contempt from within the hierarchy of our male dominant *ummah*? Our convictions so overpower our fears that these considerations lose importance. Since dialogue can only happen effectively among equals, Muslim women must reclaim their true identity lost over centuries of male domination. We go back to the same Holy Scriptures where God addresses all human as, "O Believing men and women" (Qur'an 33:35), leaving no doubt as to moral and spiritual equity. We must focus on the Qur'anic injunction that the righteous among us are those who perform good deeds, regardless of sex, color, or creed.[6]

On the international scene, Muslim women's movements are gaining access to the education in the basic religious writings and laws of Islam. Azar Nafisi, an Iranian professor, writes about the influential women in classical Persian literature.[7] Yasmeen Murshed in Bangladesh teaches women to write legislation enhancing their political rights, and Norani Othman in Malaysia leads a movement to reinterpret Muslim law.[8] The Sisterhood Is Global Institute was established in 1984 in Bethesda, Maryland. Led by Mahnaz Afkhami, an Iranian-American Muslim, this international organization works for human rights focusing on the rights of women as equal and necessary participants in social and religious circles.[9]

Domestically, Muslim women are also writing and publishing and reinterpreting the holy and the canonized scriptures of Islam from a feminist perspective. Riffat Hasan, a pioneer in such undertakings, is a professor at the University of Louisville in Kentucky. She is regarded with great respect among Muslim scholars in the United States as an organizer and facilitator of dialogue between government officials, academic persons, religious/interreligious organizations, and media specialists. Amina McCloud, Amina Wadud-Musin, Azizah al-Hibri, Lila Sied Ameen Fahlman, Sharifa Al-Khitab, and Zohra Husaini are some

---

6   There are numerous verses in the Qur'an with the same general theme, among them 4:36, 4:1 24- 125, 5:93, 7:42, 16:97.
7   The New York Times "Muslim Women's Movement Is Gaining Strength." Barbara Crossette. 12 May 1996: International Section.
8   Ibid. NYT.
9   Ibid. NYT.

of the many prominent Muslims who attempt to seek reconciliation through different media and channels. Audrey Shabbas and Tasnim Benhalim are working hard at all educational levels in the area of education about Islam and the Arab World. They organize workshops for educators and train them to be sensitive to the faith and its people. Yvonne Haddad, a Lebanese-American Christian woman, an Islamist who teaches at Georgetown University, has written several books on Islam and Muslims. Her efforts should be appreciated in that she portrays a positive and honest picture of Islam to her fellow Christians so that Islam is not only seen from the naturally biased eye of its followers. She travels all over the United States giving lectures, holding workshops and panel discussions engaging people of faith in dialogue. The Center for Muslim - Christian Understanding, established at Georgetown University in 1993, is yet another example of opening up arenas for dialogue and discussion among diverse faith groups. I need to point out that there are countless men who are working shoulder - to shoulder with their Muslim sisters. If we are to answer our calling and fulfil God's command to establish a just and moral social order within our country and our communities, we have to work together as peers and colleagues. Women and men, the highest of God's creation or *ashraf ul makhlooqat* presupposes the doctrine of stewardship of this planet earth when we hold hands to do this work in sincere humility.

In this area of west Michigan, which is known for its religious conservatism and where the locals jokingly point out that the number of churches outnumber the population, I have been intensely involved in Interfaith dialogue for the last seven years. The beautiful landscape of these Great Lake States is dotted with steeples glorifying the Almighty, signifying the solid presence of Christianity and the diversity of its ecumenical community. There are four major colleges with religious affiliation in my area. The Grand Rapids Area Center for Ecumenism is home to more than seven hundred churches. The Interfaith Dialogue Association, established in 1991, serves as a link between the conservative religious majority and a number of minority faiths represented here. Every month for the last six years people of faith have sat together face-to-face to discuss and dialogue. The annual interfaith conference held in the fall is co-sponsored by these organizations giving it a unique flavor of grass roots simplicity and academic intensity. "Common Threads", a weekly radio program, airs dialogue between faith communities on issues ranging from racism to human rights, prophets and avatars to sex, sin, and symbolism. The zeal and enthusiasm to embrace and accept others is indeed active here as is our submission to God's will to uplift the human soul to majestic heights. To refer to an example from the recent past, I point to the tragedy of the Oklahoma City bombing, in which Muslims were the initial suspects, in April 1995. As America mourned the tremendous loss and suffering of its sons and daughters, the Muslim Community of Grand Rapids called on all faith communities to join together in prayer. This was an unprecedented event in the history of this community where Hindus and Buddhists, Jews and Jains, Christians and Zoroastrians, Muslims and Bahais mourned, and prayed in unison. Our doctrines, theologies, and histories did not matter in those moments of ultimate spiritual sharing as we stood before our One and Only God.

We are at a crossroads. We owe it to the generations that inherit this world to show a record of reconciliation or at least our collective efforts to achieve that goal. History will record that in 1992 and in 1996, President Bill Clinton's inauguration was highlighted by a religious service where an imam, a rabbi, and a minister offered blessings. The opening sessions of the United States Congress also begin with similar interfaith services, celebrating the unique diversity of this nation.

Muslim women all over North America will continue this work of reconciliation, to redefine our boundaries and serve as intermediaries in this sacred quest. This work is not new to us, and neither are its challenges. Our communities and our families have depended on us for centuries to nurture morality, ethics, and spirituality. In the name of God we answer this call and make it our Jihad – our struggle to preserve this world for our children and our children's children and honor our covenant as stewards of this earth.

The Lawful and The Prohibited: Our Need, Our Obsession

Shahid Athar

"Oh you who believe, make not unlawful the good things which God has made lawful for you, but commit no excess for God loves not those who commit excess" (5:90).

L iving as a Muslim in a non-Muslim society is difficult but not impossible. We are to enjoy what is permitted and avoid what is forbidden. Sometimes this distinction is easy and sometimes it is not. There are situations that fall in the gray zone and, according to the Traditions, we are also to avoid that which is doubtful. However, what is not appropriate is that we like to do things which are wrong because of a cultural habit that we have formed and justified. In addition, there are things that we must do: for example, attending Friday prescribed congregational prayer, but we find an excuse not to do so. Thus, we should not try to make what is forbidden, permissible, and what is permissible, forbidden, because it is only up to God to do so. Also, sometimes we are not able to define priorities of certain situations. For example, someone may be very careful in choosing the blessed slaughtered (*halal*) meat because that is permissible, but not careful in performing the five daily-prescribed prayers, which are obligatory. On the Day of Judgment, we will be first questioned about our prescribed prayers long before we will be questioned about what kind of meat we ate.

The late Dr. Fazlur Rahman once wrote an article entitled "How to Revive Islam From the Debris of It's Past." By past, he meant the past 1,300 years because some Muslims have not tried to figure out how Islam flourished and developed after the first one hundred years, especially when they went to non-Muslim societies in Africa, Europe, Asia, and the Far East. By the debris, he meant all the cultural and regional influences on Islam, which have covered the beauty and essence of pure way of life by such practices. Thus, in order to see the true beauty of

343

Islam, we have to remove that debris and uncover the pure Islam while still making adjustments to different climates in which Islam finds itself. Thus, I am going to divide our concerns with the prohibited and permissible into different areas and at the end, I will present an actual survey of opinions of different Muslim scholars in the United States on the same questions.

The number one concern is related to our diet. In Islam, Muslims are told not to eat pork, pork products, alcohol, and dead meat. The difficulty is that lard is mixed in may food items, or lard products like gelatin are present, or enzymes from swine or pork are part of the ingredients. Similarly, in many medicines, alcohol is present to a certain degree. My humble suggestion would be, to make a habit for ourselves, and our children to read the labels of all food items and medicines before we ingest them. It is a blessing in this country that we can know what we are eating. In most of the other countries, including Muslim countries, food ingredients are not given on the label; therefore we don't know what we are taking in. We should use items which are of vegetable shortening only, and do not have gelatin or enzyme products in them. Similarly, we should try to avoid any oral medicines, which have alcohol in them, if we can find a substitute. Many cough medicines are now being developed without alcohol. It may happen, although rarely, that a medicine cannot be dissolved in water or other ingredients, or especially in injectable forms; therefore, for those essential medicines, we ask God's forgiveness.

In terms of Islamically slaughtered meat, the controversy in whether God's Name has been invoked or saying, "I begin in the Name of God, the Merciful, the Compassionate" should be done at the time of slaughter or at the time of cooking or at the time of eating the food, or preferably, all three. Again, there is no consensus among Muslim scholars if the meat eaten by the people of the book is acceptable to Muslims or not. Many say "yes" using the verse in the chapter al-Maida giving this permission. On the other hand, those who object, say that those verses apply to food in general and not for meat because for meat the verse they quoted is from 16:115, which says, "Do not eat any meat over which name of other than God has been invoked." In either case, the *halal* meat is a healthier meat because the blood and blood products have been drained and the chances of infection and anti-body formation are much less. For the same reason, kosher meats are acceptable to some Muslims although, again, at the time of slaughtering, Jewish rabbi do not use God's Name on each individual animal, but do a prayer in mass. My own suggestion is that one should use only the *halal* meat if that is available to that person or if it is within driving distance. If *halal* meat is not available and one cannot live without meat, then one has to decide between being a vegetarian versus invoking God's Name at the time of eating the meat. The worse situation will be that those two groups, while insisting on being right, accuse the other group of infidelity or ingratitude and hurt the feelings of the other Muslims and earn the displeasure of God.

The second item is social mixing and dress code for men and women. Both men and women in Islam have a dress code, so while women should cover their bodies, except face, hands, and feet, men should also be in appropriate dress. The other aspects of dress are that it should not be too tight or too thin, and should apply to both sexes. Muslim women constantly complain that when they put on the head cover, they are identified as Muslim women and thus discriminated against by society. What is the identification for Muslim men who do not have a beard or do not have a cap? Here again are questions of priorities and cultural biases. Some women consider the sari of Indo-Pakistani women an un-Islamic dress because it sometimes reveals portions of the belly. Now on the other hand, the Indo-Pakistani women do not like the skirt showing part of the legs of women as appropriate Islamic dress and consider it as Anglo- French culture. The point I am making is that in Islam, there is nothing like the Arab dress or Pakistani dress. Many Arab Christian women also dress the same way as Arab Muslim women and Pakistani Christian women dress the same way as Pakistani Muslim women. In order to be identified as a Muslim, the women and men should know the guidelines of Islamic dress and try to design their dress according to this. A nice booklet by Dr. Jamal Badawi is available on the title, "The Dress Code in Islam."

In the area of social mixing, the separation of the sexes is emphasized very much in Islam. By this, mixing is meant non-business, intimate mixing. Muslim women in the past and even now in societies where Islam is practiced, have conducted their regular business whether in terms of teaching or nursing by the side of men if both of them have their Islam etiquette in their dress code, manners and talking. Neither of them should dress or behave in 'a way to incite the other nor should they talk in a romantic way to make some suggestions. Other than that, they can mix while conducting a business or running an organization. Women should be allowed to go to the mosque, to pray, and to participate in other important activities in the mosque. However, there should be separate areas for them for such purposes.

Interaction with non-Muslims is another tricky situation. We are asked to spread the message of Islam and give missionary work and take care of our neighbors, even if they are non-Muslims, help the poor and needy, even if they are non-Muslims, but how do we do these without mixing with them? My solution to this situation is not that we have to stay inside our home or inside our mosques and let those seekers of missionary work visit us. We have to take ourselves and our religion out of the closet and into the open air to expose non-Muslims to practicing Muslims and Islam. The best way we can do this is, first, at the work place, where we do meet non-Muslims and from our words and mostly from our actions and appearance, we let them know we are Muslim and available to answer any questions they may have about Islam and be prepared to answer those questions. Thus it implies that we must learn and practice Islam first before we go out on this venture. Secondly, we don't have to be forceful in giving such preaching of Islam rather than just give the necessary information and praying to God to accept our effort and give guidance to those who seek it. We have to be pleasant in manner and have wisdom as outlined in the Quran and know the techniques of giving missionary work. However, we must choose our playground. We should not play games on their ground, but should engage in discussions on our terms. We must participate in the interfaith process and visit synagogues and churches, while allowing non-Muslims to visit us during our social functions like the Festival or the post-sunset ending of the prescribed fast so that they may witness the practices of Islam. As far as our children are concerned, we have no choice. Our children will mix with non-Muslims, because they do in their schools anyway. We have to set the rules for after-school hours, that is where they should mix. If they must meet and mix with non-Muslim children of the same sex, it has to be in a Muslim's house and not in non-Muslim houses where the rules of the game may be entirely different.

SOME HORROR STORIES

Now I am going to describe some of the obsessions with priorities of permissible and prohibited which give the wrong messages. These are real stories and not made up for this article. A Muslim scholar visits my house for a social function. He was not sure I would serve him *halal*

346

meat so he brings his own food. That surprises everyone else and hurts my feelings. A devout Muslim woman visits the house of another Muslim in a social gathering. Before the food is served, she asks, "Do you serve permissible meat?" The host, obviously hurt, replies, "My faith is very strong, but I do have *halal* meat for those who have weak faith." The questioner should have used "*halal*" rather than permissible or should not have asked any question at all. The third situation in this area: after my lecture about Islam, a Muslim woman came forward and asked me if a McDonald's hamburger is permissible. While answering her, I had to look the other way because her dress was very inappropriate.

Another situation occurred in a Muslim country. A group of Muslims were arguing whether wearing a platinum ring is permissible for men or not. One group said it was permissible because only gold is mentioned in the Traditions, and the other group said it is not permissible because platinum is costlier than gold and therefore should have the same restrictions. I patiently listened to their discussion while the call to the evening prescribed prayer was being recited from the nearby mosque. I went to offer my prescribed prayer at the mosque. When I came back, none of those people had prayed and they were still arguing about permissible and prohibited. In this regard, a question was asked from me, "Who is better, a Muslim who never performs the prescribed prayer or the one who prays occasionally when in the company of Muslim friends or Muslim boss?" The answer is neither. The former is a disbeliever and the latter is a hypocrite.

Another situation mentioned to me by a young man was that his parents were so strict that they never allowed him to talk to Muslim girls in his mosque or social functions in the community so he did not know any of them. Since he grew up only knowing non-Muslim girls at public school and college, he is going to marry one of them. (I am not justifying his reasoning or actions.)

I was told that in Detroit, a certain Muslim opened a grocery and meat store. He wrongfully included pork in his meat business store. Muslims obviously did not like it and objected to it in a very forceful way: first, by complaining to him, then by defaming him to those in the mosque, even to those who evidently did not know him and thirdly, by picketing in front of his shop and labeling him a disbeliever. Finally, this person gave up and he had a sign in front of his shop one day when they came to picket. The sign said, "Yes, I am a non-Muslim so please leave me alone." The lesson is that a Muslim is not to push a half-Muslim into disbelief, but try to bring him back by wisdom and beautiful manners if he can do that. Maybe this brother needed more education. Maybe he needed a rich person to buy all his pork meat and throw it in the trash or whatever, but to drive him to declare that he is a non-Muslim was not the best thing to do.

Several years ago, I mailed a questionnaire to about twenty prominent Muslims in the U.S. to assess their opinion of lawful and prohibited in social situations, while interacting with non-Muslims and the opposite sex. I asked them questions giving real situations from my own experience. Twelve out of the twenty returned my questionnaire with a response and a comment. They are as follows:

1. In Islam, men and women should not shake hands. However, several of my female patients, especially older ladies for whatever reason, extend their hand to shake hands. What should I do? Eight of the respondents said that I should go ahead and shake hands, as my intentions are pure. Two said that I should never shake hands with women.

Discussion: Even though those who said that it is allowed, they agreed that one should try to avoid shaking hands as much as possible and keep the hands busy otherwise. Two of them who did not approve used the saying of Prophet Muhammad that, "I am a man who does not shake hands with woman," and other sayings, "It is better to be clubbed with a rod of iron in your head than to touch a woman to whom you are not related by Divine Law." The "touch" here is a sexual touch rather than casual shaking of hand. In the case of a male physician, when he takes the hand of his female patient in his hand, he is increasing her confidence and offering a form of psychological treatment. Similarly, Muslim nurses who helped the injured during the battles in the days of the Prophet, had to touch men in order to provide treatment. But those days, taking care of Muslims, not sex, was on the mind of the people. "All of our actions will be judged by our intentions," according to a Tradition of the Prophet.

2. At the annual faculty staff banquet, which I had to attend, wine was being served at the table, to which all of them accept except me. What should I do? Three out of ten said, I should leave the table where wine is being served while seven out of ten said, I should do nothing and sip my ice tea.

Discussion: Several other comments came to light. One was that maybe the non-drinkers should have a table of their own and if one has to sit at a table where wine is being served, he must explain to others why he is not drinking, giving himself a chance to explain Islam. One of the learned scholars mentioned that in his company, when non-Muslims are drinking, it is their business provided that we do not serve, handle, facilitate, or promote the act of drinking. He said that we should not back out of all such occasions and activities in which non-Muslims are drinking, and Muslims have to attend those gatherings because of their status or position.

3.   I am traveling on a plane, tired from lack of sleep, beverages are being served, and my neighbor in the next seat orders a small glass of wine. However, the old lady cannot open the bottle herself and asks me to open it. What should I do?

Seven of the respondents said that I should refuse to open the bottle and three said I should quietly open it and go to sleep.

Discussion: Opening this bottle is equal to serving wine and one should not offer wine to anyone, that one should politely explain to the lady that this is against our religion. Another respondent suggested I should push the call button so that an attendant may come and open this bottle and relieve me from this dilemma.

4.   My friends and patients know that I am a Muslim and I do not celebrate Christmas. But during Christmas-time, they send me many Christmas gifts, candies, and cards, etc. What should I do?
None of the respondents suggested that I should refuse to accept these gifts and all ten suggested that I accept the gifts and thank them and maybe send a nice gift back during Eid or other Muslim holiday.

Discussion: The learned scholar who wrote a five-page long response to my questionnaire, mentioned that Prophet Muhammad accepted gifts from non-Muslims and sent gifts back to Jews and Christians. However, we must explain to our Muslim friends why we do not celebrate Christmas or the birth of any prophet; we must reciprocate their good will by giving them gifts, including gifts of Islamic literature on our occasions.

5. I invited a new non-Muslim faculty member to my house for dinner. He (out of his ignorance about Islam and me), brings a bottle of champagne with him. What should I do?

Six respondents said that I should ask him to take it back while five said that I should take it and destroy it.

Discussion: The learned scholar mentioned that I should take it and destroy it after he leaves, better than in front of the children of my family to remind them we don't drink. We should also explain to our guest why we don't drink. It was suggested that returning the bottle to the guest and asking him to destroy it may embarrass him as he meant well.

6. In my office (although I am a Muslim and don't celebrate Christmas), my good secretaries are Christians, and consider this office as their second home, and want to have a Christmas tree or some decorations. What should I do?

Three out of twelve said I should not allow them to have a Christmas tree since it is my office and the boss sets the rule and they should respect my feelings. Eight out of twelve said I should let them practice their religion as my office is their office as well and a Christmas tree is a more cultural tradition, than a religious symbol. However, I wonder what these eight would say if my secretaries were Hindus and wanted to display an idol of Rama during Diwali.

7. At the hospital, many colleagues, patients, nurses, etc., while walking or in the elevator, will say to me "Have a nice Christmas" or "How was your Christmas?" What should I say?

All said, I should give appropriate, short response, i.e., "have a nice day!" and move on.

Comment: Islam is simple and asks us to be polite and humble and even meet bad with goodness and politeness and good nature is missionary work in itself. Goodness of conduct constitutes half of religion.

In conclusion, the guiding Islamic principles in the lawful and the prohibited are:

1. Everything is permissible except that which is specifically prohibited.
2. To make things lawful and to prohibit is the right of God only "It is not fitting for a believer, man or woman, when a matter has been decided by God and His Messenger, to have any option about their decision: if anyone disobeys God and His Apostle, he is indeed on a clearly wrong Path" (33:36).
3. To prohibit the lawful and permit the unlawful is equal to polytheism (associating partners to God).
4. What is permissible is sufficient and what is unlawful is superfluous.
5. Whatever leads to unlawful is also unlawful. Based on this, the mixing of the two sexes and serving or selling wine is prohibited.
6. Good intentions do not make wrong acceptable. For an action to be acceptable the intentions are to be pure and the action itself must be pure as well. There is no concept of Robin Hood in Islam.
7. Doubtful things (*makruh*) are also to be avoided according to the Tradition of Prophet Muhammad: "The permissible is clear and the prohibited is clear. Between the two, there are doubtful matters, which people don't know are permissible or prohibited. One who avoids them to safeguard his religion and his honor is safe, while one who engages in a part of them, he may be doing the prohibited."
8. The Law of Prohibition applies to everyone alike, rich or poor, average citizen and the highest official, the illiterate and the scholar. In many Muslim societies, the rich and the powerful get away with all the wrong doings while the Divine Law is being enforced on the Muslim masses. To the contrary, Prophet Muhammad said, "if my daughter Fatima is caught stealing, her hand will be cut off as well."
9. The necessity makes the exception (that is, permission to eat pork if no food is available to save life).
10. Given a choice, a Muslim should take the lesser of two evils. For example, a Muslim has a choice to buy a house on mortgage in a nice neighborhood versus raising his family in a rented apartment in a dingy neighborhood infested with drug dealers and violence. Which one should he choose?

I will let the reader ponder on this one.

Note:

Those who responded were Dr. T. B. Irving, Dr. M. S. Meghahed (Buffalo), Imam A. M. al-Khattab (Toledo), Dr. Hassan Hathout, Dr. Maher Hathout, Dr. Mahmood Rashdan, Dr. Jamal Badawi, Dr. Muzzamil Siddiqui, Dr. A. S. Hashim, Dr. Moazzam Habib (Indianapolis), Imam Shakir el-Sayyed (Plainfield, ISNA), and one preferred to remain anonymous.

VII

WORKS OF DA'WAH

Islamic Movement
In America – Why?

Shamim A. Siddiqi

The world has reached the stage where international communism is dead. The demise of the Soviet Union has rewarded the United States of America with the claim to be the only superpower of the world. America is championing the cause of freedom, and free market economy, mixed with liberalism, in every sphere, to establish a "New World Order." But her pursuit is half-hearted, full of compromises and double standards — strong against weaker nations, like Iran, Iraq, Haiti, Cuba, and Sudan, but timid against the giants with huge foreign markets like China, India, or where other Western interests take precedence. America has thus become hypocritical in the manifestations of her ideals, which are for symbolic gestures only. As such, there is a big gap in improvement both on the ideological side and in the exercise of her political will to carry out her goal and vision to a successful end around the world.

On the other hand, Islam, which stands for justice, equality, and peace, possesses a superb ideology (a profound, benevolent, and all-encompassing concept of life), advocates a comprehensive guidance for the human society, both in individual and collective spheres, presents the perfect model of prophet Mohammed for mankind to follow in every walk of life, is being ignored by the Muslim countries themselves. The Muslim countries so far, failed to produce a practical model of Islam and teachings in the present context of the world anywhere on the surface of the earth.

Humanity is, thus, standing today in gloom and total frustration. Neither could the lone superpower and its European allies could deliver the good to mankind nor could the Muslims present a model of a modern Islamic state in accordance to Allah's *Deen* anywhere in the world.

In the present global state of affairs, when both the superpower and the Islamic movements around the world are trying to produce and present a model of their respective ideologies, and when none could succeed so far, it is desirable to find out what is the best place where both ideologies could be implemented in a homogeneous way.

What America professes to advocate is security of life, liberty, pursuit of happiness, democratic process, human rights, family values and a free-market economy. Islam emphasizes these and many more values of its own concept of life in a very refined way, with all its checks and balances, so that only the good of each remains and flourishes and the evil is eliminated. To attain the values, which Islam advocates, an Islamic society creates an environment of God-consciousness (*Taqwa*), a sense of accountability after death and the concept of Amanah or trust. These are the dominating concepts of the Islamic way of life. They go a long way in producing the character, which can guarantee the implementation of values that are only cherished by America, but refined, implemented and accomplished by Islam. Islam provides the loving model of Prophet Mohammed to follow and get inspiration from his life-pattern. Islam, if embraced and followed properly, will produce that responsible character in American men and women that may transform America into a model society for mankind to aspire. In other words, America provides the appropriate place where its values can be welded into predominant Islamic values to produce the best model of Islam through democratic or a true representative process. America may turn out to be the laboratory of Islam for the 21st century.

It is, therefore, in a positive response to an urgent call of the time that a genuine effort should be made to introduce Islam to the people of America, interwoven with the values, which are equally cherished in this country, in a palatable manner. It requires long-term planning, a devoted and dedicated team of workers, and an organized effort.

But here is the great tragedy. There are Muslims who live in America. They are a part of the socio-cultural-educational and economic process of this country. They have their homes and hearth on this land. They are enjoying the luxuries and benefits of the system, but at the same time do not want to improve America's growing sickness. They dream of bringing revolution to some distant lands of Asia, the Middle East, or Africa. They do nothing except condemn America as a society of the "*Kuffar*" (infidels), but enjoy its material benefits. They are indeed accountable to Allah and to their progenies for the inactivity to do good to the land, which provides them the bread, butter, and all other luxuries day in and day out.

It is therefore, incumbent, that the issue of building the Islamic

356

Movement in America is discussed in detail. I will pinpoint the inherent logic behind this urgency and bring forward the reasons for its essentiality.

OBLIGATIONS OF MUSLIMS

Qur'an ordains in verse 33 of *Surah* 41 and verse 67 of *Surah al-Maidah*. Every Muslim has to fulfill the responsibility of *Shahadah Alannas* (witness to mankind). This directive is for all times to come. If a Muslim does not call the people of the land to the fold of Islam through organized *Da'wah* efforts, he or she is actually supporting the *Batil* structure of the American society.

OBLIGATIONS AS CITIZENS

As citizens of America, Muslims are sailing in the same boat in which America is sailing. If the boat sinks, Muslims will sink with it. If the boat survives, Muslims will keep floating along with it. But the tragedy is that the boat is sinking slowly - morally, economically, and politically, and the Muslims are unmindful of the forthcoming tragedy. As America is beset with innumerable problems, it is the Muslim's moral and religious obligation to come forward with Islamic solutions for America's problems. As citizens of America, Muslims have the right to disseminate and launch upon a campaign for the propagation of Islam as an alternate way of life to the people of the land, and not exercising this right and duty is concealment of the truth (*Kitmanul-Haq*).

BETTER DA'WAH OPPORTUNITIES

Efforts toward the establishment of Allah's Deen or *Khilafah Ala Minhaje-Nabuwah* (establishing Khilafah on the pattern of Prophet Mohammed) are going on in different Muslim countries under different names and styles. But the environment is not congenial for the rule of Islam as a power anywhere in the Muslim world. In every Muslim country, the power bases are not the masses but vested interests who are bent upon perpetuating the power in their hands by all means. Also, the interference of the Western powers in the internal affairs of the Muslim countries is rampant, with devastating effects on the social, economic, and political aspects of life. Human rights are violated everywhere. In short, most of the Muslim countries today stand socially

Westernized, morally corrupt, politically exploited and economically ruined with no will or vision of their own. Muslim masses have no say in the affairs of their own countries. They stand as silent spectators. They are no longer the decisive factor in deciding their own future and fate in terms of the ideology they love most.

Thus the possibilities for the emergence of an Islamic state anywhere in the Muslim world are remote in the near future. Current Islamic movements around the world are lacking in *Hikmah*, well-formulated approaches, solution to problems, inspiring models, resources, smooth sailing at home, political will and a "team" of dedicated brothers and sisters which is prepared to give all that they possess for the Deen of Allah. The Islamic movement from Jakarta to Casablanca is the same, more or less.

However, the circumstances in America are better and more conducive for building an Islamic movement to establish and prosper than in other parts of the world. America is a government of law. Democratic processes are deep-rooted in the body-politic of the country. Human rights are guaranteed through its constitution. The judiciary is independent and strongly defends and protects human rights against all kinds of encroachments and violations. Freedom of speech is perhaps limitless and unfettered. Rights of movements, mobilization of faith and conviction are all guaranteed and protected. America, thus, provides the right environment for the spread of Islam here, which the Muslim world has failed to offer so far to its adherents.

Muslims of America can plan and implement *Da'wah* at least until the vested interests of the land create impediments which is always inevitable regardless of Muslim or a predominantly Christian country. That is the well-defined process ordained by Allah in the Qur'an (*Surah Al-Ankabut*; Verses 2-3 and *Surah Al-Baqarah* Verses 155-56). The stages of trial and tribulations come to polish the commitments of a Muslim *Da'ee*, and strengthen his or her character. It is now incumbent upon the Muslims of America to concentrate whole-heartedly in building a solid Islamic Movement in America starting of course, from their own houses.

The Islamic Movement in America will be another front besides the Islamic Movements in the other countries, to pave the way for a success of the movements in the Muslim world. The success of the Muslim world now depends on how soon the Muslims of America are able to build up their own indigenous movement for the spread and introduction in the body-politic of this country.

AMERICA: A HETEROGENEOUS COUNTRY

America has a unique position in the community of nations. It is a heterogeneous country. People from almost all nations of the world now comprise the nation of America. It depicts a rainbow of nationalities and different cultures. America is a country of immigrants and its doors are still open. Every year, more than a million people migrate to this land of opportunities. Everyone contributes to its diversity wherein lies its strength. They contribute to its economy, enjoy the benefits of constitutional guarantees and materialistic bounties along with the curses of liberalism in every walk of life. Here the Muslims can carry out the mission of their life to a great extent unhindered, through its democratic process and constitutional safeties, available under law, to each and every citizen, irrespective of race, color, faith, or ethnic background. America is thus, better set to build the Islamic Movement in comparison to the rest of the world.

Muslims of America are generally well off — many are financially affluent, and highly educated. They realize their unique position where Allah in His infinite mercy has placed them. They must also realize their responsibility as a *Da'ee* in a foreign land.

AMERICA: MATURED FOR CHANGE

America is the citadel of capitalism, which has reached its zenith and is now slowly drifting down the hill. The material progress in America is due not necessarily to capitalism but the extraordinary research and development programs carried out in the public and private sectors. Capitalism and liberalism have actually created gigantic problems for this country, which needs to be resolved. Some of the major problems are: the growth of a lopsided economy, unbalanced budgeting, frequent cycles of recession and fear of inflation, ever-increasing gaps in the economy of the have and the have-nots, dismantling the family system and corroding family values, general moral decadence, increasing tolerance of the gay culture, sexual anarchy, etc. The list of problem is endless.

In the midst of these growing problems the echo of the 1992 presidential election was "change." Bill Clinton came to power uniquely through raising the slogan of change. But none of the political parties has a program to change the character of the people. Though the moral decay is eating away the vitals of this supra-nation, the leaders are beating about the bush, crying to protect the family values and bring "change", simply as slogans. Amidst this promise of change, it makes no difference who comes to power. The social, economic, and political condition of America has gone beyond repair. No Band-Aid treatment is going to work. The main cause of this deterioration lies somewhere else! It lies in denying the authority of the Creator while living on His earth and enjoying His bounties and believing or behaving as if this is the only life and there is no accountability after death. This has made humans irresponsible, reckless and unreliable in both their individual and collectives life. The denial of the Supreme authority and the negligence of the concept of accountability in the Hereafter have resulted in unbalanced society and an economy, which is uncertain and bereft of Barakah (blessings). The verdict of the Qur'an is very clearly: "But he who turns away from remembrance of Me, he/she will face a narrow (tight or depressed) economy, and I will bring him/her blind to the assembly on the Day of Resurrection." (20:124)

America today stands at the crossroads. Its economy is uncertain. Its political institutions have gone corrupt. Its moral values are withering away. Its resources are thinning out. Both home and foreign fronts are staggering. America needs a change. These moments offer immense opportunities to the Muslims of America to come forward and present Islam to the inhabitants of this great country as an alternate way of life in an eloquent but organized and disciplined manner. It will be possible only when this responsibility will be undertaken, not by individuals, but by an organized, disciplined, and indigenous Islamic Movement of America.

Socialism never made any headway in America. It was never akin to the taste of the American people. Capitalism and its evil effects are being harvested by the American society as a whole. At this juncture, if an Islamic movement is built up in America which pinpoints the shortcomings of capitalism, elaborates the fallacies of democracy with vivid illustrations from its own system, exposes the devastating consequences of the liberal life-style, there is every possibility that the American people may think of changing over to a better system, a better ideology. Here, it may be observed that the Christian Church has been and is condemning the system too, but it could not and cannot produce an alternate to capitalism. Hence, it could not succeed. Islam presents an alternative to the prevailing system. There is thus, every possibility, that the people of the land will be attracted to the Islamic system of life.

It is therefore, essential that is brought to the attention of the American intelligentsia as well as the masses, as an alternate way of life.

A GAME OF REBOUND FROM THE MUSLIM PERSPECTIVE

War strategies in the present context of the world have changed and been given new dimensions. It is now mostly fought on enemy land by propaganda campaign and attracts propaganda literature. Muslims have to take the issue of restoration of *Khilafah*, with the wisdom of a Momin. This is the *Hikma* of the Deen and the Muslims have to resolve how to get the campaign expedited on all fronts.

The Muslim leadership of the Islamic Movements in the world must also support the Muslims of America in this worthy cause. This in fact, is the strategy of rebound; playing the game in America and reaping the harvest in the Muslim world. The Ummah as a whole has to play this game of rebound as the only way to check and eliminate the interference of the Anglo-American-French-Zionist hege-monies in the affairs of the Muslim world.

The *Ummah* failed to provide and present to the Russian people Islam as an alternative way of life or an Islamic society as an alternative to communism and capitalism anywhere in the world to attract them and serve as model for humanity to follow. As such, they fall back on capitalism and liberal democracy. There was no other choice before them. In its wake, Muslims lost a great opportunity to guide the destiny of mankind. We have missed the bus. Let us not do it again!

FUTURE PROSPECTS

A successful Islamic movement in America will muster public opinion against her interference in the internal affairs of the Muslim world and the political leadership will then have no choice but to refrain and give up the game of interference. This is possible only when Muslims of all backgrounds take a united step. A successful Islamic movement in America will herald an era of introducing and spreading Islam in the Caribbean, South America and elsewhere in the Northern Hemisphere. An organized *Da'wah* effort can bring this change anywhere. However, the blatant interference of America in the affairs of the Muslims must be accepted as a challenge by the Muslims who must work toward "*Iqamatudeen*" or rule of God in America.

Marketing Islam In the U.S.: A Strategy for Dignity, Harmony, and Prosperity

Aqueel A. Ansari

It is generally, and quite often emotionally, argued that Islam is the best product in the marketplace. It is customary for a marketer to position his product as the best product. The question is if the buyers perceives it top be as such. A CEO of a company that markets Islam today has second thoughts, given the performance of the product, if he should continue marketing it. Over one billion buyers, and yet the marketers shy-away from a product demo when potential buyers ask for one!

It is proposed to develop a strategy for marketing Islam in the U.S. Why the U.S.? A lot of literature exists on marketing Islam in the West, a term that is used to refer to Western Europe and America. The West represents too broad a geography to devise a meaningful strategy. The product and the strategy for its marketing must relate to the realities of the marketplace. The West is no longer a function of space alone; its mind-set influences man and society practically everywhere. The U.S. constitutes a major force in the creation and promotion of this mind-set. It is no wonder that history locates the center of the Western civilization in the U.S. No marketer can ignore this marketplace but only to his own detriment, especially if he claims to represent the best product, though he may find entry to the market quite challenging. If he is able to market his product effectively in the U.S., tremendous opportunities await him in the global market. More importantly, we, who live in the U.S. seeking to establish our roots here, are place strategically to seize the opportunity. It is reasonable to direct our efforts to marketing Islam in the U.S.

The paper deals with a topic that is large in scope. It is not intended to address the topic in its entirety, but it certainly seeks to understand the nature of the product, to identify direction of our efforts, and to develop a strategy consistent with the direction. The paper is based on materials presented in Satanic Whispers and Echoes of Truth (Ansari, A: Awareness Publishing, 1994).

An attempt to assess marketability of a product must include an in-depth study of its nature, worthiness, and value as well as knowledge of competitors in the marketplace and their products. The purpose of this exercise is to learn to position the product right and to guarantee customer satisfaction of existing and potential buyers. It is generally argued that a successful marketing strategy positions the product right to respond effectively to preference of buyers and realities of the market.

Nature of the Market

A market is defined by nature of the product traded in it. The auto market, for example, refers to a market where automobiles are traded. The auto market may be divided by the types of autos traded. You may have separate markets for Chevy, Honda, and Pontiac. A market does not necessarily refer to a place; it includes places where autos are traded. Yet it may be divided by its geography. You may divide the U.S. for example, into eastern, northern, southern, and western markets. If we wish to market Islam, it is imperative to know the nature of its product and realities of market(s) it seeks to target.

Our concern here is with a market that deals in a special product, the life of man on earth. The market offers a variety of lifestyles. Islam too offers a lifestyle of its own. The Arabic word for lifestyle is *Deen*. The marketer should make immediate note of the fact that Islam is not alone in the market. In fact, the market is crowded with a variety of *Deen*. The Qur'an refers to this reality in Chapter 109: 6, as it distinguishes its lifestyles from all other lifestyles. This verse points to a yet another reality. Man is free to buy his lifestyle. Accordingly, the marketer of the *Deen* of Islam offers it as a choice only. But he must work hard to establish the worthiness and value of his product and to relate it to the worthiness and value of the competitor's products in the marketplace. This gives man the opportunity to effectively exercise his freedom of choice.

The nature of lifestyle is determined by the mind-set or the perception it offers. A lifestyle is characteristically different from another in its perception of life. The Qur'an articulates perception of life in terms of someone or something man worships (109: 2-5). The dictionary meaning of worship is intense love or admiration. When man experiences intense love for something, he is said to worship it. Likewise, when he admires someone, he is said to worship him. The word connotes intensity only when the object of worship signifies exclusion of all other objects. The object of worship based upon the perception of life then becomes the focus of his life. If man develops, for example, intense love for wealth, it becomes the object of his worship as he directs his efforts in its pursuit. Man, therefore, prefers a lifestyle simply because he prefers one object of worship to the exclusion of all others. The marketer should know that the choice of an object of worship continues the fundamental choice; it is fundamental because all other choices in life become subordinate to it. An attempt to market the *Deen* of Islam must clarify the fundamental choice to distinguish it clearly from the competing lifestyles. the buyer should know that the worthiness and value of the lifestyles he buys relates to the fundamental choice.

Products and Competitors

Man shops for a perception of life that is consistent with the lifestyle of his choice. Though the market offers numerous perceptions, we may group them, for the sake of clarity, into two broad categories. We may refer to the first category as the mind-embodied perception. This perception give man his body with its mind as body and mind perish, man's life on earth begins in birth and concludes in death. He lives to cater to his body and mind, and he uses the power of his mind to civilize him. The body with its mind becomes the focus of life. The object of worship is success, which is measured in terms of possession, power, and prestige, as they relate to body and mind.

Because resources on earth are limited and man has a short span of life, the mind-embodied perception promises him success only if he competes with fellowman. When the majority buys a mind-embodied perception, society institutionalises and promotes competition as the basis of social order. Life becomes a contest and the world an arena where winners find prosperity and losers experience misery. Alienation and frustration may cause losers to resort to violence. Win or lose, man lives in constant fear - fear of losing, fear of misery, or fear of injury.

Who are the marketers of the mind-embodied perception? You may view them as specialists of mind. I prefer to label them the Rationalists. He represents the ruler and the ruling elite in society. His identity varies with geography and age. He is the tribal chief, king, aristocrat, constitutional monarch, republican, military dictator, communist, socialist, or democrat. But regardless of age and geography, the authority he assumes come from a single source - the power of making laws. When man buys the mind-embodied perception, the package includes the rationalist as the lawgiver.

We now turn to the next perception of life. We may refer to it as the soul-embodied perception, because it gives man his soul. Though body and mind perish upon death, soul of man continues to live. This perception divides life into two segments, one before and the other after death. The earthly life is temporal, whereas the life after death is eternal. As soul is the residue upon death, it caters to it in the earthly life. The focus of life becomes the salvation of soul in the life after death. Accordingly, it discounts the value of earthly life. Man may win or lose here, but what matters is if soul finds salvation in the life after death. This is generally how it positions its product to compete with the mind-embodied perception.

How does it cater to soul of man? When he buys a soul-embodied perception, it comes with a religion of its own. In fact, every religious markets a soul-embodied perception. Religion offers man a deity or a pantheon of deities that it declares holy as well as a body of rites and rituals the practice of which it recommends. Man thus becomes the faithful of the religion he practices. This is how he caters to his soul to find salvation. When the majority buys a soul-embodied perception, society institutionalizes its religion as the basis of culture.

The discussion points to a major misconception about the nature of competition in the marketplace. The two perceptions are generally considered to compete with one another, because the mind-embodied and soul-embodied perceptions offer contradictory lifestyles. The truth is that the two perceptions are complementary products, and as such they should not even compete. Man may buy mind-embodied perception to cater to his body and mind, whereas he may still buy a soul-embodied perception to cater to his soul. This is how a smart buyer, historically speaking, competes in the arena to secure prosperity in the earthly life, and yet he practices a religion to ensure salvation in the life after death. The coexistence of two perceptions in history confirms their complementary nature. Man is willing to live two contradictory lifestyles to become whole: body, mind, and soul. In it lies the conflict and anxiety man experiences throughout history as he juggles with two objects of worship taking turns to worship the one while tossing the other up in the air.

While the two perceptions do not compete in the marketplace, the mind-embodied perceptions compete with one another, as do the soul-embodied perceptions. For example, socialism and capitalism, both being mind-embodied perceptions, compete with one another. Likewise, Taoism finds its competitor in Buddhism, both being soul-embodied perceptions. The discussion is relevant to positioning the perception of Islam. The marketer must determine if it competes with the one or the other category of perceptions in the marketplace.

We may continue our discussion of the soul-embodied perception. Who are its marketers? You may view them as specialists of soul. I prefer to label them as Traditionalist. He represents the priest and the priestly class. His identity varies with the religion he markets. Like the Rationalist, he too seeks authority, which the role of intermediary confers upon him; he position himself as the intermediary between man and his deity. As the intermediary, he formulates and interprets religious laws and establishes rites and rituals for every occasion. When man buys a soul-embodied perception, which comes with a religion of its own, the package includes the Traditionalist as the intermediary.

Historical evidence suggests that the Traditionalist carefully protects his role of intermediary as therein lies the very basis of his authority. He needs a credible customer base to maintain his share of the market, which enables him to wield authority. This is why the market of soul-embodied perceptions becomes highly competitive. This is why he campaigns ceaselessly always looking for converts to become the faithful of his religion. He does not hesitate to instill prejudice, intolerance, or even hatred, to maintain his share of the market.

This is a serious charge, as it calls for further explanation. Religion, any or all, is built around some man as its founder or originator, who is declared a hero, portrayed as superhuman, or even deified. When you practice a religion, it calls upon its faithful to adore and revere its hero; it is generally made a part of its body of rites and rituals. It is a common human feeling to let race, language, and geography become the basis of relationship between man and fellowman, especially if he adores the fellowman as the founder or originator of the religion he practices. This is how religion divides man and fellowman along lines of race, language, and geography of its hero. This is how history pitches the faithful of one religion against the faithful of another.

When a religion attempts to transcend the culture of its hero, it creates new barriers to divide the faithful. This is how history pitches the faithful of one culture against the faithful of another, both practising the same religion. Historical evidence confirms the division of all religions into sects, denominations, and factions to accommodate cultural differences of the faithful. While the faithful of one religion experiences prejudice, intolerance, or even hatred against the faithful of another, the experience is equally is equally shared by the faithful of one sect against the faithful of another of the same religion.

It would be unfair to single out the Traditionalist for his prejudice and intolerance. The Rationalist also employs prejudice, intolerance, or even hatred, to market his perception. The nature of political economy characterizes the social order he seeks to establish. The form of government and the type of economic system specify the nature of political economy. He simply combines a form of government with a type of economic system to produce a variety of political economies. It gives him the flexibility to combine monarchy, dictatorship, or democracy with capitalism; totalitarian government with communism; and aristocracy and democracy with socialism. He innovates or modifies the nature of political economy in response to age, culture, and geography of society. This is how the Rationalist divides man and fellowman according to the nature of the political economy. The history pitches, for example, capitalism against communism, or capitalism with democracy against capitalism with monarchy. Regardless of the form of government or the type of economic system that specifies the nature of the political economy, competition constitutes the basis of social order designed to keep man and fellowman busy in the arena while the Rationalist stays in control.

Though the Traditionalist does not cater to the body and mind of man, he too builds elaborate structures like the Rationalist does, including monuments, shrines, and houses of worship. He therefore needs the political economy of the Rationalist. This explains his willingness to coexist and even cooperate with the Rationalist. This enhances competitive edge of the Traditionalist, as the Rationalist becomes the patron of his religion and the perception of life it promotes. The Rationalist is equally eager to become patron of the religion of Traditionalist, because the former is aware of the authority the latter derives from his control of the soul of man. In fact, the Rationalist envies the customer loyalty that the Traditionalist has come to enjoy, as the majority of his buyers pass on their religion to the next generation. This is why the two manage to coexist, although history portrays them as antagonists. The marketer of Islam should make special note of the inter-generational customer loyalty.

Generally, a buyer carefully weighs the worthiness and value of his lifestyle before he exercises the freedom of his choice to buy a perception of life. The faithful with inherited perception however is unwilling to trade his perception for another simply because he is not the buyer of the perception he inherits.

The shared arrangement exists throughout history. Man buys from the Rationalist a mind-embodied perception for the privilege of competing for prosperity ion the arena, whereas he pays the Traditionalist for salvation of his soul. But regardless of the perception or combination of perceptions he buys, man continues to live with prejudice and in misery. It is reasonable to conclude that the market is ready for a perception of life that makes him whole. Does the *Deen* of Islam offer such a perception? This inquiry is next.

Lifestyle of Submission

Unlike the *Deen* of the Rationalist or the *Deen* of the Traditionalist, the *Deen* of Islam offers man a lifestyle that is designed to make him whole. It spares him the shared arrangement of the Rationalist and Traditionalist, which is characteristic of a life of conflict and anxiety. Islam distinguishes its *Deen* from all other *Deen* in terms of perception of life it offers. You may refer to it as the true or the original perception to distinguish it from the mind-embodied or soul-embodied perception. I prefer the term "original", because it is a good strategy to position your product in the market as original. It also happens to be a statement of fact, because it is ancient as man himself. In fact, it is more ancient than man on earth. It is by design of the traditionalist that he traces it only as far back as the seventh century AD. We shall return to discuss the point further.

We may describe the nature of the original perception in one word - Dignity. The dictionary defines dignity s worthiness and value. By definition, a product commands value when it is worthy of its design. That is, it does what it is designed to do. For example, a lawn mower is designed to mow grass. It therefore commands value as long as it mows grass. Likewise, if the life of man is to command value, it must be worthy of its creation. But how does the life of man become worthy of its creation? The answer again lies in one word - submission. Islam literally means submission. The original perception restores dignity of man if he buys the *Deen* of Islam or the lifestyle of submission.

The buyer should know that submission constitutes the universal law of creation. The sun, the earth, the moon, and everything between them exist with dignity as each of them submits to become worthy of its creation. The earth, for example, is designed for dual motion; it spins at its axis as it revolves around the sun. The spinning creates night and day, whereas the change of season is caused by its revolution. The earth submits to dual motion to seek its worthiness. The lifestyle of man must be in agreement with the universal law of submission to become worthy of his creation.

The forgoing discussion distinguishes submission by design from submission by choice. All created beings, except man, submit by design; they have no choice but to do what they are designed to do. Man alone is given the choice, and he is free to choose submission. Accordingly, he is equipped to make the right choice - the choice of submission. It is the right choice as it alone restores the dignity of man.

Let us pursue the freedom of choice, as it is relevant in marketing Islam. It is in keeping with this freedom that he is created with an unmatched power of mind. Even the Rationalist distinguishes man from the rest of the creation by the power of his mind; this is how he becomes rational. The buyer of original perception is asked to evaluate the nature and consequence of the choice of submission. The marketer of Islam is to make a rational and reasonable appeal to the buyer to examine the worthiness and value of the lifestyle of submission. Once the buyer submits to the critical examination his uncritical faith and unquestionable rites and rituals, designed for ostentatious care of the soul, the Traditionalist has tough time maintaining a credible customer base. Once the buyer is made aware of his failure by design to deliver prosperity, the Rationalist too cannot hold his ground for long. An effective strategy for marketing the lifestyle of submission is to challenge both the buyers and the competitors simply on the merit of the product itself.

The buyer is made aware of a yet another aspect of the freedom of choice. He is accountable for the choices he makes. The great power of mind and the resources of the universe are placed at his command to enable him to buy the lifestyle of submission to restore his dignity. Accountability makes the choice a serious business of life; it relates to the fundamental choice in life. A buyer is customarily held accountable if he buys the wrong product. The marketer of Islam ought to explain that inter-generational transfer of faith is consistent with accountability. First, if man is created with the freedom of choice, inheriting faith denies man the right to exercise his freedom of choice. The fellowman or even his parents cannot and should not make the choice for him. Second, man is not accountable for the choices of others; he is accountable only for the choices he makes. But if he lets others make the choice for him, he is still accountable for his choice (of letting others make it for him). Accountability gives man no choice but to defend his right to freedom of choice as we kill as his right to exercise it.

Historically, the perception-of-life market is not a free market. The Rationalist manipulates the market to stay in control or else he risks losing his authority as the lawgiver. The Traditionalist coexists with the Rationalist to secure his share of the market or else he too risks losing his authority as the intermediary. A challenging task for he marketer of Islam is to unveil the secrets of the shared arrangement, which exists by design to keep the buyer from exercising his freedom of choice.

How does the original perception of life restore dignity of man? When man buys the original perception, he buys the lifestyle of submission. But he submits to whom or what. In short, what is the object of his worship? Man submits to the one true deity, invisible, and unseen, which proclaim his unity and singularity as the creator of the heavens, the earth, and everything between them. Man acknowledges throughout history universality of the one true deity regardless of race, language, religion, or geography. The universally acclaimed deity becomes the object of his worship. Man submits to it to become worthy of its creation.

The earth submits to orbiting and revolving to become worthy, but what does man submit to in order to become worthy? Man may speculate but he does not know. The deity tells man what he must do to become worthy. This explains nature and purpose of the revealed knowledge. The book, *Satanic Whispers and Echoes of Truth*, establishes the unity and universality of the revealed knowledge. Man is asked simply to do what is good and right to become worthy. The buyer may find it reasonable as he discovers unity of purpose in diverse forces of nature operating in harmony to do what is good and right. But does man know what is good and right? Again, man may speculate, but he and his fellowman cannot always agree on it. The deity, therefore, takes upon itself to let man know what is good and right? This explains the appointment of messengers to whom the deity reveals the knowledge of what is good and right. It is they who bring to man the revealed knowledge.

The lifestyle of submission vests all authority in the deity, who alone is the Lord and master of the universe it creates. Its buyer accepts the deity not only as the object of his worship but also as the lawgiver, because it alone knows what is good and right. The Rationalist however supplants authority of the deity to become the lawgiver. He may not deny the deity, but he certainly rejects its messengers and the revealed knowledge they bring to man. Why? Because he claims to know what is good and right. This is why he claims authority, he argues, to make laws designed to do what is good and right. This is how he justifies the use of force to enforce his laws. The marketer then advises the buyer to refer to history. The historical performance of the Rationalist confirms that he does not know what is good and right.

The lifestyle of submission binds man and his deity in a direct relationship. Man is accountable to the deity, who alone is the lawgiver. The Traditionalist generally accepts the deity, but he certainly compromises its authority by assuming the role of intermediary. He invents religion around some man, and glorifies him as its founder or its originator. He, thus, rejects messengers of the deity and the knowledge revealed to them. If he accepts a messenger as the founder of his religion, he compromises once again authority of the deity as he misrepresents the messengers. For the Traditionalist markets the religion he invents to become its intermediary and not the lifestyle of submission the messengers offer. The historical performance of the traditionalist tells the buyer that he too does not know what is good and right, nor does he have any business mediating between man and his deity.

Man becomes worthy of his creation when he does what is good and right as the deity reveals it. It frees his body and mind from the Rationalist as he learns to submit to none but the deity. It rescues his soul from the Traditionalist as he learns to establish a direct relationship with the deity. His life now begins to command value. His life is rid of conflict and anxiety, as he no longer juggles with two or more objects of worship. He submits to the one true deity to become whole, his body, mind, and soul. This is how the buyer of the original perceptions restores dignity in life.

The buyer soon discovers that he cannot practice the good and right in the privacy of home as the Rationalist recommends or in the designated houses of worship the Traditionalist prefers. He also discovers that many of the goods he seeks to practice are incompatible with the goods of the Rationalist or the Traditionalist. Examples include usury or interest, alcohol, intoxicants, gambling, pornography, extravagance, homosexuality, sex outside marriage, abortion, and inconsistency of behaviour.

The lifestyle of submission directs him to relate to fellowman in accordance with the principles of benevolence, justice, and truth. It gives him a totally different perspective on cultural, social, political, and economic issues, as they relate to the basis of power, role of authority, nature of government, economics of mass production and mass consumption, distribution of wealth, relationship of haves and have-nots, division of the property of the deceased, relationship of the sexes, adoption of children, and nature and scope of education.

The revealed knowledge establishes universal brotherhood as man and fellowman are descended from one primal couple. Even if they choose different lifestyles, it does not constitute a basis for prejudice. You do not hate a buyer simply because he is not your customer. After all, he is free to exercise his freedom of choice. Moreover, the possibility does exist that someday he may choose to become your customer.

The choice of different lifestyles does not justify competition either. Man does not have to compete with fellowman to become prosperous. True, resources on earth are scarce, but it cannot be the justification for the Rationalist's prescription for competition. The revealed knowledge distinguishes between needs and desires. The needs of man are limited, whereas his desires are unlimited. The limited resources of earth can never satisfy unlimited desires at all. Thus argues the Rationalist to create the basis for competition. It is however not a solution to the problem. The winner does come out ahead, but the loser may not have enough even to cater to his needs. The evidence of history confirms the proposition. This is how the Rationalist, in every age, creates islands of prosperity in the vast ocean of misery Yet man is generally unwilling to forgo desires and to become content with needs. But the marketer of Islam quickly points out that the deity does not want man to forgo but, simply, postpone his desires. Man is asked to cater only to his needs in the earthly segment of his life, but his desires must wait as they will be fulfilled in the next life when he inherits the kingdom of the deity. This is in keeping with the wisdom that everything has its time and place.

It does not take a genius to figure out that competition is a prescription of the winners, who establish it in the basis of social order to legitimatize extravagance and indulgence of the winners and the misery of the losers. The arena with its rulers becomes fair and just, and none ought to complain. But the revealed knowledge establishes cooperation as the basis of social order consistent with the availability of resources on earth. It however redefines prosperity. Man becomes prosperous when his needs are met, and society becomes prosperous when it meets the needs of all. It becomes possible when man ceases to compete to win and begins to cooperate to share. He who has more than his needs shares with he who does not have enough. Man buys the lifestyle of submission to become worthy, and worthiness does not lie in fulfilment of desires but in striving to do what is good and right.

Once the buyer restores his dignity and does what is good and right, it becomes clear to him that it is good to have his dignity, but it is not good enough. He is in constant danger of losing his dignity until society seeks to establish and promote what is good and right. The greater good lies in his striving to establish what is good and right in the society. Therefore, he sets out to restore the dignity of fellowman. It ought to restore the marketer of Islam that in every buyer he finds a new marketer of his product.

When the practice of what is good and right grows, it sets moral example in the society. When the lifestyle of submission becomes the choice of the majority, moral example becomes the basis of power in society. This is how the lifestyle of submission, based upon the original perception of life with the deity as his object of worship, establishes what is good and right, restores dignity of man and fellowman, and creates a social order where harmony is traded for prejudice and prosperity for misery.

A Marketing Strategy: Challenges and Opportunities

The lifestyle of submission offers a perception of life that is exclusive and distinct. It is exclusive as it alone guarantees prosperity in both the earthly life and the next life. While the Rationalist promises prosperity in the earthly life, the Traditionalist gives an expectation of it n the next life. Neither is able to restore dignity or deliver prosperity. It is distinct as it clearly separates its buyers from the rest in terms of its unique object of worship. It even asks it buyers to proclaim, "I do not worship what you worship, and you do not worship what I worship." (109: 2-3).

The marketer of Islam must guard carefully the integrity of the product, which is beyond any reasonable doubt, the best product in the market. A competitor seldom hesitates to benefit from any resemblance his product may have with the best product. The original perception does not resemble the mind-embodied perception, any or all, as it shall never accept the Rationalist as the lawgiver, regardless of the nature or end of his political economy. This explains the growing discontent of buyers,

374

especially the buyers in Asia and Africa, who seriously question the worthiness and value of Islam as they continue to live in misery. While the Rationalist is guilty of product misrepresentation, the buyer is equally responsible for the wrong product he buys.

The soul-embodied perception of the Traditionalist constitutes a more serious threat for its apparent similarity with the original perception. The market performance confirms that the Traditionalist deliberately markets his soul-embodied perception as the original perception. He even introduces himself as the marketer of the lifestyle of submission to market the religion of Islam. He appears credible in his presentation as the package he markets includes the Qur'an. Though he recites the Qur'an, he does not know what is good and right, and yet he skilfully uses it as a basis for theological interpretations he construes or the rites and rituals he innovates. This explains why the market can no longer distinguish the *Deen* of Islam from numerous soul-embodied perceptions in the market. This explains how the buyer becomes the faithful to the religion of Islam, practising its rites and rituals to cater to his soul. This explains why the Rationalist continues to be the lawgiver as he simply secures the authority of the Traditionalist as intermediary in return for his support. The shared arrangement is designed to give the Rationalist undisputed authority in society.

The *Deen* of Islam is not a religion, as it never intends to market a soul-embodied perception. Moreover, it bears no reference to any man as its founder or originator. The Qur'an refers to Islam as *Deen-il-lah*, a lifestyle the deity creates from its creation (110: 2). But the traditionalist, who needs a man to create a religion around him, discovers in the messenger of the Qur'an, its founder. He becomes his servant to become the intermediary, expresses intense love or adoration (worship?) for him, glorifies his person to glorify himself, and even celebrates his birthday to give the faithful an occasion for religious festivity.

The foregoing discussion explains why the Traditionalist traces Islam back to the seventh century AD only. This explains why its faithful experiences prejudice against the faithful of other religions. This explains why Islam fails to restore dignity, establish harmony, and deliver prosperity. This explains why Islam experiences division into sects and factions. This is why the faithful experiences Sunni Islam or Shi'a Islam or some faction of either. This is why there are supposedly over one billion buyers, yet the product commands no value, because Islam exists as a religion of the traditionalist and not the *Deen* of the deity. In reality, the soul-embodied perception of the religion of Islam has caused its original perception to become practically extinct in the market. The greatest challenge the marketer now faces lies in reestablishing integrity of the product and introducing it once again as a new product. It is essential to restoring the buyer's confidence.

The Traditionalist, especially in Asia and Africa, has held the soul of the man for centuries, and man has been unable, generally for fear of injury, to challenge his role as intermediary. The situation in the U.S. however, is not quite as serious yet. True, the Traditionalist is busy marketing Islam as a religion; he is learning to seek protection of the Rationalist to improve his cash flow (e.g., registering as a non-profit organization to avoid taxes); he benefits from services of interest-based financial institutions; and now he enters the political arena for a share in gains of the political economy. True, communities are developing along sectarian and ethnic lines, reinforcing prejudice, conflict, and even violence; fund-raising is actively pursued to build elaborate houses of worship and prestigious community centers; growing numbers of Sunni *mullahs* and *Shi'a imams*, trained in the theological institutions of the Traditionalist, are imported to take charge of the faithful to promote sectarian and ethnic causes; and schools are designed for the *mullahs* and *imams* to teach our children the religion of Islam to preserve their sectarian and ethnic heritage. The Asian and African scenario appears to replicate itself in the US. While the Traditionalist caters to his soul, the faithful in the US are busy serving the Rationalist as they compete in the arena to become prosperous. They too act like the smart buyer, who juggles the two objects of worship, taking turns to worship the one while tossing the other up in the air.

To repeat, the situation in the US, however, is not quite as serious yet as the roots of the religion of Islam are only of recent origin. Though the Traditionalist appears to be gaining in the marketplace, the shared arrangement between the Traditionalist of Catholicism, Protestantism, and Judaism as well as the Rationalist constitutes a formidable barrier to marketing the religion of Islam. The apparent gain may be explained by growth in ethnic populations of Asian and African origin, resulting from natural increase and immigration. The Traditionalist of Islam may expect to build a stable customer base largely through inter-generational transfer of faith, but the larger society shall remain insulated from his sphere of influence.

The marketer of the lifestyle of submission should not be

overwhelmed by the odds against him. He may lack the resources to go for an all out campaign for product promotion. but he should never lose sight· of the nature, worthiness, and value of product. He has the best there is, and there is no competition. It is only a matter of time. He is not in a hurry as he sets for himself a long-term planning horizon. He works without fear of mockery or injury and with sincerity and wholeheartedness for the sake of the deity alone.

He offers the buyer the fundamental choice (the choice of object of worship) as he appeals to the power of his mind. He explains the worthiness and value of the lifestyle of submission. He then encourages him to critically examine the worthiness and value of competing lifestyles. The outcome is certainly not his concern. "..... Whosoever wishes may get on the path of his Lord." (73: 19). He is not worried about his share of the market. "... But a few acknowledge with gratefulness." (67: 23). Yet there exists in every buyer a potential marketer. He persists in striving to ensure availability of the product in the market.

He clearly states that the lifestyle of submission has nothing to do with any religion, especially the religion of Islam. Truth is one but religions are many. He distinguishes his buyers from the faithful of all religions. The Qur'an labels its buyers Muslim, because they make a voluntary choice of submission to do what is good and right as the deity reveals. Moreover, its buyer does not and cannot inherit the lifestyle, because every buyer must exercise his freedom of choice to become Muslim.

The package he offers does not include an intermediary. He positions himself only as a teacher of the revealed knowledge, who is always willing to learn and share knowledge of what is good and right. Every buyer learns to read *Salat*, be it regular *Salat* or *Salat* of *Jumaa, Idul Fitr, Idul Adha,* and funeral. While he is able to prepare body of the deceased for burial, he is ready to perform ceremony of nikah (wedding). There is no intermediary to oblige him; he must be able and ready to respond to an occasion. The buyer knows that these are not rituals, and he does not have to hire a specialist of soul to perform them. These comprise the good he must learn to practice.

As every buyer is a potential marketer, so he is a teacher of the revealed knowledge. He does not have to be a professor or scholar; he simply learns and relearns but only to share the knowledge of what is good and right. The buyer studies the Qur'an as the textbook of what is good and right. But the Qur'an is revealed in Arabic, and the audience is English speaking. Do you have to know Arabic to buy the lifestyle submission? The product is designed for buyers everywhere. Is it the wish of the deity that the whole world should become Arabic speaking? It is not reasonable to make such an assumption.

The Qur'an uses the language of its time and place to communicate what is good and right. The deity has revealed the knowledge before, e.g., in Pali, Hebrew, Greek, and Aramaic. The deity does not prefer one language to another. The deity creates language to communicate. The Qur'an constitutes the final and complete source of revealed knowledge. As long as he markets the lifestyle of submission to promote what is good and right, the marketer is not limited to Arabic in his choice of language. The Qur'an in Arabic exists as the standard for man and fellowman to refer to, regardless of race, language, and geography. The marketer in the US is therefore free to use English, which is the language of his time and place. A major task however includes a translation of the Qur'an that rids it of theological themes and explains its concepts, principles, and rules emphasizing their relevance to challenges of his time and opportunities they offer his buyers. But he does not have to wait until the desired translation becomes available.

How does the marketer position his product? The buyer no longer takes campaigns and slogans at the face value. Harmony and prosperity have become catchwords largely due to performance of competitors in the market. He is fed up with speeches, lectures, and sermons. He is tired of surveys and questionnaires designed to reduce his personal preferences to demographic profiles. He does not trust marketers as they care about products and buyers. This is how they have come to view marketers, and the buyer is always right.

The marketer makes the buyer the focus of his campaign as he relates to one buyer at a time. He shows how the product is designed to benefit the buyer. He is in the business of life and lifestyle, so he shows how his life may command value if he chooses to restore dignity. The marketer positions his product with respect to dignity. Who does not seek worthiness and vale in life? The marketer challenges his competitions to do just that. More importantly, he challenges the buyer to use the power of his mind to take charge of his life and exercise his freedom of choice to seek dignity.

Though he does not discriminate between buyers, he singles out his target group that is known to experience the greatest need for the product. The social order, designed for competition, creates winners and losers. The losers comprise the majority in the market, and the competitions generally ignore them. The historical performance of the market suggests that the group of losers show strong preference for the lifestyle of submission. The explanation lies in the nature of the product, which alone restores dignity of its buyers. Having lost in the arena and having nowhere to turn to, it constitutes the perfect target group. The losers are everywhere. They are in urban centers or rural areas, downtown or suburbia. They are adolescent, youth, and adult. They comprise a culturally diverse group. The marketer targets the group to build a stable base without threatening the competitors in the early phase of his campaign. Initially, he may even earn their approval for his benevolence and service.

As he builds his customer base one at a time, the organization of the community of buyers becomes a major marketing strategy. The community may not necessarily exist in space but it certainly does in time. The community reinforces buyers to do what is good and right while it encourages them to subordinate their subsequent choices to the fundamental choice. This is the first community of buyers, and it constitutes the lead or the core community. Its members may live in separate communities in one or fifty states. The core community assumes the role of the marketer, who now becomes its member. We shall now refer to the core community as the marketer.

The Traditionalist is always hung up on space to create a community. He needs territory to build his community even at the expense of prejudice, hatred, and violence. He follows in the footsteps of his patron, the Rationalist, to build elaborate houses of worship and expensive centers to secure his authority as intermediary in the community. Unlike the Traditionalist, the core community does not build as does not relate to a contiguous space. The *Deen* of Islam transcends space as it markets a lifestyle based upon the original perception of life. Its focus is man whose dignity it seeks to restore. Yes, it too builds, but it builds the character of man, who submits to the universal deity to do what is good and right. This is the "mandate of heaven."

The core community, however, resides in the society, and society refers to a territory in space. Once the core community is organized, the marketer has the choice to target the whole society or a segment of it as defined by its geography. I prefer the strategy that targets one community at a time. It allows the marketer to learn from its learning experiences and to conserve its resources as it concentrates its efforts on one community at a time.

Once the marketer selects the target community, it works out a detailed marketing plan designed to establish what is good and right in the community. The plan contains three sections. The first section relates to marketing the lifestyle of submission. It organizes local buyers into a local group to build a local customer base; the size of the base is not critical. It prepares teachers, who learn and relearn only to share what is good and right in the community.

The second section outlines areas of research to specify immediate needs of the target group, especially the needs the marketer may relate to and satisfy. The purpose of this exercise is to develop community programs, however small in size though not necessarily limited in scope, to cater to specific needs. It prepares public servants, who implement community programs to serve the target group. The local group may engage in fund-raising for specific programs.

The third and final section examines social, economic, and political issues in the community, especially the issues that relate to the target group. The purpose of this exercise is to come up with an agenda of what is good and right to address major issues in the community. It researches and prepares position papers on relevant issues. The local group capitalizes on every opportunity it gets, and it even creates, where possible, opportunities of its own, to communicate its position on what is good and right to respond to live community issues. It makes its presence felt at public meetings, including town council meetings and meetings of county commissioners. It taps carefully local media resources to promote its campaign, publicize its programs, and articulate its position on relevant issues.

The marketer must answer two questions as they relate to the marketing strategy for the target community. First, there is much good as well as much evil. Does the plan address all good and all evil? The marketer follows the rule of hierarchy, which simply states that good and evil are arranged in hierarchical structure. When a buyer or a community secures that which is good, more good will follow. Likewise, when extreme evils are eradicated, minor evils die out. The marketer therefore begins to address good and evil in the community. You may refer to *Satanic Whispers and Echoes of Truth* for a detailed discussion of the hierarchy of good and evil.

Next, how long does the marketer work with a target community before it moves on to target the next community? The marketer works with a long-term horizon, and it is never in a hurry to enjoy benefits of its effort. Marketing the lifestyle of submission is a mission, and missions are seldom accomplished in one lifetime. You seldom eat fruits of trees you plant. The plan, however, ought to bear some reference to time. Generally, once the local group is operational, the marketer is ready to target the next community. It however continues to monitor progress of local groups.

Moving Ahead

The lifestyle of submission begins with the premise that all men are created equal. It therefore rejects outright competition as the basis of social order, because it is futile for equals to compete. It further establishes that man cannot be lawgiver of fellowman, because he who makes laws wields authority. Again, it is futile for an equal to exercise power over an equal. Likewise, man cannot be an intermediary between the deity and fellowman, because an intermediary wields authority. Once again, it is futile to become an intermediary of an equal. The lifestyle of submission vests all authority in the deity, who alone is the Lord of the universe it creates.

Man experiences conflict and anxiety as long as his body, mind, and soul are loosely connected. There exists in the market no single lifestyle or a combination of two or more lifestyles to make him whole. It is in the nature of man to pursue one object of worship to experience unity of life. The lifestyle of submission confirms unity and universality of truth, and it evidences in the one true deity, invisible and unseen, its unique object of worship. It is unique, because it is alone worthy of worship by man, regardless of race, religion, language, and geography. It is unique, because it alone constitutes the common denominator between man and fellowman. It is unique, because it postulates in submission the universal law for its creation. It is unique, because it establishes the universal citerion to distinguish good from evil, right from wrong. It is unique, because it alone guarantees prosperity in this world and in the next.

Man seeks to live in harmony with fellowman in pursuit of prosperity, because dependence is in the nature of life. If society fails to deliver harmony and prosperity, he must critically examine the worthiness and value of his lifestyle. The fundamental choice he makes not only his lifestyle but also the nature of relationship he seeks to establish with fellowman. The historical evidence confirms widespread prejudice and misery man experiences in everyday society. Man is born free to live the lifestyle of his choice. If he still values dignity, harmony, and prosperity, the time is now to evaluate his options in the market and look for an alternative lifestyle. He now has the opportunity to examine and verify the lifestyle of submission. He must, for his dignity depends on it. Only when the lifestyles of submission becomes the choice of the majority does society prosper in harmony.

The Future of Da'wah
in North America

Larry Poston

I n recent years the subject of *da'wah* has become a topic of considerable interest among Muslims in North America. A plethora of articles and books have appeared both in English and Arabic that deal with this subject from a variety of angles. Western writers—both scholarly and popular—have noted the steady increase in the number of converts to the Muslim faith. An article in the Wall Street Journal proclaims in its headline that "Islam is Growing Fast in the U.S., Fighting Fear and Stereotypes." U.S. News and World Report has observed that "Islamic worship and lifestyles are becoming an increasingly familiar part of the American tableau. It is said to be the nation's fastest growing religion ..."

But what may be said of the future of Islamic *da'wah* in North America? Will Muslim da'is become increasingly successful in their missionary work, or do the reports mentioned above represent only a temporary advance?

As we attempt to answer these questions it is important to note at the outset the differences in orientation and focus of Muslims living in the West. In seeking to classify the approximately six million Muslims currently resident in the United States and Canada with respect to their beliefs as to how Muslim missionary activity should proceed, two general philosophies of da'wah can be distinguished. These may be called, respectively, the "defensive-pacifist" and "offensive-activist" approaches.[1] The first characterizes the attitude of those Muslims who are concerned

---

1 Particularly recommended are the following: Sadiq Amin, *Al-Da'wah al-Islamiyya: Faridah Shari'iyya wa Darura Bashariyya* (Aman: Jam'iyya Amman al-Matabi' al-Ta'awuniyya, 1987); *Christian Missions and Islamic Da'wah: Proceedings of the Chambesy Dialogue Consultation* (London: The Islamic Foundation, 1976); Ahmad von Denffer, *Key Issues for Islamic Da'wah* (Delhi: Hindustan Pub., 1983); Anwar Al-Jindi, *Afaq Jadida lil-Da'wah al-Islamiyya fi 'Alam al-Gharb* (Beirut: Mu'assasa al-Risala, 1984); Muhammad Khurshid, *Da'wah in Islam* (Houston: Islamic Education

solely or primarily with the retention and maintenance of their own Islamicity and not with the extension of that Islamicity to the non-Muslims around them. The second applies to those who are desirous of converting non-Muslims to Islam and of transforming non-Muslim society so that it will reflect Islamic values and beliefs.

The defensive-pacifist orientation is a consequence of the factors, which spurred the early waves of Muslim immigration to the United States and Canada. The ideological and theological hindrances to the residence of a Muslim in the *dar al-kufr* were mitigated by pragmatic considerations such as the need to escape the increasingly chaotic conditions of Eastern Europe and the Middle East. Muslim immigrants quickly adopted the spirit of American individualism and this enabled them to blend into the communities in which they chose to reside. Organizations were established which mainly reflected the various national origins, ethnic backgrounds, and sectarian beliefs of the different Muslim populations. There have been few concerted efforts to subsume these differences under a larger Islamic umbrella.[2]

The adherents of the activist group consist primarily of a minority of earlier immigrants who have resisted absorption into the melting pot and thus have become only minimally assimilated into American society. These individuals are convinced that assimilated Muslims are incapable of bearing a credible witness to the society around them. It is believed that it is impossible for them to offer an alternative to prevailing social conditions because identification with and acceptance of those conditions are implied in their own lifestyles. Activists maintain that they must distinguish themselves in specific ways from American society so that their lives present a contrast to the lifestyles that surround them.

Other activists are found among the new immigrants who are being injected into North American communities at the rate of 25,000 to 35,000 per year. While many of these would have been considered nominal

Council, n.d.); *Manual of Da'wah for Islamic Workers* (Montreal: Islamic Circle of North America, 1983); Khurram Murad, *Da'wah Among Non-Muslims in the West* (London: The Islamic Foundation, 1986); Yahiya Emerick, *How to Tell Others About Islam*; Shamim Siddiqi, *Methodology of Da'wah: American Perspective* (New York: Forum Islamic, 1989); Shamim Siddiqi, *The Da'wah Program* (New York: Forum Islamic, 1993); Larry Poston, *Da'wah in the West: Muslim Missionary Activity and the Dynamics of Conversion to Islam* (New York: Oxford University Press, 1992).

2 R. Gustav Niebuhr, "American Moslems", *The Wall Street Journal* (October 5, 1990): 1.

Muslims in their home countries, an interesting psychological phenomenon occurs when they enter a non-Muslim country. Yvonne Haddad and Adair Lummis have observed in their extensive study of Muslim communities that "many have found their consciousness about religious identity enhanced in the American context as people question them about the basic tenets of their religion."[3] A considerable number of Muslims, then, become activists when they become aware of their minority status in the midst of a predominantly Judeo-Christian nation. Such awareness results in a re-examination of the tenets of their inherited faith. But such an evaluation is often not grounded in a clearly defined Islamic ethos and thus lacks coherence. This results in an inability to distinguish between ethnic, nationalistic, and truly Islamic concerns. Very few have, thus far, succeeded in attaining to a supra-cultural form of Islam not identified with a specific ethnic or national background, although Yvonne Haddad and Jane Smith note that newer "mosque and center communities have attempted to reconstitute themselves into self-consciously more Islamic and less ethnically stylized organizations."[4]

Muslim organizations that can be classified as activistic are multiplying and increasing in size, but for the most part they are still small, unorganized, poorly staffed, and poorly funded. An article appearing in the December 1986 edition of *Arabia: The Islamic World Review* traces the origin of organizations concerned with *da'wah* to Muslim immigrants influenced by contact with or the writings of Maulana Maududi, Syed Qutb, Syed Nursi and other such personages. But few of these organizations have been able to maintain their emphasis on outreach and have instead succumbed to the nationalistic and ethnic interests noted previously:

Because of the fact that these organizations failed to grasp the nature of western society and its dynamics they have yet to leave any significant imprint on their new countries. Most of these *da'wah*

---

3 Jeffrey L. Sheler, "Islam in America", *U.S. News and World Report* (October 8, 1990): 69.

4 Hyphenated terms such as "offensive-activist" and "defensive-pacifist," while admittedly clumsy, are necessary because of the varying usages of these terms in contemporary English-speaking societies. The word "offensive," for instance, can have the meaning seen in the phrase "taking the offensive," which communicates the idea of "taking the initiative" (the meaning I am using here). It can, however, also be used as a term signifying derogation, such as in the phrase "what he said is offensive to me," which is not the way I am using the term. Adding "activist" to "offensive" gives the former the meaning that I intend.

organizations have now become ethnic groups with an emphasis on preserving their specific cultural and social identity.[5]

The author of this article criticizes even those few organizations that have retained an activistic focus for their failure to evolve a "da'wah language" which could attract Westerners, their corresponding failure to produce literature suitable for educating Westerners about Islam, their lack of competent, properly educated leadership, their failure to provide programs for training Islamic workers, and their failure to encourage self-evaluation, criticism and discussion of their goals, objectives, strategies, and methodologies. Perhaps the most deadly observation made is that, because of the pre-eminence of national and ethnic interests, the organizations often work in isolation from, and occasionally in opposition to, each other.

It appears that it has been the inability of Muslim groups in North America to establish a commonly accepted hermeneutic for the contextualization of Qur'anic precepts in Western societies that has led to such a divided front. Simply stated, there are some who refuse to adapt any Qur'anic precept to Western ways, requiring instead that Western society be transformed to accommodate Muslim law. Others are willing to bend in certain instances on an interim basis, recognizing the exigencies of a technologically oriented and pluralistic society. A case in point that relates specifically to the subject of *da'wah*: some Muslims feel themselves constrained by Qur'anic injunctions (i.e. *Al-Baqarah*: 256) not to compel others to adopt their faith. But they have begun to understand that in a pluralistic society such as that which exists in America it is the religion that is the most visible and forceful in presenting its claims that gains the most publicity and, hence, exercises the greatest amount of influence and wins the greatest number of converts. Some have noted that, while the number of Jews living in North America is roughly equivalent to that of Muslims, the Jewish people exercise an influence in nearly every area of society that is out of all proportion to its size. At the same time, other Muslims are repulsed by the idea that

---

5 The formation of the Islamic Society of North America is certainly the most ambitious attempt to produce a larger unity, and it has enjoyed limited success. There are, however, several issues that remain to be resolved even within this organization. See, for instance, the chapter by Steve A. Johnson entitled "Political Activity of Muslims in America", in Yvonne Yazbeck Haddad (ed.), *The Muslims of America* (New York: Oxford University Press, 1991).

adherents of the Islamic faith must join the carnival atmosphere of American evangelical movements if they are to compete successfully for the souls of men and women. Until the issue of a common hermeneutic is resolved (assuming that it is capable of resolution), the Muslim community in the West will most likely continue to subdivide ad infinitum.

Because of the Muslims' preoccupation with such issues, at least two windows of opportunity for effective *da'wah* activity have already closed. The first opened in the 1960s and was analyzed by Jacob Needleman, an authority on contemporary religious movements in America. In a book entitled *The New Religions*, Needleman identified the features deemed by Westerners to be the most attractive elements of Zen Buddhism, Subud, Transcendental Meditation and other religious groups new to the American scene. He discovered that young Americans were searching primarily for religious faiths that were self-centered in the sense that they supplied solutions to individual as well as societal difficulties. Buddhism, for instance, was perceived as providing release from one's personal suffering, and was therefore appealing. Needleman noted that the traditional Judeo-Christian religious systems certainly contained such individualistic aspects but that these dimensions of Western religion had in the course of time been "overlaid" or "neglected."[6]

Second, the new religions accentuated the mind as opposed to the emotions. But Needleman notes that traditional Christianity and Judaism early on abandoned reason to secular philosophers and thus lost their appeal to thinking men and women. He states that:

> "The exclusion of the mind from the religious process is one of the central characteristics of our religious forms. It was not always so, but by and large it is so now. We may be willing to grant religion the power to move us and stir us to the 'depths' of our emotions, but we reserve the autonomy of our reasoning for ourselves."[7]

Closely associated with this observation was the fact that, surprisingly, the liberated young people of the 1960s were seeking a faith, which

---

6 Yvonne Haddad and Adair Lummis, *Islamic Values in the United States* (N.Y.: Oxford University Press, 1987), p. 22.

7 Yvonne Yazbeck Haddad and Jane Idleman Smith (eds.), *Muslim Communities in North America* (Albany: State University of New York Press, 1994), p. xxix.

involved ritual, discipline, and method. They were attracted to the rigor and discipline of meditation exercises and willingly submitted themselves to the commands of their gurus. According to this observation, the movement of Reformed Judaism and traditional Christian denominations away from liturgy and ritual—which was perceived by Christian and Jewish leaders to be a necessary adaptation in light of the informality and "looseness" of the times—turned out to be their undoing and resulted in the loss of a significant number of young people to Eastern religions.

The third source of appeal was found in the fact that Christianity and Judaism were perceived as being religions which underestimate or denigrate human potential. The Pauline teaching regarding a sinful nature as inherent in every individual by virtue of the original failure of Adam and Eve in Eden and the Jewish concept of the *yezer ha-ra* serve only to remind people of their inability to progress spiritually beyond a certain point. The possibility of attaining "sinless perfection" is essentially heretical in these faith systems and is relegated to sects beyond the pale of orthodoxy. The new religions, on the other hand, emphasized the possibility of individuals attaining tremendously advanced states of being in the here and now. Needleman shows how the Western concept of the "holy man" was (and is) essentially flawed in that such a one was holy only in a strictly spiritual sense. The Eastern religions, said Needleman, "with their practical methods involving work with the body, the attention, the intellect and memory, [and] the training of the emotions" essentially supplanted the Western view of holiness and opened whole new worlds of possibilities for human beings to improve themselves. The fatalistic ideas inherent in Oriental religion were carefully excised before their transference to the West, and so there remained no pessimistic doctrines involving such negative theological concepts as those mentioned above. Needleman contends that this was to the liking of the Woodstock generation who sang of their longing for a return to "the Garden."

Measuring Islam by these three characteristics, one would conclude that this religion had great potential for expansion in the Western context. Research by this author has shown that conversions by Westerners to the religion of Islam from the late 1800s through the 1980s have been motivated by five specific factors. These are as follow:

1) The perceived simplicity of Islam as opposed to the complexity of Christian and Jewish systems of belief.
2) The perceived rationality of Islam as opposed to the alleged

irrationality of such Christian beliefs as the Trinity, the incarnation and resurrection of Jesus, the prevalence of the miraculous and the supernatural, etc.

3) The perception of Islam as an essentially "this-worldly" religion as opposed to the "other-worldly" orientation of (in particular) Christianity.

4) The perception of Islam as a religion espousing the universal brotherhood of mankind as opposed to the racism which is endemic in Christianity and the segregationism so characteristic of both Christianity and Judaism.

5) The perception of Islam as a religion without human mediators as distinguished from the priestly concept found in the Christian and Jewish faiths.[8]

How do the above-mentioned characteristics accord with Needleman's observations regarding the attractiveness of the new religions he investigated?

Because the Muslim faith acknowledges no mediators between the individual and God it may certainly be considered self-centered. There are *few—if any*—accountability structures built into the various Islamic structures found in America, ensuring that the practice of the faith is strictly voluntary. Islam's emphasis upon reason is apparently also very attractive, and this accord well with Needleman's observations regarding the new religions' preoccupation with the mind as opposed to the emotions. Muslims are fond of claiming that their faith is "the thinking man's religion" and that the precepts of Islam are in precise accordance with all modern scientific discoveries.[9] Finally, Islam stresses the ritual of prayer and the disciplines of fasting and almsgiving, and deems important the memorization of Qur'anic verses and traditions of the Prophet. For young people enamored of a disciplined spiritual lifestyle, Islam supplies a very adequate model. Thus it would seem that this religion contains all of the characteristics that were found to be appealing to Western young people.

---

8 "Muslim Organizations in the West: An Overview," *Arabia: The Islamic World Review*, December 1986: 24.

9 Jacob Needleman, *The New Religions* (New York: E.P Dutton, 1970), p. 13.

The problem is, of course, that Needleman's observations were made in 1970 during what was the culmination of the wave of spiritual experimentation begun in the 1960s. And as Jackson Carroll observed in his study of religion in America, "in the 1970s there [was] a marked change. The upheaval and turmoil of the 1960s [gave] way to what appear to be disillusionment, cynicism, and a groping for direction."[10] Already in 1976, Martin Marty, the University of Chicago historian of modern Christianity, wrote that:

> "The New Religions now have their cultic place under the sun
> and they will continue to influence and suffuse other religious
> groups. But even as I write they draw less attention than they
> did. Their most effervescent period may well be past."[11]

The observations of Needleman, Carroll, and Marty taken together imply that, had Muslims mobilized in force and espoused a specific strategy for da'wah during the 1960s and early 1970s, they might well have attracted large numbers of followers due to the social and spiritual dynamics present during that period of time. Certainly the Muslim Student Association realized significant gains during those years, but this organization appears to be the exception rather than the rule. It was able to observe and to imitate Christian parachurch organizations such as Campus Crusade for Christ, the Navigators, and InterVarsity Christian Fellowship, all of which enjoyed rapid growth during the late 1960s and early 1970s. But for the most part, Muslims in America failed to analyze and were unprepared for this situation, the majority of them being so assimilated into their surrounding culture that they were unmindful of any personal responsibility with regard to da'wah activity. Ethnic concerns were given priority rather than matters, which involved the ummah as a whole. Consequently we find that today when awareness of the importance of da'wah is increasing, the culture of America has changed in a way which makes what would previously have been attractive elements of Islam less relevant or not relevant at all.

---

10 Ibid., p. 15.

11 For a more detailed exposition of these factors, see Larry Poston, *Islamic Da'wah in the West: Muslim Missionary Activity* and the *Dynamics of Conversion to Islam* (New York: Oxford University Press, 1992), chapter 10.

The second recent window of opportunity for Islamic *da'wah* was the eight year Reagan administration (1980-1988). During this era there arose a new emphasis upon conservative ethics and morality on the part of a sizable portion of American society. Reagan's outspokenness with regard to the issues of abortion, homosexuality, chemical dependency and the like were due to and accompanied by an increase in conservative religious values. Here again, Muslims enjoyed a distinct advantage over traditional Christian and Reformed Jewish denominations, which during the 1960s and 1970s adopted relatively liberal moral values. Even Christian evangelicals—noted for their exclusivism with regard to non-Christian religions—recognized the appeal of the Muslim Shari'a. Kerry Lovering, the publications secretary of the evangelical missions organization known as the Sudan Interior Mission (now SIM International), wrote in 1979 that "Christianity ... has failed miserably ... it is now Islam that offers salvation from the drunkenness, sexual license, political corruption, violence, blasphemy and corrupt lifestyles that afflict 'Christian' nations."[12] This was the evaluation of a Christian writer who understood the potential of an Islamic appeal to morality better than Muslims did, for Muslims did not grasp this opportunity to demonstrate their distinctiveness. Instead America saw the rise of such movements as Christian Reconstructionism (also known as Theonomy), an ideology derived from conservative elements of Protestant Christianity which advocates the return of the entire nation to the laws and standards of the Mosaic Covenant as recorded in the Pentateuch. This movement and others like it continue to advance because of their emphasis upon conservative moral ethics, social justice, and law and order, all of which appeal to citizens who are increasingly frustrated with the apparent failure of civil rights legislation and current techniques of law enforcement.

But now that both the Reagan and Bush eras have drawn to a close, the direction which American society will take is still unclear and the Muslims of America find themselves faced with the problem of a constantly moving target. In order to become or to remain appealing, they must be able to adapt the precepts of their faith to the constantly changing trends of thought in America. Such adaptations would require planning and strategies which are consistently being updated and which

---

12 See such works as Osman Bakar, *Tawhid and Science: Essays on the History and Philosophy of Islamic Science*, and K. Ajram, *The Miracle of Islamic Science* (Buffalo Grove, IL: Knowledge House, 1993).

would allow Islam to maintain unadulterated its supra-cultural aspects while simultaneously emphasizing various facets of the religion which accord with contemporary culture. Capable, creative, and brilliant leadership is essential here, but this is an area in which by its own admission American Islam suffers a vital lack.

Although the elements discussed by Needleman may no longer exercise a significant appeal and the conservatism of the Reagan and Bush eras may be on the wane, there yet remain certain traits within the American ethos which Martin Marty believes have become so ingrained into the people as a whole that there is no danger of them disappearing in the foreseeable future. These traits include pluralism (a commitment to allowing all religious expressions access to "the public square," experimentalism (the willingness of Americans both to seek and to practice spiritual alternatives to traditional religion), scripturalism (preference for adherence to a written revelation), a positive view of Enlightenment thinking (an acceptance of principles of logic and reason as the primary tests for truth), and voluntarism ("the principle or tenet that the Church and educational institutions should be supported by voluntary contributions instead of by the State").[13] Each of these characteristics is to an extent favorable to the growth and expansion of Islam in America. Pluralism and experimentalism are generic traits, assuring Islam of a hearing as a religious alternative and making it possible for newcomers to practice the precepts of the faith without fear of social ostracism. The Muslim emphasis upon and commitment to the Qur'an as the revelation of God accords well with the ideas inherent in the concept of scripturalism. The emphasis of the religion upon reason makes it a viable alternative for those who are repulsed by the emotional emphases of a large portion of contemporary Christianity, and its lay-orientation endows it (at least in theory) with characteristics of voluntarism. It can thus be concluded that the Muslim faith still has potential for exercising a profound influence upon American society. But it is the contention of this writer that these advantages will avail Muslims nothing unless they are able to effect certain changes within the ethos of American Islam.

First, unless Muslims develop an indigenous American leadership, Islam will retain a distinctly foreign character, which in the 1990s will not be advantageous for its growth and expansion. In the 1960s and

---

13 Jackson W. Carroll et al., *Religion in America: 1950 to the Present* (New York: Harper and Row, 1979), p. 7.

early 1970s the guru from the Indian subcontinent or from Sri Lanka was appealing due to the exoticness of his identification with things foreign to America. But this preoccupation with exoticness is, for the most part, a thing of the past, and one sees a renewed emphasis in the spiritual sphere (even as it is seen in the area of economics) upon indigenous or "home-grown" ideas and personages.[14] This fact, combined with the essentially negative image which Islam retains due to its portrayal in the American media, leads us to believe that unless American converts are trained as quickly and thoroughly as possible for positions of leadership (which would in itself serve to begin the transformation of the perception of the religion by the masses as foreign), Islam will continue to be categorized as an essentially alien cult.

Second, Muslims would have to increase tremendously their efforts to transform the stereotypical image of Islam as consisting mainly of Iranian and Libyan terrorists, Black activists, male chauvinists and the like. That many are aware of this need is evidenced by the emphases of organizations such as the International Institute of Islamic Thought, strategically located in a suburb of the nation's capital. But the approach of these agencies is often flawed. The philosophy of the IIIT, for instance, is predicated upon a belief that the most influential persons in America are the college-educated, and hence one of the chief objectives of this organization is the preparation of college-level textbooks.[15] But this assumption is only partially true. The mass media (e.g. television, motion pictures, and even paperback novels) exert a greater and more lasting influence than does a college education due to the ongoing nature of the former. A single college course in Islam (assuming that one is offered and that students enroll) enjoys a duration of perhaps ten to fifteen weeks, while a television program or paperback bestseller can occupy the minds of Americans for months or even years. Thus a transformation of the image of Islam can only be effected through the above-mentioned media, not through academia.

Third, if the anti-Christian polemic of writers and speakers seeking to imitate the rhetoric of such personages as Ahmad Deedat does not cease, Muslims may well create a situation precisely the opposite of that

---

14 Martin E. Marty, *A Nation of Behavers* (Chicago: University of Chicago Press, 1976), p. 206.

15 Kerry Lovering, "Tough at Home, Aggressive Abroad: Islam on the March", *Muslim World Pulse*, August 1979, p. 6.

which they wish to produce. Historians have noted the role played by the Christian missionary movement of the 19th century with its often inflammatory rhetoric in sparking the renewed vigor seen among the major world religions today. The potential exists for Islam to duplicate this phenomenon in the reverse. Direct attacks upon Christian teachings such as the divinity, crucifixion, and resurrection of Jesus may indeed cause some persons to forsake the Christian faith (just as Christianity has been able to attract a number of converts from Islam), but such attacks will most likely serve mainly to increase the interest of nominal Christians in the precepts of their culturally-inherited faith and in so doing solidify their commitment to the Christian religion. Public debates of the nature of those staged between Deedat and Christians such as Jimmy Swaggart and Josh McDowell—seen by an increasing number of Americans on videotaped recordings—have made both Christians and Jews increasingly aware of Muslim *da'wah* activity in the Western world. Evangelical Christians in particular are beginning to discuss ways in which this activity can be mitigated. Evangelicals will not surrender secularized Americans to Muslim *da'is* and will seek to stem the rising tide of conversion to Islam both by renewed efforts to proclaim their own message and by efforts to reclaim as many converts as possible.

Fourth, Muslims would do well to realize that despite the observation that nationalistic and ethnic interests have served to hinder da'wah efforts, the pursuit of the kind of unity envisioned by nearly all Muslims concerned with this subject is a vain pursuit. Individuals and organizations who in an era characterized by the prevailing pluralistic and individualistic mindset continue to strive for a national or international union of Muslim organizations will inevitably be frustrated in their ambitions. The very limited success of Christian ecumenicists in their endeavor to create a World Council of Churches serves to illustrate this point. It is admittedly troublesome that such diversity exists within religious faiths, but this must be accepted as an irreversible and inevitable historical development. Time and effort would be better expended upon more achievable goals at local levels of social interaction.

Finally, an internal and personally oriented missiological approach espoused by such thinkers as Khurram Murad[16] would have to be

---

16 See Martin E. Marty, *Religion and Republic* (Boston: Beacon Press, 1987), pp. 36-48.

adopted by a majority of Muslims and would have to be expanded and continually developed. The ambivalence arising from the fact that both the Qur'an and the historical traditions of Islam support an external and institutional strategy of proselytization[17] would have to be resolved once and for all. Such a resolution would of necessity have to include various means for mobilizing the mass of Muslim laymen through instruction regarding the responsibility of each individual to be involved in da'wah and through training in the principles and techniques of outreach. While it is doubtful that the majority will ever become convinced that the only justification for their continued residence in the *dar al-kufr* is to function as missionary agents (an idea espoused by al-Faruqi, among others[18]), unless a concept similar or analogous to this is promoted, Muslims in America will continue to become assimilated into and secularized by the surrounding culture.

The dream of a Muslim America is deeply embedded in the minds of many Muslims. With regard to the present influence of Islam upon the American ethos, Isma'il al-Faruqi wrote just prior to his assassination that:

> "The Islamic vision endows North America with a new destiny worthy of it. For this renovation of itself, of its spirit, for its rediscovery of a God-given mission and self-dedication to its pursuit, the continent cannot but be grateful to the immigrant with Islamic vision. It cannot but interpret his advent on its shores except as a God-given gift, a timely divine favor and mercy."[19]

On a tour of the United States in 1977, Dr. Abdel-Halim Mahmoud

---

17 A concrete example of this is the fact that little (if any) consideration has been given to the common practice of adopting an Arabic name upon conversion to Islam. While this may have merit within the community itself, it serves to maintain and even increase the aura of foreignness which characterizes the Muslim faith. As long as converts continue publicly to use Arabic names, their credibility will suffer.

18 This thinking is expounded in Ismail al-Faruqi's work entitled *The Islamization of Knowledge*: General Principles and Workplan, published by the International Institute of Islamic Thought.

19 The internal-personal approach to missionary outreach is predicated upon the belief that salvation is obtained only by individuals making deliberate and conscious choices with regard to their religious allegiances. Such choices are made "internally" in the

of al-Azhar University was asked if American Muslims might one day try to replace the Constitution of the United States with Shari'a law. He answered: "We cannot deny such a possibility."[20] And Musa Qutub of the Islamic Information Center of America is fond of quoting an ancient tradition that in the latter days Islam will spread from the West to the East, and he intends to make his center a training institution to prepare workers for this task.[21] Sulayman Nyang concurs with this idea when he surmises that "American Muslims could one day be one of World Islam's major pillars of support", and that "U.S. Muslim Centers . . . will play an important role in the cultural development of their brethren elsewhere in the Muslim world."[22]

If the changes outlined above are effected or occur at some future point, it is conceivable that Muslims would become a missionary force to be reckoned with. But if not, then these goals will never become reality and the dream of an Islamic America will remain only a wistful dream.

---

sense that they consist of intellectual and emotional activity (involving "the heart" and "the mind"). Thus external rituals, liturgies, or similar practices are deemed unnecessary to effect salvation, although they may be useful in expressing salvation attained through an intellectual/emotional decision. Accordingly, the goal of missionary work is to elicit such internally made choices from individuals. For a more complete discussion of this concept, see Poston, Da'wah in the West, chapter 3.

20 The external-institutional approach to missionary work is the opposite of the internal-personal approach (see the previous note). It is predicated on the belief that salvation is primarily obtained through an external conformity to a particular status or set of regulations or religious practices (i.e. baptism, circumcision, obedience to legal precepts, "good works", etc.), and thus seeks to elicit outward conformity to whichever practices or forms are deemed essential by a specific religious system.

21 See Isma'il Raji al-Faruqi, "Islamic Ideals in North America," in The Muslim Community in North America, ed. Earle Waugh, Baha Abu-Laban, and Regula B. Qureshi (Edmonton: University of Alberta Press, 1983), p. 268.

22 Ibid., p. 270.

AMERICAN MUSLIMS
AT THE MILLENNIUM
AND BEYOND

American Muslims at the Millennium and Beyond

Saiyad Fareed Ahmad
Saiyad Nizamuddin Ahmad[1]

Introduction

The Quran exhorts man to *Consider the flight of time* [Surat Al-Asr (103):1], for indeed *man is bound to lose himself* [Surat Al-Asr (103):2]. There can be no more timely counsel than this, especially in these twilight years of the twentieth century. A century that has seen much tumultuous and catastrophic change. A century in which we have heard the constant refrain from the West and Westernizing elites of the "immense possibilities" and "untapped potentials" offered by "science" and "technology. " Yet above this triumphalist chorus the cool voice of dispassionate reason is seldom heard. Indeed, the frank stock-taking of whence we have come and whither we are going, the solemn contemplation of what tomorrow is to bring in the light of present realities, is a task that is all too often faced with great apprehension if not fear. To some extent, such trepidation is understandable, for indeed who knows the future? Being fully cognizant of the fact that only Allah truly has knowledge of the future, in the spirit of the exhortation to "consider the flight of time, " we shall offer in these pages an analysis of the problems and prospects, the predicament and promise of the American Muslims on the eve of the millennium, and beyond. A word about the "millennium" is in order. The proper and legitimate calendar of the Muslims is the lunar *Hijri* calendar. However, among the many tumultuous changes wrought against the Islamic world by colonialism and

---

1 Saiyad Fareed Ahmad is Associate Professor in the Department of Sociology and Anthropology, International Islamic University, Kuala Lumpur. Saiyad Nizamuddin Ahmad is a doctoral candidate in Near Eastern Studies, Princeton University where he is writing on Islamic law. The authors are deeply indebted to Saiyad Salahuddin Ahmad for his criticisms and proof reading.

the perverse mania for things Western that continues to plague Muslims, is the use of the Gregorian calendar. This is not to say that Muslims have not in their history made use of a solar calendar as well, but it always remained subservient to the lunar one. The great mathematician, Omar Khayyam, helped to devise a solar *Hijri* calendar which was and remains the most accurate solar calendar ever, but he always used lunar Hijri dates in his writings.[2] Thus, we hasten to point out that the so-called millennium as a temporal benchmark should have no particular significance for Muslims. We are resorting to its use simply because it is one of the many trappings of Western culture that all too many Muslims, especially American Muslims, have made their own. Furthermore, the Gregorian calendar has, rightly or wrongly, acquired the status of an almost universal convention and throughout the world people from all walks of life are presently gazing hard into their crystal balls about what the future might bring.[3] The present article is simply an attempt to critically evaluate the condition of the American Muslim community and the directions it may take in its future development and growth, "millennium" or no "millennium."

The Limits of Prognostication

As human beings we live in the past as well as the future and of course in the present. No one can reasonably claim that the past, present, or future is irrelevant to our lives.[4] At the same time, we look to the future in the hope that many of our present problems will be solved and our

---

2 Seyyed Hossein Nasr, "Why We Should Keep the Hijrah Calendar," in his Islamic Life and Thought, (Albany: State University of New York Press, 1981), 216–7.

3 The fascination with "the future" has spread far and wide. The critical need for a coherent vision of the future is palpable in nearly every aspect of global society. This is especially true in the US and most European societies. Many sociology and anthropology departments offer courses on futurology or the sociology of the future. The current upsurge of such interest is visible in the banking industry, the government (especially in the context of foreign policy), private industry and the public. A number of organizations and groups have emerged that are concerned with the future-such as the Commission on the Year 2000, the Institute for the Future, and the World future Society. The general awareness about the future globally has generated a sort of "futurist" movement and it is growing all the time. A wide spectrum of techniques and methods are pressed into service in forecasting the future generally involving computer models.

4 Of late, interesting information on how we conceive time has emerged especially in

goals achieved. Yet accurately predicting the future remains a hazardous venture as the record of failed predictions in the social sciences amply demonstrates.[5] The innumerable variables involved in the processes of social change, conflict, and competition contribute to the limitations endemic to the predictive enterprise.

The Future of Islamic Religiosity and Spirituality

Any consideration of the future of religion, especially Islam, is a question that evokes conflicting, subjective, polemical, even highly emotional responses. What is the future of Islam in America? Will it survive at all? Dr. Muhammad Abdul-Rauf, an eminent Al-Azhar educated scholar, resident for many years in America thinks it will:

> In my opinion, based on personal experience and direct observation, and also inspired by the outlook of Islam itself, one can safely assert that Islam and its basic values have every chance not only to survive intact in America but also to flourish in honor and dignity. Islam has a long history of expansion outside its original territory, always surviving as a religion, under all geographic and climatic conditions. It has always been invaded by powerful cultural influences, but has remarkably resisted all attempts at changes and modification,

---

the existential perspective. Piaget claims all cognition must be grounded in a "present active-reflective process." Since cognition springs from present-active experience, the present time is a source of knowledge in its own right; it has a possibility for new knowledge that must be respected and promoted. The present does not appreciate and rediscover what was already known; it adds to the heritage of knowledge. Presently two theories on time are in vogue: linear and circular. The theory of linear time suggests that past, present, and future come in this order and follow the same sequence. In the circular theory, past, present, and future are all present simultaneously.

5 Despite all the progress made in the social and behavioral sciences in the previous decades, both measurement and prediction remain mired in a gamut of problems. The only thing that can be said with certainty is that there are some measuring devices, which are better than not having any. For problems of measurement and prediction in the social sciences, see Aaron V. Cicourel. Method and Measurement in Sociology, (New York: Free Press, 1964), 247; Claire Seltiz, et al., Research Methods in Social Relations, (New York: Holt, Rinehart, and Winston, 1966), 145.

co-existing with, and even absorbing cultural patterns not in conflict with its religious framework. [6]

The resiliency of Islam and Islamic institutions in vastly differing times and climes is truly remarkable. The vast geographic spread and immense cultural diversity of the Muslim peoples is a fact of world history making it the first truly global civilization. From Morocco to Indonesia and Central Asia to South Africa Muslims are to be found preserving a common core of values and ideals reflected in their literature, art, architecture, and traditional costumes. In America, Muslim peoples from nearly every corner of the Islamic world are to be found. Such a situation is unprecedented in Islamic history and thus presents a unique, and challenging set of problems and will demand equally innovative, creative answers. However, this highly variegated conglomeration of Muslims is not the only unprecedented feature of the Muslim predicament in America. Whatever lands Islam traveled to in the past and whichever civilizations it encountered, it moved in a world in which the "sacred, " that is to say religion and the life of faith, regardless of what religion, was paramount in human life. This was true in Zoroastrian Persia, Christian Syria, Egypt, Hindu India, and Taoist/Confucian/ Buddhist China. In all of these societies human life was regulated on the basis of some understanding of "sacred categories" and traditions. This is emphatically not the case with modern Western civilization, of which America is the most widely known, if not the main, representative.

The dominant religion in the West these days is secularism. Since the so-called Renaissance, the West has increasingly based its way of life on secular categories. Doubtless, some of these secular categories, particularly the notion of freedom of religion, and other so-called "civil liberties" protected by America's First Amendment to its constitution, have allowed Muslims to organize themselves and propagate their faith in a manner which is not even possible in some countries where the majority population is Muslim. Yet, on the other hand, if there are certain freedoms guaranteed by US laws, the history of social upheaval in this century bears witness to the inequality and hypocrisy of American society toward nearly every minority group especially those who lack

---

6 Muhammad Abdul-Rauf, "The Future of Islamic Tradition in North America, " The Muslim Community in North America, Earle H. Waugh, Baha Abu Laban, and Regula Qureshi, Eds. , (Calgary: University of Alberta Press, 1983), 316.

economic privilege. Moreover, and this is critical for Muslims to realize, there exists a subtle but undeniable tendency inherent in American social institutions that, covertly or overtly, undermines religion and the life of faith—whether it be that of Muslims, or Jews, or any other religion. The overall cultural mood of American society is what has been called the "culture of disbelief."[7] A case in point is the latest defeat of the resolution on prayer in schools (June 1998).

Yet, the issue at hand is more complex than the mere notion of the separation of so-called church and state. On the one hand, one is guaranteed freedom of religion, yet on the other, the overall societal institutions, be they educational, economic, legal, political, even medical, are designed to categorically ignore religion, if not directly undermine it. The increasingly decadent, crass materialistic and sensualistic mass-culture and the over-all climate of immorality in the lives of the most common citizens up to the Chief Executive, pose a difficult challenge to the preservation of any religious values and Islamic values in particular.

For Islam, to survive in America, nay anywhere, Muslims must see that their children are brought up Islamically. This cannot be done merely through weekend schools and the like. Muslims will have to strive to make a much vaster network of their own educational institutions from kindergarten to university level. A number of Islamic schools providing primary, elementary, and secondary school education do exist in the U. S, but there will have to be many, many more. Ideally, every Muslim child should be able to attend an Islamic school. Furthermore, Muslims, in the next century, will have to strive to establish their own universities. What we have said about educational institutions applies, *mutatis mutandis*, to all other institutions as well.

One aspect of education in which American Muslims have been shockingly negligent is in establishing even basic institutes for traditional Islamic education, i. e. in the classical Islamic curriculum studied to specialize in the religious sciences such as *tafsir*, *hadith*, and especially *Sharia*. There is a crying need for such institutes in which the rudiments of Arabic grammar, syntax, rhetoric, basic *fiqh*, Quran and *hadith* are taught. It is not practical at this stage to hope for *madrasas* of the caliber of Al-Azhar, Zaytuna, Qarawiyyin, Deoband, Nadwat al-

---

7   Stephen L. Carter, The Culture of Disbelief: How American Law and Politics Trivialize Religious Devotion, (New York: Anchor Books, 1994).

Ulama, Qum, or Najaf to be established, but institutes where the basics could be learned would then enable those who have the inclination to go abroad and pursue higher Islamic studies in those illustrious centers of learning. Muslims should work with such *madrasas* in establishing prepatory institutes in America. This is more important than it might seem. All too many children of Muslim immigrants are encouraged to devote themselves to professions that are perceived as prestigious and lucrative such as medicine, engineering, and of late, law. Rare indeed, if not totally non-existent, is the young Muslim who is encouraged to strive to become a *faqih*, a *muhaddith*, a *mufassir*, and so on. Another important reason which discourages the young generation to enter religion as a profession is the lack of job prospects and competitive salaries.

One of the many complaints one hears about scholars brought from abroad to serve the needs of the Muslim community, is that they do not understand American society, that they do not know English well (if at all), that they do not relate to American converts and to Muslims who have been raised here or lived most of their adult lives here, and so on. If this were not problem enough, those persons who are American converts or have spent most of their lives in America and do understand its society, language, etc. rarely (if at all) have any formal training in Islamic sciences. Obviously one cannot expect a scholar coming from abroad to be able to understand the problems and concerns of American Muslims as well as they themselves do. Hence, it is of the utmost importance that Muslims begin to establish institutions to train their own Islamic scholars. It is only through strong social institutions, especially in education, that the deleterious effects of the "culture of disbelief" can be fought.

The "culture of disbelief" represents an external obstacle to the survival of Islam in America. A perhaps much more decisive obstacle is the internal obstacle of what, for want of a better term, we shall call nationalistic and sectarian bickering. It seems that no Muslim community in America is immune to such poisonous tendencies. Nationalistic bickering takes the form of rivalry on the basis of national origin and often linguistic proclivity. Such conflict manifests itself in many ways such as Arab vs. non-Arab, Pakistani vs. Indian or Bengali, Farsi speakers vs. Pushtu speakers, Urdu speakers vs. non-Urdu speakers (Bengalis, Punjabis, Sindhis and so forth), immigrant Muslims vs. indigenous (most of whom are African-Americans), *etc*. Sectarian bickering manifests itself in at

404

least as many ways as well, if not more; thus we have Sunnis vs. Shiis, Deobandis vs. Barelwis, *muqallids* vs. non-*muqallids*, sufis vs. non-sufis, Wahhabis/Salafis vs. everybody else *etc.* An immense amount of time and energy is wasted in such pursuits mostly concerned with non-issues, and thus contributes to the weakening of Muslim unity and makes it very difficult if not impossible to realize truly unifying and constructive goals. By indulging in such bickerings, Muslims end up frittering away their energies and resources. American Muslims in the next century will have to learn to set aside their differences and work for their common betterment and "Ummatic unity. " Some of the chief causes responsible for such conflict, dissension, and religious intolerance could perhaps be removed by a dispassionate attempt to understand the issues at hand and by educating people in an enlightened way about the proper practice of their religion.

There seems to be an increasing trend among people in the West for a quest for inner meaning and spirituality. Dissatisfaction and disillusionment with modern, depersonalized mass societies in which norms and values are changing and eroding, has made relating to others and to oneself increasingly difficult for almost everyone. This is likely to send many people in search of the security and familiarity of religion. We strongly feel and project that religion—especially of the Eastern variety—in the coming century will experience increased growth. This is already happening in the case of the global Islamic resurgence for the last two decades and as it continues to spread everywhere, it has not been without its effects in North America as well. A similar phenomenon is occurring in other spheres of life as well, like the popularity of Eastern medicine especially Chinese herbal medicine, acupuncture, Tibetan Buddhist medicine, Hatha Yoga, and Ayurvedic medicine.[8] These things augur well for the future acceptance of things more substantial and meaningful, like seeking the solace of religion. However, acceptance of religion is a far more complex process and is not on par with accepting alternative medicine or health practices.

When we consider the possibility whether Islam will acquire increasing or diminished relevance in the coming century, or whether it will survive

---

8 In this regard see Jan van Alphen and Anthony Aris, Eds. , Oriental Medicine: An Illustrated Guide to the Asian Arts of Healing, (Boulder: Shambhala, 1995) and Richard Gerber, MD, Vibrational Medicine: New Choices for Healing Ourselves, updated edition, (Santa Fe: Bear and Company, 1988).

in America at all, we do not necessarily mean its physical or numerical survival, although it is certainly important. Numerical strength, in the so-called democratic forms of society, is without a doubt helpful, but it is the quality and not the quantity that is ultimately important. What is of crucial significance and critical importance, is the caliber of commitment and faith of human beings imbued with path-breaking qualities and attributes and not those who are culturally or nominally Muslims. Islamic history is replete with examples of challenges which Muslims not only faced, but emerged from in a dominant position with renewed zeal and vigor. Thus, despite the negative image propagated by its enemies as a "fundamentalist threat" both in America and the Muslim world, Islam is not in danger of disappearing, but is rather poised to expand. In America, and elsewhere in the world, Islam is the fastest growing religion. Even if we discount some of this as propaganda designed by our detractors to induce hysteria in the local population, the fact remains that Islam is gaining adherents from numerous quarters; furthermore, to acknowledge this is not to brag about it, but only an admission of what is happening in the world. In sum, our argument is that Islam in America is not only "here to stay" but is destined to make its mark in the next century, *in sha Allah*. We assert this fact with full awareness of the complete absorption and assimilation of the African Muslims during that most ignoble chapter in American history—the era of slavery—as so poignantly and painfully depicted in Alex Haley's historical novel, *Roots*. However, we do not want to downplay the threat of assimilation and absorption in any way since these factors are ever-present in American society. Muslims must remain ever-vigilant. Their greatest strength in resisting the threat of assimilation rests in maintaining strong families and extended familial ties, values, and religious education. As pointed out above, the greatest danger is that of secularism especially as manifested in the form of a superficial life -style that is completely devoid of any higher purpose and meaning. The widely prevalent "think positive" and "feel good" culture has a special appeal for the younger generation. We cannot completely isolate our youth from everything American. If we completely exclude them from activities and not provide them with healthy, wholesome opportunities to engage their time and attention, reaction and rejection will follow. Intelligent and creative parenting based on love, compassion, understanding and reasoning is what is desirable. A strong youth movement is an absolute imperative in the coming century which can provide them avenues and channels to engage their attention. Survival and maintenance of one's own identity in a culture like America has to be an act of will and determination with a commitment to follow one's life-style regardless of anything. Despite everything, we feel that Islam has a future in America.

Over the years, estimates of the Muslim population in America have varied from 3. 6–8 million. But a more realistic figure, which is quoted by many reliable sources is 6. 5 million. According to Ali M. Kettani, Afro-Americans have contributed about 3–4% per year to the Muslim population in the US.[9] It seems realistic to assume that Muslim immigration to the US will decline because of the scare tactics of some vested interest groups, but indigenous conversion will go up 6–8%. Based on the estimated population of 6. 5 million from 1960–1995, one could possibly extrapolate that by the year 2030, the Muslim population will reach 13–16 million. Hence, Islam will not only continue to surge, but it will make all around progress in the coming century, *in sha Allah.* Some people even envision that America and Canada will be in the vanguard of Islamic resurgence and revival. Perhaps, this idea may be a little far-fetched, but American Muslims, without a doubt will play an important role in the coming century, *in sha Allah.*

Islamic Identity: Growing Up Muslim in North America

Problems related with Muslim identity in North America are perhaps, the most hotly debated. According to some, Muslims suffer an identity "crisis" in North America, while others characterize maintaining a Muslim identity as "*jihad*", while still others think that they have a "dual' or "multiple" identity i. e. they try to be Muslim and American at the same time. We do not mean to suggest that this cannot be done but the fundamental questions related with identity are whether American Muslims will remain Muslims true to their faith, or will they become entangled with other badges of identification. Will they be able to maintain themselves as an active, dynamic and vibrant community? Or will they be absorbed and assimilated like the earlier generations? Do they need a survival strategy? Talking of survival though seems defeatist and apologetic. An active, dynamic orientation that has been the hallmark of Muslim identity

---

9 Ali M. Kettani, al-Muslimun fi uruba wa amrika, 2 vols. , (Dar al-Idris: 1976), figures also quoted in his lecture at the University of Petroleum and Minerals, Dhahran, Saudi Arabia, Monday January 24, 1977.

throughout Islamic history is the best strategy. No compromises should be made on this issue.

These questions are of immense importance for Muslims everywhere. Under the impact of colonial rule and modernization, westernization and secularization, Muslims went through periods of not only confused identities, but ends and means as well. Modern Muslims surprisingly are a most unreflective sort, and thus something of an embarrassment to Islam. The modern script of Islam is a script of intellectual lethargy and masterly inactivity—a sort of lapse that has already lasted half a millennium. As challenges to Islam and Muslim identity have emerged across nations and societies, Muslims have always struggled to meet them. As Islamic resurgence has spread, people are increasingly returning to Islam with increased awareness and consciousness of their identity. These include not only the poor and the down-trodden, but also the educated and the affluent "elites."

As noted, Muslims in the United States face a variety of challenges as far as the issue of identity is concerned. They bear a variety of identities such as, ethnic, religious, occupational, racial, regional and a horde of others. These are not altogether new, as these are similar to those faced by other minority groups in America. In order for us to suggest what might happen to Muslim identity in the future, we need to analyze these challenges. At the heart of the issue is how to lead an Islamic way of life in a hostile non-Islamic society. Prejudice and hostility drives some people to hide their identity. The core issues relate to the faith and practice of its rites and rituals because Islam as a total and complete way of life is misunderstood by the local people as well as by contemporary Muslims, for many of whom even offering the five daily prayers becomes a problem.

Ideally speaking, there is no identity crisis in Islam. Most Muslims clearly know who they are, what their mission in life is, and where they are headed. Compared to other religious faiths, most Muslims are still doing a fair job of socializing their children into their religious way of life. There are no secrets about how to raise their children Islamically either. But their efforts are deterred and frustrated by lack of time, involvement with "earning a living", competing with many agencies of socialization, and the predominant appeal of the American culture of nihilism and hedonism. By and large, these factors can be grouped under societal and cultural, upon which individuals, usually, do not have control. We agree that the issue of transmitting a clear, unmistakable

408

Islamic identity is problematic in America, but there are widespread factors which create a sort of conduciveness for sticking with their culture and religion, such as marriage; which remains the norm, low divorce rate, strong family ties, the desire to raise their children Islamically, and high average annual income. There are other factors which are conducive to imparting a clear Islamic identity to children. These include a religious home, practicing Muslim parents, transmission of religious values and norms through enlightened Islamic education, love, compassion, and understanding minus authoritarianism, and contact with an active Muslim community. The quintessence remains parental commitment, dedication, and education.

Education for the New World

No subject is of more vital concern, present or future, than education. If there is any one factor that cannot only ensure our survival, as far as things are humanly possible, but also our continued existence as an active vibrant community, then that factor is education. Even though it appears certain that most Muslim children will be at the mercy of the public school system until quite sometime into the next century, American Muslims must not neglect the educational challenge. It is our prediction that the issue of education and the educational agenda will move to the forefront of debate as the crisis of culture and identity deepens and the Muslim community begins to strike deeper roots in America and acquires greater institutional sophistication. Other likely changes include the growth of educational institutions and an increase in trained, certified Muslim teachers, the proliferation of un-biased textbooks and other instructional materials. If Muslim schools are able to multiply sufficiently— and they will have to multiply many fold—they would serve as a beacon of light and haven for Muslims as the public schools become more and more mired in violence, drug addiction, and so on. If the mania for multiculturalism is able to win the "culture war" against the conservative right and maintain itself into the next century, we may find the study of Islam better incorporated in classes on comparative religion, world history, or politics.

In the final analysis, all education and learning depends on well trained, dedicated, skilled teachers. They are instrumental in molding our young people. Excellent books and curricula are also necessary. Given the growing market for Islamic literature perhaps they will be produced, but market or no market, their development is an urgent need. In any case, it is only dedicated teachers who can translate such books and curricula into reality, and they are not as easily produced as books. Indeed, they are a rare breed. A step toward remedying the need for a pool of dedicated Muslim teachers would be a teacher's training institute. We cannot expect anyone else to train these kind of teachers for us. Also, unfortunately, not many people will opt for the teaching profession unless they are offered competitive remuneration. We will have to provide monetary incentives and rewards in the form of fellowships and scholarships to help qualified students to acquire the necessary credentials. As Muslim businesses grow, and charitable organizations become more sophisticated in investing and fund-raising, such institutes could be endowed as *waqfs*.

The Political Conundrum

American Muslims have been completely marginalized as far as the political system is concerned. The reasons for this are many and varied. It is not our intention here to analyze the causes for their lack of political participation but to examine the issues of political power and prestige and what Muslims might accomplish in this sphere in the coming "millennium."

Such an examination should be viewed against several critical events that have unalterably changed global politics. These include the anticipated and predicted demise of communism and socialism, the Gulf war, the recent nuclear explosions by "non-violent" India followed by those of Pakistan, the emergence of the Islamic Republic in Iran, and the global Islamic resistance that is not going away despite all efforts by its detractors. After "the triumph of the West", a sense of decline and the limits of power of the West, as contending reverse theses have emerged. Many in the West increasingly seem to feel that their civilization appears to have taken a wrong turn. After the historic process known as the "world revolution of Westernization," which has not only been instrumental in causing the global violence and world wars, the rise of communism and fascism, decolonization, Third World dictatorships, and contemporary terrorism,[10] – one is witnessing the emergence of global interdependence.

---

10 Theodore H. von Laue, The World Revolution of Westernization: The Twentieth Century in Global Perspective, (oxford: Oxford university Press, 1987).

Socio-economic forces such as the information and computer revolution, cultural globalization and the American obsession with the so-called "new world order" are complicating matters further. Hostilities and prejudices among nations and societies have not entirely disappeared, but new realities are constantly emerging.

One such reality is the presence of a large number of Muslims who have taken up citizenship in many western societies including America. This not only makes these nations multicultural and multireligious but also raises the prospect of the normalization of a Muslim presence in the West and all the numerous rights that should come with it. Muslims have to contend and live with American law[11]– which not only is in conflict with Islamic law (*Sharia*), but also does not show any respect for it either. It has effected them through immigration laws, religious liberty laws, and hate crime legislation. It is evident from various legal decisions during the last couple of decades, that it has not looked kindly upon Muslims, although, through the efforts of groups such as CAIR (Council for American- Islamic Relations), the courts gradually have become more responsive. The battle for social and political rights is not going to be easy. On some pretext or another, Muslims will have to face some kind of prejudicial treatment. They will have to develop an infrastructure of organizations which can strive to secure their legal and political rights and their eventual participation and acceptance in the American political system. This cannot happen suddenly, but *in sha Allah* gradually. People and politicians do not like to give up power easily. It seems that for better or worse, Muslim voter registration and education, Muslim congressmen and senators, will become a reality— whether Muslims or non-Muslims like it or not. Vested interest groups, the politics of race and ethnicity and its subversive influence have always played a role in American politics. It is an inevitable product of the way the American political system is organized. Zionist hegemony and influence peddling in American politics plus so-called "Arab-Israeli peace initiatives" will continue to cast their shadows on the life of American Muslims. What happens in the Muslim countries abroad also affects American Muslims directly or indirectly.

---

11 Kathleen Moore, "Muslim Commitment in North America: Assimilation or Transformation?, " The American Journal of Islamic Social Sciences, vol. 11, no. 2, 1994, 223–244.

Another threat that will shape the political participation of American Muslims, is the imposition of Western order in the name of global order. Global Islam finds itself at cross-purposes with the Western order of Pax Americana. The latest neo-colonialist program, euphemistically termed the "new world order" (which other countries have ever been consulted to form this order?) is being imposed on the Muslim societies. Presently, most Muslim countries are completely under the influence of Western governments, especially America. But in the coming century, any such imposition of a particular view as global will be increasingly resisted not only by the Islamic world but by Muslims living in the western world. Western political hypocrisy, double standards, political corruption, money laundering, and ethical and moral bankruptcy, have already engendered a reaction that lowers the prospect of the acceptance of all things Western. Many such fallacious ideas and theses like "unlimited growth, " "international economic order, " and "modernity and modernization theory, " have been discarded before. Some of these ideas will be touched upon in the next section. Any world order in which world faiths do not have a major share in shaping it is not even worth considering. That the changing world is a challenge to all major faiths is acknowledged by most people. No amount of tinkering with the present international order can save it. Under the impact of newer developments like global interdependence, power cannot be separated from morality. The only solution to the present impasse would be to radically depart from popular, present day doctrines and replace them with a religious perspective sufficient to transform secular outlooks.

The American political scene, as far as American Muslims are concerned, is presently polarized between two extremes—one position advocates political participation of some sort, and the other counsels Muslims to shun political involvement and participation. The former position is based on the idea that, at present, Muslims are by-passed and marginalized and for this they should blame themselves, whereas the later position visualizes that American politics is a filthy endeavor which will smear the pristine qualities of Islam and the Muslims without any substantial gain. The supporters of political participation are of the view that, now that so many Muslims have chosen to become citizens, political involvement and participation is unavoidable if they want to make a mark. The inevitability argument does not impress those who seek political avoidance because according to them one "cannot join the system and beat it. " Both positions have their pluses and minuses. If it is true that sooner or later Muslims will have to be part of the political system, then a beginning must be made sometime. It appears plausible that any gains in the beginning would be more symbolic than real. For instance, it seems highly implausible that there would be a Muslim president even in the next century or that they would ever form a majority party in Congress. A few token senators, congressmen, and mayors here and there would not make much of a dent in the firmly entrenched special interests. Neither will these be able to sway American public opinion in favor of Muslims or win friends for them. The American political system is far too convoluted for accomplishing such objectives. Winning political power and participation in America is contingent upon several other variables; chief among them is a political base. In addition, economic power represented especially by the business and commercial interests sponsors and buys the political power. It seems to us that the odds are stacked against the Muslims as far as their political participation is concerned.

In the intervening period, what is needed is to accomplish a number of things that will, in the long run, strengthen the Muslim community's power base. We now make up about 3% of the US population. We are the second largest religious minority. We need to become a strong, cohesive community and develop a trusted leadership which can generate and procure finances to carry out educational plans and programs which will develop ethically and morally oriented future leaders. Muslims can help clean up the political system by producing leaders which can uphold truth and justice as their highest value and act as the real role models for the political system. This is what we are good at and this is what we must do in the next century. Also in the short run, we should practice block voting, that is, we should vote as a block for those politicians whose political viewpoints are akin to our viewpoints. For building a powerful base of committed leaders, the American Muslims should be in the vanguard of problem solving for every kind of people. We need to have our own public treasury (Bait -al -Mal) which can take care of our needs. As we are accomplishing these goals, simultaneously we need to build a strong, positive image of Islam in America, which is at the bottom of everything including political power. This is truly an awesome responsibility that awaits us in the next century.

Modernity, Post-Modernity and Beyond[12]

What sort of society will take shape in the next century? Will American society become more conducive to Muslims? Questions like these come to one's mind while considering the future Muslim presence in America.

American society has undergone many transitions in its two centuries of history, and at present it is one of the fastest changing societies in the world. It is claimed that it has moved from being an industrial society to a post-industrial society, and now it is claimed that it is changing into a "post-modern" society. This claim is premised on the idea that the Western societies have been undergoing rapid changes and that they have entered, or are on the verge of entering a new era in their history. These new changes are of such magnitude and intensity that the label of "modernity"—it is held—no longer adequately characterizes them, hence the necessity of discarding old theories and labels.

"Modernity" and "post-modernity" are terms that are being bandied about everywhere, but often too casually. Endless discussions have ensued over the past quarter of a century on modernity and modernism, which is now being superseded because its principles are considered no longer operative or valid. As long as the notion of modernity held sway, it denoted all kinds of progress, changes and development. The concept of modernity itself was later on construed as a cultural movement, and strange and contradictory as it might seem, in some ways, it represented a critical reaction against modernity. At its core is the idea of change and flux—the notion of an incessant, continuous creation of the new. The new must replace the old—change for the sake of change— regardless of anything, not even knowing where such change will lead. As a result, change has become the ultimate value and the measure of everything. Things that change are accorded prestige and value, and what does not, is considered unworthy and devoid of any value. It is this mentality of seeking change in everything that has created a tendency among many Muslims not to follow Islam unless it is perceived as "modern. " Now even modernism, however, is deemed outmoded and is being replaced by the notion of post-modernism.

---

12 In writing this section we have benefited immensely from an excellent work by Krishan Kumar, From Post-industrial to Post-modern Society: New Theories of the Contemporary World, (London: Blackwell,1995).

The dominant discernible theme among post-modernists is cultural because its main concern from the very beginning has been cultural modernism. Emphasis is placed mostly on the rejection and discarding of ideas associated with modernism. A concern with decentralization, dispersal, and the renewed importance of place, are characteristic features of post-modernism. However, the side by side existence of contradictory and conflicting ideas within postmodernism is particularly ubiquitous. Of particular significance is its peculiar notion of knowledge. Knowledge itself is considered to be a cultural product in the ideology of postmodernism. As such their are no universal truths. There is no one "privileged discourse" and all is relative.

Muslims have had a tumultuous encounter with modernity and modernism. The debate and discussion is still on in may societies. We are told by the West that most of our problems will disappear if we can "modernize" Islam. In other words, modernization has always been presented as a panacea for all our ills. Post-modernism, like its predecessor has no respect for religions, but in its emphasis on acceptance of differences, variety, pluralism, and traditions—a euphemism for religions—one can expect some more tolerance and better treatment. It seems to us that the Islamic cultural realm will suffer a tremendous onslaught from post-modernist relativism, as it did under the sway of modernism. American Muslims and their children will have to be prepared to face its influence . There is rarely any facet or aspect of our life which is safe from post-modernist critique With its increasing popularity, this trend will grow. If nothing else, our young generations may be forced to study it for a very long time.

In the end, it must be made absolutely clear that Islam is not a mere cultural artifact subject to intellectual fads and fashions such as the ideational flux of modernism or the relativist musings of postmodernism.

The Clash of Civilizations,[13] – The Crash of Western Civilization,[14] – and Civilizational Dialogue[15]

Global politics has taken on an interesting meaning since the publication of Huntington's book which offers penetrating analysis and, at the same time, suggests that "In the emerging era, clashes of civilizations are the greatest threat to world peace, and an international order based on civilizations is the surest safeguard against world war."[16] – This specter of civilizational war has assumed additional meaning for Muslims, because since the fall of communism and socialism Islam has replaced this traditional arch enemy of the West. Under the euphemism of a "fundamentalist threat," the Western powers, in their sinister alliance with international hegemonistic Zionism are trying to demonize Islam wherever they can.

In case of a civilizational war, whose side would the American Muslims take? What role would they play in such a conflict ? Would they encounter the kind of concentration camp experience the Japanese Americans had to undergo during the Second World War ? It is true that after a very long struggle, the American government admitted its crimes and Japanese Americans were awarded some token compensations for their suffering and humiliating treatment. This sinister episode leads one to believe that in a war situation between Americans and Muslims, perhaps, a worst scenario may be in store for them. One can only hope that such a situation might not arise.

Presently, three major competing theses, namely the clash of civilizations, crash of civilizations, and civilizational dialogue are percolating. Both processes of international conflict and global order are simultaneously at work at any particular point in time. The crash of Western civilization makes an interesting addition to the debate because a clash will happen only if the West continues to exist. The decay and crash of Western civilization has already begun and, at the present, is

---

13 Samuel P. Huntington, The Clash of Civilizations and the Remaking of World Order, (New York: Simon and Schuster, 1996).
14 Jacques Attali, "The Crash of Western Civilization: The Limits of the Market and Democracy, " Foreign Policy, No. 107, 1997, 54–63.
15 Anwar Ibrahim, "The Need for Civlizational Dialogue, " Intellectual Discourse, 2, 1994. 101–5.
16 Samuel P. Huntington, Ibid., 321.

in process but it is given a short shrift. However, it may also be added here that civilizations just do not disappear instantly and it takes a while before they completely disintegrate and disappear. Huntington does acknowledge that "far more significant than economics and demography are problems of moral decline, cultural suicide, and political disunity in the West."[17] – Under moral decay, he includes the increase in antisocial behavior, family decay, a decline in "social capital", general weakening of the "work ethic", and decreasing commitment to learning and intellectual pursuits. One could possibly add a horde of others, because when one looks at American society, it has every conceivable social problem that one could imagine and is adding to its woes all the time. The worst part of the whole situation is that they do not look at some of their problems as problems. All kinds of justifications and rationalization are offered for their existence. In a footnote, Huntington further presents a prediction from Quigly with which he agrees but thinks that it may not happen because of lack of support. Quigly asserts:

> Western civilization did not exist about AD 500, it did not exist in full force about AD 1500, and it will surely pass out of existence at sometime in the future, perhaps before AD 2500.[18]

Another person who has similar views and is predicting a similar fate for the Western civilization is Jacques Attali, a French intellectual. In his seminal article, he has offered a very interesting and stimulating analysis. He warns the disintegration and decimation of communism have spawned a post-cold war triumphalism that is premature and misplaced. His main argument is that two of the central and pivotal values of Western society, i. e. the market economy and democracy are flawed and contain some built in tendencies which could lead to its eventual demise. He argues:

> Despite the prevalent belief that the market economy and democracy combine to form a perpetual motion machine that

---

17 Ibid., 304.
18 Cited in Ibid., 303. The original reference is Caroll Quigley, The Evolution of Western civilizations: An Introduction to Historical Analysis, (Indianapolis: Liberty Press, 1979; first published by Macmillan in 1961), 127, 164–6.

propels human progress, these two values on their own are in fact incapable of sustaining any civilization. Both are riddled with weaknesses and are increasingly likely to break down. Unless the West and particularly its self appointed leader, the United States begins to recognize the shortcomings of the market economy and democracy; Western civilization will gradually disintegrate, and eventually self-destruct.[19]

The key phrase in the above quote is that it will slowly disintegrate and self-destruct. According to Attali, the major threat to American society has to do with factors inherent in it, not external to it. We feel this to be a strong argument and that all the xenophobia displayed against the "Islamic threat" is totally misplaced and ill-conceived. He is also of the opinion that a total collapse is imminent unless Western societies are willing to drastically restructure their market economy and democracy. The crash, can only be averted by seeking honest answers to some of the most fundamental issues related to the core of liberal democracy and market mechanism. Western civilization should try to attain humility and modesty about its own values. He suggests that "the fact the West may disagree with some aspects of Islam as applied in some countries—the status of women, for example- does not mean that there is nothing to learn from Islamic societies."[20] – The West can also learn from Asian societies as well. It is this kind of attitude and spirit that can avert the clash of civilizations. The crude exercise of power, arrogance, double standards, and domination should be replaced by mutual understanding, respect, and an amicable approach to conflict resolution.

This brings us to a third major perspective, which is emerging in response to the clash scenario, which is that of "civilizational dialogue." One of its greatest advocates is Anwar Ibrahim, the Deputy Prime Minister of Malaysia. The need for a dialogue between nations and civilizations is increasingly being sought after and recommended as a means of conflict resolution by many prominent Muslims.[21] – The idea,

---

19 Jacques Attali, Ibid., 56.
20 Ibid., 62. For this point see also Charles, Prince of Wales' speech, "A Sense of the Sacred: Building Bridges Between Islam and the West," delivered at a seminar of the British Foreign Office at Wilton Park, December 13, 1996. This speech is reproduced in an abbreviated form in Impact International, vol. 27, no. 1, January 1997, 20–4.
21 Anwar Ibrahim, Ibid.

after all, is not new; what is new is its increasing urgency and the readiness of civilizations to use dialogue as a means of resolving disputes. It is true that the cold war is over, but the unchained beast of nuclear weapons remains; the recent explosions by "non-violent" India and Pakistan have brought the horrors of a nuclear war on the sub-continent. One rash move could still trigger unimaginable death and destruction.

This disaster could be averted provided differences could be settled through a constant dialogue between Muslim and Western nations at the international level, and locally between American Muslims and the two other monotheistic faiths. Some of this dialogue between individuals and groups is already taking place at the informal and formal level in North America. But there remain some insurmountable hurdles to a dialogue between the West and Islam. There exist all kinds of obstacles to understanding; especially the elements of conflict today are much more complex. In the words of Nasr, on the Muslim side:

> Today, as far as the Islamic world is concerned, the causes behind such terrible acts (terrorism) are the loss of hope, unbearable pressures (often, reported directly or indirectly by the West), and desperation before forces that are destroying one's religion and civilization. Hatred is a fire that consumes and annihilates, but the fire cannot be put out unless one inquires about its causes. Otherwise, as soon as one fire is put out another one is ignited.[22]

On the Western side, he continues:

> There is no possibility of creating understanding between the West and the Islamic world until, on the Western side, people realize that the absolutization of the West's worldview at a particular moment in time, when combined with powerful economic "interests" that are usually against the interests of others, bring about impatience with and even hatred of other worldviews. This has happened to such an extent that today many people in the West who are opposed to friendship with

---

22 Seyyed Hossein Nasr, "Islam and the West: Yesterday and Today, " The American Journal of Islamic Social Sciences, vol. 13, no. 4, 1996, 556.

the Islamic world, because of their own political and economic agendas, also oppose any mention of the harmony and peace that dominated most of the life of Jews and Christians within the Islamic world before modern times. They even seek to arouse Christian and Jewish enmity against Islam, although many of them are not themselves, for the most part, serious followers of either religion.[23]

Apart from the above reasons which act as a barrier to dialogue between the Islamic world and the West, there are many others. The fundamental question that needs to be settled as a prerequisite to a dialogue is whether the "Islamic Threat" is a myth or a reality. If it is for real, then the "clash" is not only highly likely but imminent at some future date. Esposito thinks that the threat is overblown and based on some erroneous and prejudicial views of Islam in the West; in fact, he tried to separate fictitious elements from the factual, genuine and appropriate grievances from cultural bias, prejudicial and stereotypical views from what is actually happening in the Muslim world. A fostering of a genuine understanding and mutual appreciation between Islam and the West is highly recommended by him.[24]

Dovutoglu thinks that the matter is far more serious than what superficially appears at the surface. He suggests that a dialogic situation necessitates a classification of civilizations in terms of self perceptions. Western civilization sees itself as "strong and rigid; one that has a metaphysically well established worldview and an exclusivity that provides the quality of impenetrability. " This kind of self-perception is characterized by him as "egocentric illusion" because it enables the West to harbor an illusion that it is the "primary mover"; that it constitutes the center of the world. As opposed to this, Islamic civilization is strong and flexible. It has a worldview which is divinely ordained, comprehensive, inclusive, integrative and metaphysically sound. It absorbs influences from other cultures and civilizations provided borrowed elements do not contradict Islamic Sharia. And since, it is open to penetration by other civilization, lacks "overweening arrogance" in its self perception, does not have the "prime mover" complex and no periphery because to Allah

23 Ibid.
24 John L. Esposito, The Islamic Threat: Myth or Reality, (New York: Oxford University Press, 1992), 243.

belong the East and the West, change is possible. Given these basic anomalies and contradictions in their worldview, Davutaglu concluded that chances for civilizational dialogue are remote.[25]

The issue of a dialogue is both supported by many and opposed by some. Difficulties to dialogue remain but obstacles to understanding can be overcome. Whether one likes it or not, the destinies of Islam, the Christian West, and Judaism are intertwined and connected together and they cannot be severed in the long run. The long term relationship between these monotheistic faiths ought to be conducted on the basis of universal, permanent truths and not on what is ephemeral, transient, relativistic, whims and fancies which are based upon the desire for power, greed, self-assertion and domination. The sooner the West realizes that the bond and the affinity at the religious level is far closer and stronger, the better off the world would be and economic and cultural cooperation can be strengthened leading to trust, tolerance, and mutual respect.

History has placed American Muslims in a situation where they will have to play a critical role in the future and bear a heavy responsibility to mediate between an unlikely scenario of a "clash" between Islam and the West. Their very presence and growth in the future will in part discourage such a possibility. One the one hand, they will have to become a median community in a society of extremes, on the other, they will have to become an active, assertive, vibrant community working towards not only achieving their goals but also contributing effectively and constructively to society. Muslims will have to enhance their participation and contribution at all the levels of society. We can especially make our mark on the American society in the area of ethics and morality, which in recent years has drastically declined.

The role that is amply suited for the American Muslims and augurs well into the next century, is to become religiously, economically, politically, culturally strong and start exerting our influence on other Muslim societies by exporting our experiences to these societies because they are faced with similar problems. Influence of the American Muslim community will grow locally as well as internationally in the next century. As resources of the community increase and diversify, it can start acting

---

25 Ahmet Davutoglu, "The Clash of Interests: An Explanation of the World (Dis)order, "Intellectual Discourse, vol. 2, no. 2, 1994, 107. See also his article in "The Possibility of Civlizational Dialogue, " International Institute of Islamic Thought (Malaysia), Newsletter, no. 16, December 1997, 1.

as catalytic agents of change because of the conduciveness that already exists-things that come from America are relatively more acceptable to the world. Internally, it will have to focus on *Dawah* activities to make Islam more popular and accelerate conversion. Not discounting odds, opportunities and possibilities for *Dawah* in A merica are immense.

Lastly, the American Muslims will have to develop their clout and leverage to a point where they can start influencing American foreign policy toward Muslim countries. This will happen if our numbers keep growing and we become religiously and economically more powerful. This is all a distinct possibility provided we keep developing our human capital as Islamic personalities despite challenges to the contrary.

A Century of Islam in America : A New Vision for the Millennium[26]

Our presence in North America is both a challenge and a vast opportunity. The material presented above attempted a critical analysis of selected aspects of Muslim life in America and offered some solutions, directions and predictions for the next century. We have completed a century of our presence and are poised to start the next century. Our incessant struggle and survival was not without problems and neither will the next century. As stated at the outset, the start or end of a century does not have any religious significance in Islam except that it is believed that a mujaddid will appear in the beginning of every century (of the Islamic calendar) to purge Islam of all innovations and reform it from any impurities that may have crept into it.

Islam is our destiny—it has given us a meaning, purpose, and a sacred direction in life. We must always assess our performances, achievements, and failures, past and present. We must adopt a realistic posture without looking for easy solutions or magical formulae and understand the magnitude of the problems currently being faced. Our response must stem from Islam and must be inspired by its spirit. Islamic civilization, regardless of differences in time and space, must follow its own principles and develop according to its own worldview and lifestyle; any imposition of external norms and values must be avoided.

---

26 Yvonne Yazbeck Haddad, A Century of Islam in America, (Washington, D. C., American Institute for Islamic Affairs, 1986), 1.

How can we ensure our continued presence in North America and also strike deeper roots as time advances? First, there is a dire need and necessity for having the US Islamic agenda for the coming century. This idea has been with us for at least two to three decades. Many organizations have had their own plans and programs, but we have not seen any complete, detailed , national, Islamic agenda for the millennium. We feel strongly that it should be prepared in the next two years either by a national task force or by the joint effort of a number of organizations. A blueprint for the next century is badly needed to chart the course. Some of the ideas offered by various authors could be used as core ideas for developing such an agenda. Many documents, to the best our knowledge, exist at the local level and they should all be consolidated into a national one. The Islamic Society of North America (ISNA) could be such an organization to take the initiative to finalize such a document. It should take all factors into account. All local and national resources should be mobilized for achieving this goal.

We are at the beginning of a new social order. This might sound like a fantastic leap of imagination specially when the recent past has been filled with many setbacks for the Islamic world. Many people have an erroneous impression that Islam is a civilization that is no more. Islam, without doubt, is a unique global civilization. It is religion, culture, and civilization all put together. Decay does not touch it; in fact, to the contrary, as time passes, its truth becomes more self-evident. Its Divine character remains pristinely intact. It is also not like any other religion, it is not merely a collection of some moral or ethical values, or social or cultural system. It is also not a man-made system where something is in today and other things are out tomorrow. It is a combination of transcendental truths, articles of faith and essential doctrines of belief, of mutual relationship of abd and mabud —the Lord and the servanthood. If such is the reality and scope of Islam, to harbor doubts about its presence in the West in the next century is unrealistic. Not only will it make its presence felt but will flourish. The doubts expressed by some regarding its existence in the West are related more to Muslims than Islam.

Muslims of America face difficult problems. We must find solutions to these problems within the Islamic framework and tradition. This will necessitate a complete and total revival of the great Islamic tradition of knowledge which once was our glory. A complete turnaround of devoting our young talent to seek Islamic knowledge from the "cradle to the grave" must be established. Our solutions can be worked out in light of this knowledge. We can even help solve some of the problems faced by Americans which are common to most modern, industrial societies. Some of these general American problems have also become the problems of Muslims in this society. These include, but are not limited to, the assimilation or transformation of Muslims and their communities, possibility of a dialogue with the West, disintegration of the challenge of modernity and the emergence of post-modernistic chaos, the issue of identity, the need to reform our educational system, and political isolation versus participation in the American political system. It is not up to one individual or community to resolve these problems on its own; we must seek national cooperation and support to develop viable solutions

In conclusion, what we are suggesting is that our vision for the future must have Islam as its foundation. Any time and every time Muslims have moved away from Islam they have faced humiliation and an abundance of problems. Over the last century, Muslim nations have tried numerous alien ideologies without any marked improvement in their overall condition. It is high time that the Muslims put their complete faith and practice in Islam again. Only then can this vision of Islam as a global civilization and hope for the future become a reality.

Notes:

1 Saiyad Fareed Ahmad is Associate Professor in the Department of Sociology and Anthropology, International Islamic University, Kuala Lumpur. Saiyad Nizamuddin Ahmad is a doctoral candidate in Near Eastern Studies, Princeton University where he is writing on Islamic law. The authors are deeply indebted to Saiyad Salahuddin Ahmad for his criticisms and proof reading.
2 Seyyed Hossein Nasr, "Why We Should Keep the Hijrah Calendar, " in his Islamic Life and Thought, (Albany: State University of New York Press, 1981), 216–7.
3 The fascination with "the future" has spread far and wide. The critical need for a coherent vision of the future is palpable in nearly every aspect of global society. This is especially true in the US and most European societies. Many sociology and anthropology departments offer courses on futurology or the sociology of the future. The current upsurge of such interest is visible in the banking industry, the government (especially in the context of foreign policy), private industry and the public. A number of organizations and groups have emerged that are concerned with the future-such as the Commission on the Year 2000, the Institute for the Future, and the World future Society. The general awareness about the future globally has generated a sort of "futurist" movement and it is growing all the time. A wide spectrum of techniques and methods are pressed into service in forecasting the future generally involving computer models.
4 Of late, interesting information on how we conceive time has emerged especially in the existential perspective. Piaget claims all cognition must be grounded in a "present

active-reflective process. " Since cognition springs from present-active experience, the present time is a source of knowledge in its own right; it has a possibility for new knowledge that must be respected and promoted. The present does not appreciate and rediscover what was already known; it adds to the heritage of knowledge. Presently two theories on time are in vogue: linear and circular. The theory of linear time suggests that past, paresent, and future come in this order and follow the same sequence. In the circular theory, past, present, and future are all present simultaneously.

5 Despite all the progress made in the social and behavioral sciences in the previous decades, both measurement and prediction remain mired in a gamut of problems. The only thing that can be said with certainty is that there some measuring devices, which are than not having any. For problems of measurement and prediction in the social sciences, see Aaron V. Cicourel. Method and Measurement in Sociology, (New York: Free Press, 1964), 247; Claire Seltiz, et al. , Research Methods in Social Relations, (New York: Holt, Rinehart, and Winston, 1966), 145.

6 Muhammad Abdul-Rauf, "The Future of Islamic Tradition in North America, " The Muslim Community in North America, Earle H. Waugh, Baha Abu Laban, and Regula Qureshi, Eds. , (Calgary: University of Alberta Press, 1983), 316.

7 Stephen L. Carter, The Culture of Disbelief: How American Law and Politics Trivialize Religious Devotion, (New York: Anchor Books, 1994).

8 In this regard see Jan van Alphen and Anthony Aris, Eds. , Oriental Medicine: An Illustrated Guide to the Asian Arts of Healing, (Boulder: Shambhala, 1995) and Richard Gerber, MD, Vibrational Medicine: New Choices for Healing Ourselves, updated edition, (Santa Fe: Bear and Company, 1988).

9 Ali M. Kettani, al-Muslimun fi uruba wa amrika, 2 vols. , (Dar al-Idris: 1976), figures also quoted in his lecture at the University of Petroleum and Minerals, Dhahran, Saudi Arabia, Monday January 24, 1977.

10 Theodore H. von Laue, The World Revolution of Westernization: The Twentieth Century in Global Perspective, (oxford: Oxford university Press, 1987).

11 Kathleen Moore, "Muslim Commitment in North America: Assimilation or Transformation?, " The American Journal of Islamic Social Sciences, vol. 11, no. 2, 1994, 223–244.

12 In writing this section we have benefited immensely from an excellent work by Krishan Kumar, From Post-industrial to Post-modern Society: New Theories of the Contemporary World, (London: Blackwell, 1995).

13 Samuel P. Huntington, The Clash of Civilizations and the Remaking of World Order, (New York: Simon and Schuster, 1996).

14 Jacques Attali, "The Crash of Western Civilization: The Limits of the Market and Democracy, "Foreign Policy, No. 107, 1997, 54–63.

15 Anwar Ibrahim, "The Need for Civlizational Dialogue, " Intellectual Discourse, 2, 1994. 101–5.

16 Samuel P. Huntington, Ibid. , 321.

17 Ibid. , 304.

18 Cited in Ibid. , 303. The original reference is Caroll Quigley, The Evolution of Western civilizations: An Introduction to Historical Analysis, (Indianapolis: Liberty Press, 1979; first published by Macmillan in 1961), 127, 164–6.

19 Jacques Attali, Ibid. , 56.

20 Ibid. , 62. For this point see also Charles, Prince of Wales' speech, "A Sense of

the Sacred: Building Bridges Between Islam and the West, " delivered at a seminar of the British Foreign Office at Wilton Park, December 13, 1996. This speech is reproduced in an abbreviated form in Impact International, vol. 27, no. 1, January 1997, 20–4.

21 Anwar Ibrahim, Ibid.

22 Seyyed Hossein Nasr, "Islam and the West: Yesterday and Today, " The American Journal of Islamic Social Sciences, vol. 13, no. 4, 1996, 556.

23 Ibid.

24 John L. Esposito, The Islamic Threat: Myth or Reality, (New York: Oxford University Press, 1992), 243.

25 Ahmet Davutoglu, "The Clash of Interests: An Explanation of the World (Dis)order, " Intellectual Discourse, vol. 2, no. 2, 1994, 107. See also his article in "The Possibility of Civlizational Dialogue, " International Institute of Islamic Thought (Malaysia), Newsletter, no. 16, December 1997, 1.

26 Yvonne Yazbeck Haddad, A Century of Islam in America, (Washington, D. C., American Institute for Islamic Affairs, 1986), 1.

APPENDIX 1*

Islamic Center Directory, United States

The following directory contains Masjids and Islamic Centers in the United States, as originally compiled by ISNA, and since has been extensively updated by MSA of the USA and Canada. The Directory has been prepared in alphabetical order according to state, and in order of zip codes.

Alabama

Masjid Al-Quran, 3424 26th St North, Birmingham, AL 35207 Phone: 205-324-0212

Birmingham Islamic Society, 1810 25th Court South, Homewood, AL 35209 Phone: 205-879-4247

Masjid As-Saabiqoon, 3501 Jefferson S.W., Birmingham, AL 35221

Islamic Center of Tuscaloosa, 832 11th Ave., Tuscaloosa, AL 35401 Phone: (205) 556-0685

Tuscaloosa Islamic Center, 728 22nd Ave., Tuscaloosa, AL 35401

Masjid Al-Islam, 903 Columbus Road, Aliceville, AL 35442

Islamic Society of Tuscaloosa, P.O. Box 625, Tuscaloosa, AL 35486 Phone: 205-758-6962

Huntsville Islamic Center, 1645 Sparkman Drive, Huntsville, AL 35816 Phone: 205-721-1712

Huntsville Islamic Center, 814 Lee Drive, Huntsville, AL 35816 Phone: 205-534-4117

Masjid Sajdullah, 4421-#2 Bonnell Drive, Huntsville, AL 35816

Tuskegee Islamic Community, 1508 Adam St., Tuskegee, AL 36088 Phone: (205) 727-9936

Tuskegee Islamic Community, 1313 Franklin Road, Tuskegee, AL 36088 Phone: (334) 724-9837

Masjid Qasim Bilal El-Amin, 2425 Lark St., Montgomery, AL 36108 Phone: (205) 281-8474

Masjid An-Nur, 312 B Street Rear, P.O.Box 81, Anniston, AL 36202 Phone: (205) 238-9041

Islamic Center of Dothan, 211 Jeff St., Dothan, AL 36303-4155 Phone: 205-792-9186

Masjid Baitul Haqq, 509 Aurelie St., Mobile, AL 36604 Phone: (205) 432-2609

Mobile Islamic Center/Masjid Al-Islam, 1559 Duval St., Mobile, AL 36605 Phone: 205-473-4100

---

* The primary source for all appendices is the MSA/ISNA.

Islamic Society of Mobile, 63 East Dr., Mobile, AL 36608 Phone: 334-343-4695

Islamic Dawah Center of Prichard, 911 S. Wilson Ave., Prichard, AL 36610,

Islamic Society of Mobile, 5463 Moffat Road, Mobile, AL 36618

Masjid Muhammad, No. 69, 3424 26th St N., Birmingam, AL 36625

Mobile Islamic Center, PO Box 6353, Mobile, AL 36660

Selma Islamic Center, 2820 Citizens Parkway, # 19, Selma, AL 36703

Muslim Center, 1310 1/2 First Ave., Opelika, AL 36801 Phone: 205-749-6997

Muslim Community Association (MCA), 338 Armstrong St., Auburn, AL 36830 Phone: 205-821-8307

Alaska

Ar-Rashid Mosque, 1315 Latouche#A, Anchorage, AK 99501 Phone: 907-258-2951

Arizona

Masjid Muhammad, 1046 W Buckeye Rd., Phoenix , AZ 85001

Islamic Center, 5743 N. 35th Ave., Phoenix, AZ 85017 Phone: (602) 433-1377

Islamic Center, 2242 N. 60th Ave., Phoenix, AZ 85017

Islamic Community Center of Phoenix, 5301 N. 30th Dr., Phoenix, AZ 85017 Phone: 602-249-0496

Masjid Jauharatul Islam, 4615 S. 16th St., Phoenix, AZ 85040

Masjid Jauharatul Islam, 102 W S Mountain Ave., Phoenix, AZ 85041 Phone: (602) 268-6151

Islamic Community Center, P.O. Box 944, Tempe, AZ 85280-0944 Phone: (602) 921-3874

Islamic Cultural Center, 131 E 6th St., Tempe, AZ 85281 Phone: 602-894-6070

Muslim Community Mosque, 1797 W. University Dr. # 167, Tempe, AZ 85281 Phone: (602) 829-9465

Islamic Center of Tucson, 901 E 1st St., Tucson, AZ 85719 Phone: 602-624-3233

Islamic Center of Flagstaff, 1515 S. Yale St #3-1, Flagstaff, AZ 86001 Phone: 602-773-1714

Masjid Ibrahim, 2075 Airway Ave., Kingman, AZ 86401 Phone: 602-757-8822

Arkansas

Muslim Association of Arkansas, UAPB Box 111, Pine Bluff, AR 71601

Masjid Ameen Zakariyya, 1717 Wright Ave., Little Rock, AR 72202 Phone: 501-372-1942

Masjid Al-Baiyina, 1219 W. 20th Ave., Little Rock, AR 72216 Phone: (501) 374-1541

Islamic Center of Jonesboro, 118 S.Rogers St., Jonesboro, AR 72401 Phone: 501-935-2658

Masjid Hamzah, 807 N. Leverett, Fayetteville, AR 72701 Phone: 501-442-4155

California

Masjid Bilal, 4016 S Central Ave., Los Angeles, CA 90000 Phone: 213-233-7274

Masjid Umar Ibn Alkhattab, 1025 Exposition Blvd., Los Angeles, CA 90007 Phone: 213-733-9938

Masjid Felix Bilal, 4016 S. Central, Los Angeles, CA 90008

Masjid Al-Huda, 733 Hindry Ave #212A A-107, Los Angeles, CA 90009 Phone: (310) 568-9932

Masjid Asabiqun, 4608 S Central Ave., Los Angeles, CA 90011

Masjid Felix Bilal, 4016 S. Central, Los Angeles, CA 90011 Phone: 213-233-7274

Masjid Ibadillah, 2310 W Jefferson Blvd., Los Angeles, CA 90018 Phone: 213-734-9940

Masjid Al Mumin, 1635 S Andrews Pl., Los Angeles, CA 90019 Phone: 213-737-8682

Islamic Center of Southern California, 434 S Vermont Ave., Los Angeles, CA 90020 Phone: 213-382-9200

Hollywood Masjid, 5545 Carlton Way, Hollywood, CA 90027 Phone: 213-957-0464

Masjid Ibne Taymiah, 10915 Venice Blvd., Los Angeles, CA 90034 Phone: 310-202-0432

Musalla Commerce, 25538 Garfield Ave., Commerce, CA 90040 Phone: 213-887-9089

Masjid As Salam, 2900 W Florence Ave., Los Angeles, CA 90043 Phone: 213-758-4033

Masjid Bilal Ibn Rabah, 5446 S. Crenshaw Blvd., Los Angeles, CA 90043 Phone: 213-291-0105

Masjid Al Rasol, 11211 S Central Ave., Los Angeles, CA 90059 Phone: 213-566-0341

Masjid Bilal Ibn Rabah, 5721 Ruthellen St., Los Angeles, CA 90062

Muslim Brothers of America, 128 S Wetherly Dr., Beverly Hills, CA 90211

Islamic Center of Beverly Hills, 505 S. Beverly Dr. Box 735, Beverly Hills, CA 90212 Phone: 310-859-0404

Islamic Cultural Center, 106 N. Alameda Blvd., Compton, CA 90221

Masjid Ikhlas, 1333 E Compton Ave., Compton, CA 90221 Phone: 213-537-3146

Masjid A-Rashid, 2212 E. Compton Blvd., Compton, CA 90223 Phone: 310-537-3142

Islamic Society of West Los Angeles, 4117 Overland Ave., Culver City, CA 90230 Phone: 213-838-7255

Islamic Center of Hawthorne, 12209 Hawthorne Way, Hawthorne, CA 90250 Phone: 310-978-4036

Jamat-e-Masjidul Islam, 820 Java St., Inglewood, CA 90301 Phone: 213-419-9177

Islamic Education and Research Center, 1918 W. Artesia Boulevard, Torrance CA 90504 Phone: 310-532-7755

Islamic Center of South Bay, PO Box 10057, Torrance, CA 90505

Masjid of Allah, 7925 Serapis Ave., Pico Rivera, CA 90660

Muslim Community of Cerritos, 16619 Valleyview, Cerritos, CA 90701 Phone: 213-926-1914

The Islamic Center of South Bay, 25816 Walnut St., Lomita, CA 90717 Phone: 213-534-1363

Masjid Al Shareef, 2104 Orange Ave., Long Beach, CA 90810 Phone: 213-591-7137

Muslim Center, 3184 N Olive Ave., Altadena, CA 91001 Phone: 213-684-6988

Muslim Community Center, 922 E Mendocino St., Altadena, CA 91001 Phone: 818-791-7290

Masjid Al-Taqwa, 2551 N. Fair Oaks Ave., Pasadena, CA 91001 Phone: 818-398-8392

Masjid Qurtuba, 1121 E. Huntington Dr., P.O.Box 872, Duarte, CA 91010 Phone: 818-305-0077

Al-Fatiha Islamic Center, 1125 Orange Ave., Monrovia, CA 91016 Phone: 818-357-0465

Islamic Center of Conejo Valley, 2700 Borchard Blvd., Newbury Park, CA 91320

Northridge Islamic Center, 8424 Tampa Ave., Northridge, CA 91324 Phone: 818-885-9107

Islamic Center of Santa Clarita Valley, 26477 Golden Valley Rd #D, Saugus, CA 91350 Phone: 805-296-8423

Hilal Islamic Center, 8741 Laurel Canyon Blvd., Sun Valley, CA 91352 Phone: 818-954-0208

Islamic Center of Corona and Norco, 1820 Fullerton Suite 330, Corona, CA 91719

Islamic Center of Rancho Cucamonga, 9395 Feron Blvd Suite B, Rancho Cucamonga, CA 91730

Islamic Center of San Gabriel Valley, 19164 E. Walnut Drive North, Rowland Hights, CA 91748 Ph: 818-964-3596

Islamic Center of Claremont, 3641 N Garey Ave., Pomona, CA 91767 Phone: 909-593-1865

Muslim Educational Society - Cal Poly, 3801 W. Temple Ave., Pomona, CA

91768 Phone: 909-595-7800

Masjid Gibrael, 1301 E Las Tunas Dr., San Gabriel, CA 91776 Phone: 818-285-2573

Islamic Education Center, 659 Brea Canyon Rd. Suite 2-3, Walnut, CA 91789 Phone: 909-594-1310

Islamic Information Center of America, 7516 La Jolla Blvd., La Jolla, CA ????? Phone: 619-454-7763

Islamic Center of Lakeside, 10390 Mountain View Ln., Lakeside, CA ????? Phone: 619-596-0020

Masjid Al-Taqwa, 2575 Imperial Ave., San Diego, CA 92102 Phone: 619-239-6738

Islamic Association of San Diego, 3872 50th St., San Diego, CA 92105 Phone: 619-461-7441

Islamic Center of San Diego, 7050 Eckstrom Ave., San Diego, CA 92111 Phone: 619-278-5240

Islamic Services Foundation, 7710 Balboa Ave., Suite #219B, San Diego, CA ????? Phone: 619-279-1994

Islamic Society of San Diego, 4935 Curry Dr., San Diego, CA 92115

The American Islamic Group, P. O. Box 711660, San Diego, CA 92171-1660 Phone: 619-268-8189

Masjid Aisha, 1369 N. Willow Ave # B-11, Rialto, CA 92376

Musalla - Victorville, 14036 Hesperia Rd., Victorville, CA 92392

Islamic Development Center, 24436 Webster St., Moreno Valley, CA 92453

Islamic Society of Riverside, 1038 W Linden, Riverside, CA 92507 Phone: 714-683-8631

The Islamic Society, 2530 Thayer St., Riverside, CA 92570

Islamic Center of Saddleback Valley, 22622 Lambert St, Suites # 407-8, Lake Forest, CA 92630 Ph: 714-454-2868

Fullerton Mosque, 413 West Ave #A, Fullerton, CA 92631 Phone: 714-447-3194

Islamic Society of Indo-China, 737 West Gage Ave., Fullerton, CA 92832

Masjid Gibrael, 1301 E Las Tunas, San Gabriel, CA 92642

Islamic Society of Orange County, 9752 W. 13th St., Garden Grove, CA 92644 Phone: (714) 531-1722

Islamic Society of Orange County, 5051 Berean Ln., Irvine, CA 92667

Islamic Society, 9752 13th St., Santa Ana, CA 92703 Phone: 714-531-1722

Masjid 'Umar al Farooq, 1839 Mountainview Ave., Anaheim, CA 92802 Phone: 909-399-4708

Yemeni Association Mosque, 1122 High St., Dolano, CA 93215 Phone: 805-725-9940

Dar-ul-Islam Mosque, 2822 W James St #A, Visalia, CA 93277 Phone: 209-732-6402

Muslim Center, 1221 California Ave., Bakersfield, CA 93304

Bakersfield Mosque, 701 Ming Ave., Bakersfield, CA 93307 Phone: 805-836-9055

Masjid Al-Ihsan, 1115 E. Planz Road, Bakersfield, CA 93307 Phone: 805 397-9913

Islamic Society of San Luis Obispo, 108 Mustang Dr #104, San Luis Obispo, CA 93405 Phone: 805-541-6298

Islamic Center of Northern Valley, 2763 W. Ave L #274, Lancaster, CA 93536

Masjid of Antelope Valley, P.O.Box 902846, 1125 E. Palmdale Blvd., Palmdale, CA 93590 Phone: 805-224-1111

Squaw Valley Islamic Settlement, P.O.Box 517, Dunlap, CA 93621

Masjid Fresno, 2111 East Shaw Ave., Fresno, CA 93710 Phone: 209-222-6686

Monterrey Mosque, 1131 10 St, Fireside Lodge Conf Rm., Monterrey, CA 93940 Phone: 408-373-4172

Monterey Bay Islamic Center, ?????, Monterey Bay, CA ????? Phone: 408-375-0692

Islamic Center of Mountain View, 607-A West Dana Street, Mountain View, CA 94040 Phone: (415) 938-9047

Masjid Al-Jame, PO Box 5730, 373 Alta Vista Drive, South San Francisco, CA 94083 Phone: 415-876-9763

Masjid Al-Falah, PO Box 1424, San Francisco, CA 94101

Masjid Al-Noor, 3004 16th St. #102, San Fransisco, CA ????? Phone: 415-552-8831

Islamic Center of San Francisco, 400 Crescent Ave., San Francisco, CA 94110 Phone: 415-641-9596

Muslim Mosque, 850 Davisadero St., San Francisco, CA 94117 Phone: 415-563-9397

Islamic Community of Northern California, PO Box 410186, San Fransisco, CA 94141 Phone: 415-552-8831

Islamic Society of San Francisco, 20 Jones Street, 3rd Floor, San Francisco, CA ????? Phone: 415-863-7997

Masjid Al-Falah, PO Box 421424, San Francisco, CA 94142

Al-Baqi Islamic Center, 1435 East Bayshore Road, East Palo Alto, CA 94303 Phone: 415-321-9278

Alameda Mosque, 707 (??) Height St., Alameda, CA 94501

Concord Afghani Mosque, 1545 (??) Monument Blvd, 2nd Flr., Concord, CA 94520

Fairfield Mosque, 902 Union Ave., Fairfield, CA 94533 Phone: 707-426-5768

Islamic Society of East Bay-SF, 3535 Capitol Ave., Fremont, CA 94538 Phone: 510-795-7137

Masjid Imam Muhammad Abdullah, 1540 C Street, Hayward, CA 94541

Muhajereen Masjid, 27949 (??) Leidig Ct., Hayward, CA 94544

Islamic Center of Livermore, 379A South Livermore Ave., Livermore, CA 94550 Phone: 510-373-6499
Masjid Muhammad, PO Box 1708, Pittsburg, CA 94565
Vallejo Mosque, 727 (??) Sonoma Blvd., Vallejo, CA 94590
Masjid Waritheen, 1652 47th Ave., Oakland, CA 94601 Phone: 415-436-7755
Al-Islam Mosque, 8210 Macarthur Blvd., Oakland, CA 94605 Phone: 510-638-9541
Abu Bakr Mosque, 948 (??) 62nd St., Oakland, CA 94609
Muhammad Mosque, 2014 San Pablo Ave., Oakland, CA 94612
Islamic Center, 2510 Channing Way, Berkeley, CA ????? Phone: 510-549-9465
Berkeley Mosque, 2288 Fulton St #306, Berkeley, CA 94704 Phone: 415-549-9465
American Muslim Alliance, 2154 University Ave., Berkeley, CA 94704 Phone: 510-849-0510
Islamic Society of West Contra Costa County, 1110-36th Street, Richmond, CA 94804 Phone: 510-236-8130
Islamic Society, 781 Bolinas Rd., Fairfax, CA 94930
Islamic Center of Mill Valley, 62 Shell Rd., Mill Valley, CA 94941 Phone: 415-383-0617
Islamic Center of Santa Cruz, 4401 Capitola Road #2, Capitola, CA 95010 Phone: 408-479-8982
MCA of San Francisco Bay Area, 1755 Catherine St., Santa Clara, CA 95050 Phone: 408-246-9822
Bay Area Islamic Center, 3003 Scott Blvd., Santa Clara, CA 95054 Phone: 408-970-0647
Islamic Center of San Jose, 325 N. Third Street, San Jose, CA 95112 Phone: (408) 947-9389
South Bay Islamic Association, 325 N 3rd St., San Jose, CA 95112 Phone: 408-947-9389
Hussaini Center, 4597 Alum Rock Ave., San Jose, CA 95127
Al Hilal Center, 2272 Trade Zone Blvd., San Jose, CA 95131 Phone: 408-274-4219
Islamic Center, 514 Lanfair Ave., San Jose, CA 95136
Stockton Islamic Center, 1130 S Pilgrim St., Stockton, CA 95205 Phone: 209-466-9101
Masjid As-Sadiq, 1545 Julian St., Stockton, CA 95206
Stockton Student Mosque, 1219 El Monte St., Stockton, CA 95207 Phone: 209-474-3184
Lodi Mosque, 210 Poplar Ave., Lodi, CA 95240 Phone: 209-333-9619
Islamic Center of Merced, 2322 Ashby Rd., Merced, CA 95348 Phone: 209-725-8167
Modesto Mosque, 1445 Carpenter Rd., Modesto, CA 95351 Phone: 209-576-8149

Musalla Santa Rosa, 912 Link Lane, Santa Rosa, CA 95401 Phone: 707-578-8424

Islamic Center of Davis, 539 Russell Blvd., Davis, CA 95616 Phone: 916-756-5216

Islamic Society of Folsom, 99 Cablo Circle #81, Folsom, CA 95630 Phone: 916-985-0356

Woodland Mosque, 1023 North St., Woodland, CA 95695 Phone: 916-666-4706

The Islamic Center, 3425 Sacramento Blvd., POB 5572, Sacramento, CA 95817

Islamic Center of Greater Sacramento, 411 (??) V St., Sacramento, CA 95818

Masjid An-Noor, 7320 14th Ave., Sacramento, CA 95820 Phone: 916-457-3233

Masjid As-Sabur, 4911 15th Ave., Sacramento, CA 95820

Baitul Llah Islamic Information Center, 4123 12th Avenue, Sacramento, CA 95817 Phone: (916) 455-2902

Masjid Abraham, 3449 Rio Linda Blvd., Sacramento, CA 95838

Islamic Center of Chico, 1316 Nord Ave., Chico, CA 95927 Phone: 916-342-5889

Islamic Center of Live Oak, 2825 First St., Live Oak, CA 95933 Phone: 916-695-8945

Islamic Center of Yuba City, 3636 Tierra Buena Rd, Yuba City, CA 95993 Phone: 916-671-6702

Colorado

Bism Rabbik Foundation, 8223 S. Quebec St., Suite I121, Englewood, CO 80112-3173
Phone: 303 306-0777

Mountain State Islamic Association, 2715 Humboldt St., Denver, CO 80205 Phone: (303) 296-0948

Denver Islamic Society, 3501 Easbury Ave., Denver, CO 80210

An Nur Masjid, 2124 S Birch PO Box 24653, Denver, CO 80222 Phone: (303) 759-1985

Denver Islamic Society, PO Box 24653, Denver, CO 80224 Phone: 303-375-1985

Dar Makkah Foundation, P.O. Box 24046, Denver, CO 80222 Phone: 303-695-1989

Colorado Muslim Society, 2071 South Parker Rd., Denver, CO 80231 Phone: 303-696-9800

Denver International Airport Mosque, 6th Floor Mezzanine, Denver International Airport, Denver, CO ?????

Islamic Center of Boulder, 1530 Culver Ct., Boulder, CO 80303 Phone: 303-444-6345

Islamic Center of Golden, 818 14th St, P.O.Box 944, Golden, CO 80402
Phone: (303) 279-0589

Islamic Center of Fort Collins, 900 Peterson St., Fort Collins, CO 80521
Phone: (303) 493-2428

Greenley Islamic Center, 1600 8th Ave., Greenley, CO 80631

Islamic Society of Colorado Springs, 4820 Rusina Road Suite C, Colorado
Springs, CO 80907
Phone: (719) 528-5463

Pueblo Mosque/ Pueblo Islamic Society, 32 Martha Ln., Belmont, Pueblo, CO
81001 Phone: 719-546-0137

Connecticut

Daar-ul-Ehsaan, 980 Hill St., Bristol, CT 06010 Phone: (203) 589-4512

The Islamic Association of Greater Hartford, 1781 Wilbur Cross Highway
Berlin, CT 06037 Phone: (203) 829-6411

Islamic Center of Connecticut, 1 Madina Drive (68 White Rock Drive),
Windsor, CT 06095-0624 Ph: 203-728-9637

Masjid Muhammad, PO Box 20130, 155 Hungerford St., Hartford, C T 06120
Phone: 203-728-9637

Islamic Center of New London, 23 Connecticut Ave., New London, CT 06320
Phone: (203) 442-6321

Islamic Community of Fairfield County, 57 Pepper St., Monroe, CT 06468
Phone: 203-261-6222

Masjid Muhammad - New Haven, 64 Carmel St., New Haven, CT 06511 Phone:
203-562-0594

Masjid Al-Islam, 624 George St., New Haven, CT 06511 Phone: 203-777-
8004

Masjid Al-Islam, 840 Dixwell Ave., Hamden, CT 06514 Phone: 203-772-0417

New Haven Islamic Center, 2 Prudden St., West Haven, CT 06516 Phone: 203-
933-5799

Bridgeport Islamic Society, PO Box 5171, Bridgeport, CT 66601

Masjid Al-Aziz, PO Box 9041, 679 Fairfield Ave., Bridgeport, CT 06601
Phone: (203) 368-3766

Masjid An-Noor, 1300 Fairfield Ave., Bridgeport, CT 06605 Phone: 203-579-
2211

University of Bridgeport Masjid, P.O.Box 1106, Southport, CT 06606 Phone:
203-576-4531

Albanian American Muslim Community, 38 Raymond St., Waterbury, CT 06706
Phone: (203) 879-3680

Albanian Community Center, 21 Long Meadow Dr., Wolcott, CT 06716

United Muslim Masjid (Masjid Rahman), 219 W. Main St., Waterbury, CT
06722 Phone: 203-756-6365

Islamic Society of Western Connecticut, 388 Main Street Danbury, CT 06810
Phone: 203-744-1328

Qadri Masjid, 4 Elton Court, Norwalk, CT 06851 Phone: 203-852-0847
Islamic Community of Fairfield County, P.O. Box 106,Norwalk, CT 06852-0106 Phone: (203) 261-6222
Islamic Community of Fairfield County, 2 Tierney St., Norwalk, CT 06852 Phone: 203-866-5274
Muslim Center, 109 Tresser Blvd 3D, Stanford, CT 06902 Phone: 302-324-4105
Stamford Musallah, 77 Judy Lane, Stamford, CT 06906 Phone: 203-327-5878
Farmington Masjid, UCONN Health Center., Farmington, CT Phone: 203-742-9464

Delaware
Masjid Ibrahim, 28 Salem Church Road, Newark, DE 19711
Phone: (302) 733-0373
Islamic Society of Delaware, 109 Dutton Dr, PO Box 533, New Castle, DE 19720
Muslim Center, 301 W 6th St., Wilmington, DE 19801 Phone: 302-571-0532
Masjid uz Zumar, Route 1 #500, Smyrna, DE 19977

District of Columbia
The Ansaru Allah Community, 816 Rhode Island Ave NW, Washington, DC 20001
Masjid Muhammad, 1519 4th St NW, Washington, DC 20001
Washington Masjid, 1519 Fourth St. N.W., Washington, DC 20001
Emerson Masjid, 1311 Emerson St NW, Washington, DC 20008
The Islamic Center, 2551 Massachusetts NW, Washington, DC 20008 Phone: 202-332-8343
Jazal Mosque, 2141 Leroy Place NW, Washington, DC 20008
Masjid Baitullah, 438 Kenyon St NW, Washington, DC 20010
Masjid Ul-Ummah, 770 Park Road NW, Washington, DC 20010
Hanafi Madhab Center, 7700 16th Street NW, Washington, DC 20011
Masjid Muhammad, 1519 Fourth St NW, Washington, DC20011
Muhammad Mosque #4, 1615 Kenilworth Ave NE, Washington, DC 20019
Masjid Ush Shura, 3109 Martin Luther King Jr Ave SE, Washington, DC 20032 Phone: (202) 322-2937
Association of Latin American Muslims, P.O. Box 57285, Washington, DC 20037 Phone: 202-483-3467

Florida
Islamic Center of Daytona Beach, PO Box 1903, Daytona Beach, FL 32015 Phone: 904-252-3501
Masjid Al-Salaam, 702 W Monroe St., Jacksonville, FL 32202 Phone: 904-355-7001

Jacksonville Masjid, 2242 Commonwealth Ave., Jacksonville, FL 32209 Phone: 904-387-6910
Islamic Center of Northeast Florida, 2223 St. Johns Bluff Rd So, Jacksonville, FL 32246 Phone: 904-646-3462
Al Ansar Mosque, 1020 W Pensacola St., Tallahasse, FL 32304 Phone: 904-681-9022
Masjid Muhammad, 115 Bragg Dr., Tallahasse, FL 32304
Mosque Al-Mujahideen, Rt 2, Box 124, Laurel Hill, FL 32567
Gainesville Islamic Center, 302 NW 4th Ave., Gainesville, FL 32601
Islamic Center of Gainesville, 1010 W University Ave., Gainesville, FL 32601 Phone: 904-378-9416
Masjid Al-Muslimeen, 412 NW 17th St., Gainesville, FL 32608
Islamic Soc. of Central Florida, 1005 N Goldenrod Rd., Orlando, FL 32807 Phone: 407-273-8363
Islamic Center of Orlando, 15433 Ruby Lake Road, Lobe Honorista, FL ????? Phone: 407-438-0266
Islamic Society of Brevard County, PO Box 1167, Melbourne, FL 32901 Phone: 305-984-4129
Islamic Center of S. Florida, 507 NE 6th St., Pompano Beach, FL 33060-6225 Phone: 305-946-2723
Masjid Al Ansar, 5245 NW 7th Ave., Miami, FL 33127 Phone: 305-984-4129
Masjid Annour, 13774 S.W. 88 St., Miami, FL 33174 Phone: 305-383-6669
Masjid Miami, 7350 NW 3rd St., Miami, FL ????? Phone: 305-261-7622
Masjid/ Muslim Community Association of South Florida, 4305 NW 183rd St., Miami, FL ?????Phone: 305-624-5555
Masjid Noor-i-Islam,10600 Stirling Rd., Cooper City, FL ????? Phone: 305-434-3855
Masjid Nur Islam, 6750 NW 27th Way, Fort Lauderdale, FL 33309
Masjid Tawhid, 1557 N.W.5th St., Ft. Lauderdale, FL 33311
Sunrise Mosque, 2542 NW Franklin Park Dr., Fort Lauderdale, FL 33311 Phone: 305-581-6295
Islamic Center, 3369 College Ave # 209, Fort Lauderdale, FL 33314
Masjid Salahuddin, 2820 Griffin Rd., Dania, FL ????? Phone: 305-981-7569
Bismillah Islamic Center, 2304 N. Florida, Tampa, FL 33602
Masjid Al-Hamdulillah, 1936 Martin Luther King Blvd., FL Tampa, 33602
Islamic Society of Tampa Bay Area, 7326 E Sligh Ave, Tampa, FL 33610 Phone: 813-621-9890
Islamic Society of Tampa Bay, 11104 61st St., Temple Terrance, FL 33617
Islamic Dawah Center, 1936 W. Martin Luther King Blvd., Tampa Bay, FL ?????
Muslim Center, 6013 N 48th St., Tampa, FL 33675 Phone: 813-626-8608
Islamic Comm. for Palestine, PO Box 82009, Tampa, FL 33682 Phone: 813-980-2572
Islamic Center of Daytona Beach, PO Box 1903 Daytona Beach, FL 33701

Mosque, 700 Bernel Road, South Daytona, FL ?????
Muslim Center, 922 9th St S., St Petersburg, FL 33701 Phone: 813-866-3314
Masjid Al-Qaadir Mu'minun, 2343 23rd Ave S., St Petersburg, FL 33712
Center for Islam and Cultural Awareness, Post Office Box 2994 Fort Myers,
FL 33902 Phone: 941-332-7833
Islamic Center of SW Florida, PO Box 2979, Fort Myers, FL 33902 Phone:
813-768-1207
Islamic Center Munich, 365 5th Ave S., Ste 222, Naples, FL 33940
Islamic Center, 795 Mirado Lane, Port Charlotte, FL 33952 Phone: (813)
629-2964
Muslim Association,16 Applewood Dr, P.O.Box 307, Brantford, FL 34206
Islamic Society of Pinellas County, PO Box 494, Pinellas Park, FL 34664
Phone: 813-546-3162
Jami Al Salam, 504 Skinner Blvd., Dunedin, FL 34694 Phone: (813) 447-8736
Islamic Centre of Kissimmee, 2350 Old Vineland Rd., Kissimmee, FL 34746
Phone: 407-390-1100

Georgia
Islamic Society, 4082 Macedonia Road, Powder Springs, GA 30073
Masjid Al-Momineen of Stone Mountain, P.O Box 984, Stone Mountain, GA
30086-0984 Phone: (404) 294-4058
Masjid Al-Huda, 120 Brumblow Rd 1-9, Carrolton, GA 30117 Phone: (404)
830-6812
Muslim Center, 315 N 3rd St., Griffin, GA 30223 Phone: 404-228-7924
Bilal ibn Rabah Islamic Center, 120 Hamilton St., La Grange, GA 30240
Phone: (706) 884-4431
Masjid Bilal ibn Rabah, 200 Carver St., La Grange, GA 30240
Muslim Center, 208 Hamilton St., La Grange, GA 30240
Masjid Atlanta City, PO Box 54815, Atlanta, GA 30308
West End Community Masjid, 547 West End Place, Atlanta, GA 30310 Phone:
(404) 758-7016
Islamic Center, 589 Ralph McGill Blvd NE, Atlanta, GA 30312
Masjid Al Muminun, 1127 Capitol Ave., Atlanta, GA 30315 Phone: 404-586-
9562
Atlanta Masjid of Al-Islam, 735 Fayetteville Rd SE, Atlanta, GA 30316 Phone:
404-378-4219
Masjid al-Mujtahideen, 1281 McPherson Ave., Atlanta, GA 30316-1605 Phone:
404-533-5154
Al-Farooq Masjid of Atlanta, 442 14th St NW, Atlanta, GA 30318 Phone:
(404) 874-7521
Masjid Al-Hidayah, 9 Perimeter Way N.E. Suite 150D, Atlanta, GA 30339
Phone: (404) 953-6806
Chamblee Masjid, 3301 Henderson Mill Road #P2, Carrollton, GA 30341

Gainesville Community Mosque, 512 Summit St., Gainesville, GA 30501 Phone: (404) 532-5687

Medina Masjid, Route 3, P.O.Box 399, Commerce, GA 30529 Phone: (404) 355-9431

Al-Huda Islamic Center, 2022 S Milledge Ave., Athens, GA 30605 Phone: 404-548-4620

Al-Huda Islamic Center, P.O. Box 962, Elberton, GA 30635 Phone: 404-283-7510

Dalton Islamic Center, 843 McAfee St., P.O.Box 3033, Dalton, GA 30719 Phone: 706-226-9841

Masjid Muhammad, 612 Beaufort Ave., Augusta, GA 30901 Phone: 404-766-2808

Muslim Community Center, 912 Laney Walker Blvd., Augusta, GA 30901 Phone: (706) 724-9739

Islamic Community of Fort Gordon, P.O. Box 7628, Fort Gordon, GA 30905

Islamic Society, 148 Morehead Dr., Martinez, GA 30907

Islamic Center of Augusta, 3416 Middleton St., Augusta, GA 30907 Phone: (706) 868-7278

Islamic Society of Augusta, PO Box 4594, Martinez, GA 30907 Phone: 404-863-5416

Islamic Center Middle Georgia, ???? Etwood Dr., Macon, GA 31204 Phone: (912) 757-9003

Muslim Center, 2031 E. Napier Ave., Macon, GA 31204 Phone: (912) 745-4068

Masjid Ma'un, 107 E. Martin Luther King St., Hinesville, GA 31313

Masjid Jihad, 117 E. 34th St., Savannah, GA 31401 Phone: 912-236-7387

Muslim Center, 109 Old Blaylock Ln, P.O.Box 70006, Albany, GA 31707 Phone: (912) 431-1144

Masjid Al-Noor, 837-1/2 5th Ave., Columbus, GA 31901

Masjid Muhammad, 2742 Spenola St., Columbus, GA 31906 Phone: 404-322-5074

Hawaii
Islamic Center, 1395 Aleo Place, Honolulu, HI 96822 Phone: 808-947-6263

Islamic Information Office, 1935 D Aleo Place, Honolulu, HI 96822 Phone: (808) 423-0998

Idaho
Islamic Center of Boise, 328 N. Orchard, Boise, ID 83706 Phone: (208) 377-5217

Islamic Center of Moscow, P.O.Box 4025, 316 Lilley St., Moscow, ID 83843 Phone: 208-882-8312

Muslim Community of Palouse, 920 S Logan, Moscow, ID 83843 Phone: 208-882-1149

Illinois

Islamic Society of Northwest Suburbs, 3890 Industrial Dr., Rolling Meadows, IL 60008 Phone: 708-253-6400

Islamic Association of Des Plaines, 480 Potter Rd., Des Plaines, IL 60016 Phone: 708-824-1100

Islamic Association Des Plaines, 9202 Greenwood Opp. Gold Mills, Des Plains, IL 60016

Islamic Foundation North, 100 Wimbledon Ct., Lake Bluff, IL 60044 Phone: 312-295-6795

Islamic Cultural Center-Greater Chicago, 1810 N Pfingsten Rd., Northbrook, IL 60062 Phone: 708-272-0319

Dar-ul-Islam, P.O.Box 1906, Palatine, IL 60078-1906, Phone: (847) 397-2200

Albanian American Islamic Center, 5825 St. Charles Rd., Berkeley, IL 60103 Phone: 708-544-2609

Islamic Center of North America, PO Box 484, Bellwood, IL 60104 Phone: 312-829-2255

Islamic Community of Illlnois, 8 O'Hare Ct., Bensenville, IL 60106 Phone: 708-766-6466

Muslim Society of Bloomingdale, 1523 Bourbon Pkwy, Streamwood, IL 60107 Phone: 708-717-7668

Islamic Society of Northern Illinois Univ., 721 Normal Rd., Dekalb, IL 60115 Phone: 815-758-6203

Islamic Community Center, 345 Heine Ave., Elgin, IL 60123-3213 Phone: 312-695-3338

Elmhurst Islamic Center, 844 Geneva Ct., Elmhurst, IL 60126 Phone: 312-941-9228

Muslim Society, 1785 Bloomingdale Rd., Glendale Heights, IL 60139 Phone: 708-653-7872

Islamic Society of Northern Illinois University, 721 Normal Road, Dekalb, IL 60155 Phone: 815-756-4955

Islamic Foundation, 300 W Highridge Rd., Villa Park, IL 60181 Phone: 708-941-8800

Midwest Islamic Center, 1081 W. Irving Park Road, Schaumburg, IL 60193 Phone: 708-894-9650

American Islamic Association, 8860 St. Francis, Frankfort, IL 60423 Phone: 815-469-1551

Al-Masjid ul-Ummat As-Salaam, 3422 West 159th Street, Markham, IL 60426 Phone: (708) 596-3692

Harvey Islamic Center, 15406 Turlington Harvey, IL 60426 Phone: 708-333-4165

South Suburban Islamic Ctr of Harvey, 15200 S. Broadway, Harvey, IL 60426 Phone: 312-331-4165

Islamic Foundation Libertyville, 356 Brainerd Ave., Libertyville, IL ?????
Phone: 708-367-6522

Muslim Association of Bollingbrook, 420 Seminole Ln., Bolingbrook, IL 60439 Phone: 312-739-0127

Masjid Al-Islam, 560 East Frontage Rd, Bolingbrook, IL 60440 Phone: 708-972-0701

Muslim Center, 523 Oak Ave., Lockport, IL 60441

American Islamic Association, St Francis Rd & 88th Ave, Box 168 RR #4, Mokena, IL 60448 Phone: 219-922-4519

Mosque Foundation of Chicago, 7360 W 93rd St., Bridgeview, IL 60455 Phone: 708-430-5666

Mosq ` Foundation, 9001 Turnberry Dr., Burr Ridge, IL 60521

Islamic Foundation of Greater Chicago, PO Box 1101, Oak Brook, IL 60521

Islamic Center of Naperville, PO Box 428, Naperville, IL 60566 Phone: 708-713-7417

Napervill Masjid, 450 S. Olesen Dr., Naperville, IL 60540 Phone: 708-355-3733

Downtown Islamic Center, 218 S. Wabash, 5th Floor, Chicago, IL 60604 Phone:312-939-9095

Masjid Al-Asr, 24 N. Pulaski Rd., Chicago, IL 60607

As-Salaam Center, 4819 S Ashland Ave., Chicago, IL 60609 Phone: 312-247-2666

Masjid/American Islamic College, 640 W. Irving Park Rd., Chicago, IL 60613 Phone: 312-281-4700

Nigerian Islamic Association, 932 W. Sheridan, Chicago, IL 60613 Phone: 312-665-2451

Masjid Al-Fatir, 1200 E 47th St., Chicago, IL 60615 Phone: 312-268-7248

Islamic Center of Chicago, 4035 N. Damen Ave., Chicago, IL 60618 Phone: 312-477-0003

Westside Muslim Center, 24 N. Pulaski Rd., Chicago, IL 60618 Phone: 312-722-8005

Masjid Muminun, 8607 1/2 S. Ashland Ave., Chicago, IL 60620 Phone: 312-238-3974

National Islamic Center, 734 W 79th St., Chicago, IL 60620

Masjid-e-Dawah, 4103 W. Madison, Chicago, IL 60624

Masjid-e-Kausar, 4542 N. Whipple (Basement), Chicago, IL 60625 Phone: 312-267-2512

Wallen Community Center, 1701 W. Wallen Ave., Chicago, IL 60626 Phone: 312-274-1184

Mosque of Umer, 11405 S Michigan Ave., Chicago, IL 60628 Phone: 312-660-0399

Al Takaful, PO Box 29090, Chicago, IL 60629 Phone: 312-475-8373

Masjid Al-Anaak, 2506 W 63rd St., Chicago, IL 60629 Phone: 312-434-2400

Masjid Al-Muhajireen, 4158 W. 63rd Street, Chicago, IL 60629 Phone: 312-581-1083

Qassam Mosque & Cultural Center, 13247 W 63rd St., Chicago, IL 60629 Phone: 312-436-8083

Turkish American Cultural Alliance, 3845 N. Harlem Ave., Chicago, IL 60634 Phone: 312-725-3655

Masjid Al-Latif, 1114 W. Foster Ave., Chicago, IL 60640

Masjid Al-Taqwa, 955 W. Foster Ave., Chicago, IL 60640 Phone: 312-769-5486

Islamic Community Center of Ilinois, 4003 W. Montrose Ave., Chicago, IL 60641 Phone: (312) 725-5020

Muslim Community Center, 4380 N Elston Ave., Chicago, IL 60641 Phone: 312-725-9047

Masjid-e-Rahmat, 6412 N. Talman, Chicago, IL 60645 Phone: 312-761-6065

Masjid-e-Tahoora, 6448 N. Seeley, Chicago, IL 60645

Masjid Al-Qadir, 2312 E. 75th St., Chicago, IL 60649

Masjid Elijah Muhammad, 7351 S Stony Island Ave., Chicago, IL 60649

Masjid Ar-Rahman, 5330 W. Division Ave., Chicago, IL 60651 Phone: 312-379-0002

The Islamic Community, PO Box 53398, Chicago, IL 60653

Northside Mosque, 1017 W. Roscoe St., Chicago, IL 60657 Phone: 312-743-9364

Jamia Masjid, 6340 N. Campbell, Chicago, IL 60659 Phone: 312-743-9364

Masjid Hameedia, 1456 W. Elmdale, Chicago, IL 60660 Phone: 312-274-2435

Masjid-e-Noor, 6151 N. Greenview, Chicago, IL 60660 Phone: 312-743-9364

The Islamic Community Center, PO Box 4332, Chicago, IL 60680

As-Salaam Masjid, 4819 S Ashland Ave., Chicago, IL 60690

Masjid Al-Latif, 1114 W. Foster Avenue, Chicago, IL 60640

Masjid Al-Huda Al-Islami, 7400 West Addison, Chicago, IL ?????

O'Hare Airport, Terminal 2 Chapel, Mezzanine Floor, Chicago, IL ????? Phone: 312-280-6807

Muslim Community Center, 5921 Darlene Dr., Rockford, IL 61109 Phone: 815-397-3311

Islamic Center, 334 West Wheeler St., Macomb, IL 61455 Phone: 309-833-3875

Central Illinois Mosque & Islamic Center, 106 5 Lincoln, Urbana, IL 61801 Phone: 217-352-6689

Islamic Center, PO Box 2262 Stn A, Champaign, IL 61820

Masjid Quincy, c/o Hatim Adam, #505 S. 24th St., Quincy, IL 62301 Phone: 217 228 9527

Muslim Center, 255 E Orchard, Decatur, IL 62521 Phone: 217-422-0149

Islamic Society of Greater Springfield, 1316 E Bruce St., Springfield, IL 62703 Phone: 217-787-1594

Islamic Center of Greater Centralia, 224 S Broadway, Central City, IL 62801 Phone: 618-533-3080

Islamic Center of Carbondale, 321 S Cedarview, Carbondale, IL 62901 Phone: 618-529-1168

Islamic Center of Carbondale, 512 W College, Carbondale, IL 62901 Phone: 618-549-6378

Indiana

ISNA Headquarters/Masjid, P.O. Box 341, Plainfield, IN 46168 Phone: 317-839-8157

Masjid Al-Fajr, 2846 Cold Spring Road, Indianapolis, IN 46222 Phone: 317-923-2847

Daniel Mohammed Islamic Center, 2040 E. 46th St., Indianapolis, IN 46226 Phone: (317) 251-9796

North West Indiana Islamic Center, 9803 Colorado St., Merrillville, IN 46307 Phone: (219) 756-7622

Masjid Muhammad, PO Box 629, Michigan City, IN 46360

Muslim Center, 302 E 10th St., Michigan City, IN 46360 Phone: 219-872-5607

The Islamic Center, PO Box 710 Brown Rd., Michigan City, IN 46360

Gary Muslim Center, 607 W Sth Ave., Gary, IN 46401

Masjid Al-Amin, 3702 W. 11th St., Gary, IN 46404P hone: 219-949-1854

Gary Masjid, 1473 W. 15th Ave., Gary, IN 46407 Phone: 219-885-3018

Islamic Society of Michiana, PO Box 170, Notre Dame, IN 46556 Phone: 219-291-4236

Masjid Mujahideen, 431 S Dundee, South Bend, IN 46619

Great News Islamic Center, 310 S. Dundee, South Bend, IN ?????

South Bend Masjid Muhammad, 1125 W Thomas, South Bend, IN 46625

Angola Islamic Center, PO Box 191, Angola, IN 46703 Phone: 219-665-9225

Islamic Center of Fort Wayne, 1111 Chute Street, Fort Wayne, IN 46803 Phone: 219-423-2432

Masjid Al-Fatihah, 511 E. Leith St., Fort Wayne, IN 46806 Phone: 219-456-6826

Al-Hidayaa Center, 1117 Largo Drive, Fort Wayne, IN ????? Phone: 219-432-6605

Islamic Association of Indiana, 409 E Elm St., New Albany, IN 47150-3320 Phone: 812-945-4000

Islamic Center of Muncie, 1717 N. Ball Ave., Muncie, IN 47304 Phone: (317) 288-8014

The Islamic Center, 809 E 8th St., Bloomington, IN 47401 Phone: 812-332-5130

Muslim Center, 1332 Lincoln Ave., Evansville, IN 47714 Phone: 812-682-4632

West Lafayette Al Masjid, 1022 1st St., West Lafayette, IN 47906 Phone: 317-743-8650

Iowa

Masjid, 1221 Michigan Ave., Ames, IA 50010-3951 Phone: (515) 292-3683

Masjid Dar-Ul-Argam, 1221 Michigan Ave., Ames, IA 50014 Phone: 515-292-3683

Masjid Muhammad, PO Box 1432, Des Moines, IA 50314 Phone: 515-243-9154

Islamic Center of Des Moines, 6201 Franklin Ave., Des Moines, IA 50322 Phone: 515-266-7591

Masjid Al-Noor Islamic Center, 728 W 2nd St., Waterloo, IA 50701 Phone: 319-233-2671

Islamic Society of Iowa City, P.O. Box 1502, Iowa City, IA 52240, Phone: 319-354-6167

Islamic Association of Cedar Rapids, 2999 First Ave SW, Box 1425, Cedar Rapids, IA 52404 Phone: 319-362-0857

Islamic Council of Iowa, PO Box 5813, Cedar Rapids, IA 52406 Phone: 319-396-4719

Islamic Service Group, PO Box 521, Cedar Rapids, IA 52406 Phone: 319-362-3711

Kansas

Islamic Center of Lawrence, 1300 Ohio St., Lawrence, KS 66044 Phone: (913) 749-1638

Muslim Community Association, 1224 Hylton Heights, Manhattan, KS 66502 Phone: 913-776-8543

Islamic Society of Wichita, 3104 E. 17th St, Wichita, KS 67214 Phone: 316-687-4946

Islamic Association of Mid Kansas, 3406 W Taft, Wichita, KS 67213 Phone: (316) 945-0472

Kentucky

Masjid Muhammad, Kentucky State Reformatory, Lagrange, KY 40032

Masjid Abdullah Muhammad, 3020 Magazine St.,Louisville, KY 40203

Islamic Cultural Association, 4005 N Upper River Rd., Louisivlle, KY 40207 Phone: 502-893-9466

Islamic Center of Louisville, 1715 S 4th St., Louisville, KY 40208 Phone: 502-634-1395

Muslim Center, 1142 S 42nd St., Louisville, KY 40211 Phone: 502-772-1143

Masjid Muhammad, 1917 Magazine, Louisville, KY 40211 Phone: 502-772-9503

Masjid Bilal Ibn Rabah, 572 Georgetown St., Lexington, KY 40508 Phone: 606-233-4827

Islamic Center of Lexington, 649 South Limestone Street, Lexington, KY 40508 Phone: 606-255-0335

Masjid Muhammad, 940 Whitney Ave., Lexington, KY 40508

Islamic Center, 2816 Ring Road East, Elizabeth Town, KY 41042 Phone: (502) 765-7190

Louisiana

Masjid Abu Baker Al-Siddeeq, 4425 David Dr., Metairie, LA 70003 Phone: 504-887-5365

Masjid Yaseen, 7527 W. Judge Perez Dr., Arabi, LA 70032, Phone: (504) 277-9222

Masjid Taubah, 448 Realty Road, Gretna, LA 70056 Phone: (504) 392-3425

Jefferson Muslim Association, PO Box 640758, Kenner, LA 70064 Phone: 504-888-9364

Masjid of Al-Islam, 2626 Magnolia St., New Orleans, LA 70113 Phone: (504) 895-6731

Bilal Ibn Rabah Center, 717 Teche St., Algiers, LA 70114

New Orleans Islamic Center, 1911 St. Claude Ave., New Orleans, LA 70116 Phone: (504) 944-3758

Masjid Rahmah, 7103 Burthe St., New Orleans, LA 70118 Phone: (504) 866-3879

Masjid Al-Ghurba, 6244 Waldo Dr., New Orleans, LA 70148 Phone: (504) 282-0700

Masjidur-Rahim, 1238 N. Johnson St., New Orleans, LA 70187 Phone: 504-827-0017

Masjid Muhammad, Rte. 5, Box 135E, Slidell, LA 70458 Phone: 504-641-0150

Slidell Masjid of Al-Islam, 37482 Browns Village Rd., Slidell, LA 70460-9361 Phone: 504-641-3172

Islamic Center of Lafayette, 1117 Johnston St., Lafayette, LA 70501 Phone: 318-235-1472

Islamic Society of Lake Charles, 501 Hudson Dr., Westlake, LA 70669 Phone: (318) 439-3783

Muslim Center, S6s4 Packard St., Baton Rouge, LA 70801

Islamic Center of Baton Rouge, 820 W Chimes, Baton Rouge, LA 70802 Phone: 504-766-6015

Masjid Sabiqun, 740 E. Washington St., Baton Rouge, LA 70802

Islamic Association of Greater Shreveport, 3769 Youree Dr., Shreveport, LA 71105 Phone: 318-861-7990

Masjid At-Taqwa, 2510 Morningside Drive, Shreveport, LA 71108

Masjid Muhammad, PO Box 9202, Shreveport, LA 71109

Islamic Association of Greater Shreveport, 2950 E Texas #528, Bossier City, LA 71111 Phone: 318-747-8929
Masjid, 9203 Midvale Dr., Shreveport, LA 71118 Phone: (318) 687-6827
Masjid Muhammad, 2414 Oak St., Monroe, LA 71202 Phone: (318) 387-8596
Islamic Center of N. Eastern Louisiana, NLU Box 5305, Monroe, LA 71212
Islamic Center of North Louisiana, 203 S. Homer St., Ruston, LA 71270
Phone: (318) 255-6902

Maine
The Islamic Center of Maine, P.O. Box 267, Orono, ME 04473

Maryland
Islamic Community Center of Laurel, 7306 Contee Road, Laurel MD 20707
Phone: 301-317-4584
Imamia Center, PO Box 275, Lanham, MD 20801
Dar-adh-dhirk Masjid, 4323 Rosedale Ave., Bethesda, MD 20814 Phone: 301-907-0997
Muslim Community Center, 9229 E Parkhill Dr., Bethesda, MD 20814
Islamic Center of Maryland, 2 Leatherbark Court, Germantown, MD 20874
Phone: 301-869-1011
Islamic Society of Maryland, 601 E Franklin Ave., Silver Spring, MD 20901
Phone: 301-577-2891
Muslim Community Center, 15200 New Hampshire Ave., Silver Spring, MD 20905 Phone: 301-384-3454
Islamic Society of Baltimore, 6631 Johnny Cake Rd, PO Box 7647, Baltimore, MD 21207 Phone: 301-247-4869
Progressive Islamic Community, 2701 W Belvedere Ave., Baltimore, MD 21215
Masjid Walter Omar, 3401 W. North Ave., Baltimore, MD 21216
Masjid Ul-Haqq, 514 Islamic Way, Baltimore, MD 21217 Phone: (410) 728-1363
Masjid As-Saffat, 1335 W. North Ave., Baltimore, MD 21217 Phone: 410-669-0655
Masjid Muminum, 2642 Hartford Rd., Baltimore, MD 21218 Phone: 301-467-8798
Muslim Community Services, 1420 Harberson Rd., Baltimore, MD 21228
Phone: 301-744-7753
Jamaatal-Muslimeen, P.O. Box 10881, Baltimore, MD 21234 Phone: 410-692-2641
Masjid Al-Inshirah, 6004 Liberty Rd., Baltimore, MD 21244
The Islamic Society of Del Marva, P.O. Box 2053, Salisbury, MD 21802
Phone: (410) 341-4023
The Hurlock Muslim Center, Cambridge, MD Phone: (410) 673-7914

Massachusetts

Islamic Society of Western Mass., 377 Amostown Rd., West Springfield, MA 01105 Ph: 413-788-7546

Islamic Center of West Massachusetts, 57 Chaplin Terrace, Springfield, MA 01107

Masjid At-Tawhid, 111 Oak St., Springfield, MA 01109

Masjid Al-Baqi, 495 Union St., Springfield, MA 01109 Phone: (413) 732-9288

Islam Society of Greater Worchester, 57 Laurel St., Worchester, MA 01604 Phone: 508-842-8242

Islamic Center of Boston, 126 Boston Post Rd., Wayland, MA 01778 Phone: 508-358-5885

Selimiye Jamii (Masjid), 105 Oakland Ave., Methuen, MA 01844

Islamic Center of New England, 74 Chase Drive, Sharon, MA 02067 Phone: 617-784-0434

Masjid Al-Hamidulillah, 724 Shawmut Ave., Boston, MA 02119 Phone: 617-442-2805

Masjid Al-Noor, 28 Circuit St., Boston, MA 02119 Phone: 617-427-1542

Masjid Al-Quran, 35 Intevale St., Boston, MA 02121 Phone: 617-445-8070

The Islamic Multi Service Organization, 7 Long Ave., Allston, MA 02134 Phone: 617-562-1433

Islamic Society of Boston, 204 Prospect St., Cambridge, MA 02139 Phone: 617-876-3546

Muslim Prayer Room, MIT, Religious Activities Center, Building W11, Room W11-110, 40 Massachusetts Ave., Cambridge, MA 02139 Phone: (617) 258-9285

Islamic Association of Massachusetts, P.O. Box 535, Everett, MA 02149 Phone: 617-381 6666/ 617-381 9555

Islamic Center of New England, 470 South Street, Quincy, MA 02169 Phone: 617-479-8341

Wentworth Islamic Society, 131 Coolidge Ave #526,Watertown, MA 02172 Phone: 617-581-3193

Jamaa Masjid of Boston, 1380 Soldiers Field Road, Boston, MA 02215 Phone: (617) 961-4563

Mosque of New England, P.O.Box 222, Seekonk, MA 02771 Phone: 508-336-9040

Michigan

The Cultural Association, PO Box 628, Franklin, MI 48025 Phone: 313-855-3977

Islamic Community Center, 4215 Middlebelt, W. Bloomfield, MI 48033

Islamic Association of Greater Detroit, 879 W Auburn St., Rochester, MI 48063 Phone: 810-852-5657

447

Islamic Council Detroit, 64 Duncan Dr., Troy, MI 48098
Muslim Community Assn. of Ann Arbor, 2301 Plymouth Rd., Ann Arbor, MI 48105 Phone: 313-665-1772
American Muslim Society, 9945 W Vernor Hwy, Dearborn, MI 48120 Phone: 313-842-9000
Al-Qur'an and As-Sunnah Society of North America, PO Box 1589, Dearborn, MI 48121-1589
Islamic Center, 37311 Phipps Street, Inkster, MI 48141 Phone: 313-562-2175
Muslim Community of W Suburbs of Mich., PO Box 52668, Livonia, MI 48152 Phone: 313-349-3926
American Muslim Society of Dearborn, 17514 Woodward Ave., Detroit, MI 48203
Masjid Al-Nur, 318 Pilgrim, Detroit, MI 48203
Masjid Muhammad, 11529 Linwood Ave., Detroit, MI 48206 Phone: 313-868-2131
International Muslim House, 1741 Berry Park#303, Detroit, MI 48208 Phone: 313-872-6651
Detroit Masjid, 17346 Plainview, Detroit, MI 48219
Masjid Al-Haqq, 4118 Joy Road, Detroit, MI 48227 Phone: 313-897-9218
The Islamic Center of Detroit, 15571 Joy Rd., Detroit, MI 48228
Al-Mumineen Mosque, PO Box 32485, Detroit, MI 48232 Phone: 313-537-2234
Muslim Center, 1605 W Davison Ave., Detroit, MI 48238 Phone: 313-883-3330
Federation of Islamic Assoc., 25351 Five Mile Rd., Redford Twp., MI 48239
Tawheed Center, 31598 Bristol Ln., Farmington Hills, MI 48339 Phone: 313-489-1255
Masjid Al-Madrashah, 3129 Clio Rd., Flint, MI 48504
Masjid Mu'min, 64043-A Clio Rd., Flint, MI 48504 Phone: 313-785-4001
Flint Islamic Center, 614 W Homes St., Flint, MI 48505 Phone: 313-789-7716
Flint Masjid of Al Islam, 402 E Gillespie, Flint, MI 48505 Phone: 313-787-6591
Dyewood Islamic Society of N. America, 5271 N Dyewood Dr., Flint, MI 48532 Phone: 313-230-9226
Masjid Abdur Rahman, 1 14 N 4th St., Saginaw, MI 48601
Islamic Soc of Greater Lansing, 920 S Harrison Rd., East Lansing, MI 48823 Phone: 517-351-4309
The Islamic Center, 110 Intnl Ctr, Michigan St., East Lansing, MI 48824
Islamic Center of Mt Pleasant, 907 McVey St., Mt Pleasant, MI 48858 Phone: 517-772-5206
Walim Mahmoud Islamic Center, 235 Lahoma, Lansing, MI 48915 Phone:

517-882-1883
Kalamazoo Islamic Center, 3018 W Michigan Ave., Kalamazoo, MI 49007
Phone:616-381-6611
Din Al-Fitrah Islamic Center, 1174 Jefferson, Grand Rapids, MI 49507
The Islamic Center, 515 Dicksinson SE, Grand Rapids, MI 49507

Minnesota
Masjid Muhammad, 3759 4th Ave South, Minneapolis, MN 55409 Phone: (612) 827-4858
Masjid An-Nur, 1729 Lyndale Ave, North, Minneapolis, MN 55411
Islamic Center of Minneapolis, 1128 6th St SE, Minneapolis, MN 55414 Phone: 612-379-8269
Islamic Center, 4056 7th Ave NE, Columbia Heights, MN 55421 Phone: (612) 781-9111
Islamic Center of Minnesota, 1401 Gardena Ave NE, Fridley, MN 55432 Phone: 612-571-5604
Rochester Islamic Center, 322 Broadway South, Rochester, MN 55904 Phone: 507-282-8087

Mississippi
Masjid Al-Bayyinah, 374 Issaquena Ave., Clarksdale, MS 38614
Masjid Bilal, J.F.K. Music Building, Highway 61, North Mound Bayou, MS 38762
Community of Islam, 1210 Crawford St., Vicksburg, MS39180
Masjid Muhammad, 1208 Jones Ave., Jackson, MS 39204 Phone: 601-362-1170
Mississippi Muslim Association, 2533 Old McDowell Rd., Jackson, MS 39204 Phone: 601-373-0825
Masjid Mohammed, P.O.Box 941, Quitman, MS 39355 Phone: 601-776-5444
Masjid Al-Huda, 118 N. 31st Ave., Hattiesburg, MS 39401 Phone: (601) 268-8742
Masjid Muhammad, 903 Elizabeth Ave., Hattiesburg, MS 39401 Phone: 601-544-9828
Masjid Al-Halim, 8 Al-Halim Rd., Sumrall, MS 39482 Phone: (601) 736-8540
Masjid Muhammad, 307 E. Division St., Biloxi, MS 39530
Biloxi Islamic Center, 205 Keller Ave., Biloxi, MS 39530 Phone: (601) 432-7650
Muslim Center, 501 1/2 Keller Ave., Biloxi, MS 39530 Phone: 601-323-0910
Masjid Al-Haque, Route 2, Box 517A, Silver Creek, MS 39663 Phone: (601) 587-0245
Islamic Center of Mississippi, 204 Herbert St., Starkville, MS 39759 Phone: 601-323-6559

Islamic Association of Mississippi, PO Box 701, MSU, Starkville, MS 39762
Phone: 601-323-6559
Masjid Al-Islam, 254 North Hickory Street, Canton, MS ?????

Missouri
Dar-al-Islam, 517 Weidman Rd., Manchester, MO 63011 Phone: 314-394-7878
Masjid At-Taqwa Wa-Jihad, 3333 Union Blvd., St. Louis, MO 63105
Masjid Al Mu'minun, 1434 N Grand Ave., St. Louis, MO 63106 Phone: 314-531-5414
Islamic Center of St Louis, 3834 Westpine St., St Louis, MO 63108 Phone: 314-531-3584
Massged Alakhella, 5178 Deerfield Circle #2, St Louis, MO 63128 Phone: 314-843-4474
Potosi Correctional Center, Rte 2, Box 2222 (3a-13), Mineral Point, MO 63660
Islamic Center of Warrensburg, 143 E. Culton, Warrensburg, MO 64093 Phone: 816-747-9442
Masjid Inshirah, 4302 Prospect, Kansas City, MO 64130
Masjid Muhammad, 2715 Swope Pkwy, Kansas City, MO 64130 Phone: 816-924-5483
Masjid Omar, 2700 E 49th St., Kansas City, MO 64130
Masjid Ahmed, 5501 Cleveland Ave., Kansas City, MO 64140
Islamic Society of Greater Kansas City, 8501 E 99th St., Kansas City, MO 64141 Phone: 913-469-8317
Islamic Center of Central Missouri, 201 S Fifth St., Columbia, MO 65201 Phone: 314-875-0578
Islamic Center of Rolla, 1306 N. Elm St., Rolla, MO 65401 Phone: 314-341-7360

Montana
The Islamic Center of Billings, PO Box 121, Billings, MT 59103-0121 Phone: 406-656-8832
Muslim Community of Bozeman, 1145 S. Pinecrest Dr., Bozeman, MT 59715 Phone: (406) 587-7162

Nebraska
Masjid Muhammad, 2934 N. 24th St., Omaha, NE 68111
Islamic Center of Omaha, 3511 N 73 St., Omaha, NE 68134 Phone: 402-571-0720
Islamic Foundation of Lincoln, P.O.Box 84133, 3636 N. First St., Lincoln, NE 68501 Phone: (402) 475-0475
Islamic Community, P.O.Box 795, S. Sioux City, NE 68776 Phone: (402) 494-5152, (Phone: 712) 239-5320

Nevada

Masjid As-Sabur, 711 W. Morgan Ave., Las Vegas, NV 89106 Phone: (702) 647-2757

Islamic Society of Nevada, 4730 E. Desert Inn Road, Las Vegas, NV 89121 Phone: (702) 433-3431

Islamic Center of Reno, 1295 Valley Road, Reno, NV 89512 Phone: (702) 786-2522

New Hampshire

Islamic Society of Merrimack Valley, 230 Main St., Salem, NH 03079 Phone: (603) 893-1112

Islamic Society of Seacoast Area, P.O. 52, Durham, NH 03824 Phone: 603-749-4689

New Jersey

Muslim Foundation Inc., 22 Tomar Ct, PO Box 390, Bloomfield, NJ 07003 Phone: 201-338-7710

Jami Masjid of Boonton, 604 Birch St., Boonton, NJ 07005 Phone: 201-334-9334

Islamic Center of East Orange, 61 Lincoln St., East Orange, NJ 07017-2304 Phone: 201-672-6690

Albanian American Muslim Society, 43 Monroe St., Garfield, NJ 07026

Masjid Al-Wadud, 698 Bloomfield Ave., Monclair, NJ 07042 Phone: 201-678-3632

Islamic Educational Center of North Hudson, 4613 Cottage Place Union City, P.O.Box 5548, N. Bergen, NJ 07047 Phone: 201-330-0066

Masjid Mohammed, 112 Park St., Orange, NJ 07050 Phone: 201-674-9882

United Islamic Center, 408 Knickerbocker St.,Paterson, NJ 07051

Masjid-ullah Muhammad, 321 Grant Ave., Plainfield, NJ 07060 Phone: 201-561-6797

Muslim Community Masjid, Newark, PO Box 721, Lyndhurst, NJ 07071

Muslim Community of New Jersey - Woodbridge, P.O.Box 865, Woodbridge, NJ 07095 Phone: 908-634-8968

Masjid Al-Haqq, 685 Springfield Ave., Newark, NJ 07101 Phone: (201) 621-9228

Islamic Cultural Center, PO Box 1064, 24 Branford Pl., Newark, NJ 07101 Phone: 201-748-8153

Daar Al-Hadeeth, PO Box I 561, Newark, NJ 07102

Masjid Mohammad, 257 S. Orange Ave., Newark, NJ 07103 Phone: 201-623-3500

Turkish Mosque of America, 103 Elmwood Ave., Newark, NJ 07104 Phone: 201-482-6333

National Islamic Association, 239 Roseville Ave., Newark, NJ 07107 Phone: 201-482-8996

451

Denullah Masjid, 69 Van Ness Pl., Newark, NJ 07108
Baith Quraish, 69 Custer Ave., Newark, NJ 07112
Islamic Center Newark, 210-216 Clinton Pl., Newark, NJ 07112 Phone: 201-824-3764
Masjid Newark, I 324 Clinton Place, Newark, NJ 07112
Newark Community Masjid, 214 Chancellor Ave., Newark, NJ 07112 Phone: 201-926-8927
Masjid Al Hadi, 9 Broad St., Elizabeth, NJ 07114 Phone: 908-351-7238
Muslim American Dawah Center, P.O.Box 269, Elizabeth, NJ
An Juman-e-Islamia, 146 Jewett Ave., Jersey City, NJ 07302
Muslim Federation of New Jersey, 2 Chopin Court, Jersey City, NJ 07302 Phone: 201-433-0057
Jamaat Ibad Er-Rahman, 26 Gifford Ave., Jersey City, NJ 07304
Jersey City Mosque, 539 Bergen Ave., Jersey City, NJ 07304 Phone: 201-433-8304
Masjid Al-Iman, 360 Woodward St, P.O.Box 3236, Jersey City, NJ 07304 Phone: 201-491-5575
El-Taweed Center, 984 West Side Ave., Jersey City, NJ 07306 Phone: 2014321773
Islamic Center of Jersey City, 17 Park St., Jersey City, NJ 07306 Phone: 201-451-8030
Islamic Center of New Jersey, PO Box 6607, Jersey City, NJ 07306
Masjid Al-Salaam, 2824 Kennedy Blvd., Jersey City, NJ 07306
Masjid As-Salaam, 984 West Side Ave., Jersey City, NJ 07306 Phone: 201-332-9588
Masjid Muhammad, 297 Martin Luther King Dr., Jersey City, NJ 07306 Phone: (201) 435-6845
Masjid Al-Nasr, 383 Oldham Road, Wayne, NJ 07470
Turkish Muslim Mosque, 32 Chestnut St., Paterson, NJ 07501 Phone: 201-345-1083
Islamic Center of Passaic and Patterson, 245 Broadway, Paterson, NJ 07501 Phone: 201-279-4151
United Islamic Center, 408 Knickerbocker Ave., Paterson, NJ 07503 Phone: 201-345-6584
American Muslim Association (New World Masjid), 501 Getty Ave., Paterson, NJ 07503 Phone: 201-278-3666
Islamic Foundation (Masjid Jalalabad), 61 Van Housten St., Paterson, NJ 07505 Phone: 201-279-6408
Masjid An-Nur, 18 Fair St., Paterson, NJ 07505 Phone: 201-357-0122
Jamaet Ibad El-Rahman Mosque, 272 N 8th St., Prospect Park, NJ 07508 Phone: 201-956-6969
Masjid MSA-Passaic Community College, Prospect Park, NJ 07508
Karacay Turkish Mosque and Cultural Center, 92 Ballentine Dr., North Haledon, NJ 07508

Islamic Center of Passaic County, 152 Derrom Ave., P.O.Box 2697, Paterson, NJ 07509 Phone: 201-278-7070

Masjid An-Nur Ahlus-Sunnah, 18 Fair Street, Paterson, NJ 07524

Mosque Foundation, 80 Grandview Ave., North Caldwell, NJ 07647

Masjid MSA-Bergen Community College, 75 Azalea St., Paramus, NJ 07652

Islamic Teaching Center, 90 Cedar St., Ridgefield Park, NJ 07660

Darul-Islam Masjid (Muslim Community of Bergen), 320 Febry Terrace, Teaneck, NJ 07666 Phone: 201-692-7730

Admiral Family Circle Islamic Community, 509 Cedar Lane 2nd Floor, Teaneck, NJ 07666

Islamic Center of Fairleigh Dicks, 1000 River Rd., Teaneck, NJ 07666 Phone: 201-836-6382

Islamic Center of Asbury Park, 209 Bond St, 401 Sewall Ave., NJ 07712 Phone: 908-988-8406

Islamic Society of Monmouth County, 496 RedHill Road, Middletown, NJ 07748 Phone: 908-671-3321

Oakhurst Masjid, 1 Klein St., Oakhurst, NJ 07755 Phone: 908-531-8606

Saut-ul-Islam, PO Box 1653, Burlington, NJ 08016

Masjid Al-Mubeen, 21 E. High St., Glasboro, NJ 08028 Phone: 609-881-5427

Masjid Al-Muhajireen, Rt 2, Box 118, Cedar Ave., Hammonton, NJ 08037 Phone: 609-561-6759

Masjid Free Haven, 280 Ashland Ave., Lawnside, NJ 08042 Phone: 609-546-2995

Masjid Shahada, 1504 Route 206, Mount Holly, NJ 08060 Phone: 609-265-9370

Shia Association of N. America, 144 Jacqueline Ave., Delran, NJ 08075 Phone: 609-461-2221

Quba School & Islamic Center, 1311 Haddon Ave., Camden, NJ 08103 Phone: 609-541-6782

Admiral Family Community Center,1268 Park Blvd., Camden, NJ 08103 Phone: 609-541-0301

Masjidun-Nur Islamic Learning Center, 1231 Mechanic St., Camden, NJ 08104 Phone: 609-365-2428

Masjid Muhammad, 1071 S. Cole Plaza, Atlantic City, NJ 08401 Phone: 609-347-0788

Masjid Muhammad, 107 N Center St., Atlantic City, NJ 08401

Masjid Muhammad of Al-Islam, 500 Ward Ave., Bordentown, NJ 08505 Phone: 609-298-0500

Islamic Society of Central Jersey, P.O.Box 2039, Princeton, NJ 08543 Phone: 908-329-8126

Masjidul Taqwa, 1001 E State St., Trenton, NJ 08609 Phone: 609-541-3482

Masjid An-Nur, 311 Bellevue Ave., Trenton, NJ 08618

Masjid As-Saffat, 25 Oxford St, 541 W. State St., Trenton, NJ 08618 Phone: 609-392-9141

Masjid Ul-Jihad, 10 Sanhican Drive, Trenton, NJ 08618

Islamic Center of South Jersey, 612 Garfield Avenue, Palmyra, NJ Phone: 609-786-7440

Islamic Society of Ocean County, P.O.Box 4684, Toms River, NJ 08754 Phone: 908-363-1940

Muslim Center of Middlesex County, 142 School St, PO Box 306, Piscataway, NJ 08854 Phone: 908-572-9246

Islamic Society, 5 Hastings Road, Old Bridge, NJ 08857

Muslim Center of Somerset County, P.O. Box 852, Somerville, NJ 08876-0852 Phone: (908) 526-1837

Kafala Community Services, P.O. Box 1067, New Brunswick, NJ 08901 Phone: (908) 214-1547

Noor-ul-Islam, 949 Patton St., New Brunswick, NJ 08902

New Brunswick Islamic Center, 167 Remsen Ave, P.O.Box 481, New Brunswick, NJ 08903 Phone: 908-214-1547

New Mexico

Masjid As-Sabiqun, 1619 Del Monte SW, Albuquerque, NM 87105

Islamic Center of New Mexico, 1100 Yale Blvd SE, Albuquerque, NM 87106 Phone: 505-865-4796

Masjid Muhammad, 901 Edith SE, Albuquerque, NM 87106

Dar-al-Islam, PO Box 180, Abiquiu, NM 87510 Phone: 505-685-4515

Masjid Al-Iman, P.O.Box 146, Abiquiu, NM 87510 Phone: (505) 827-3867

Islamic Society of Socorro, 907 1/2 Annette St., Socorro, NM 87801 Phone: 505-835-3111

The Islamic Center of Las Cruces, 1065 E Boutz, Las Cruces, NM 88001 Phone: 505-522-3363

Portales Islamic Center, 912 W. 15th Lane, Portales, NM 88130 Phone: 505-359-6874

Islamic Center, S. San Francisco & Ocampo, Santa Fe, NM ????? Phone: (505) 988-5122

New York

International Community Center, 145 W 27th St #6E, New York, NY 10001

Masjid Manhattan, 12 Washington Place, New York, NY 10003

Muslim World League, 134 W. 26th St., New York, NY 10001 Phone: (212) 627-4033

BMOC Muslim Society, 199 Chambers St., New York, NY 10007

Masjid Manhattan, 12 Warren St, 2nd Fl., New York, NY 10007 Phone: 914-471-2978

Madina Masjid, 401 E. 11th St., New York, NY 10009 Phone: 212-533-5060

Masjid Al-Farah, 245 W Broadway, New York, NY 10013 Phone: 212-431-4882

Masjid Ar-Rahman, 80 Madison Ave., New York, NY 10016 Phone: 212-868-6666

Islamic Conference, 130 E 40th St, 5th Fl., New York, NY 10016 Phone: 212-883-0140

International Islamic Community, Room# S-1767 U.N. Secretariat, New York, NY 10017

Islamic Fellowship of Hunter Center, 695 Park Ave #121 N 320, New York, NY 10021 Phone: 212-772-5083

Islamic Center of New York, 1 Riverside Dr., New York, NY 10023

Masjid Malcolm Shabazz, 102 W 116th St., New York, NY 10026 Phone: 212-662-2200

Mosque of Islamic Brotherhood, 130 W 113th St., New York, NY 10026 Phone: 212-662-4100

International Muslim Society, 110 W 130 St., New York, NY 10027

Alianza Islamica (for spanish speakers), 1708 Lexington Ave., New York, NY 10029 Phone: 212-427-1142

Islamic Center (Jumah Only), 1 Riverside Dr., New York, NY 10029 Phone: 212-722-5234

The Islamic Center of New York, 1711 3rd Ave., New York, NY 10029 Phone: 212-722-5234

Jihad Society, 2130 1st Ave #812, New York, NY 10029

Al Islam America, PO Box 362, New York, NY 10039

Mostazafan Foundation of New York, 500 5th Ave, 34th Fl., New York, NY 10110

Islamic Society of Mid-Manhattan, P.O.Box 1107 FDR Station, New York, NY 10150

Masjid Ar-Rahman, 29 East 29th St., Apt. 1, New York, NY Phone: (212) 213-4430

The Islamic Center - Green Point, 602 Leonard St., Green Point, NY Phone: (718) 383-6344

Staten Island Masjid, 117 Venduzer St., Staten Island, NY 10301

Staten Island Masjid, 230 Benzigen Ave., Staten Island, NY 10301

Staten Island Masjid, 100 Grand View Terrace, Staten Island, NY 10308 Phone: 718-984-6806

Muslim Majlis of Staten Island, 104 Rhine Ave, PO Box 209, Staten Island, NY 10314 Phone: 718-442-6674

Jihad Society of New York, 635 River Ave., Bronx, NY 10451

Islamic Federation of America, 115 E 168th St., Bronx, NY 10452 Phone: 212-538-6515

Islamic Senior Citizen Club, 936 Woodycrest Ave., Bronx, NY 10452 Phone: 212-585-1564

Makky Jamme Masjid, 115 E. 168th St., Bronx, NY 10452 Phone: 212-681-5943

Masjid Taqwa wa-Jihad, 901 Anderson Ave., Bronx, NY 10452 Phone: 718-538-2474

Sunna wa Jamaat, 2058 Ryer Ave., Bronx, NY10452

Baitus Salaam Jame Masjid, 2703 Decatour Ave., Bronx, NY 10458 Phone: 212-733-0991

Baitul Aman Islamic Center, 2351 New Bold Ave., Bronx, NY 10462 Phone: (718) 904-8828

Masjid Quba, 3520 Dekalb Ave #1F, Bronx, NY 10467 Phone: 718-515-9071

Parkchester Jame Masjid, 1203 Virginia Ave., Bronx, NY10472 Phone: 718-828-4194

Islamic Society of Westchester & Rockland, 22 Brookefield Rd., Mt. Vernon, NY 10552 Phone: 914-668-8786

Masjid Yusuf Shah, 10 S. 2nd Ave., Mt. Vernon, NY 10552 Phone: 914-699-8677

Sunnatullah Masjid, 354 Hunter St., Ossining, NY 10562

Masjid Tawheed, 1000 Main St, P.O.Box 2561, Peekskill, NY 10566 Phone: 914-734-2304

Islamic Cultural Center, 10 Hutchinson Purchase St., Purchase, NY 10577 Phone: 914-253-9400

Islamic Center, 883 Balfour St., Valley Stream, NY 11580 Phone: (516) 825-5104

Islamic Science Foundation, PO Box 250, Purchase, NY 10580

Masjidul Jihadul Akbar, PO Box 364, Middletown, NY 10940 Phone: 914-342-0663

Muslim Peace Fellowship, PO Box 271, 521 North Broadway, Nyack, NY 10960 Phone: (914) 358-4601

Islamic Center of Rockland, P.O.Box 562, Valley Cottage, NY 10989 Phone: 914-634-5617

Islamic Center of Astoria, 21-23 30th Dr., Astoria, NY 11102 Phone: 718-699-5083

Ghousia Jama Masjid, 25-86 31st St., Astoria, NY 11102 Phone: 718-728-2601

Shah Jalal Masjid/ Astoria Islamic Foundation, 25-67 31st St., Astoria, NY 11102 Phone: 718-204-2337

Masjid Al-Birr, 36-05 30 St., Astoria, NY 11102 Phone: 718-784-0336

Astoria Islamic Center, 21-27 27th St., Astoria, NY 11105 Phone: (718) 278-6677

Masjid Dawudi, 143 State St., Brooklyn, NY 11201 Phone: 718-875-6607

Al-Kalima, 191 Atlantic Ave., Brooklyn, NY 11201

Masjid Nur Al-Islam, 3324 Church Ave., Brooklyn, NY 11203

Masjid An-Nur, 1071 New Lots Ave., Brooklyn, NY11208 Phone: 718-827-4879

Masjid Ikhwa, 1135 Eastern Pkwy., Brooklyn, NY 11213Phone: 718-493-0461

Ansar of Islam Inc., 676 St Mark Ave., Brooklyn, NY 11216

Majlis Ashura of NYC, 1221 Atlantic Ave., Brooklyn, NY 11216 Phone: (718) 638-2169

Masjid Abdul Muhsi Khalifah, 120 Madison St., Brooklyn, NY 11216 Phone: 718-783-1279

Masjid Al-Muminin, 1221 Atlantic Ave., Brooklyn, NY 11216Phone: 718-789-0291

Al-Masjid Al-Jamia, 806 St. Johns Place, Brooklyn, NY 11216 Phone: (718) 875-6607

African Islamic Mission, 1390 Bedford Ave., Brooklyn, NY 11216 Phone: 718-638-4607

Masjid Al-Taqwa, 1266 Bedford Ave., Brooklyn, NY 11216 Phone: 718-622-0800

Masjid-e-Khalifa, 1174 Bedford Ave., Brooklyn, NY

Al-Farouq Masjid, 552-4 Atlantic Ave., Brooklyn, NY 11217 Phone: 718-488-8711

Dar Al Quran Association, PO Box 330, Atlantic Ave Station Brooklyn, NY 11217

Bangladesh Muslim Center, 1013 Church Ave., Brooklyn, NY 11218 Phone: 718-282-9230

Masjid Nur Al-Islam, 21 Church Ave., Brooklyn, NY 11218 Phone: 718-435-3237

Masjid of the Crimean Turks, 4509 New Utrecht Ave., Brooklyn, NY 11219

Islamic Society of Bay Ridge, 68-07 5 Ave., Brooklyn, NY 11220 Phone: 718-439-4992

Masjid Fatih, 59-11 8th Ave., Brooklyn, NY 11220 Phone: 718-438-6919

Ansar Allah Community, 719 Bushwick Ave., Brooklyn, NY 11221

Islamic Hall of Knowledge, 548 Hart St., Brooklyn, NY 11221

Universal Order of Love, 544 Hart St., Brooklyn, NY 11221

Masjid As-Salaam, 85 Nassau Ave., Brooklyn, NY 11222 Phone: (718) 383-1238

Albanian American Islamic Community, 1325 Albemarie Rd., Brooklyn, NY 11226

Makki Masjid, 1089 Coney Island Ave., Brooklyn, NY 11230 Phone: 718-859-4485

Masjid Abu Bakr As-Siddiq, 115 Foster Ave., Brooklyn, NY 11230 Phone: 718-833-0011

Umar Masjid/ Islamic Center of Brighton Beach, 230 Neptune Ave., Brooklyn, NY 11230 Phone: 718-648-0887

Saut ul Islam, PO Box 167, Brooklyn, NY 11230

Masjid Ammar Ben Yaser, 4315 8th Ave., Brooklyn, NY 11232 Phone: 718-972-8858

Masjid Alarqam, 651 Banner Ave., Brooklyn, NY 11235 Phone: 718-646-0960

Masjid Al-Muslimeen, 1928 Fulton St (near Ralph Ave), Brooklyn, NY Phone: 718-771-1506

Masjid Ar-Rahman, 330 86th Street, Brooklyn, NY

Masjid Hazrat-i-Abu Bakr, 141-49 33rd Ave., Flushing, NY 11354 Phone: 718-358-6905

Masjid Jamal Uddin Afghani, 149 Cherry Ave., Flushing, NY 11355 Phone: 718-463-8007

Muslim Center of New York - Flushing, 137-58 Geranium Ave., Flushing, NY 11355 Phone: 718-445-2642

American Muslim Mission Center, 105-01 Northern Blvd., Corona, NY 11368 Phone: 718-779-1060

Islamic Center, 101-03 43rd Ave., Flushing, NY 11368 Phone: (718) 478-6653

The Islamic Center/ Masjid AlFalah, 42-12 National Street, Corona, NY 11368 Phone: 718-476-7968

Islamic Society, 79-01 Broadway, Flushing, NY 11373

Masjid Al-Tawfiq, 85-37 Britton Ave., Elmhurst, NY 11373 Phone: 718-779-1519

Islamic Center of Queens, 57-16 37th Ave., Woodside, NY 11377 Phone: 718-803-3747

Masjid Al-Muqaam, 5011 Queens Blvd., Flushing, NY 11377

United Muslim Organization, 94-30 41st Road, Flushing, NY 11377

United Albanian American Islamic Foundation, P.O.Box 4102, Flushing, NY 11386 Phone: 718-381-3853

Islamic Center, 80-40 223rd St., Queens Village, NY 11407

Masjid Al-Qasas, 19103 Linden Blvd., St. Albans, NY 11412

Masjid Al-Abidin, 104-14 127th St., Richmond Hill, NY 11419 Phone: 718-848-8759

The Islamic Foundation, 91-04 182 Pl., Hollis, NY 11423 Phone: 718-523-5046

Islamic Group, 89-41 Springfield Blvd., Queens Village, NY 11427 Phone: (718) 740-3299

Jamaica Islamic Center, 85-37 168th St., Jamaica, NY 11432 Phone: 718-739-3182

Masjid Al-Jamiyah, 107-54 Sutphin Blvd., Jamaica, NY 11435 Phone: 718-658-3632

Masjid Umar Ben Abdel Aziz, 88-29 161st St, P.O.Box 707, Jamaica, NY 11435 Phone: 718-291-1190

Masjidul Istiqaamah, 139-36 87th Rd., Briarwood, NY 11435 Phone: 718-262-0329

Imam Al-Khoei Islamic Center, 89-89 Jamaica Van Wyck Expwy, Jamaica, NY 11435-4123 Phone: 718-297-6520

Muslim Center, 105-01 Northern Blvd., Jamaica, NY 11468Phone: 718-779-1060

Al-Nur Islamic Center, 678 Front St. #E, Hampstead, NY 1550-4505 Phone: 516-883-6905

Masjid Taha, 195 Nassau Road, Roosevelt, NY 11575 Phone: (516) 483-3431

Islamic Center of South Shore, 202 Stuart Ave., Valley Stream, NY 11580 Phone: 516-285-1274

Islamic Center Long Island, 835 Brush Hollow Rd., Westbury, NY 11590 Phone: 516-333-3495

Masjid Daral-Quran, 1514 E 3rd Ave., Bay Shore, NY 11706 Phone: 516-665-9462

Crimean Islamic Society, 24 Greene Dr., Commack, NY 11725

Islamic Center of Huntington, P.O.Box 274, East Northport, NY 11731. (Phone: 516-754-4828)

Long Island Muslim Society, 3066 Hempstead Tpke., Levittown, NY 11756. (Phone: 516-796-1725)

Islamic Association of Long Island, PO Box 0593, Selden, NY 11784 Phone: 516-496-9661

Islamic Unity and Culture Center of Plav-Gusinje, 31-33 12th St., Long Island City, NY Phone: (718) 274-2016

Al-Jamiyat Islamic Center, PO Box 241, 221 Meritt,Wyandanch, NY 11798. Phone: 516-491-1164

Muslim Center, 1305 Straight Path, Wyandanch, NY 11798 Phone: 516-643-8175

Project Allahu Akbar Community Center, 133 N. 22nd St., Wyandanch, NY 11798. Phone: 516-491-1164

Masjid Muhammad, PO Box 200, Coxsackie, NY 12051-0200

Masjid Al-Hidaya, 2339 15th St., Troy, NY 12180. Phone: 518-274-0137

Abdul Muhaimin Islamic Center, P.O.Box 737, Schenectady, NY 12301, Phone: 518-377-2951

Islamic Center of Capital District, PO Box 81, 21 Lansing Rd., Schenectady, NY 12301. Phone: 518-294-6518

Islamic Community of Ulster County, 70 Brodhead Rd., Shohokan, NY 12494. Phone: 914-657-8464

Masjid Al-Rasheed, 8 Eliza Street, Beacon, NY 12508 Phone: 914-831-7903

Masjid Al Jihad Al Akbar, 25 Washington Terrace, Newburgh, NY 12550

Mid-Hudson Islamic Association, 125 All Angels Road, Wappinger Falls, NY 12590 Phone: 914-297-0882

Masjid-ul Mutakabbir, PO Box 21, 462 Main St., Poughkeepsie, NY 12601 Phone: 914-471-4559

Masjidul-Ikhlas, P.O.Box 836, Monticello, NY 12701

Masjid of Islamic Unity, 2503 South Salina St.,Syracuse, NY 13205 Phone: 315-471-9744

Islamic Society of Central NY, 925 Comstock Ave., Syracuse, NY 13210 Phone: 315-637-7536

Muslim Center, 843 Salt Springs Rd., Syracuse, NY 13224 Phone: 315-445-0987

American Muslim Community Center, 2504 S. Salina St., Syracuse, NY 13225 Phone: 315-478-3556

Islamic Center of Northern NY, P.O. Box 432, Watertown, NY 13601

Islamic Center, 427 State St., Carthage, NY 13619 Phone: 315-493-4945

Islamic Organization of Southern Tier, 37-39 Carroll St., Binghampton, NY 13901 Phone: 607-724-9954

Islamic Center of Medina (Shi'a), 414 West Ave., Medina, NY 14103 Phone: 716-798-9806

Islamic Center of West Valley, 10482 Fritz Road, West Valley, NY 14171 Phone: 716-942-3474

Masjid Muhammad, 615 Michigan St., Buffalo, NY14202

Masjid Daru-as-Salaam, 75 East Parade, Buffalo, NY 14211 Phone: 716-896-0725

Masjid Nu'man, 1373 Fillmore Ave., Buffalo, NY 14211 Phone: (716) 891-8766

Masjid Zakaria (Darul Uloom Al-Madania), 182 Sobieski St., Buffalo, NY 14211

Islamic Center, 3268 Main St., Buffalo, NY 14214

Islamic Society of Niagara Frontier, 40 Parker St., Buffalo, NY 14214 Phone: 716-683-1840

Lackawanna Islamic Mosque, 154 Wilkesbarre Ave., Lackawanna, NY 14218 Phone: 716-825-9490

The Islamic Society of Niagara Frontier - Amherst Center, 110 Heim Rd., Amherst, NY 14228

As Sabiqun Islamic Center, 518 Broadway, Elmira, NY 14504

Sufi Masjid, 1529 Fuller Rd., Waterport, NY 14571

Masjid Taqwa, 370 North St., Rochester, NY 14605 Phone: 716-325-9200

Masjid Mujahadin, 46 Glover, Rochester, NY 14611

Turkish Society of Rochester, 2841 Culver Road, Rochester, NY 14622 Phone: 716-266-1980

Islamic Center of Rochester, P.O.Box 23266, Rochester, NY 14692 Phone: 716-442-0117

Jamestown Islamic Society, 99 Hallock St., Jamestown, NY 14701 Phone: 714-373-3404

Jamestown Islamic Society, 112 Whitehill Ave., Jamestown, NY 14701

Islamic Society of Southern Tier, 209 Arland Ave., Olean, NY 14760 Phone: 716-373-3404

Islamic Association of Finger Lakes, 432 Main Street, Big Flats, NY 14814 Phone: 607-562-3869

Ithaca Muslim Community, Cornell, 218 Anable Taylor Hall, Ithaca, NY 14853 Phone: 607-277-6706

North Carolina

Islamic Society of Charlotte, 3313 Chilham Pl., Matthews, NC 23105Phone: 704-542-8314

Community Mosque of Winston-Salem, 1326 East 3rd Street, Winston-Salem, NC 27101 Phone: (910) 724-5554

Masjid Muhammad, 1500 English St., Winston-Salem, NC 27105 Phone: 919-724-0258

Masjid Al-Mu'minun, 1500 Harriett Tubman Blvd, Winston-Salem, NC 27105 Phone: 910-724-0258

Islamic Center of Greensboro, P O Box 987, 107 N Murrow Blv'd (3rd Floor), Greensboro, NC 27402 Phone: (910) 370-9204

Masjid Al-Ummil Ummat, 2109 Martin Luther King Drive, Greensboro, NC 27406

The Islamic Group, 825 C W Florida, Greensboro, NC 27415

Masjid Seifullah, 110 South Haywood St., Raleigh, NC 27601 Phone: (919) 839-0710

Masjid Seifuddin, 110 Lord Anson Dr., Raleigh, NC Phone: 919-212-0588

Islamic Community Development Center, 8213 Wynnewood Drive,Raleigh, NC 27604

Islamic Assoclation of Raleigh, 3020 Ligon St., Raleigh, NC 27607 Phone: 919-467-0826

Masjid Ar-Razzaq, 1009 W Chapel Hill St., Durham, NC 27701

Jamaat Ibad Ar-Rahman, PO Box 1590, Durham, NC 27702-1590

Islamic Center, 1511-13 Memory Lane, Rocky Mount, NC 27801

Muslim Center, 917 Dickerson Ave., Greenville, NC 27835

Islamic Society of Gastonia Mujahideen, 826 Springdale Ln., Gastonia, NC 28052 Phone: 704-867-2489

Islamic Society, 3313 Chilham Place, Matthews, NC 28105 Phone: (704) 537-9399

Islamic Society of Greater Charlotte, 5012 Split Oak Dr., Charlotte, NC 28212 Phone: 704-537-3485

Brittany Masjid, 2619-3 Milton Road, Charlotte, NC 28215

Masjid Muhammad, 1230 Beatties Ford Rd., Charlotte, NC 28216

Masjid Ash-Shaheed, 2717 Tuckaseegee Road, Charlotte, NC Phone: 704-394-6579

Masjid Omar Ibn Sayyid, 1831 Murchison Road, P.O.Box 286, Fayetteville, NC 28302 Phone: 910-488-7322

The Islamic School and Social Center of Fayetteville, 2030 Rosehill Rd., Fayetteville, NC Phone: (910) 630-3136

Al-Kahf Center, Rt 2, Box 433B, Dudley, NC 28333

Masjid Muhammad, 719 1/2 Castle Street, Wilmington, NC 28401 Phone: 919-343-8034

Masjid Muhammad, 711 S 8th St., Wilmington, NC 28401

New Bern Islamic Center, 1726 Washington St., New Bern, NC 28560
Muslim Center, 703 2nd St Dr SW, Conover, NC 28613
Muslim Center, PO Box 7371, Asheville, NC 28807 Phone: 704-253-6428

North Dakota
Islamic Society of Fargo-Moorehead, PO Box 5223, Fargo, ND 58105 Phone: 701-298-3610
Minot Islamic Society, 1440 32nd Ave SW #10, Minot, ND 58701 Phone: 701-852-8070

Ohio
Islamic Society of Greater Columbus, 580 Riverview Dr., Columbus, OH 43202 Phone: 614-262-1310
Masjid Al Islam, 1677 Oak St., Columbus, OH 43203 Phone: 614-252-0338
Muhammad Mosque, 440 Fairfield Avenue, Columbus, OH 43203 Phone: 614-252-2626
Islamic Foundation of Central Ohio, 325 Crain Ave., Columbus, OH 43205 Phone: 614-245-3251
Masjid Deen Al-Fitrah, 815 E. Mound St., Columbus, OH 43206
Ahl Sunnat wal Jamaat, PO Box 151151, Columbus, OH 43215
Muslim Center, 431 Evans Rd., Marion, OH 43302 Phone: 216-581-4935
Islamic Center of Greater Toledo, 25877 Scheider Rd., Perrysburg, OH 43551
The Muslim Community Center, 724 Tecumseh, Toledo, OH 43620 Phone: 419-385-0609
Masjid Saad, 4346 Secor Rd., Toledo, OH 43623 Phone: 419-292-1492
Toledo Islamic Academy, 4346 Secor Rd., Toledo OH 43623 Phone: 419-292-1493
Masjidul-Haqq, 828 Ewing St., Toledo, OH 43607 Phone: 419-241-9522
Masjid Al-Madinah, 1300 Reid Ave., Lorain, OH 44052 Phone: 216-244-1361
Masjid Bilal, 7401 Euclid Ave., Cleveland, OH 44103
Masjid Dhul-Qarnain, 5618 Luther, Cleveland, OH 44103
Masjid Al-Warithdeen, 7301 Superior, Cleveland, OH 44103
Masjid Al-Ansari, 3520 E. 116th St., Cleveland, OH 44105,
Islamic Mosque of Cleveland, 12740-42 Lorain Avenue, Cleveland, OH 44111 Phone: 216-941-0120
First Cleveland Mosque, 13405 Union Ave., Cleveland, OH 44120
Masjid Muhammad, 431 Evans Rd., Marion, OH 44120
Islamic Center of Greater Cleveland, 6055 W. 130th St. Parma, OH 44130 Phone: 216-362-0786
Islamic Society of Greater Kent, 325 Crain Ave., Kent, OH 44240 Phone: 216-678-4252
Jaffery Union of NE Ohio, 1460 Manchester Road, Akron, OH 44314 Phone:

(330) 745-2410

Islamic Society of Greater Youngstown, 1670 Homewood Ave., Youngstown, OH 44501 Phone: 330-743-3742

Islamic Center, PO Box 418, Youngstown, OH 44501 Phone: 216-743-3030

Masjid Muhammad, 131 Woodland Ave., Youngstown, OH 44501 Phone: 216-743-3030

Muslim Brotherhood, 851 Fairfax Ave., Youngstown, OH 44505

Islamic Society of Northeastern Ohio, 4848 Higbee Ave NW, Canton, OH 44718-2528 Phone: 216-492-7827

Islamic Center of Greater Cincinnati, 8090 Plantation Drive, Cincinnati, OH 45069 Phone: 513-755-3280

Cincinnati Islamic Center, 3809 Woodford Rd., Cincinnati, OH 45213

Islamic Association of Cincinnati, 2515 Fairview Ave., Cincinnati, OH 45219

Islamic Association of Cincinnati, 3668 Clifton Ave., Cincinnati, OH 45220 Phone: 513-621-6558

Masjid Ar-Raheem, 1432-34 Elm St., Cincinnati, OH ?????

Islamic Community Center, 299 E Market St., Xenia, OH 45385 Phone: 513-376-4111

Muslim Center, PO Box 244, Dayton, OH 45401 Phone: 513-423-4031

Islamic Center of Dayton, 26 Josie St., Dayton, OH 45403 Phone: 513-879-3951

Dayton Islamic Center, 2170 Malvern Ave., Dayton, OH 45406

Masjid of Islam, 637 Randolph St., Dayton, OH 45406

Miami Valley Islamic Association, 1800 S Burnett Rd., Springfield, OH 45505 Phone: 513-322-3266

Muslim Center, 743 W Liberty St., Springfield, OH 45506 Phone: 513-323-8781

Masjid An-Nur, 743 W. Liberty St., Springfield, OH ?????

Islamic Center of Athens/MSA of Ohio University, 13 Stewart St., Athens, OH 45701 Phone: 614-594-3890

Islamic Center, 435 S Collette St., Lima, OH 45805 Phone: 419-277-6765

Masjid Abu-Bakr El-Saddik, 332 W Buckeye St., Ada, OH 45810 Phone: 419-634-3000

Oklahoma

Islamic Society of Norman, 420 E Lindsey, Norman, OK 73069 Phone: 405-364-5341

Islamic Society of Edmond, UC Box 4113, 100 N University Dr., Edmond, OK 73083 Phone: 405-340-4160

Islamic Society of Edmond, 525 N University Dr., Edmond, OK 73034 Phone: (405) 741-1077

Islamic Society of Greater Oklahoma City, 2809 N Indiana, OK 73106 Phone: 405-524-4341

Masjid Al-Mu'minun, 1322 NE 23rd, Oklahoma City, OK 73111 Phone: 405-

424-1471

Muslim Center, PO Box 2134, 2016 Cache Rd., Lawton, OK 73245 Phone: 405-855-5203

Islamic Dawah Center, 1621 S.W. Pennsylvania, Lawton, OK 73501

Muslim Community of Al-Jihad, PO Box 514, Granite, OK 73547 Phone: 405-535-5216

Tulsa Dawah Muslim Community, 17643 S. Tacoma, Mounds, OK 74047

Islamic Society of Stillwater, 616 N Washington St., Stillwater, OK 74075 Phone: 405-744-4034

Islamic Society of Tulsa, 431 S Birmingham, Tulsa, OK 74104 Phone: 918-622-9364

Islamic Community Center, 1213-1/2 E. Pine St., Tulsa, OK 74106

MCA Ponca City Chapter, 2500 Wildwood, Ponca City, OK 74604 Phone: 405-762-7732

Oregon

Bilal Mosque Association, 4115 SW 160th Ave., Beaverton, OR 97007 Phone: 503-591-7233

Islamic Society of Greater Portland, 9775 SW Pawnee Path, Tualatin, OR 97062 Phone: 206-574-5216

Muslim Community Center of Portland, 3801 N.E. Martin Luther King Blvd., Portland, OR 97211 Phone: 503-281-7691

Masjid As-Sabr, 10200 SW Capitol Hwy, Portland, OR 97219 Phone: 503-293-6553

Salman Al-Farsi Islamic Center, PO Box 35, 610 N.W. Kings Blvd., Corvallis, OR 97339 Phone: 503-758-0329

The Islamic Society of Eugene, 1856 W Broadway, Eugene, OR 97403 Phone: 503-485-0899

Pennsylvania

Nasab Islamic Center, 2007 Center Ave., Beaver Falls, PA 15010

Muslim Community Center of Greater Pittsburgh, 233 Seaman Lane, Monroeville, PA 15146 Phone: 412-373-0101

Masjid Mumin, 537 Paulson Ave. East Liberty, Pittsburgh, PA 15206 Phone: 412-363-1237

Islamic Center of Pittsburgh, P.O.Box 19763, Pittsburgh, PA 15208 Phone: 412-682-5555

Masjid Attawheed, 1001 East Entry Drive, Pittsburgh, PA 15216 Phone: 412-571-1003

First Masjid of Islam, 1831 Wylie Ave., Pittsburgh, PA 15219:

Masjid Al-Awwal, 1911 Wylie Ave., Pittsburgh, PA 15219 Phone: 412-471-1036

Masjid Al-Nur/ An-Nur Islamic Center, 303 Trenton, Wilkinsburg, PA 15221

Phone: 412-363-3545

Masjid Pittsburgh, 7222 Kelly St., Pittsburgh, PA 15224 Phone: 412-241-8850

Islamic Center of Pittsburgh, 4100 Bigelow Blvd., Oakland, PA Phone: 814-682-5555

Masjid Al Fajr, 2009 W 3rd St., Chester, PA 15334

Islamic Society of Greater New Castle, 1229 Finch St, P.O.Box 722, New Castle, PA 16103 Phone: 412-656-0760

Islamic Cultural Center of Erie, 9 East 12th St., Erie, PA 16501

Islamic Society of Central Pennsylvania, PO Box 10185 Calder Square, State College, PA 16805 Ph: 814-238-3017

Masjid Muhammad, 1725 Market St., Harrisburg, PA 17103 Phone: 717-238-2272

Islamic Center, 1725 Martin Luther King Blvd., Harrisburg, PA 17104 Phone: 717-238-2272

Islamic Society of Greater Harrisburg, 407 North Front Street, Steelton, PA 17113 Phone: 717-939-3107

Islamic Society of Susquehanna Valley, 4th and Arch St., Sunbury, PA 17801 Phone: 717-286-9995

Islamic Center of Lehigh Valley, 20 North 9th St., Emmaus, PA 18049 Phone: 610-965-6752

IPA of North America, 842 Hamilton Mall #33, Allentown, PA 18101 Phone: 215-432-6355

Stroudsburg Islamic Center, RR 7, Box 7498, Stroudsburg, PA 18360, Phone: 717-421-4108

Islamic Association of NE Pennsylvania, 679 Carey Ave., Wilkes Barre, PA 18702 Phone: 717-824-7246

Masjid al-Noor (Islamic Center of NorthEastern PA), P.O. Box 5061, WilkesBarre, PA 18710 Phone: 823-9660

Masjid As Sabiqun, 19 W 3rd St., Chester, PA 19013 Phone: 215-872-1019

Masjid Al Fajr, 2009 W 3rd St., Chester, PA 19015 Phone: 215-494-5554

Jamia Masjid, 4300 Spruce St., Apt. C104, Philadelphia, PA 19104

International Muslim Brotherhood, 4637 Lancaster Ave., Philadelphia, PA 19121

Masjid Salfia, 3116 Ridge Ave., Philadelphia, PA 19121 Phone: 215-232-9475

Al-Aqsa Islamic Society, 1501 N. Germantown Ave., Philadelphia, PA 19122 Phone: 215-765-2743

Makkah Mosque, 1319 W Susquehanna Ave., Philadelphia, PA 19122 Phone: 215-978-9508

Masjid Al Hashar, 2832 N 22nd St., Philadelphia, PA 19122

Albania Mosque, 157 West Girard Ave., Philadelphia, PA 19123

Masjid Bawa Muhaiyaddeen, 5820 Overbrook Ave., Philadelphia, PA 19131

Phone: 215-879-6300

Philadelphia Masjid, 4700 Wyalusing Ave., Philadelphia, PA 19131 Phone: 215-877-8600

Minaret Muhammadi Ministry, 1900 N 54th St Philadelphia, PA 19131-3134

Masjid Al-Hashr, 2823 N 22nd St., Philadelphia, PA 19132 Phone: 215-225-2084

Muslim Society of Delaware Valley, 2209 N Front St., Philadelphia, PA 19133 Phone: 215-634-1102

The Muhammad Family, 6032 N Camac St., Philadelphia, PA 19141-3228

Masjid Muhajadeen, 413 S 60th St., Philadelphia, PA 19143 Phone: 215-471-5526

Islamic Council of Delaware Valley, 918 E Sedgwick St., Philadelphia, PA 19150

Masjidullah, 7700 Ogontz Ave., Philadelphia, PA 19150 Phone: 215-424-8022

Muslim Society of Delaware Valley, 157 Girard Ave., Philadelphia, PA 19154

Islamic Center of Coatesville, 710 E Lincoln Hwy, Coatesville, PA 19320

Masjid Al-Bedayah, 516 Walnut St., Coatesville, PA 19320 Phone: 215-380-8561

Islamic Society of Greater Valley Forge, 958 Valley Forge Road, Devon, PA 19333 Phone: 610-688-2209

Islamic Center of Chester County, 1001 Pottstown Pike, West Chester, PA 19380 Phone: 610-344-9488

Islamic Society of Chester County, Mail Box 3042, West Chester, PA 19381 Phone: 215-444-1415

Norristown Masjid, 931 Green St., Norristown, PA 19401 Phone: 215-275-8668

Rhode Island

Masjid Al-Islam Inc., 40 Sayles Hill Road, North Smithfield, RI 02896 Phone: (401) 762-0107

Masjid Muhammad, 234 Pavillion Ave., Providence, RI 02907 Islamic Center of Rhode Island, 582 Cranston St., Providence, RI 02907 Phone: 401-274-3986

South Carolina

Afroamerican Islamic Umma Inc., 1139 Copeland St # 125, Newburg, SC 29108

Masjid At Taqwa, 701 Russell St NE, Orangeburg, SC 29115-6047 Phone: (803) 534-2281

Masjid Al-Muslimin, 1929 Gervais St., Columbia, SC 29201 Phone: 803-254-7542

Masjid As-Salaam, 5119 Monticello Rd., Columbia, SC 29203 Phone: (803)

466

252-9477

Masjid Muhammad, 4000 Monticello Road, Columbia, SC 29203

Charleston Muslim Center, 1998 Hugo Ave., Charleston, SC 29405 Phone: 803-554-1773

Islamic Society of Charleston, 195 Line St., Charleston, SC 29403 Phone: (803) 722-3483

Islamic Association of Charleston, 2370 Otranto Rd., Charleston, SC 29406 Phone: 803-722-4158

Masjid Muhammad/Florence Masjid, 410 N. Coit St., Florence, SC 29501 Phone: 803-669-9982

Conway Islamic Center, 1808 Race Path Ave.,Conway, SC 29526 Phone: (803) 397-0811

Islamic Society of Greenville, PO Box 25721, 2701 Wade Hampton Blvd., Greenville, SC 29615 Phone: 864-292-2219

Muslim Center, 808 Geinsberg Dr., Anderson, SC 29621 Phone: 864-766-0924

Masjid Muhammad, 1019 Arlington Ave, P.O.Box 10301, Rock Hill, SC 29731 Phone: (803) 328-5865

South Dakota

Islamic Society of Brookings, 803 13th Ave., Brookings, SD 57006 Phone: 605-697-6187

Tennessee

Islamic Center of Nashville, 2515 12th Ave S., Nashville, TN 37205 Phone: (615) 385-9379

Muslim American Community Center, 2416 Batavia St., Nashville, TN 37208

Muslim Community Center, 2418 Batavia St., Nashville, TN 37208 Phone: (615) 320-5126

Muslim American Community, 2420 Batavia Street, Nashville, TN 37208

Masjid Al-Islam, 2508 Clifton Ave., Nashville, TN 37209 Phone: (615) 329-1646

Masjid Qur'aan wa Sunnah, 2805 Gallatin Pke., Nashville, TN 37215 Phone: 615-226-5965

Muslim Community Center, 504 Kilmer St., Chattanooga, TN 37404 Phone: 615-624-2098

Chattanooga Muslim Center, 1410 Cemetery Ave., Chattanooga, TN 37408 Phone: 615-756-4917

Muslim Community of North East Tennessee, PO. Box 23557, Johnson City, TN 37614 Phone: 615-928-0753

Masjid Muhammad, I 709 College St., Knoxville, TN 37921 Phone: 615-637-8172

Muslim Community, PO Box 51511, Knoxville, TN 37950 Phone: 615-974-

9343

Masjid Annoor, 100 Thirteenth Street, Knoxville, TN 37916 Phone: 423-637-8172

Lake County Muslim Community, Rt 1, Box 330, Tiptonville, TN 38079

Masjid Muhammad - Al Muminun, 4412 S. Third St., Memphis, TN 38109 Phone: (901) 789-1904

Masjid Al-Noor, 3529 Mynders Ave., Memphis, TN 38111 Phone: (901) 324-5002

Muslim Society of Memphis, 1065 Stratford Rd., Memphis, TN 38122 Phone: 901-685-8906

Muslim Center, Jackson, TN 38301

Texas

Islamic Society of Texas, 1817 Independence Dr., Grand Prairie, TX 75052 Phone: 214-641-7131

Islamic Society of Irving, 230 1/2 E Grauwyler, Irving, TX 75061 Phone: 214-721-9136

Islamic Association of N Texas, 840 Abrams Rd., Richardson, TX 75081 Phone: 214-231-5698

Muslim Marriage Service, 13618A Co. Rd. 748, Rosharon, TX 77583 Phone: (713)-595-3450

Islamic Mosque at Texoma, PO Box 2666, Sherman, TX 75090 Phone: 903-786-3395

Masjid Ansar Allah, 4410 Second Ave., Dallas, TX 75210

Dallas Masjid of Al-Islam, 2604 S Harwood St., Dallas, TX 75215 Phone: 214-421-3839

Masjid Ansar-Allah, 3455 Roberts Ave., Dallas, TX 75215 Phone: 817-654-1947

Islamic Association of North Texas, 840 Abrams Rd., Richardson, TX 75243

Islamic Services Foundation, Box 742342, Dallas, TX 75374-2342 Phone: 214-907-9007

Islamic Society of Arlington, 100 Madinah Dr., Arlington, TX 76010 Phone: 817-461-8415

Al-Qur'an was-Sunnah Society, 1526 S Center St., Arlington, TX 76010 Phone: 817-548-3134

Islamic Society of Denton, 1105 Green Lee St., Denton, TX 76021 Phone: 817-566-5927

Masjid Ansar Allah, PO Box 883, Fort Worth, TX 76101-0883

Masjid Hassan, 1201 E Allen Ave., Fort Worth, TX 76104 Phone: 817-927-9871

Islamic Association of Terrant County, 4801 Fletcher Ave., Fort Worth, TX 76107 Phone: 817-737-8104

Masjid Shakir Dawan, 2605 Ennis Ave., Fort Worth, TX 76111

Masjid Al-Seddiq, 2432 New Robinson Rd., Waco, TX 76706 Phone: 817-662-5054

Islamic Society, 11815 Adel Rd., Houston, TX 77014 Phone: 713-537-1946

First Talim Masjid Muhammad, 505 East 401/2 St., Houston, TX 77018

Masjid Muhammad, 505 East 40 1/2 St., Houston, TX 77018

Islamic Center, 14561 S Main, Houston, TX 77035 Phone:713-729-7666

Islamic Society, 1209 Conrad Sauer Dr., Houston, TX 77043-4306 Phone: 713-464-4720

Masjid Muhammad, 11830 Corona Ln., Houston, TX 77072 Phone: 713-498-6666

Houston Masjid of Al-Islam, 6641 Bellfort Ave., Houston, TX 77087

Islamic Society, 8803 Old Galveston Rd., Houston, TX 77089 Phone: 713-947-0394

Islamic Society of Greater Houston, 3110 Eastside Dr., Houston, TX 77098 Phone: 713-524-6615

Islamic Center, 10415 Synott, Sugarland, TX 77478 Phone: 713-495-3403

Galveston Islamic Society, 2642 Gerol Dr., Galveston, TX 77551 Phone: 409-744-4129

Islamic Society of Triplex, 1270 West cardinal Dr., Beaumont, TX 77705 Phone: 409-842-5349

Islamic Center, 1503 Lakewood Village, Baytown, TX 77752

Islamic Community of Bryan, 417 Stasney St., College Station, TX 77840 Phone: 409-846-4222

Islamic Center of San Antonio, 11216 Javalin Trail, Helotes, TX 78023 Phone: 512-695-5373

Masjid Muhammad, 1702 Hayes, San Antonio, TX 78202 Phone: 512-224-5767

Islamic Center of San Antonio, PO Box 290402, San Antonio, TX 78280-1802 Phone: 512-927-3887

Islamic Society of Kingsville, PO Box 949, Kingsville, TX 78364 Phone: 512-592-7870

Rio Grande Valley Islamic Center, 501 E. Pike Blvd, P.O. Box 421, Weslaco, TX 78596
Phone: 210-969-8549

Austin Mosque, 1906 Nueces St., Austin, TX 78705 Phone: 512-442-6317

Muslim Center, PO Box 18812, Austin, TX 78744 Phone: 512-441-6031

Islamic Center of Amarillo, 601 Quail Creek Dr., Amarillo, TX 79121 Phone: 806-358-1615

Muslim Center, PO Box 5842, Lubbock, TX 79403 Phone: 806-762-5979

Islamic Center of the South Plains, 3419 LaSalle Avenue, Lubbock, TX 79407 Phone: 806-797-8026

Islamic Association of West Texas, 4604 Tammy Cove, Midland, TX 79703 Phone: 915-699-5208

Muslim Association of West Texas, PO Box 9386, Midland, TX 79708 Phone:

915-694-5814
Islamic Center of El Paso, 1600 N Kansas, El Paso, TX 79902 Phone: 915-593-1381

Utah
Ogden Islamic Society, 5392 S 1900 W#C, Roy, UT 84067 Phone: 801-479-0589
Islamic Society of Salt Lake City, 740 S. 700 East, Salt Lake City, UT 84102 Phone: 801-364-7822
American Muslim Cultural Association, P.O. Box 561, Logan, UT 84321-0561, Phone: 801-753-5787
Logan Islamic Center, 748 N 600 E., Logan, UT 84321 Phone: 801-753-2491

Vermont
Islamic Society of Vermont Inc., P.O. Box 476, Essex Junction, VT 05453 Phone: (802) 388-3227

Virginia
Jamaat Al Muslimeen, PO Box 43, Annandale, VA 22003
Islamic Community Center of Virginia, 6010 Columbia Pike, Annandale, VA 22003-9453 Phone: 703-578-1895
Islamic Center of Northern Virginia, 4420 Shirley Gate, P.O.Box 789, Fairfax, VA 22030 Phone: 703-941-6558
World Assembly of Muslim Youths (WAMY), P.O. Box 8096, Falls Church, VA 22041 Phone: 703-931-7239
Dar Al-Hijra, 3159 Row St., Falls Church, VA 22044 Phone: 703-536-1030
International Islamic Society, PO Box 5132, Falls Church, VA22044
Islamic Center of Northern Virginia, PO Box 4336, Falls Church, VA 22044
All Dulles Area Muslim Society (ADAMS), 500 Grove Street, Herndon, VA 22070 Phone: 703-318-0529
Muslim Association of Virginia, P.O.Box 2551,Woodbridge, VA 22193
Masjid Muhammad, 2911 I5th E Broad St., Richmond, VA 23201
Masjidullah of Richmond, 2211 North Ave., Richmond, VA 23222 Phone: 804-321-9778
Masjid Bilal, PO Box 8064, 400 Chimborzazo Blvd., Richmond, VA 23223 Phone: 804-226-4099
Islamic Center of Virginia, 1241 Buford Rd, PO Box 35051, Richmond, VA 23235 Phone: 804-320-7333
Islamic Center of MCV, PO Box 726, Richmond, VA 23298
Masjid Bilal Ibn Rabah, 2837 Villa Circle 2, Norfolk, VA 23504
Norfolk Masjid, 3401 Granby St., Norfolk, VA 23504 Phone: 804-623-2628
Masjid William Salaam, 614 W. 35th St., Norfolk, VA 23508
Masjid Muhammad, 1145 Hampton Ave., Newport News, VA 23607 Phone:

804-245-6514
Muslim Community of Tidewater, 530 Lasalle Ave., Hampton, VA 23661
Phone: 804-723-2892
Mosque & Islamic Ctr of Hampton Roads, 22 Tide Mill Ln., Hampton, VA
23666 Phone: 804-838-4756
Siraj Muslim, 185 Revelle Dr., Newport News, VA 23802The
Orthodox Muslim Group, PO Box 1000, Fed Ref of Petersburg, Petersburg,
VA 23803
Petersburg Islamic Center, 503 W. Washington St., Petersburg, VA 23803
Phone: 804-861-9562
Muslim Center, 1106-08 E 26th St., Norfolk, VA 24016 Phone: 804-627-
1538
Masjid An-Nur, 2227 Clifton Ave., Roanoke, VA 24017
Islamic Society of New River Valley, 1302 North Main St., Blacksburg, VA
24060 Phone: 540-961-5210
Islamic Center of Blacksburg, P.O. Box 11629, Blacksburg, VA 24062-1629
Masjid Muhammad, 1011 W Fayette St., Maninsville, VA 24112
Danville Masjid, 206 Burrett St., Danville, VA 24541

Washington
Islamic Center of Eastside, 15100 SE 38th St. 101, Suite # 786, Bellevue,
WA 98006 Phone: 206-746-0398
Masjid Al-Taqwa, 1911 S.W. Campus Dr, P.O.Box 317, Federal Way, WA
98023
Evergreen Islamic Institute, PO Box 1762, Lynnwood, WA 98036 Phone: 206-
523-2855
Masjid Dar al-Arqam, 6210 188th St. SW, Lynnwood, WA 98036 Phone: 206-
774-8852
Omar Al-Farooq Mosque, 5507 238th St. SW, Mountlake Terrace, Seattle, WA
98043 Phone: 206-776-6162
Downtown Muslim Association, 1111 3rd Ave, Suite 2870, Seattle, WA 98107
Phone: (206) 723-7491
Jamiul Muslimun Mosque, 5945 39th Ave S., Seattle, WA 98118 Phone: 206-
723-7677
Al-Yasin Mosque, 2210 Cherry St., Seattle, WA 98122 Phone: 206-329-9457
Iah San Mosque, 12516 22nd Ave NE, Seattle, WA 98125 Phone: 206-365-
7120
Islamic Center of Seattle, 1420, NE, Northgate Way, Seattle, WA 98125
Phone: 206-363-3013
Al-Multaqa al-Islamia, P.O. Box 75704, Seattle, WA 98125 Phone: 206-778-
5352
South Seattle Islamic Center, 3040 S. 150th St., Seatac, WA 98188
Mas'alah Muslim Center, 6114 S. Ainsworth, Tacoma, WA 98408

Tacoma Islamic Center, 2010 Bridgeport Ave SW, Tacoma, WA 98409 Phone: (360) 565-0314

Islamic Center, 2523 S Ainsworth, Tacoma, WA 98415 Phone: 206-383-4862

An-Nur Mosque, 8005 Martin Way, # 12, Olympia, WA 98506 Phone: 206-459-1993

Islamic Society of SW Washington, 2109 NW 47th Avenue, Camas, WA 98607

Pullman Islamic Center, 1155 Stadium Way, Pullman, WA 99163 Phone: 509-334-7600

Spokane Islamic Center, E. 505 Wedgewood, Spokane, WA 99208 Phone: 509-482-2608

Islamic Centre of Tri-Cities, PO Box 464, 3100 Van Diesen, Richland, WA 99352 Phone: 509-375-5071

West Virginia

Muslim Center, PO Box 1124, Charleston, WV 25325

Islamic Association of West Virginia, 325 Central Ave.,Logan, WV 25601 Phone: 304-752-7649

Muslim Assoc. of Huntington, 1628 13th Ave., Huntington, WV 25701 Phone: 304-522-3455

Islamic Center of Morgantown, PO Box 140, Morgantown, WV 26507 Phone: 304-598-7396

Wisconsin

Islamic Association of Greater Milwaukee, 16860 Golf Pkwy, Brookfield, WI 53005

Albanian American Islamic Society, 6001 88th Ave, P.O.Box 361, Kenosha, WI 53140 Phone: (414) 654-0575

Islamic Foundation Libertyville, 3322 15th St., Kenosha, WI 53144 Phone: (414) 552-8239

Muslim Community Center, 1636 N 14th St., Milwaukee, WI 53205

Northside Islamic Center, 2401 W. Vine, Milwaukee, WI 53205

Masjid Sultan Muhammad, 2475 N. M.L. King Drive, Milwaukee, WI 53212

The Islamic Center, 1956 Linden Ave., Racine, WI 53403

Muslim Center, 419-21 High St., Racine, WI 53404

Masjid Al-Haqq, 1146 Wisconsin Ave., Beloit, WI 53511

Islamic Center of Madison, 21 N Orchard St., Madison, WI 53715 Phone: 608-251-4668

Masjid-us-Sunnah, P.O.Box 5387, Madison, WI 53705-5387 Phone: (608) 277-1855

Islamic Center, 527 2nd St. W, Altoona, WI 54720 Phone: 715-831-1560

Fox Valley Islamic Society, 103 Kappel Dr., Appleton, WI 54915 Phone: (414) 722-7860

Wyoming
The Islamic Center of Laramie, 903 Harney St., Laramie, WY 82070 Phone: 307-721-8810

Tourist Destinations
(Not meant to be a complete list)

Bermuda
Masjid Muhammad, #1 Cedar Ave, P.O.Box HM1508, Hamilton, Bermuda HMSX

The Virgin Islands
Virgin Islands Islamic Society, 84-85 Herman Hill, PO Box 659, Kingshill, St. Croix, VI 00851

The West Indies
Masjid-Ur-Rahman, 20 IERE Village Princess Town, Trinidad, West Indies Phone: 001-809-557673
Muslim Community of Dominica, Ross University School of Medicine, P.O.Box 266, Portsmouth, Commonwealth of Dominica West Indies.

APPENDIX 2

Islamic Center Directory, Canada

The information compiled here initially comes from ISNA's directory of Masajid and Islamic Centers, the compilation published by the Muslim World League Office in Toronto, Ont., and the Muslim Guide to Toronto, published by Ethno Lingua in Mississauga, Ont. Additions and corrections have also been added from various sources.

Atlantic Provinces

Muslim Association of Newfoundland, Suite 75, Box 51 St John's, NF A1C 5H4 Phone: 709-726-9005

Islamic Assoc. of the Maritimes, 42 Leaman Dr., Dartmouth, NS B2Y 5Y2 Phone: 902-420-1676

Maritime Muslim Academy, 6225 Chebucto Road, Halifax, NS B3L 1K7 Phone: 902-429-9067

Islamic Assoc. of the Maritimes, Box 443 Stn. "M" Bedford Row, Halifax, NS B3J 2P8 Phone: 902-469-9490

Islamic Information Centre, 8 Laurel Lane, Halifax, NS B3M 2P6 Phone: 902-445-2494

Muslim Association of New Brunswick, 1100 Rothsey Rd. Saint John, NB E2H 2H8 Phone: 506-693-7713

Prince Edward Island Muslim Group, 12 Poplar Ave., Charlottetown, PE C1A 6S7 Phone: 902-566-0678

Quebec

Islamic Cultural Centre, C.P. 8817, Ste. Foy, QC G1V 4N7 Phone: 418-832-9710

Trois Riviers Mosque, 3009 Blvd., De Forges, Trois Riviers, QC G8Z 1V3 Phone: 819-373-3891

Nour El-Islam Mosque, 4675 Rue Amiens, Montreal, QC H1H 2H6 or H1H 5L5

As-Sunnah An-Nabawyah Assoc., 7220 Hutchinson St., Montreal, QC H3N 1Z1 Phone: 514-844-2029

Al-Sunnah Al-Nabawiah Mosque, (Address not available) Phone: 514-278-8441

El-Kairouane Mosque, 3726 Rue Jean Talon Est., Montreal, QC H2A 1X9 Phone: 514-728-2922

Masjid as-Salam, 16 Ontario St., Montreal, QC ??? ???

Fatih Sultan Mehmed Mosque, 7387 Rue St Laurent, Montreal, QC H2R 1W7 Phone: 514-272-0009

Al Oumma Al Islamaya Mosque, 1590 Boul St Laurent, Montreal, QC H2X 2S9 Phone: 514-843-7866

Al-Ummah Mosque, 20-70 Clark, Montreal, QC H2X 2R7 Phone: 514-843-7866

Al-Ummah Al-Islamia Mosque, 1245 Rue St. Dominique, Montreal, QC H2X 2W4 Phone: 514-879-8677

Fatima Mosque, 2012 St Dominique, Montreal, QC H2X 2X1 Phone: 514-285-1893

Islamic Society of McGill, 3480 McTavish #b09 Montreal, QC H3A 1X9 Phone: 514-284-5107

Islamic Society of Concordia, 2090 MacKay, Montreal, QC H3G 2J1

Mountain Sights Mosque, 7835 Montain Sights #83, Montreal, QC H4P 2B1 Phone: 514-737-7586

Al-Bait Ul-Mukarram, No Address Given, Phone: 514-737-8671

Muslim Community of Quebec, 7445 Chester Ave NDG Montreal, QC H4V 1M4 Phone: 514-484-2967

Islamic School of Montreal, 7435 Chester Ave., Montreal, QC H4V 1M4 Phone: 514-484-8845

Information Centre on Islam, 2054 St-Denis #2, Montreal, QC H2X 3K7 Phone: 514-844-2029

Islamic Center of West Island, 3683 St. Jean Blvd., Dollard Des Ormeaux, QC ??? ??? Phone: 514-624-5748

Dorval Mosque, No Address Given, Phone: 514-633-5353

Jamia Islamia Mosque, 2144 Rue St Helene, Longueuil, QC J4K 3T6 Phone: 514-674-4433

Jamia Islamia Mosque, No Address Given, Phone: 514-442-2303

Islamic Center of Quebec, 2520 Chemin Laval Rd., Ville St Laurent, QC H4L 3A1 Phone: 514-331-5582

Islamic Assoc. of Longueuil, 417 Cartier #5, Longueuil, QC J4K 4B7 Phone: 514-651-9492

Makkah Al-Mukarramah Mosque, 11900 Boul Gouin, Pierrefonds, QC H2Z 1V6 or H8Z 1V6

Islamic Centre of South Montreal, 1885 Rue Nielsen, St Hubert, QC J4T 1P1 Phone: 514-443-3482

Islamic Circle of North America, P.O. Box 24530, 1155 Rome Blvd., Brossard, QC J4W 3J1 Phone: 514-637-2755

Ontario

The Ottawa Muslim Association, PO Box 2952 Stn D, 257 Northwestern Ave., Ottawa, ON K1P 5W9 or K1Y 0M1 Phone: 613-725-0004

Islamic School of Ottawa, 10 Coral Ave., Nepean, ON K2P 5Z6 Phone: 613-727-5066

Ottawa Muslim Community Circle, P.O. Box 5706, Merivale Depot, Nepean, ON K2C 3M1

Muslim Arab Youth Association, P.O. Box 741 Stn "B", Ottawa, ON K1P 5P8 Phone: 613-745-0837

Islamic Shia Ithna-Asheri Association of Ottawa, 37 Brady Ave., Kanata, ON K2K 2R2 Phone: 613-592-8368

Islamic Society of Kingston, PO Box 2021, Kingston, ON K7L 5J8 Phone: 613-389-7613

Islamic Center of Oshawa, PO Box 1062, Oshawa, ON L1H 7H8

Oshawa Islamic Centre, 26 McGrigor St., Oshawa, ON L1H 1X7 Phone: 905-436-9310

Ja'ffari Islamic Centre, 7340 Bayview Ave., Thornhill, ON L3T 2R7 Phone: 905-881-1763 /

As-Sadiq Islamic Schools, 9000 Bathurst Street, Thornhill, ON L4J 8A7 Phone: 905-771-9917

Phone: 416-261-9112

Ihsan Muslim Heritage Society, 138 Yorkland Street, Unit 173, Richmond Hill, ON L4S 1J1 Phone: (905) 770-5696

Malton Islamic Association, 7344 Custer Crescent, Malton, ON L4T 3K7 Phone: 905-671-0891

Albanian Muslim Society of Toronto, 564 Annette St., Toronto, ON M6S 2C2 Phone: 416-763-0612

Canadian Society of Muslims, P.O. Box 143 Station "P", Toronto, ON M5S 2S7 Phone: 905-272-5959

Islamic Society of North America, P.O. Box 160 Stn. "P", Toronto, ON M5S 2S7 Phone: 416-977-2057

TARIC Mosque, 99 Beverley Hills Dr., Toronto, ON M3L 1A2 Phone: 416-245-5675

Sunnatul Jamaat of Ontario, 347 Danforth Road, Toronto, ON M4K 1N7 Phone: 416-690-2298

United Can. Muslim Assoc. of Ontario, 182 Rhodes Ave., Toronto, ON M4L 3A1 Phone: 416-462-1401

Makki Masjid, 8450 Torbram Rd., Brampton, ON L6T 4M9 Phone: 905-458-8778

Islamic Centre of Brampton, 900 Central Park Dr., Unit 98, Brampton, ON L6S 3J6 Phone: 905-458-7142

Islamic Society of Peel, P.O. Box 51034, Brampton, ON L6T 5M2 Phone: 905-458-8778

Zafar Mosque, 153 Benworth Ave., North York, ON M6A 1P6 Phone: 416-789-3445

Islamic Centre of Toronto, 2445 Homelands Dr. #45, Toronto, ON L5K 2C6 Phone: 905-823-6255

Islamic Society, 4627 Fullmoon Circle, Mississauga, ON L4Z 2A6

Masjid-El-Farooq, 935 Eglinton Ave. W., Mississauga, ON L5R 1A6 Phone: 905-858-7586

Halton Islamic Association, 4310 Fairview St., Burlington, ON L7L 4Y8
Phone: 905-333-9856

Islamic Association of St. Catherines, 117 Geneva St., St. Catherines, ON
L2R 4N3 Phone: 905-641-8007

Muslim Association of Hamilton, 1308-1310 Upper Gage Ave., Hamilton,
ON L8W 1E4 or L8W 1B4

Masjid Rasul Al-Azam, 83 Sunrise Ave., Toronto, ON

Bader Islamic Association of Toronto, 474 Roncesvalles Ave., Toronto, ON
M6R 2N5 Phone: 416-536-8343

Jami Mosque, 56 Boustead Ave., Toronto, ON M6R 1Y9 Phone: 416-769-
1192

Masjid E Noor, 277 Scott Rd., Toronto, ON M6M 3V3 Phone: 416-658-6667

Madina Masjid, 1015 Danforth Ave., Toronto, ON M4J 1M1 Phone: 416-
465-7833

Croatian Islamic Centre, 75 Birmingham St., Etobicoke, ON M8V 2C3
Phone: 416-255-8338

Bosnian Community Mosque, 4146 Dundas St. W., Etobicoke, ON M8X 1X3
Phone: 416-233-

ICNA, 100 McLevin Ave., Unit 3A, Scarborough, ON M1B 2V5 Phone: 416-
609-2452

Iranian Islamic Centre, 55 Estate Dr., Scarborough, ON Phone: 416-438-
2221

Scarborough Muslim Association, 2665 Lawrence Ave. E. Scarborough, ON
M1P 2S2 Phone: 416-750-2253

Jame Abu Bakr Siddique Masjid, 2665 Lawrence Ave. E., Scarborough, ON
M1P 2S2 Phone: 416-750-2253

Malvern Muslim Association, 28 Nahanni Terr, Scarborough, ON M1B 1B8
Phone: 416-472-1082

Imdadul Islam Centre, 26 LePage Court, North York, ON M3J 1Z9 Phone:
416-636-0044

Masjid Al-Falah, 391 Burnhamthorpe Rd. East, Oakville, ON

Cambridge Islamic Centre, 16 International Village Dr., Cambridge, ON
N1R 8G1 Phone: 519-740-6855

Cambridge Muslim Society, P.O. Box 22, Cambridge, ON H3C 1C5 Phone:
519-623-0568

Sarnia Muslim Association, 281 Cobden St., Sarnia, ON N7T 4A2 Phone:
519-336-9022

Waterloo Masjid, 213 Erb St. W., Waterloo, ON N2L 1V6 Phone: 519-886-
8470

Masjid Hussein, 65 5th Ave., Kitchener, ON N2C 1P5 Phone: 519-748-0194

Islamic Union, 325 Pioneer Dr., Kitchener, ON N2P 1K6

Canadian Islamic Organization, 29 Burr Cres., Unionville, ON L3R 9B8
Phone: 416-745-1211

Brantford Muslim Association, PO Box 174 Brantford, ON N3T 5M8 Phone: 416-756-2120

London Muslim Mosque, 151 Oxford St. West, London, ON N6H 1S3 Phone: 519-439-9451

Islamic Centre of Southwest Ontario, 951 Pond Mills Road, London, ON

Niagara Muslim Society, RR 1, Niagara-on-the-Lake, Niagara Falls, ON L2

Islamic Society of Niagara Peninsula, 6768 Lyons Creek Rd., Niagara Falls, ON L2E 6S5 Phone: 416-295-4845

Windsor Islamic Association, 1320 Northwood Dr., Windsor, ON N9E 1A4 Phone: 519-258-3552

Thunder Bay Muslim Association, P.O. Box 24026, 70 Court Street, Thunder Bay, ON P7A 4T0 Phone: 807-767-7380

Islamic Society of Sudbury, 755 Churchill Ave., Sudbury, ON P3A 4A1 Phone: 705-560-1271

Western Provinces

Manitoba Islamic Association, 247 Hazlewood Ave., Winnipeg, MB R2M 4W1 Phone: 204-256-1347

Islamic Association of Manitoba, Box 44, 900 John Bruce Rd., Winnipeg, MB R2M 4W2

Islamic Association of Saskatchewan, 3273 Montaque St., Regina, SK S4S 1Z8 Phone: 306-585-0090

Saskatoon Islamic Centre, 222 Copland Crescent, Saskatoon, SK S7H 2Z5 Phone: 306-665-6424

Islamic Centre of Swift Current, 369 Powell Cres., Swift Current, SK S9H 4C7 Phone: 306-778-3311

Salah El Deen Mosque, 195 Douglas Ave., Red Deer, AB T4R 2G2 Phone: 403-347-5812

Markaz-Ul-Islam, P.O. Box 8035, Fort McMurray, AB T9H 4H9

Islamic Centre of Calgary, 5615 14th Ave. S.W., Calgary, AB T2T 3W5 Phone: 403-242-1615

Markaz-Ul-Islam, 7907 36th Ave., Edmonton, AB T6K 3S6 Phone: 403-450-6170

Al-Rashid Mosque, 13070 113th St., Edmonton, AB T5E 5A8 Phone: 403-451-6694

Muslim Community of Edmonton, 10721-86th Ave., Edmonton, AB T6E 2M8 Phone: 403-432-0208

British Columbia Muslim Association, 12300 Blundell Rd., Richmond, BC V6W 1B3 Phone: 604-270-2522

APPENDIX 3

Islamic School Addresses in North America

United States:

Alabama
Sr. Clara Muhammad School, P.O.Box 5442, 3424 26th Street North, Birmingham, AL 35207 Phone: (205) 320-1300
Islamic Academy of Alabama,1810 25th Court South, Homewood, AL 35209 Phone: 205-870-0422
Tuskegee School,1610 Hunter St., Tuskegee, AL 36083 Phone: (205) 724-0580

Arkansas
Sister Clara Muhammad School, 2101 Izard Street, Little Rock, AR 72202
Sister Clara Muhammad School, 1219 W. 20th St., P.O. Box 16429, Little Rock, AR 72216

Arizona
Madrassah Al-Noor, 125 5th Street #7, Tempe, AZ 85281 Phone: 602-894-0764
Al-Huda Islamic School, 901 E. 1St St., Tucson, AZ 85719 Phone: (602) 624-8182

California
Foundation of American Islamic Teaching and Heritage, 2100 E. Howell # 103, Anaheim, CA 92806 Phone: (714) 939-9211
Al-Qalam Institute of Islamic Sciences, 2441 Durant Ave., Berkeley, CA 94704 Phone: 510-841-7429
Fatimah Girl's Academy, P.O. Box 8059, Fresno, CA 93727 Phone: 209-338-0203
Orange Crescent School, 9802 W. 13th Street, Garden Grove, CA 92644 Phone: 714-531-1451
Dar-al-Uloom Al-Islamiyah of America, P.O.Box 3986, Lennox, CA 90304 Phone: 213-674-2237
Al-Madinah School, 3510 W. Expositon Blvd., Los Angeles, CA 90018 Phone: (213) 296-5961
New Horizon School - LA Campus, 434 South Vermont Ave., Los Angeles, CA90020 Phone: 213-480-3145
Qurdobah School, 3420 W. Jefferson Blvd., Los Angeles, CA 90050 Phone: (213) 731-2581

South Bay Area Islamic School, 910 Al Costa Dr. Milpitas, CA 95035

Islamic Middle School, 2105 41st Ave., Oakland, CA 94601 Phone: (510) 436-0232

Sister Clara Muhammad School, 1652 47th Avenue, Oakland, CA 94601 Phone: (415) 436-7755

New Horizon School, 626 Cypress Ave., Pasadena, CA 91103 Phone: (818) 795-5186

Claremont Islamic School, 3619 N Garey Ave., Pomona, CA 91767 Phone: 909-392-9692

Al-Huda School, P.O. Box 5022, Richmond, CA 94805

Islamic Academy of Riverside, 1038 W. Linden St., Riverside, CA 92507 Phone: 909-682-1202

Islamic Middle School and Independent Study Center, 3638 University Avenue, Suite 238, Riverside, CA 92501 Phone: 909-686-9930

An-Nur Islamic School, 7320 14th Ave., Sacramento, CA 95820

Sister Clara Muhammad School, 2575 Imperial Avenue, San Diego, CA 92102 Phone: (619) 232-5910

Al-Basit Academy, 9921 Cormel Mt. Road, Suite 137, San Diego, CA 92129

Islamic School of San Diego, 7050 Eckstrom Ave., San Diego, CA 92111 Phone: 619-278-7970

Darul-Uloom Falah-e-Darain, 720 N. Fairview Ave., Santa Ana, CA 92703 Phone: (714) 547-9107

Granada Islamic School, 3003 Scott Blvd., Santa Clara, CA 95054 Phone: 408-970-0647

Silicon Valley Academy,1095 Dunford Way, Sunnyvale, CA 94087-3765 Phone: (408) 243-9333

Al-Falaq Academy, 6624 Lockhurst Dr., West Hills, CA 91307 Phone: (818) 340-0259

Connecticut

Islamic Institute of Connecticut, PO Box 320612, Hartford, CT 06132-0612 Phone: 860-246-0020

Sister Clara Muhammad School, 3284 Main St., Hartford, CT 06120

Colorado

Crescent View Academy, 10958 E. Bethany Dr., Aurora, CO 80014 Phone: (303) 745-2245

Denver Islamic School, 2071 S. Parker Road, Denver, CO 80220 Phone: (303) 696-9800

Delaware

Islamic School of Delaware, 28 Salem Church Road, Newark, DE 19713 Phone: (302) 733-0373

District of Columbia

Sister Clara Muhammad School, 1519 4th St. N.W., Washington, DC 20001
Phone: 202-387-9591

Florida

Sister Clara Mohammad School, 2242 Commonwealth Ave., Jacksonville, FL 32209

Darul Uloom Florida, 2350 Old Vineland Rd., Kissimmee, FL 34746 Phone: 407-390-1100

Islamic School of Miami,13774 S.W. 88 St., Miami, Fl.33174 Phone: 305-264-0884

Sister Clara Muhammad School, 5245 NW 7th Avenue, Miami, FL 33127

Muslim Academy of Central Florida, 1005 N. Goldenrod Road, Orlando, FL 32807-8326 Phone: (407) 382-9900

The Islamic Community School, 200 Transmitter Road, Panama City, FL 32404 Phone: (904) 744-8067

Islamic Academy of Florida, 5910 East 130th Ave., Tampa, FL 33617 Phone: 813-987-9282

Universal Academy of Florida, 7320 E. Sligh Ave., Tampa, FL 33610 Phone: (813) 664-0695

Georgia

Dar-un-Noor School, 434 14th street NW, Atlanta, GA 30318 Phone: (404) 876-5051

Islamic School, West End Community Mosque, 1128 Oak St. S.W., Atlanta, GA 30310 Phone: (404) 752-7262

Islamic School,1127 Capital Ave., Atlanta, GA 30315

Sr. Clara Muhammad School, 735 Fayetteville Road, SE, Atlanta, GA 30316 Phone: (404) 378-4319

Warith Deen Mohammed High School, 735 Fayetteville Road SE, Atlanta, GA 30316 Phone: (404) 378-4219

West End Primary School, 573 West End Place, Atlanta, GA 30310 Phone: (404) 766-8878

Sister Clara Muhammad School, 2742 Spenola St., Columbus, GA 31906

Islamic School, 2132 Line Tree Lane, Powder Springs, GA 30073 Fax: (770) 445-9779

Sister Clara Muhammad School,117 East 34th St., Savannah, GA 31401

Illinois

Aqsa School for Girls, 7360 W. 93rd Street, Bridgeview, IL 60455 Phone: 312-598-2700

Universal School, 7350 W. 93rd St., Bridgeview, IL 60455 Phone: 708-599-4100

American Islamic College, 640 W. Irving Park Rd., Chicago, IL 60613 Phone: 312-281-4700

East West University, 816 S. Michigan, Chicago, IL 60605

Madrasatun Nur, 1114 W. Foster Ave., Chicago, IL 60640

Muhammad's Development School, 823 E. 75th St., Chicago, IL 60619

Muna Madrassah, 11405 S. Michigan, Chicago, IL 60628 Phone: 312-821-9260

Sr. Clara Muhammad School, 1625 E. 74th Street, Chicago, IL 60649 Phone: 312-487-9709

Sister Clara Muhammad School, 5330 West Division, Chicago, IL 60651

Madrasah Ta'lim-ul-Islam, P.O.Box 44, Gilberts, IL 60136 Phone: 708-428-5725

College Preparatory School of America, 331 West Madison, Lombard, IL 60148 Phone: 708-889-8000

Islamic School of Mortan Grove, 8601 North Menard St., Morton Grove, IL 60053 Phone: 708-470-8801

Iqra International Educational Foundation, 7450 Skokie Blvd., Skokie, IL 60076 Phone: 312-226-5694

The Islamic Foundation School, 300 W. Highridge Road, Villa Park, IL 60181 Phone: 312-941-8800

Indiana

Al-Amin Elementary School, 3702 West 11th Avenue Gary, IN 46404 Phone: 219-949-1854

Madrasa-tul-Ilm, 2846 Cold Spring Rd., Indianapolis, IN 46222 Phone: 317-923-0328

Sister Clara Muhammad School, 954 E. 30th St., Indianapolis, IN 46218

Kansas

An-Noor Islamic School, 3104 E. 17th St., Wichita, KS 67214 Phone: (316) 651-0303

Kentucky

Sister Clara Muhammad School,1917 W. Magazine St., Louisville, KY 40211

Louisiana

Mosque Academy, 820 W. Chimes St. #101, Baton Rouge, LA 70802

Sister Clara Muhammad School, 2700 Magnolia St., New Orleans, LA 70113 Phone: (504) 895-6731

Sister Clara Muhammad School, 717 Teche St., New Orleans, LA 70114 Phone: (504) 362-6758

Sister Clara Muhammad School, 2924 Greenwood Rd., Shreveport, LA 71109

Maryland

Al-Rahmah School, 6631 Johnnycake Road, Baltimore, MD 21244 Phone: (301) 747-4869

An-Nur Institute for Islamic Studies and Arabic Language, 10012 Harford Road Baltimore, MD 21234 Phone: 410-663-9677

Islamic Community School, 1335 W. North Avenue, Baltimore, MD 21227 Phone: (301) 669-0655

Sister Clara Muhammad School, 514 Wilson St., Baltimore, MD 21217

Al-Huda School, PO Box 10550, Silver Spring, MD 20914-0550 Phone: 301-879-2903

Muslim Community School, 7917 Montrose Road, Potomac, MD 20854 Phone: (301) 340-6713

Massachusetts

Islamic Elementary School, 1380 Soldiers Field Road, Boston, MA 02215 Phone: (617) 961-4563

Islamic Society of Boston/Weekend Islamic School, 204 Prospect St., Cambridge, MA 02139 Phone: 617-876-3546

Sister Clara Muhammad School, 150 Magnolia St., Dorchester, MA 02125 Phone: (617) 289-4037

Al-Hamra Academy Elementary School, Times Square Plaza, 200 West Main Street, unit 4, Northborough, MA 01532 Phone: 508-393-0171

School of Islamic Studies, 84 Chase Drive, Sharon, MA 02067 Phone: (617) 784-0519

Al-Hamra Academy, P.O. Box 377, Shrewsbury, MA 01545

Michigan

Michigan Islamic Academy, 2301 Plymouth Road, Ann Arbor, MI 48105 Phone: (313) 747-1710

Crescent Academy International, 40440 Palmer Rd., Canton, MI 48188 Phone: 313-729-1000

Al-Ikhlas Training Center, 4001 Miller St., Detroit, MI 48211 Phone: (313) 925-0880

Darul-Arqam Islamic School, 4612 Lonyo, Detroit , MI 48210 Phone: (313) 581-3441

Sister Clara Muhammed School, 11529 Linwood, Detroit, MI 48206 Phone: (313) 868-2131

Islamic Society of Greater Lansing, 20 South Harrison Rd., East Lansing, MI 48823

Flint Islamic School, 614 W. Home Ave., Flint, MI 48505 Phone: (313) 787-5525

Huda School and Montessori, 32220 Franklin Rd., Franklin, MI 48025 Phone: 810-626-0999

Darul-Uloom Sabil-ur-Rashad, 318 Pilgrim St., Highland Park, MI 48203 Phone: (313) 867-9428

Minnesota
The Islamic Academy of Minnesota, 3759 4th Ave South, Minneapolis, MN 55407 Phone: (612) 823-7757

Missouri
Islamic School of Central Missouri, 201 S. 5th St, P.O. Box 1241, Columbia, MO 65205 Phone: (314) 875-4633
Islamic School of Kansas City, 8501 E. 99th St., Kansas City, MO 64134 Phone: (816) 763-0322
Al-Salam Day School, 517 Weidman Road, Manchester, MO 63011 Phone: 314-394-8987
Islamic Institute of Learning, 5388 Geraldine Ave., St. Louis, MO 6 3 1 1 5 Phone: 314-381-2490
Sr. Clara Muhammad School, 1434 North Grand Ave., St. Louis, MO 63106 Phone: 314-531-5414
Sr. Clara Muhammad School, 1435 North Grand Ave., St. Louis, MO 63106 Phone: (314) 531-3118

New Jersey
Quba School & Islamic Center, 1311 Haddon Ave., Camden, NJ 08103 Phone: 609-541-6782
Islamic School of NJ, 190 Sherman Ave., Glen Ridge, NJ 07028
Al-Ghazali Elementary School, 17 Park St., Jersey City, NJ 07304 Phone: (201) 433-5002
Jamaet Ibad El-Rahman, Jersey City Mosque, 539 Bergen Avenue, Jersey City, NJ 07304 Phone: (201) 433-8304
Sister Clara Muhammad School, 257 S. Orange Ave., Newark, NJ 07103
Islamic School of New Jersey, 20-24 Branford Place, Newark, NJ 07101 Phone: (201) 624-6322
Islamic Educational Center of North Hudson, 4613 Cottage Place Union City, P.O.Box 5548, N. Bergen, NJ 07047 Phone: 201-330-0066
The Islamic Day School, 61 Lincoln Street East, Orange, NJ 07017 Phone: (201) 672-6660
Al-Huda School, 154 Ellison St., Paterson, NJ 07505 Phone: 201-742-7474
Noor-Ul-Iman School, P.O. Box 3105 Princeton, NJ 08543 Phone: 908-329-1306
Al-Hikmah Elementary School, 278 North 8th St., Prospect Park, NJ 07508 Phone: (201) 790-4700
Al-Ghazaly Junior / Senior High School, 441 North Street, Teaneck, NJ 07666 Phone: (201) 836-2555

New Mexico

Khalid Islamic School, P.O. Box 130, Abiquiu, NM 87510

New York

Islamic Elementary School, P.O.Box 6149, Bronx, NY 10451 Phone: (212) 991-4609

Al-Madrasa Al-Islamiyah, 1669 Bedford Avenue, Brooklyn, NY 11226 Phone: (718) 774-0221

Ikhwanul Tawheed Academy, 1221 Atlantic Avenue, Brooklyn, NY 11216 Phone: (718) 638-2169

Islamic Family School, 552-4 Atlantic Ave., Brooklyn, NY 11217

Islamic School of NY City, 675 4th Ave, Brooklyn, NY 11215

Al Noor School, 675 4th Avenue, Brooklyn NY11232 Fax: 718-768-7088

Darul Uloom Al-Madania, Inc.,182 Sobieski St., Buffalo, NY 14212-1506 Phone: (716) 892-2606

Sister Clara Muhammad School, 105-01 Northern Blvd., Corona, NY 11368

Al-Iman School, 89-89 Van Wyck Expwy., Jamaica, Queens, NY 11435-4123 Phone: 718-297-6520

Muslim Model School, 166-26 89th Ave., Jamaica, NY 11432 Phone: (718) 658-1199

Islamic School,151 Elk Ave., New Rochelle, NY 10804

Academy of Islam, 156 W. 119th St., New York, NY 10026

Arabic Teaching Center, 210 E. 47th St., New York, NY10017

Islamic School of Islamic Cultural Center of New York, 1711 3rd Ave., New York, NY 10029 Phone: (212) 722-5234

Sister Clara Muhammad School, 102 West 116th Street, New York, NY 10026 Phone: (212) 662-2200

Islamic Elementary School, 130-08 Rockaway Blvd., South Ozone Park, NY 11420 Phone: 718-322-3154

Razi School, 55-11 Queens Blvd., Queens, New York, NY

Sister Clara Muhammad School, 370 North St., Rochester, NY 14605

An-Nur School in Albany New York, 21 Lansing Rd North, Schenectady, NY 12304

Islamic Elementary School, P.O.Box 190099, S. Richmond Hill, NY11419 Phone: (718) 322-3154

Madrasatul Ihsan, 423 West Onondaga Street, Syracuse, NY 13202 Phone: 315-472-5040

Crescent School, 835 Brush Hollow Rd., Westbury, NY 11590 Phone: (516) 333-4939

Razi School, 55-11 Queens Blvd., Woodside, NY 11377 Phone: (718) 779-0711

North Carolina
Sister Clara Muhammad School,1230 Beatties Ford Road, Charlotte, NC 28216
Phone: (704) 596-2447
Sister Clara Muhammad School, 1009 W. Chapel Hill St., Durham, NC 27701
The Islamic School and Social Center of Fayetteville, 2030 Rosehill Rd.,
Fayetteville, NC   Phone: (910) 630-3136
Al-Iman School, 3020 Ligon St., Raleigh, NC 27606 Phone: 919-821-1699
Sister Clara Muhammad School, 1500 English St.,Winston-Salem, NC 27105

Ohio
Carter G. Woodson Academy, 3520 E. 116th St., Cleveland, OH 44105
Islamic Academy School of Arts and Sciences, 6601 Lexington Avenue,
Cleveland, OH 44106 Phone: 216-621-3738
Islamic School,1187 Hayden Avenue, Cleveland, OH 44110 Phone: (216)
249-4500
Islamic School, P.O.Box 20651, Columbus, OH 43220 Fax: (614) 262-7378
Sister Clara Muhammad School, 408 S. 17th St., Columbus, OH 43206
Sunrise Academy, 5657 Scioto-Darby Road, Hilliard, OH 43026 Phone: 614-
527-0465
Toledo Islamic Academy, 4404 Secor Road, Toledo, OH 43623

Oklahoma
Peace Elementary School, P.O.Box 906111, Tulsa, OK 74112

Pennsylvania
Muslim Community Center of Greater Pittsburgh, 233 Seaman Lane,
Monroeville, PA 15146 Phone: 412-373-0101
Habib Allah Day School, 4637 Lancaster Ave., Philadelphia, PA19121
Sr. Clara Muhammad School, 426 Mount Pleasant Ave., Philadelphia, PA 19119
Sr. Clara Muhammad School, 4700 Wialusing Avenue, Philadelphia, PA 19131
Phone: 215-877-9020
The Little Heart's Haven, 6041 Drexel Road, Philadelphia, PA 19131
Sr. Clara Muhammad School, 7222 Kelly St., Pittsburgh, PA 15208
Quranic Open Muslim, (Madrasa for Girls), 600 Campbell Street, Williamsport,
PA 17701

South Carolina
Sister Clara Muhammad School, 5119 Monticello Rd., Columbia, SC 29203

Tennessee
Islamic School, 100 13th St., Knoxville, TN 37916
Sister Clara Muhammad School, 4412 South Third Street, Memphis, TN 38109
Phone: (901) 789-1904

Islamic School,1065 Stratford Rd., Memphis, TN 38122 Phone: 901-685-8906

Islamic School of Nashville, 7335 Charlotte PK, Nashville, TN 37209 Phone: 615-352-5903

Sister Clara Muhammad School, 3316 Torbett St., Nashville, TN 37209

Sister Clara Muhammad School, 3508 Clifton Avenue, Nashville, TN 37209 Phone: 615-329-1646

Texas

Sister Clara Muhammad School, 2604 S. Harwood St., Dallas, TX 75215

Sister Clara Muhammad School,1201 E. Allen Ave., Fort Worth, TX 76104

Elementary Education Academy, 6614 Hornwood Drive, Houston, Texas 77074 Phone: 713-988-8466

Iman Academy, P.O.Box 4944, Houston, TX 77502-0944 Phone: (713) 910-3626

Islamic Learning Institute, Inc., 7603 Bellfort Suite 200, Houston, TX 77061 Phone: (713) 644-5794

Madrasat Al-Huda Schools, 6700 Sands Point, Houston, Texas 77074 Phone: 713-988-8466

Sister Clara Muhammad School, 6641 Bellfort Avenue, Houston, TX 77023 Phone: (713) 643-9580

Brighter Horizons School, 329 E. Polk St., Richardson, TX 75081 Phone: 972-907-9007

Virginia

Islamic Saudi Academy, 8333 Richmond Highway, Alexandria, VA 22309 Phone: 703 780 0606

Institute of Islamic and Arabic Sciences, 8500 Hilltop Rd., Fairfax, VA 22031 Phone: 703-641-4890

The American Open University, School of Islamic and Arabic Studies 3400 Payne St, Suite 200, Falls Church, VA 22041 Phone: (703) 671-2115

Islamic School, 555 Grove St., Herndon, VA 22070

School of Islamic and Social Sciences (SISS), P.O.Box 670, Herndon, VA 22070-4705 Phone: (703) 471-5546

Sister Clara Muhammad School,1145 Hampton Ave., Newport News, VA 23607 Phone: (804) 245-6514

Sister Clara Muhammad School, P.O. Box 1066, Norfolk, VA 23510

Clara Muhammad Boarding School, Hwy 607, P.O.Box 71, Randolph, VA 23962

Muslim Teacher's Training Center, 400 Chimborozo Blvd., P.O. Box 25594 Richmond, VA 23261

Sr. Clara Muhammad School, 400 Chimborazo Blvd, P.O. Box 8064, Richmond, VA 23223 Phone: 804-392-9538

Washington
Islamic School of Seattle, P.O. Box 22956, Seattle, WA 98122-0956 Phone: (206) 329-5735

West Virginia
Islamic Association of West Virginia, P.O. Box 8414, S. Charleston, WV 25303

Wisconsin
Sister Clara Muhammad School, 317 West Wright Street, Milwaukee, WI 53212 Phone: (414) 263-6772

Canada

Nova Scotia
Islamic Assoc. of the Maritimes, Box 443 Stn. "M" Bedford Row, Halifax, NS B3J 2P8 Phone: 902-469-9490

Quebec
El-Kairouane Mosque, 3726 Rue Jean Talon Est., Montreal, PQ H2A 1X9 Phone: 514-728-2922
Islamic School of Montreal, 7435 Chester Ave., Montreal, PQ H4V 1M4 Phone: 514-484-8845

Ontario
Islamic School of Cambridge,16 International Village Dr., Cambridge, ON. N1R 8G1 Phone: 519-740-6855
Al-Rashid Islamic Institute, R.R. #1, Cornwall, ON. K6H 5R5 Phone: 613-931-2895
ISNA Islamic Community School, 1525 Sherway Drive, Mississauga, ON. L4X 1C5 Phone: (905) 272-4303
Islamic Foundation Islamic School, 441 Nugget Avenue, Scarborough, ON. M1S 5E1 Phone: 416-321-3776
Abu Bakr Islamic School, 2665 Lawrence Avenue, East Scarborough, ON. M1P 2S2 Phone: (416) 750-2253
As-Sadiq Islamic Schools, 9000 Bathurst Street, Thornhill, ON. L4J 8A7 Phone: 905-771-9917
Madrasatul Banaat Al-Muslimaat, 10 Vulcan St., Etobicoke, ON. M9W 1L2 Phone: 416-244-8600
Islamic School of Ottawa, 10 Coral Ave., Nepean, ON. K2P 5Z6 Phone: 613-727-5066

Western Provinces

Alberta:
Calgary Islamic School, 5615 14th Ave. S.W., Calgary, AB. T2T 3W5 Phone: 403-246-9420
Hira' Arabic Cultural School, 43 Aberdare Cres. N.E., Calgary, AB.T2A 6T5 Phone: 403-248-5690
Edmonton Islamic School, 13070 113th St., Edmonton, BA. T5E 5A8 Phone: 403-454-3498

British Columbia:
British Columbia Muslim School, 12300 Blundell Rd., Richmond, BC.V6W 1B3 Phone: 604-270-2511

APPENDIX 4

Media Directory

Muslim Media

(The following is a list of well-known Muslim news media publications in North America. There are many newsletters that are also published by Muslim organizations and Islamic Centers, but their circulation is generally restricted to a limited population.)

Muslim World Monitor, Phone: 214-669-9595, Fax: 214-669-9597
Muslim Journal, Phone: 312-243-7600, Fax: 312-243-9778
Islamic Horizons, Phone: 317-839-8157, Fax: 703-742-8677
The Message, Phone: 718-658-5163, Fax: 718-526-3645
The Minaret, Phone: 213-384-4570, Fax: 213-383-9674
Crescent international, 905-474-9292, Fax: 905-474-9293
Sister! Phone: 206-467-1035, Fax: 206-467-1522

Major News Media

ABC News, Phone: 212-456-4040; World News, Fax: 212-456-2213
CBS News, Phone: 212-975-3691; Evening News, Fax: 212-975-1893
NBC News, Phone: 212-664-4971; Fax: 212-664-5705
CNN, Phone: 404-827-1500; Fax: 404-827-1593
PBS, Phone: 703-998-2150; Fax: 703-739-0775
NPR, Phone: Phone: 202-414-2000; Fax: 202-414-3329
Time Magazine, Phone: 212-522-1212; Fax: 212-522-0323
Newsweek, Phone: 212-445-4000; Fax: 212-445-5068
U.S.News & World Report, Phone: 202-955-2000
New York Times, Phone: 212-556-1234; Fax: 212-556-3690
USA Today, Phone: 703-276-3400; Fax: 703-276-5527
Wall Street Journal, Phone: 212-416-2000; Fax: 212-416-2658
Washington Post, Phone: 202-334-6000; Fax: 202-334-6097

APPENDIX 5

Muslim Financial Institutions

Abrar Investments, Inc., One Landmark Square, Level 18 Stamford CT 06901 Phone: 1-888-88 ABRAR or (203) 975-8844

Amana Mutual Funds Trust, 1300 N. State St. Bellingham, WA 98225-4730 Phone: (800) SATURNA

AMSAT International, 215 6th Ave SW, Calgary AB T2P 0R2 Phone: (403) 262-1490

North American Islamic Trust (NAIT), 10900 W Washington St., Indianapolis IN 46231 Phone: (317) 839-8150

Islamic Housing Cooperative/ Canadian Islamic Trust, P.O. Box 160 Station P Toronto, ON M5S 2S7 Phone: (416) 977-2057

Ameen Housing Cooperative (ACH), 800 San Antonio Road, Suite 1, Palo Alto, CA 94303 Phone: 415-856-0440

Failaka Investments, Inc., 207 East Ohio Street, Suite 374, Chicago, IL 60611 Phone: 630-295-9655

Hudson Investors Fund, Inc., 1117 Route 46 East, Suite 101, Clifton, NJ 07013 Phone: 800-HUDSON-4, 201-458-8000

MSI Finance Corporation, Inc., 3300 South Gessner Suite # 180 Houston, TX 77063, Phone: 1-800-872-6741 (1-800-USA-MSI1), Phone: (713) 785-9099

Samad Group, Inc., 2801 Far Hills Ave, Suite 205, Dayton, OH 45419 Phone: (513) 298-9402

Shared Equities Homes, 901 Kessler Blvd West Dr Indianapolis IN 46208-1432 Phone: (317) 251-6675

Baitul Mal Inc., One Harmon Plaza, Seacaucus NJ 07094 Phone: (201) 865-8549

Fuloo$ Incorporated, A Division of Jaguar Enterprises, 4940 Homerdale Ave Suite 101, Toledo, OH 43623 Phone: (419) 843-5248